Remediating Region

SOUTHERN LITERARY STUDIES

Scott Romine, Series Editor

REMEDIATING REGION

NEW MEDIA and the U.S. SOUTH

EDITED BY
**GINA CAISON, STEPHANIE ROUNTREE,
and LISA HINRICHSEN**

LOUISIANA STATE UNIVERSITY PRESS ‖ BATON ROUGE

Published by Louisiana State University Press
lsupress.org

Designer: Michelle A. Neustrom
Typeface: Whitman

Cover image: iStock.com/bubaone

LIBRARY OF CONGRESS CATALOGING-IN-PUBLICATION DATA

Names: Caison, Gina, 1980– editor. | Rountree, Stephanie, 1983– editor. |
Hinrichsen, Lisa, 1977– editor.
Title: Remediating region : new media and the U.S. South / edited by Gina Caison,
Stephanie Rountree, and Lisa Hinrichsen.
Description: Baton Rouge : Louisiana State University Press, [2021] | Series:
Southern literary studies | Includes bibliographical references and index.
Identifiers: LCCN 2021018584 (print) | LCCN 2021018585 (ebook) | ISBN
978-0-8071-7579-8 (cloth) | ISBN 978-0-8071-7664-1 (paperback) | ISBN
978-0-8071-7668-9 (pdf) | ISBN 978-0-8071-7669-6 (epub)
Subjects: LCSH: Southern States—In mass media. | Southern States—Civilization.
| Mass media and regionalism—Southern States. | Digital media—United States—
History—21st century.
Classification: LCC P96.S685 U674 2021 (print) | LCC P96.S685 (ebook) |
DDC 302.23—dc23
LC record available at https://lccn.loc.gov/2021018584
LC ebook record available at https://lccn.loc.gov/2021018585

CONTENTS

ACKNOWLEDGMENTS

OUR IDEA FOR *Remediating Region* emerged from countless conversations, conference presentations, and classroom discussions amid our work on *Small-Screen Souths: Region, Identity, and the Cultural Politics of Television* (2017). Grappling with the ever-shrinking televisual screen—from mammoth living room furniture to handheld smartphones—compelled us to think through the ways that mediated representations of the region migrate and proliferate across space and place. In a way, this collection was already in a state of emergence before our television collection was in print. It was there in August 2017 when one of our students asked whether she could write her television paper on a video game instead: "Are they really that different?" Well, *yes*. But also, *no. It's complicated.* And so *Remediating Region* was conceived thanks to these innumerable influences, too many to itemize here. We extend our deepest gratitude to our students and colleagues: all of whom have contributed in some way, whether herein these pages or more subtly over a dinner conversation or Twitter thread. As ever, we continue to be grateful for the professionalism and editorial guidance of the LSU Press team, most especially Series Editor Scott Romine and Acquisitions Editor James W. Long. We offer a special thanks to the Department of English at the University of North Georgia for granting this project the 2020–21 Shott Award, which funded its indexing. Most importantly, we offer thanks and apologies to our loved ones who have endured the endless glow of our screens, big and small.

NOTE ON TERMINOLOGY

EXAMINING VARIOUS MEDIA across historical periods has made us all the more aware of how language has been used to shape present realities and possible futures, both in positive and in negative ways. This process has forced us to be mindful of how we render specific language in our own work. As such, we want to clarify a few key choices for the reader. *Remediating Region* follows Lori L. Tharps's assessment in the *New York Times* that "when speaking of a culture, ethnicity or group of people, the name should be capitalized. Black with a capital B refers to people of the African diaspora" ("The Case for Black with a Capital B," November 18, 2014). However, when we, the authors and editors, refer to stereotypes meant to dehumanize and prop up myths of Black people, we have elected to use the lower-case *b* in order to detach these destructive ideas from Black humanity. We have also rendered all hashtags in their accessible format using capital letters (e.g., #RemediatingRegion) to indicate separate words, even when the original post did not. Lastly, we have made every attempt to distinguish between the U.S. South as a region of the United States versus an American South, which would refer more broadly to the hemisphere rather than any single nation-state. Producing this collection has taught us that perfection across time is impossible despite our optimism and best intentions, and we do not pretend our own choices will stand the test of time in readers' or even our own views. However, we have tried to create a print collection (a rather static artifact for such a dynamic topic) that respects in language—to the best of our present ability—the future we hope to see.

Remediating Region

INTRODUCTION

~~New~~ Media; ~~New~~ South

GINA CAISON, STEPHANIE ROUNTREE, and LISA HINRICHSEN

THE EMERGENCE OF ANY new media form often induces a particular type of fantasy in Western discourse. This fantasy often depends upon narratives of connectivity across space and time where previously "isolated" communities and individuals find *entrée* into a larger public that exists at previously unknown scales of engagement. Perhaps this new, wider world comes in the form of religious community across vast lands of an expanding empire via the written word; or, maybe it exists as an imagined national coherence induced by the spreading of daily and weekly newsprint; or, it springs forward as voices radiate into individual homes beyond an assumed metropole; or, it might appear as a global community of individuals newly connected by digital platforms and invested in the same environmental cause. In many cases, these imagined yet very real connections and communities induce at least two recurring and underlying assumptions: one, that there exists some potential for greater human connection via new media forms, and two, that these new connections across vast space will render localized, regional space a thing of the past.[1] Both of these assumptions characterize human experience of media in dichotomous terms of place (local vs. networked) and time (old vs. new). However, such simplistic dichotomies are incomplete. They fail to account for the complexities of human life and society that ever-evolving forms of technology are designed to mediate.[2]

More than twenty years ago, Jay David Bolter and Richard Grusin cautioned against these types of breaks in the increasingly digital media landscape: "like their precursors, digital media [. . .] will [. . .] function in a constant dialectic with earlier media, precisely as each earlier medium functioned when it was introduced."[3] These enduring connotations of "local/old" and "networked/new" reveal not essential features of emerging technologies but rather evolving social desires for teleological progression. Bolter and Grusin define remediation as the representation of one medium form within another, and they argue that this act of remediation is a key feature in digital new media.[4] This layering of forms and insistence on the new creates a palimpsest where each subsequent layer projects itself as pinnacle of connectivity. However, "the very act of remediation [. . .] ensures that the older medium cannot be entirely effaced; the new medium remains dependent on the older one in acknowledged or unacknowledged ways."[5] Classifying media as "new" establishes a given technology in opposition to extant social formations, rendering these formations as "old" and no longer desirable; this temporal logic thereby ushers in fantasies of ever-more connected, global, and egalitarian social lives.

Despite this optimism for a connected world that manages to escape its pejoratively provincial impulses, the idea of the region has stubbornly persisted. Like evolving forms of new media, evolving ideals of "new" and newer souths continually reemerge to leverage fantasies of social, political, and economic formations in order to constitute material conditions for humans inhabiting southern U.S. spaces and beyond. This collection asserts the compatibility of a methodology at the intersection of new media and southern studies to render visible modes of national identity formation via technologies of regional *remediation*.[6] In the pages that follow, we investigate how manifold forms of media and myth engage with the people, places, and paradigms of the U.S. South. This investigation ultimately reveals the dialogic relationship between evolving technologies of human connections and regional constructs that constitute scaled forms of community, municipality, and nation. While the relationship between old and new media forms and old and new souths may be seen to be locked in a perpetual dialectic, we advocate for approaches that begin to examine the dialogic relationship that complicates this structure. In 1994, before the current ubiquity of "new media," Ella Shohat and Robert Stam convincingly articulated the stakes of these relationships across time in the field-defining *Unthinking Eurocentrism: Multiculturalism and the Media*: "Given the inequitable distribution of power among nations and peoples [. . .] the desire for an elsewhere is often frustrated by the law of green cards and border patrols. Cross-cultural spectatorship, in other words, is not simply a utopian exchange between communities, but a dialog deeply embedded in the asymmetries of power."[7] It is these very asymmetries of power within the histories of the region and media that beg for analyses that extend the conversation from the dialectic to the dialogic. The dynamisms among media, nation, and region are especially evident when tensions between "old" and "new," material and virtual, local and national threaten the stability and sovereignty of dominant structures of public control.

Against these destabilizing conditions, media and region function to negotiate conflicts by consolidating technical, social, economic, and political change within established (indeed, very *old*) U.S. structures of power such as colonialism, global trade, enslavement, empire building, plantation systems, and ecologically extractive economies. In this way, "the South"—and all the attendant perils and possibilities such a designation entails—has remained remarkably resilient across two and a half centuries of media evolution. It has done so in the service of reifying national sovereignty in the U.S. imagination as the liberal empire's regressive regional foil.[8] As a geographic region *and* a virtual idea, the U.S. South has seemingly experienced little dissolution due to an increasingly mediated, networked national and international populace. If anything, the hypercirculation of the U.S. South has only demonstrated its remarkable fluidity and adaptation to virtually every media milestone it encounters, from the widespread European circulation of Michel Guillaume Jean de Crèvecœur's 1782 *Letters from an American Farmer* (with its essay on "Charles Town") to the "media circus" of the 1925 Scopes trial, and from the global cinematic sensation of *Gone with the Wind* to the current surge in streaming the U.S. South on smaller and smaller screens.[9] This collection accounts for how and why the notion of region endures even as it is translated into new media forms.

In composing this volume, we came to think of this phenomenon as *regional remediation*, a methodological approach that rejects "new/old" classifications of region and media in order to engage both as dynamic processes fostering continual return to previous organizing logics that each ceaselessly enacts upon the other and incorporates analyses of asymmetries of power, which often fall along racial, gendered, and class-based lines. Media has continually reimagined the South, cycling through iterations of mediated forms to attempt to remediate its image into something "new." At the same time, ever-evolving forms of technology foretell ever-broadening connectivity across geographic spaces, while such innovative mediations continually return users back to the mediated forms of region, locality, and particularity. Moreover, the very act of remediating evokes a sense of "improvement." One may remediate a property, making various changes to remove environmental contaminants such as mold. Within this action, there remains the hope to "solve the problem," to make the space safe for the future. Such hopes, however, often reveal themselves as fantasies. Spores remain; soot hides in crevices; toxic chemicals slowly seep into ground water. In the ever-escaping promise of remediation for the region, where it will finally be made safe, we see instead re-mediation, where the mediated form only reproduces the problems that came before, just in a shiny, new platform. Taken together, the scholarship in this collection looks to the U.S. South's attempts to remediate itself via new forms, media's perpetual investment in the local, and technology's role in simultaneously maintaining fantasies of the "new" while repackaging the all-too-familiar dynamics of race, class, gender, and environmental degradation that undergird many of the region's representational moments.

In contrast to several well-worn paradigms of new media scholarship, *Remediating Region* reads media genealogies through multiple contextual frames, placing present models of engagement and technology within a broad network of historical analogues and antecedents. Study of the U.S. South, for example, locates mass surveillance as something not new: contemporary technologies of geomonitoring and "dataveillance," and the possibilities of what Jerome E. Dobson and Peter F. Fisher have called "geoslavery," can be seen as stemming from plantation-based systems of surveillance and ownership that have come to organize U.S. culture-at-large.[10] Indeed, almost any survey of media depicting the U.S. South from the era of the earliest newspapers to the internet age will reveal diffuse and contradictory results about the region. The region is both the site of racial violence and stereotypes of backwardness; it is also the space where the first Indigenous newspaper was published and where social media campaigns have led to progressive changes in political leadership in states often written off as deeply regressive. Nonetheless, this collection queries both the continued optimism that new media moments produce for engaged users and the ways that firmly established ideologies of racism, classism, and sexism manage to find homes even in potentially liberatory media forms from early sound recording, to the development of color film technology, to social media platforms.[11] Rather than function as a media history of the region or as a history of southern media, this collection offers a methodological framework for reimagining regional temporalities through a close examination of the continuous reinventions of regional space through media platforms.

In some ways, an examination of the U.S. South follows the logic of contradiction laid out by David S. Roh, Betsy Huang, and Greta A. Niu in their edited collection *Techno-Orientalism: Imagining Asia in Speculative Fiction, His-*

tory, and Media (2015) as they investigate how a specific geographic space and its people can represent deeply divergent ideas across platforms that provide both comfort and challenge to a homogenized West.[12] In a similar fashion, the U.S. South has served a contradictory function for the larger nation: as a site of deeply fetishized and lauded "tradition" and a site of backward abjection. Neither of these representations can tell the entire story of the relationship between any given media form and the U.S. South on its own. In other words, conversations about media and region must always recognize a both/ and construction of possibility across subjectivity, materiality, mode, and content of mediated networks of discourse. The essays in this collection do just that. In examining how changes in information and media modify concepts of "region," this collection both articulates the virtual realities of the twenty-first-century U.S. South and historicizes the impact of "new" media on a region that has long been mediated. *Remediating Region* foregrounds that all media was once "new" media at the same time that they are always constitutive through dynamic continuity with so-called "old" media. As such, this collection interrogates the deep time of mediated space as it confirms and challenges notions of southern exceptionalism within the broader scope of U.S. exceptionalism.[13]

Against such dangerous epistemologies of teleological newness, an interdisciplinary methodology in southern and new media studies is uniquely suited. To the former, southern studies has long interrogated social, political, and economic rhetorics that emerge continually throughout the region's history, all of which have claimed to birth a "New South" at varying moments in the region's history. At each instance, those invested (both ideologically and, especially, financially) in manifesting a "New South" have deployed language of innovation to obscure recursive structures of social control. For example, in the late nineteenth century, editor Henry W. Grady of the nationally read *Atlanta Constitution* became a powerful advocate for his vision of a "New South" lifted out of economic destitution through industry and technological innovation. Grady's capitalist framework consolidated ideals of U.S. citizenship—individualism, industry, innovation—in order to unite regional factions, reconciling the North and South in the spirit of enterprise. However, the "New South" of Grady's famously electrifying speeches failed to achieve the democratic possibilities touted by industrial capitalists. Instead, it replicated embedded cultural assumptions of race, gender, sexuality, and class established in the "Old" (i.e., pre-Emancipation) U.S. South: the explicit, absolute subordination of Black and brown Americans under white patriarchy.[14] Nevertheless, narratives of ever-new(er) souths endlessly endure, imbuing the present by eliding the past.

Similarly, newness has been the subject of much disciplinary interrogation in new media studies, and necessarily so. In the introduction to their 2019 special issue on "Rethinking the Distinctions Between Old and New Media" in *Convergence,* Frederick Lesage and Simone Natale dissect the perceived dichotomy of "old" and "new" by applying narrative methodology to media history. They demonstrate how "narratives about old and new media are not mere 'stories' that circulate in the public sphere: they convey specific discourses about technology, politics and society."[15] Reading media discourses as narratives enables a rhetorical analysis that incorporates empirical observations about changing technology over time while also revealing the subjective motivations of participants—whether developers, capitalists, governments, users, or otherwise. Lesage and Natale's perspective shifts interrogation toward the purposes and functions of old/new dichotomies in crafting a narrative. After all, these narratives, together with the media texts they engage, work to simultaneously interpret and constitute individual identity: "understandings of media emerge in terms of the perceived relationships between different media and between the participants' own life stories and biographies. Distinctions between 'new' and 'old' media, in other words, are part of the process through which interactions with technology in everyday life are perceived and negotiated as part of a narrative continuum encompassing previous habits and memories as well as new experiences and encounters."[16] Individual lived experiences, encounters, habits, and memories inform the discursive processes by which a person comes to understand new media qua *new* and old media qua *old.* Doing so helps individuals both "perceive[] and negotiate[]" their relationships with the media as political objects and fellow user-participants as political subjects. Narrative engagement with teleological dichotomies of old/new works to render the "new" media text as such at the same time that it negotiates cultural relationships between individuals in the context of histories within, outside, tangential to, or even beyond the temporality of the media itself. In constituting the media as *new,* users constitute themselves in relationship to it and to others, replicating and challenging the asymmetries of power.

These users are never—nor are the content, materiality, and contexts they engage—geographically or historically neutral subjects, and neither are the ways they engage with newer media. As Safiya Umoja Noble outlines in *Algorithms of Oppression* (2018), even the seemingly apolitical math-based platforms themselves do not emerge from an objective, neutral understanding of the world.[17] Individuals, complete with all of their unexamined biases, create and disseminate the technologies that many believe offer a clear window through which to view the world. In 2021, that window is often a screen enlivened by a cache of coding that reveals more about embedded cultural assumptions of race, gender, sexuality, and class than democratic possibilities of equitable global engagement. Noble speaks back to the optimism of earlier media studies that envisioned new media as a democratic, egalitarian development. Focusing on "technological redlining," data discrimination, digital quarantining, and the algorithms that run monopolistic search engines, Noble underscores how "algorithmic oppression is not just a glitch in the system, but, rather, is fundamental to the operating system of the web," which she positions as a system driven wholly by a "profit imperative that makes money from racism and sexism."[18] The net is not neutral: rather, its foundational architecture reproduces classification systems and assumptions that accelerate oppression, in part through the way it biases information toward the stereotypic and decontextualized.

In one key example, Noble outlines the tragic outcome of Google searches about impending "race wars" by the murderer who assaulted a prayer meeting at Charleston's Mother Emanuel AME Church in 2015. As authorities discovered, his search results offered him a troubling combination of advertisement-generated and targeted misinformation that confirmed and further radicalized his already racist worldview. This moment demonstrates how persistent ideologies of the Confederacy stoked by inflammatory online vernaculars and visual cultures continue to enact horrific material realities for the people who call the U.S. South home. The fact that these search technologies are capitalist manufacture designed to optimize "impressions" (or the "watch-time" of human eyes upon the screen) helps us realize how participatory cultures are inherent to the cycle of media and how its consequences have always never been new.

Seven years before the assault and murders at Mother Emanuel AME Church, with the rise of neo-Confederate chat rooms, Scott Romine noted that all things considered, a digital Confederacy would be preferably less dangerous than a real one.[19] As the Charleston Massacre, 2017 Unite the Right rally in Charlottesville, Virginia, and 2021 violent insurrection at the U.S. Capitol have all shown, however, the digital world incubates real violence, offering channels through which hate groups can operate and organize anonymously before exploding into the physical world. Online hate does not stay online: this seemingly digital Confederacy, so central to the story of domestic terrorism, was indeed always real and expansive, having moved far beyond the geographical borders of the U.S. South through what Jessie Daniels refers to as "networked white rage."[20] New media scholarship can reveal how white southern identity depends not just on geography and history but also on a distinct sense of belonging and materiality that evolving, then-new media have facilitated for hundreds of years. Contemporary media realities, which include the rise of the aforementioned neo-Confederate online groups, white-supremacist and ethnonationalist websites, far-right podcasts, and conspiracy-minded forums that activate sentimental racist and xenophobic politics under the guise of "southern," render it essential to understand how "the South" is mobilized in new media frameworks.

However, individuals, communities of color, and Indigenous nations, as this edited collection outlines, have likewise used new media technologies to challenge the assumed synonymy of the terms "South," "Confederacy," and "white." For instance, Elias Boudinot, Elijah Hicks, and other Cherokee leaders articulated their nation's sovereignty from New Echota in the typeface of Sequoyah's syllabary and distributed this message across the continent in the pages of the *Cherokee Phoenix*. As Sherita L. Johnson outlines in the opening essay of this volume, Frederick Douglass took advantage of early photographic technologies to shape the public image of African Americans, as print media of his time often tried to dehumanize Black people visually in caricatured illustrations. Additionally, as Brian Ward chronicles in *Radio and the Struggle for Civil Rights in the South* (2006), the inability of white supremacists to segregate the airwaves fundamentally molded how young people in the U.S. South began to imagine a desegregated future. The hashtag activism of groups including Black Lives Matter has created communities that realize ideological and even material gain as they circulate necessary information directly to individuals with a desire to challenge state racism.[21] Today, big data can help a student of history visualize in time-lapse form the devastating numbers of the transatlantic enslavement economy, or understand more fully the reactionary rise of Lost Cause sentimentality through digitally tracking the evolution of Civil War commemoration.[22] These examples of media pushing the region forward into a progressive future and scrambling old "codes" of being, however, must not be used in service of erasing the profound mutability of white supremacy within changing media forms or simply as naïve techno-optimism. Rather, all of these possibilities must be held together in view in order to comprehend the long history of how region and media have often been mutually constitutive technologies in ideological and material conflict.

The consequences of regional remediation are not confined to representational affect, however. There are also effects, and these effects can be read on and through the very land itself. Specific geographies and geologies remain bound up with technological innovation and decline. For example, even today, one can climb a mountain outside Boone, North Carolina, and casually pick up mica flakes from the ground's surface. These mineral deposits made the state the leading producer of mica in the first half of the twentieth century as emergent communication technologies, including radio, depended upon this geological product. Thus, highly localized factors are often at play in how technology develops and affects specific regions in ways ranging from the environment and labor politics to cultural connectivity and evolving demographics. This "geology of media" approach as outlined by Jussi Parikka (2015) offers our investigation a significant caution against two assumptions: one, that the U.S. South is somehow exceptional in its use of deployment of media technologies in the history of the world, and two, that there is *nothing* particular about how specific places on the planet do in fact contribute to the technological development that drives media innovation.[23] Indeed, certain spaces experience exploitation due to geological realities including mineral deposits, while other spaces (or sometimes the exact same places) must bear the brunt of e-waste as the ever-evolving market of media devices renders piles of refuse across the Global South.[24] Like oil, the extraction and refinement of data involves complex supply chains of rare minerals, toxic materials, water usage, and power, all problems that cannot simply be remediated in any sense of the word. Considering this, the essays that follow attend to both the virtuality and the materiality of media and region, privileging how "the material reality of media affords interpretive flexibility while also resisting or undermining other social or cultural interpretations."[25] Eschewing hierarchical Cartesian models that might privilege abstract cognitive forms (virtual) over corporeal forms (material), *Remediating Region* underscores how the dynamism of region and media works to consolidate conflicts between imperial, neocolonial ideals of U.S. empire and the material recalcitrance of land and laborer.

In addition to examining the physical materiality of land and place in discussions of media, *Remediating Region* also attends to the particularity of individual experience in place. Tracing what John Cheney-Lippold calls the "transcoding" of lived identity into data points and logics, many recent works in new media identify points of erasure, disinformation, stereotyping, and bias, while focusing on the endurance of old systems of oppression into contemporary new media.[26] Scholarly accounts overlap with shifting popular concerns about new media engagement that has resulted in changes to technological interfaces and produced numerous journalistic pieces focusing on regulation, reliability, labor, and safety.[27] Up until recently, new media scholarship has often neglected a meaningful focus on regional and local culture, instead working within national or transnational frameworks. Today, the field is increasingly rethinking the role of "the mass" in technology and society, emphasizing instead decentralization, the "glocal," and local and particular patterns of use.[28] Our work follows suit and argues that the U.S. South—with its histories of colonialism, enslavement, global trade, empire building, plantation systems, and ecologically extractive economies—provides a long and dynamic history for understanding the pervasiveness of "the algorithms of oppression" in an ever-changing new media landscape, allowing us to understand the deeper causes for "global" questions of ideology, power structures, and economic inequality that structure new media realities.

Remediating Region is divided into three sections: "Nothing New Here: On the Long History of New Media"; "From Plantation to Platform: Capitalism and the Extractive Economy of Contemporary New Media"; and "In Formation: Mediating Identity through Space and Place." Each essay contributes to the larger interventions of the book, examining media moments from the advent of nineteenth-century religious songbooks for mass distribution through contemporary Indigenous cultural revitalization technologies. In this way, the collection is simultaneously progressive and recursive in its scope, mirroring the ways that, with our increasing access to digital archives, much "old" media continues to exist into the present through digitization projects. Each section takes up a specific question about how various media engaged the region during their own moment of emergence. While the collection leans into the present moment and more recent media platforms—what many people default to when they hear "new media"—readers will recognize that these essays never take up the "new" uncritically. Therefore, one might see that each section places any "new" moment within a trajectory of media forms and effects across the region. "Nothing New Here" outlines the deep history and recursive logic of mediated representations of the region from early photography to true crime podcasts; "From Plantation to Platform" demonstrates how

histories of exploitation in the U.S. South are monetized in the digital economy of late capitalism; and "In Formation" looks to emergent communication
platforms as locations for self-determining individual and community forms of
identity that are both ideologically and physically rooted to "southern" spaces.
Together, these sections contribute to a larger argument about regional dynamisms via evolving platforms that remain uncannily bound to static notions
of the U.S. South. As some of the essays demonstrate, however, new media
forms, regardless of their date of appearance, have allowed individuals and
groups to push back against these constructs.

Part I, "Nothing New Here: On the Long History of New Media," examines the premises of what one might call "old" or "new" media. In the first
essay, Johnson outlines how Frederick Douglass and Frances Ellen Watkins
Harper worked specifically with early photographic technology to challenge
the very idea of "image" as it concerned African American people. In the second essay, David A. Davis reveals a layered consideration of regional remediation via an analysis of the temporal logics of the immensely popular podcast
S-Town. While the podcast is often cited as a key example of new media in the
first decades of the twentieth century, Davis demonstrates how the palimpsest
of novelistic and gothic narrative technique, sound recording, and journalism
renders not so much a new take on ideas of southern culture as it does a tried
and true method of creating an "exceptional region" against the backdrop of
a gawking-eared national mainstream. In the final essay of this section, Paul
Fess illustrates how the shape-note pedagogy of songbooks illuminates a core
tension between what is labeled as a "new media" practice and what is imagined as a southern "folk" culture. He outlines how the empowerment of the
individual user, so often used as a marker of "new media," is embedded in the
nineteenth-century phenomenon. Together, these essays reveal the assumptions that undergird discussions of the new and the old, challenging readers
to expand the familiar heuristics of region and media.

Part II, "From Plantation to Platform: Capitalism and the Extractive Economy of Contemporary New Media," examines the interlocked nature of information exchange, social activity, consumption, labor, and profit, and, like Part I,
locates the origins of "new" forms of privatized governance and power realized on new media platforms in the plantation-era collapse of profit and the
social. "Platform capitalism," a term coined by German theorist Sascha Lobo,
describes the way that "platforms create a stage on which every economic
transaction can be turned into an auction."[29] Noting the way that auctions

minimize costs, particularly those associated with labor, Lobo underscores the brutal human exploitation at the core of capitalism, now amplified by digital platforms. Current network structure allows the monopolistic tendencies of capitalism's architecture to gain ever more purchase on everyday life. In tracing capitalism's erasure of the political in the "free" market, Margaret T. McGehee's "'It's a State of Mind': The Online Merch-ing of Whiteness" takes on the "uniforms" of the predominantly male white nationalists of the Charlottesville Unite the Right rally—collared shirts, khaki pants, tiki torches—to argue for how white corporeal identity comes to signal itself and sell itself, in deracinated and yet highly racist form, on the internet. In examining the networked information economy, the public sphere, and capitalist acquisition, Alexandra Chiasson's "#PlantationWedding: Fantasy and Forgetting on Instagram" explores how the plantation figures as still desirable in the digital economy. Jae Sharpe's "'We Are Mere Gardeners in the Ruins': *Kentucky Route Zero* and Modeling Collaborative Human Dignity in the Information Age" identifies how the videogame *Kentucky Route Zero* depicts the bodily and affective fallout of such desires through the creation of a fantastical and surreal landscape of gameplay. Finally, Jennie Lightweis-Goff's "GIS South: Louisiana in the Lost and Found" interrogates what she considers an "intimate cartography" of digital mapping technologies as they reveal extractive economies and their devastating exploitation of southern Louisiana.

Part III, "In Formation: Mediating Identity through Space and Place," looks to emergent communication platforms as spaces for self-determining individual and community identity that engage with various "souths" and forms of "southernness." The essays in this section collectively refute the common assumption that constructed identity performances with new media are simply inauthentic or artificial. Whether the Tunica-Biloxi Tribe of Louisiana's digital revitalization of Indigenous hand-crafted fabrication or @queerappalachia's opossum and sex-positive Instagram gallery, new media engagement can constitute individual and collective identity in physical and virtual spaces that proceed from, and indeed return to, the region. For example, in Leigh H. Edwards's essay, "Digital Souths in Interactive Music Videos: Dolly Parton, Johnny Cash, and Media Convergence," she examines the content and production of online crowdsourced videos as they constitute a "southern digital folk culture" that creates a space for fans to project distinctive versions of the U.S. South as an imagined community.[30] Austin Svedjan similarly investigates individual and community identity formations in digital spaces in

"Cultivating/Contesting Identities: The Intersection of New Media and Rural Southern Queerness," as he explores how digital engagement has fostered self-actualization for queer rural southerners while simultaneously subverting what he calls hegemonic "anti-southern normativity" inherent in mainstream representations of LGBTQ+ identity. Sam McCracken's essay, "Y'all Use *Y'all* Unironically Now, 'but Y'all Aren't Ready to Have That Conversation': Race, Region, and Memetic Twang on Twitter," examines the digital second life of *y'all* as it circulates on Twitter (2006–) as a "southern performance." He examines how the word circulates on Black Twitter as a marker of "blackness"; however, when adopted by white users, these "meme genres" appropriate and elide Black labor under the guise of "authentic" southernness. Jean-Luc Pierite's essay provides a fitting denouement to the section and the collection more broadly. In "áriyasɛma of Bits and Atoms: A Tunica-Biloxi Revitalization Movement Powered by Digital Fabrication," Pierite returns *Remediating Region* to its central premise: that the materiality of media engages dynamically with human experience over time and place in ways that subvert dichotomies of new/old and local/global. He narrates how the Tunica-Biloxi Tribe's creation of fabrication labs "unit[es] traditional practices with technology," thus participating in a deep history of "Injunuity" and innovation. While Pierite's argument concludes through particularity, it speaks to the broader exigency of *Remediating Region*. Taken as a whole, this collection exemplifies how evolving technologies mediate between past, present, and future in dialogic fashion, evoking history while ushering in not-yet-realized realities.

NOTES

1. See Tribe, "Foreword," x. Tribe outlines Manovich's important work against what came to be known as "California ideology," which offered a "deadly cocktail of naïve optimism, techno-utopianism, and new-libertarian politics popularized by *Wired* magazine." This optimistic stance (notably also characterized by a "sense of place" in California) troubled Manovich who noted on an email list-serve: "A Western artist sees the Internet as a perfect tool to break down all hierarchies and bring art to the people. In contrast, as a post-communist subject, I cannot but see the Internet as a communal apartment of the Stalin era: no privacy, everybody spies on everybody else, always present are lines for common areas such as the toilet or the kitchen." Therefore, all critiques of new media optimism must recognize that this attitude was also associated with the particularities of lived experiences in specific places on the globe.

2. See Lesage and Natale, "Rethinking the Distinctions," 582. Regarding discourses

that assert the newness of evolving technologies, Lesage and Natale assert that "the death of any medium has less to do with technological developments than with issues of social life and narrative."

3. Bolter and Grusin, *Remediation*, 50.

4. Ibid., 45.

5. Ibid., 47.

6. In using the term "technology" we invoke both material/digital innovation and Michel Foucault's use of the term to indicate a set of logics that organize knowledge within a domain of power. As we argue herein, technological innovation in newer forms of media are integral networking systems for national and regional technologies of power that denote and reify structures of place, citizenship, and agency.

7. Shohat and Stam, *Unthinking Eurocentrism*, 355.

8. Duck, *The Nation's Region*; and Greeson, *Our South*.

9. This phrase is used in numerous descriptions of the Scopes trial; see, for example, Israel, *Before Scopes*, 3.

10. Dobson and Fisher, "The Panopticon's Changing Geography."

11. Lewis, "The Racial Bias Built into Photography."

12. Roh, Huang, and Niu, *Techno-Orientalism*.

13. Zielinski's *Deep Time of the Media* is foundational to our methodology for the collection.

14. Gaston, *The New South Creed*.

15. Lesage and Natale, "Rethinking the Distinctions," 580.

16. Ibid.

17. Noble, *Algorithms of Oppression*.

18. Ibid., 10, 5.

19. Romine, *The Real South*, 236.

20. Daniels, "The Algorithmic Rise of the Alt-Right."

21. De Kosnik and Feldman, eds., *#Identity*.

22. Examples of such digital humanities projects can be found at the Voyages website (https://slavevoyages.org/), itself a transatlantic effort by a multidisciplinary team of historians, librarians, curriculum specialists, cartographers, computer programmers, and web designers, in consultation with scholars of the slave trade from universities in Europe, Africa, South America, and North America. See also Kahn and Bouie, "The Atlantic Slave Trade in Two Minutes" and Kahn, "The Landscape of Civil War Commemoration."

23. Parrika, *A Geology of Media*.

24. Hertiz and Parikka, "Zombie Media."

25. Lesage and Natale, "Rethinking the Distinctions," 582.

26. Cheney-Lippold, *We Are Data*.

27. See the 2020 series "The Privacy Project" in the *New York Times*.

28. For example, Ward and Wasserman, eds., *Media Ethics beyond Borders*; and Balnaves, Donald, and Shoesmith, eds., *Media Theories and Approaches*.

29. Cited in Olma, "Never Mind the Sharing Economy." Lobo blogs for *Der Spiegel*.

30. Edwards, "Digital Souths," in this volume.

BIBLIOGRAPHY

Balnaves, Mark, Stephanie Hemelryk Donald, and Brian Shoesmith, eds. *Media Theories and Approaches: A Global Perspective*. London: Palgrave Macmillan, 2008.

Bolter, Jay David, and Richard Grusin. *Remediation: Understanding New Media*. Boston: MIT Press, 1999.

Cheney-Lippold, John. *We Are Data: Algorithms and the Making of Our Digital Selves*. New York: New York University Press, 2018.

Daniels, Jessie. "The Algorithmic Rise of the Alt-Right," *Contexts* 17, no. 1 (2018): 60–65.

De Kosnik, Abigail, and Keith P. Feldman, eds. *#Identity: Hashtagging Race, Gender, Sexuality, and Nation*. Ann Arbor: University of Michigan Press, 2019.

Dobson, Jerome E., and Peter F. Fisher, "The Panopticon's Changing Geography." *Geographical Review* 97, no. 3 (July 2007): 307–23.

Duck, Leigh Anne. *The Nation's Region: Southern Modernism, Segregation, and U.S. Nationalism*. Athens: University Press of Georgia, 2006.

Gaston, Paul M. *The New South Creed: A Study in Southern Mythmaking*. Montgomery, AL: NewSouth Books, 1970.

Greeson, Jennifer Rae. *Our South: Geographic Fantasy and the Rise of National Literature*. Cambridge, MA: Harvard University Press, 2010.

Hertiz, Garnet, and Jussi Parikka. "Zombie Media: Circuit Bending Media Archaeology into an Art Method." *Leonardo* 45, no. 5 (2012): 424–30.

Israel, Charles A. *Before Scopes: Evangelicalism, Education, and Evolution in Tennessee, 1870–1925*. Athens: University of Georgia Press, 2004.

Kahn, Andrew. "The Landscape of Civil War Commemoration." *Slate.com*. July 2, 2015, http://www.slate.com/articles/news_and_politics/history/2015/07/civil_war_historical_markers_a_map_of_confederate_monuments_and_union_ones.html.

Kahn, Andrew, and Jamelle Bouie. "The Atlantic Slave Trade in Two Minutes." *Slate.com*. June 25, 2015. http://www.slate.com/articles/life/the_history_of_american_slavery/2015/06/animated_interactive_of_the_history_of_the_atlantic_slave_trade.html.

Lesage, Frederick, and Simone Natale. "Rethinking the Distinctions between Old and New Media: Introduction." *Convergence: The International Journal of Research into New Media Technologies* 25, no. 4 (2019): 575–89. Doi: https://doi.org/10.1177/1354856519863364.

Lewis, Sarah. "The Racial Bias Built into Photography," *NYTimes.com*. April 25, 2019. https://www.nytimes.com/2019/04/25/lens/sarah-lewis-racial-bias-photography.html.

Noble, Safiya Umoja. *Algorithms of Oppression: How Search Engines Reinforce Racism*. New York: New York University Press, 2018.

Parrika, Jussi. *A Geology of Media*. Minneapolis: University of Minnesota Press, 2014.

Olma, Sebastian. "Never Mind the Sharing Economy: Here's Platform Capitalism." Institute of Network Cultures. October 16, 2014, https://networkcultures.org/mycreativity/2014/10/16/.

Roh, David S., Betsy Huang, and Greta A. Niu, eds. *Techno-Orientalism: Imagining Asia in Speculative Fiction, History, and Media*. New Brunswick, NJ: Rutgers University Press, 2015.

Romine, Scott. *The Real South: Southern Narrative in the Age of Cultural Reproduction*. Baton Rouge: Louisiana State University Press, 2008.

Shohat, Ella, and Robert Stam. *Unthinking Eurocentrism: Multiculturalism and the Media*. London: Routledge, 1994.

Tribe, Mark. "Foreword." In *The Language of New Media* by Lev Manovich, x–xiii. Cambridge, MA: MIT Press, 2002.

Ward, Stephen J. A., and Herman Wasserman, eds. *Media Ethics Beyond Borders: A Global Perspective*. London: Routledge, 2010.

Zielinski, Siegfried. *Deep Time of the Media: Toward an Archaeology of Hearing and Seeing by Technical Means*. Trans. Gloria Custance. Cambridge, MA: MIT Press, 2006.

I

NOTHING NEW HERE

On the Long History of New Media

GINA CAISON

THE WORD "NEW" SHOULD give pause. More than a simple adjective denoting arrival, discovery, invention, or beginnings, "new" often conceals more than it reveals. It makes breaks where there are none. It effaces histories. It establishes a temporality for cultural narratives often ready to distinguish themselves from what came before. And at its worst, it makes possessions of worlds and peoples. With this in mind, it is instructive to consider how "new" media moments have intersected with fantasies of the "new" in the region currently known as the U.S. South. Indeed, the imaginary "new" signals mythologies of "discovery" that undergird processes of settler colonialism, and these devastating proclamations of "new worlds"—even if by historical accident—occurred in spaces presently called the U.S. South and the farther Souths of the Caribbean and South America. These "new worlds" often shared the intertwined practices of Indigenous genocide and land theft along with the mass enslavement of African peoples. The marketing of these spaces as "new" to European audiences and consumers obscured deep histories, and the continued offhand appeals to new worlds buttress colonialist policies in present-day nation-states of the Americas. These invocations of new worlds frequently worked in service of monetary and emergent capitalist investment in the exploitation of non-European spaces. The vector of transmission for announcing these investment opportunities was often the popular media forms of the day.

For example, Thomas Harriot and John White composed a set of remarkable documents that is often considered England's "first look" at the "Americas" on what is known presently as Roanoke Island in North Carolina.[1] Theodor de Bry compiled Harriot's writings and White's watercolors into the 1590 engraved illustrated edition of *A Briefe and True Report of the New Found Land of Virginia.*[2] (See Fig. 0.1.) The collection works within multiple literacies for a variety of audiences. While the *Report* was certainly not the first work of its kind, de Bry was, in many ways, working in an emerging genre of visual colonialism that positioned representations of Indigenous peoples as embodied advertisements alongside the Latinate alphabetic, printed script of Harriot's not-so-subtle appeals for monetary investment. The fact that audiences did not have to possess literacy in written English to understand de Bry and Harriot's core (and deeply troubling) marketing pitch—that the "Americas" were bountiful, the people beautiful and docile (and thus offensively rendered akin to nonhuman animals)—allowed them to mediate European audiences' ex-

Fig. 0.1. "How They Catch Fish," de Bry's engraving after John White's watercolor located in the Library of Congress Rare Book and Special Collections Division, Washington, DC.

periences of the space regardless of their class distinction. It traded on the capital of the "new" in a mediated form to generate money for the emerging economic engine that came to be known as settler colonialism.

The intersection of new worlds, new media, and new souths constitutes the point of departure for this first section. As we offer in the Introduction and as the first three essays of this collection illustrate: all media was once new media. Appeals to connected, egalitarian tomorrows as well as predictions of perilous futures have consistently found their way into discussions of new media forms as they have appeared on the scene. Furthermore, as Benedict Anderson and others have outlined, the advent of new media forms has often affected how humans have imagined their relationships to one another, forming community across space and pulling people together into fantasies of linked time.[3] The U.S. South is not exceptional in its use of or representation within these emergent media. All regions have been shaped by the exchange of knowledge and experiences of human connection that result from mediated versions of place. Even though the scope of reactions to new media moments remains remarkably consistent across time and place, that is not to say that there is nothing particular about how, when, and why the U.S. South (or an idea of the U.S. South) has long intersected with key moments in new media. Rather, the South finds an odd congruence with media as two amorphous nouns that are often modified by the adjective "new." Ironically, the appeal to the "new" in each case often reveals little new about either. Instead, when examined closely, new souths and new media share remarkable similarities in form and content with their predecessors. The first section of this volume seeks to pull apart assumptions of newness and assumptions of southernness to illustrate the long history of new media and their uncanny likeness to narratives of "new" souths.

As Harriot and de Bry's *Briefe and True Report* demonstrates, these mediated moments of "new found land" belie the fact that the continents that came to be called the Americas had a long media history in many textual and oral forms and that the "South" we call upon today is a relatively recent invention of space. For instance, farther south than Mississippi, Maya glyphs engraved in stone or inscribed with ink in codices often serve as one of the most recognizable forms of media to Western audiences, even today. Furthermore, when people visit the impressively large Rock Eagle Effigy Mound in present-day Putnam County, Georgia, in what are Muscogee homelands, they are viewing an object designed for some purpose of communication. (See Fig. 0.2.)

Fig. O.2. Rock Eagle Effigy Mound in Oconee National Forest
at the Rock Eagle 4H Center. Photo by the author.

Although the intended original message and audience might seem beyond many present-day viewers' grasps, it is virtually impossible not to recognize the gesture in the construction of the massive stone bird. Like all Indigenous earthworks across the region and continent, it communicates meaning. As LeAnne Howe and Jim Wilson explain, "We should think of mounds as linked chapters in the novel of Indigenous North and South America. With different characters and points of view that de-emphasize chronology and plot, but give voice to a plethora of storytellers writing on the land, we may find that earthworks are mnemonics designed to help Natives *remember* to return home for solar and lunar ceremonial events. And, by returning home, we rebuild and recreate another chapter in the book of mounds."[4] These texts are indeed very old media, yet these media continue to have their own new purpose for every generation. Moreover, at some point in some time, an innovative Indigenous person or people became inspired to create an earthwork. Others joined in under conditions that likely varied in individual motivation. The result: communities communicated their beliefs, priorities, hopes, and needs to their contemporaries and to innumerable future audiences. In turn, these future audiences' own beliefs, priorities, hopes, and needs are re-animated in each moment of reception. The old and the new circle back in on one another, proving to be mutually constitutive, in constant dialogue rather than all-consuming synthesis.

This recognition of "old" media in the Americas, however, can also cover over assumptions about the forms that communication takes, its resulting users, and the asymmetries of power that determine contemporary existence. As Paul Chaat Smith offers in the introduction to *Colonial Mediascapes*, "Let me crudely characterize the existing discourse. The winter count calendar is (kind of) like a book. The quipu is (kind of) like a computer. The petroglyph is (kind of) like words. The subtext is not so buried; what we're really talking about is this: Indians are, on a good day, (kind of) like Europeans. Just as the structure of these sentences about books and computers embeds a clear point of view on what is understood to be superior, the underlying assumption applies to the users of those things as well."[5] Media innovation occurs in multiple ways in multiple places by multiple users, and the resulting forms and our analyses do not need to buttress what Smith calls "the technological determinism that shapes much of the current discourse about the past five centuries of American history."[6] Instead, recognizing the interconnectedness between form, place, creator, and audience in addition to how each of these elements generates fundamental differences among the resulting media can help us think more critically about "new" media and "new" geographies. As Howe explains, Indigenous earthworks are not (kind of) *like* a novel. They *are* the novel of the continent. They are simultaneously old and new, innovated and innovating as twenty-first-century Indigenous people continue to write on their land for future generations invested in repairing the profound damage of "new world" narratives.

Although none of the essays in this section examine Indigenous media forms in the U.S. South, they do each offer a productive caution about the limits of the "new" as a heuristic for media or the region. Sherita L. Johnson demonstrates the use of photography by nineteenth-century abolitionists and activists such as Frederick Douglass and Frances Harper to shape their audiences' recognition of Black personhood in and of the U.S. South regardless of where they lived. These thinkers' engagement with the emerging media technology challenges conceptions of a homogenous white South and works to reclaim southern homelands for African American people. It establishes a visual counternarrative to prevalent stereotypes perpetuated in previous media forms that appeals to a reality of race and region for emancipatory ends. Despite the fact that their occasions for photography differed, Douglass's and Harper's use of technology has resonance with what some today might think of as new media phenomena in the creation of an individual avatar that aids in the sustainable independence of the self.

While Johnson limns the possibilities of how Douglass and others engaged new media technologies to challenge misconceptions of the region and their personhood within it, David A. Davis examines how a supposed new media moment in the widely popular podcast *S-Town* relies upon some of the oldest narrative tropes of the U.S. South. Regardless of claims to a new form of aural literature, Davis points out how so much of the sonic construction of the show repackages well-worn stereotypes of the region to appeal to a larger national audience still invested in southern exceptionalism. The show and its bingeable format in simultaneous release might be "new" in some regards, but as Davis argues, much of its narrative structure and content depends upon techniques from southern modernist writers, such as William Faulkner, and earlier media forms, including radio. In this way, Davis's argument offers a connection to Emily Bloom's cogent point in *The Wireless Past: Anglo-Irish Writers and the BBC, 1931–1968*, that "as contemporary global citizens try to make sense of our own complex media ecology, it is an ideal moment to attend to the wireless past in order to understand the ways in which new technologies challenge conventional understanding of literature and its publics."[7] Similarly, Davis analyzes the podcast with an eye to its construction of time and the temporal landscape it attempts to chart for the region and for its listening public, demonstrating how the new literary form is forever bound up with the old.

Paul Fess returns the section to the nineteenth century and asks readers to consider the methodological rubric for what constitutes new media analysis. Nineteenth-century songbooks, such as Benjamin Franklin White and Elisha James King's *The Sacred Harp* (1834), fostered a discourse of egalitarian structures of a shape-note singing pedagogy that became attached to ideas of southern folk traditions and communities. If one steps back into the contemporaneous moment of sacred harp singing's popularity, this individuated user-driven engagement it generated begins to bear an uncanny similarity to how one might talk about "new media" today. Thus, Fess extends methodological questions from new media studies to read an object that might otherwise be considered as "old" and tied to limited constructions of southern identity via ideas of white "folk culture." In troubling the ideas of "new" and "old" objects, methods, and questions, Fess exposes how precarious any of these designations are.

Together these essays merge questions of region, representation, and temporality. They ask audiences to consider what is "new" about new media, and each in its own way follows the lead of work by scholars such as Sandra M. Gustafson, who examines the concept of "emergent media," writing that "regardless of whether they are 'old' or 'new,' media are never static. They change internally, and they change in relation to one another."[8] Moreover, they continue a conversation about the long history of new media in regional studies best evinced by Matt Cohen's work on New England. As he elucidates, "We tend to imagine that modern anxiety of technoculture is a product of a unique situation in history."[9]Although speaking of a region that is often rendered in opposition to the U.S. South, his analysis of media, region, and techno-anxiety resonates across all considerations of region and across deep time. As he writes: "What we think of as the modern consciousness or attitude, it is widely believed, was a result of the tensions brought about by the spread of such technologies: humans' cultural and individual boundaries were challenged with increasing frequency, the world seemed smaller, and time seemed to be compressed."[10] Undoubtedly, this phenomenon has an effect that is easy to imagine as exclusively our own in the present. However, Cohen explains, "In the early colonial settlement, just such a confrontation with instrumentality and technologically induced social turmoil was the everyday experience."[11] The newness of media and of place is always in process with specific machinations of power among and between specific individuals.

This section, though, is not meant simply to historicize media in the U.S. South. Instead, these essays open the collection by theorizing how individuals engage the temporal slippage of their own present by imagining designations of the old and new as more than modifying heuristics. These slippages of identity and temporality carry through archives past and present. As Cohen offers, "Many ideas about language and human relations, about technology and communication, that fueled fear, catalyzed racial hatred, and underwrote unjust policy in the seventeenth century remain firmly embedded today."[12] *Remediating Region* begins by showing how Frederick Douglass, Frances Harper, shape-note singing communities, John B. McLemore, and Brian Reed are not merely discrete subjects and objects of the past or the present. They are nodes in a continually entangled network that binds place and time.

NOTES

1. Sloan, *A New World*. Incidentally, Harriot was the first-known person to "map" the moon using a telescope, further solidifying his investment in media technology. Although his maps were less accurate, they predated Galileo's by a few months. See Pumfrey, *Harriot's Maps of the Moon*.
2. Harriot, *A Briefe and True Report of the New Found Land of Virginia* (1590).
3. Anderson, *Imagined Communities*.
4. Howe and Wilson, "At Home in a Twenty-First-Century Mound City," 6.
5. Smith, "Foreword," xi.
6. Ibid.
7. Bloom, *The Wireless Past*, 17.
8. Gustafson, "The Emerging Media of Early America," 218.
9. Cohen, *The Networked Wilderness*, 170.
10. Ibid.
11. Ibid.
12. Ibid., 171.

BIBLIOGRAPHY

Anderson, Benedict. *Imagined Communities: Reflections on the Origin and Spread of Nationalism*. New York: Verso, 1983.

Bloom, Emily. *The Wireless Past: Anglo-Irish Writers and the BBC, 1931–1968*. New York: Oxford University Press, 2017.

Cohen, Matt. *The Networked Wilderness: Communicating in Early New England*. Minneapolis: University of Minnesota Press, 2009.

Gustafson, Sandra M. "The Emerging Media of Early America." *Proceedings of the American Antiquarian Society*. 115, no. 2 (October 2005): 205–50.

Harriot, Thomas. *A Briefe and True Report of the New Found Land of Virginia*. 1590. New York: Dover, 1972.

"How They Catch Fish." Library of Congress Rare Book and Special Collections Division Washington, DC, accessed November 7, 2020. https://www.loc.gov/pictures/item/2001696969/.

Howe, LeAnne, and Jim Wilson. "At Home in a Twenty-First-Century Mound City." In *The World of Indigenous North America*, edited by Robert Warrior, 3–26. New York and London: Routledge, 2015.

Pumfrey, Stephen. "Harriot's Maps of the Moon: New Interpretations." *Notes and Records of the Royal Society of London* 63, no 2 (October 2009): 163–68.

Sloan, Kim. *A New World: England's First View of America*. Chapel Hill: University of North Carolina Press, 2007.

Smith, Paul Chaat. "Foreword." In *Colonial Mediascapes: Sensory Worlds of the Early Americas*, edited by Matt Cohen and Jeffrey Glover, xi–xii. Lincoln and London: University of Nebraska Press, 2014.

"PICTURES AND PROGRESS"

Being "Black" and "Southern" in the Nineteenth and Twenty-First Centuries

SHERITA L. JOHNSON

The process by which man is able to posit his own subjective nature outside of himself, giving it form, color, space, and all the attributes of distinct personality, so that it becomes the subject of distinct observation and contemplation, is at [the] bottom of all effort and the germinating principles of all reform and all progress.

—FREDERICK DOUGLASS, "Pictures and Progress" (1864–65)

> Say *"race,"* the photographer croons. I'm in
> blackface again when the flash freezes us.
> My father's *white,* I tell them, and *rural.*
> *You don't hate the South?* they ask. *You don't hate it?*
>
> —NATASHA TRETHEWEY,
> "Pastoral" from *Native Guard* (2006)

TRUE TO HIS PREDICTION, Frederick Douglass's image has been preserved for more than a century. *Fugitive Slave. Abolitionist. Orator. Suffragist. Foreign Diplomat. Prolific Writer.* Douglass (1818–95) was one of the most preeminent public figures in the nineteenth century. That Douglass constructed his public identity to authenticate his humanity (as well as all African Americans') is evident by his careful manipulation of photographic media as an essential component of his "body" of works—three autobiographies, a novella, speeches, and journalism. In everything that he produced, Douglass exposed the hypocrisy of a nation that did not recognize the humanity of millions of enslaved and/or free African Americans although the principles of equality and justice are at the core of U.S. nationalism. Douglass believed that for anyone who read his writings or questioned his authority, he would also use photography to dispel myths of black people being categorized as a subspecies. He believed in the truth and objectivity of photography, a common belief in response to this then-new technology. Thus, drawing from the archive of Douglass's portraits, we see Blackness as a matter of visual substance.

Reading the Black body as text, we understand better how race was/is constructed in the physical and the photographic during the nineteenth century and today (consider the proliferation of images that reify black inferiority in the twenty-first century).[1] Douglass consistently challenged stereotypical black images imprinted in the cultural imagination of nineteenth-century white Americans. Common to the antebellum public were black figures in advertisements, for slave auctions or runaway slaves. Descriptions of skin complexions ("mulatto," "dark," "near white," or "very black"), hair textures ("bushy" or "wavy"), and other bodily features ("well set," "limp arm," or "squint eye") were used to describe enslaved African Americans as chattel property. Black caricatures of African Americans with exaggerated facial features and distorted bodies that functioned to elicit humor and shame were widely circulated in American print media and popular culture (especially in minstrelsy) throughout the nineteenth century.[2] Consequently, this textual-visual culture promoted and justified systemic racism rooted in the history of slavery, the failure of Reconstruction, and the birth of Jim Crow as Douglass witnessed in his lifetime.

Taking a (new) look at how Frederick Douglass crafted his image and contested that of the U.S. South, I examine the early years of his successful career as a writer-activist by considering how his work developed partly due to the invention and evolution of photography as new media in the nineteenth century. His escape from slavery precipitated his most rebellious act, posing first for a portrait as a fugitive. This persona helped him *become* "Frederick Douglass," a freedom fighter. As he reflects later on the process of photography, Douglass understood well the essential purpose of this new technology: "Man is able to posit his own subjective nature outside of himself, giving it form, color, space, and all the attributes of distinct personality."[3] Douglass's striking images captivate us just as he might have expected to become "the subject of distinct observation and contemplation."[4] Implicit in this exchange is the chiasmus trope Douglass used so frequently to reverse the roles of a "master-slave" relationship that he created with his reading and viewing audiences alike in which he controls the textual-visual narrative. What we may not also readily understand is a more subtle rebellious act: how Douglass's fugitive iconography signifies his southernness and how he uses it to "hack" the white/black binary of this cultural identity.[5] As such, Douglass undermines the pervasive whiteness of being and *seeing* "southern" as produced by racial privilege and systemic oppression. What Douglass articulates in his writings—a sense of belonging in/ to a "place"—also transmits in his photographs. That his image was/is widely circulated, perhaps now more than ever digitally, alters how we understand southern space and place as it was/is reshaped by new media.

In addition to reading Douglass's use of his own image, taking a closer look at Frances Ellen Watkins Harper (1825–1911), as another exiled southerner, also brings into focus a sense of place and image in the nineteenth and twenty-first centuries. Harper and Douglass are a study in contrasts to consider the importance of southernness as a critical lens for examining photography as new media. How they used the medium to construct public selves as fugitive and free antagonized the white South as much as their abolitionist orations did. Harper and Douglass, as I see them, remain rooted in their southern origins despite their transatlantic excursions and rhetoric of national belonging. Their attachment to "home" was mitigated by memories of places and a people despite the restrictions of law and customs that prevented or delayed their return to the region.[6] Douglass and Harper understood how southernness was codified by the capitalism of slavery and, later, the terrorism of lynching. That "southernness," defined as such, remains so—as a veiled justification of Confederate pride and "heritage" in popular discourse—is grounds for my deconstructive analysis of Douglass and Harper as regional outcasts. Troubling also is how even as Black southerners this seems to be the case. Placed in an urban context and both having spent their formative years in Baltimore, Maryland— from which they fled and/or were expelled—Douglass and Harper are neither stereotypical nor romanticized Black southerners as were/are figures such as Uncle Tom, the mythical black rapist, mammy, and Aunt Jemima in America's cultural imagination.[7] These were the parameters of being "black" and "southern" in the nineteenth century that framed Douglass and Harper as fugitive and free. At this juncture in the twenty-first century, to see them as southerners undercuts this cultural identity at its root.

Becoming Frederick Douglass: "Fugitive Iconography"

My concerns with the aesthetics and politics of new media are bolstered by scholarship on Frederick Douglass's life as a public intellectual that has presented an archive of photography revealing just how much his image is essential to the study of American print culture as it developed during his lifetime. In *Picturing Frederick Douglass,* for example, the editors catalogue a massive collection of rare images to survey the life of the iconic leader. We can see just how much Douglass embraced this new technology, starting with the invention of the daguerreotype in 1839.[8] Douglass had escaped slavery only the year before, and he would spend almost a decade reconstructing his identity as a free man using this new technology. *Picturing Frederick Douglass* reintroduces him to audiences in the twenty-first century as a young man, unsure of himself, but with a fascination for photography that matches his passion for abolition.

In the act of *becoming* "Frederick Douglass," the slave born "Frederick Augustus Washington Bailey" had many aliases as a fugitive. He did so to escape detection by slave hunters. This fugitive act of running and hiding in the public, however, makes paradoxical the legitimacy of belonging that Douglass embraces in his writings about being southern as a fugitive and free man. The paradox is even more apparent in Douglass's early photographs when he appears framed in daguerreotypes as captured by the photographer, though he eludes slave hunters while yet a fugitive. In 1841, Douglass sat for his earliest-known portrait, a daguerreotype featuring him in a dark suit and high-collared white shirt with a patterned necktie in a knot. (See Fig. 1.1.) He stares directly into the camera with a "look of artful defiance."[9] Having to pose for several minutes for the exposure time captured Douglass the fugitive—temporarily. He took three other known daguerreotypes as a fugitive slave from 1843 to 1847.[10]

In her look at the textual-visual representation of the enslaved runaway in antebellum print culture, Sarah Blackwood explains what black fugitives supposedly looked like in prephotographic visual technologies and how Frederick Douglass and Harriet Jacobs contested such representations in their writings. The stock image of the enslaved runaway found commonly in fugitive slave notices—"as in the act of running"—annoyed Douglass the most, Blackwood reveals.[11] What I find most interesting about Blackwood's archival recovery is just how slave advertisements make visible the black/white binary of southernness that Douglass undercuts in his commentary about fugitive slave notices. He detested the image not only because of its dehumanizing effect, but perhaps also because Douglass did not *see* his southern self in this stock image. Writing to his former master, Thomas Auld, in 1848 an open letter published in *The North Star,* ten years after his escape, Douglass thinks that Auld should not be surprised to find again "[his] name coupled with mine, in any other way than in an advertisement, accurately describing my person, and offering a

Fig. 1.1. Earliest-known portrait of Douglass, 1841. Courtesy of Greg French.

large sum for my arrest."[12] The figure of the runaway slave, implicit in his gesture here although Douglass rejects it, could not encapsulate his experience
of being southern; it was only a manufactured racial type that he refuses to
use in describing himself, as he also did in his own printing house.[13] Douglass
professed that he loved "freedom more" than living enslaved in the South, yet,
he (and other fugitives) "want to live in the land of our birth."[14] While it may
have been in the U.S. South where the figure of the runaway slave appeared
most frequently in slave advertisements, northern foundries manufactured
and sold the stock image to southern printing offices.[15] And, if we focus more
on the blackness of the figure of the runaway slave, we may not also recognize
the whiteness of the slave market in which these fugitive slave notices were
created and circulated, especially throughout the South. In the samples that
Blackwood cites, for example, advertisements describe enslaved African Americans of all complexions, trades, body types, gender, and ages as runaways
and as chattel property for hire or for sale. The owners and general public are
implicitly white but only once identified as such (e.g., "negroes were enticed
away by a white man"). The juxtaposition of slave advertisements with that of

a portrait studio draws Blackwood's attention since it illustrates further the "absurdity" of racial binaries—daguerreotypes of white clients and a stock image as "negro portraiture"—in pre–Civil War print culture.[16] I want to tease further here the assumption that *southerners* refers only to white people who may pose for a daguerreotype in portrait studios and/or place an advertisement for the sale and/or recapture of slaves in antebellum print culture.

Douglass also used photography to present his southern self on his own terms, often as a fugitive, though not in the "act of running." And, if in these early 1840s images Douglass was consciously crafting his public persona, we understand better his engagement with racial discourses and politics as an abolitionist when we recognize especially how Douglass must have appeared to white southerners. His fugitive photographs offer a counterdiscourse about enslaved Black bodies, an individual subjectivity and not a collective inhumanity, in ways similar to how we now use digital platforms to create online identities. Jennifer Gonzales asks us to consider how we are defined based on the culture we consume today in a media-saturated environment, and to what degree the internet allows us to create "new (and multiple) subject positions in virtual worlds or social network sites like Facebook."[17] The internet, like early photography, enables us to enter a neutral zone to create selves that are not totally devoid of historical specificity for racial identities; it is therefore important to recognize how some images "work against" the perpetuation of stereotypes in cyberspace.[18]

Douglass believed that with photography "men of all conditions may see themselves as others see them."[19] The mirror he holds up to himself—*that is,* in the photograph—is *not,* however, how white southerners saw him as a fugitive slave. A caricature of Douglass, for example, featured on an anti-abolition pamphlet's cover, *Abolition Fanaticism in New York* (1847), is the mirrored-image of a zip coon minstrel figure that Douglass would not have recognized as his authentic self, but it is one that the publishers surely knew white southerners would appreciate seeing, something so foreign and unlike themselves.[20] (See Fig. 1.2.) Published in his birthplace of Maryland, the pamphlet disseminates Douglass's speech as a warning to white southerners about "what happens to 'a runaway [. . .] when he reaches the abolition regions of the country.'"[21] The black figure is dressed elegantly, as Douglass would have appeared, but stands stiffly as if frozen in a lecturing pose with its right hand extended and the left hand holding a top hat. Its mouth is curled open as if speaking. With the buffoonish facial features—a thick, dropped lower lip and wide eyes—this figure appears dignified in dress only. Otherwise, it is another stock image of a black male "cooning" or performing as a dignitary, as was common for actors (especially white) to portray in the minstrel tradition.

Antebellum photography as new media, however, enabled Douglass to pioneer face recognition (as we might understand it today) for public encounters with a fugitive slave. The pose that he perfected in his 1840s daguerreotypes became his signature look during the early phase of his career until the Civil War era. His stern gaze and physical strength identify Douglass as a freedom fighter. Owing to the popularity of his two autobiographies—*Narratives of the*

Fig. 1.2. Cover of *Abolition fanaticism in New York: Speech of a runaway slave from Baltimore, at an abolition meeting in New York, held May 11, 1847.* Library of Congress Book/Printed Material Division, Washington, DC.

Life of Frederick Douglass, An American Slave (1845) and *My Bondage and My Freedom* (1855)—which featured his likeness, Douglass capitalized on the face of the fugitive.[22] It became the face of a movement representing one human race. Ironically, Douglass's use of a photographic medium also upended the public surveillance of the fugitive as no longer objectified as *other,* nor identified by what Joy Buolamwini calls the "coded gaze," the implicit biases now found in standard facial recognition technologies.[23] Her research reveals technological flaws that could have a devastating effect on humanity (e.g., like "spreading a virus" of racism). Since "algorithmic biases" are "like human biases" that may lead to "exclusionary experiences" and "discriminatory practices," Buolamwini warns, advances in facial recognition technology must rely on more diverse samples of the population—in compiling data and providing employment opportunities—to create a "full spectrum of inclusion." Such practices could also prevent racial profiling as consequence of public surveillance.[24]

The glitches in facial recognition technology today hearken back to the antebellum era, when prephotographic visual technologies failed to distinguish Black bodies as property, and the stock image of the enslaved only identified a discriminatory target filtered by the "coded gaze." Thus, Douglass used photography to undermine the apparatus of enslavement and thereby expose the implicit biases of the U.S. public-at-large. Confident that "men of all conditions and classes can now see themselves as others see them, and as they will be seen by those [who] shall come after them," he presented a true image of himself, as distinguishable by photographic lens as by the human eye.[25] Indeed, "Douglass embraced photography as a great democratic art" in its accessibility and affordability.[26] Photography was a means to achieve progress by equalizing all, as Douglass believed that "man is the only picture-making animal in the world."[27] But, if Douglass "nor his peers recognized any contradiction between photography as art and as a technology" that could be used to manipulate images through various processes, what *truth* then could Douglass find in photographs?[28]

To demonstrate, ideologically, Gonzales examines digital artwork that produces universal subjects by manipulating physical features to emphasize common attributes of humankind. Morphing images to create artificial cross-racial identification has its appeal for "transcending differences." But what cannot be replicated is *the experience of difference,* as Gonzales contends, revealing "how people live their lives [. . .] based on] the privileges or discriminations that attend racial differences."[29] Gonzales cites an earlier study by Mark Hansen to undermine the paradox of universal, online subjectivity.[30] Hansen illustrates how "digital art can produce affective states in the user that might ultimately lead to recognizing incongruities or incommensurabilities between categories of identity and embodied singularity."[31] Hansen's analysis of a video game, "Catch a Nigger in Cyberspace," illustrates his claims about the possibilities of racial erasure that Gonzales finds troubling.[32] As she explains, users choose options to explore cyberspace, and the wrong choice puts the user in the role of a black male, a fugitive figure who appears to be running toward "a promising future or into a labyrinth hostile territory."[33]

In the way the game allows the player to artificially experience the fugitive's flight and potential arrival in a utopian cyberspace, Douglass offers his former master an opportunity to enter a paradoxical world that is strange yet familiar. In a decade, Douglass had evolved into a southern gentleman—acquiring the material and cultural accoutrements of respectability but not chattel property—like his former master. Thus, when Douglass invited Thomas Auld to a virtual tour of the former fugitive's new home in Rochester, New York, he did so by contesting the capitalism of slavery and thereby redefined Black southernness as an alternative lived experience and distinct identity: "So far as my domestic affairs are concerned, I can boast of a comfortable a dwelling as your own with a wife and four children."[34] Douglass teases, "[his children] are all in comfortable beds, and are sound asleep, perfectly secure under my own roof. There are no slaveholders here to rend my heart by snatching them." While Auld had a chance to play in his own version of "Catch a Nigger" game, relief of his frustrations—in losing valuable chattel, the immorality of slavery itself—is the affective response Douglass anticipates of Auld. Ironically, the interplay exacerbates more: "How, let me ask, would you look upon me, were I some dark night in company with a band of hardened villains, to enter the precincts of your elegant dwelling and seize the person of your own lovely daughter Amanda [. . .] make her my slave—compel her to work, and I take her wages—place her name on my ledger as property?"[35] The truth of Black humanity is mirrored in the doubled images of the master-slave relations, with Douglass's reversal again of the subject positions. The two men appear as equals, fathers and husbands, protectors and proprietors. As Douglass concedes, there "is no roof under which [Auld] would be more safe than mine."[36]

Picturing "southerners" as Douglass does, by transposing his likeness onto his former master, demonstrates that he might have understood well photography as technology. Morphing images of a slaveholder and fugitive slave, however, Douglass accounts for *the difference of lived experiences*. He forgoes writing a narrative about his own "prosperity and happiness" to remind Auld instead of the atrocities the enslaved yet experienced—torture and abuse, sale and separation. "Say not that this is a picture of fancy," Douglass chides.[37] What Douglass asks us to consider is how identity may be constructed as myth when reality is multidimensional. This is most certain in trying to define "the South" and "southerners." How might our twenty-first century conceptions of regional distinction and fluidity, for example, aid in the recovery of different types of "southerners" in the nineteenth century?

Picturing Southerners: Frederick Douglass and Frances Harper

Understanding the U.S. South and "southerners" today requires taking a new look at no other time than the pre–Civil War era, its people, and the places they called "home." With the expulsion of many Indigenous peoples, the arrival of refugees, the acquisition of foreign properties, and the admixture of new languages, customs, and religions, "the South" of the nineteenth century produced an array of multicultural "southerners."[38] To consider who contributed to such changes and how they claimed a space, hostile or hospitable, is the challenge of archival recovery and a more thorough analysis of nationalism that prompted the formation of a Confederacy and the cultural hegemony it manifests in southern studies.[39] For now, though, I turn to another familiar face in a picture gallery of Black southerners, Frances Ellen Watkins Harper, who also imagined that progress was certain. Like Douglass, Harper was also a native of Maryland, but she was born free in Baltimore in 1825.[40] While most scholars ignore Harper's claims of being and belonging, I consider her legal status and early life in the urban U.S. South as essential to (re)constructing the region's cultural identity and literary history.[41] That her activism aligns with Douglass as their careers in the abolitionist and women's rights movements coincide throughout the nineteenth century leads me to consider also the fugitive/free binary as another determinant of southernness, especially for African Americans.

Harper does not appear *southern* enough considering her experience of freedom—from circumstances of birth rather than from "fugitivity," as compared to Douglass; hence, his overwhelming presence in southern studies overshadows Harper's placement often at the margins. Manisha Sinha reasons that, for Douglass, fugitivity was "an epistemological standpoint that served as the best intellectual and polemical riposte to the proslavery argument," which made Douglass an exceptional abolitionist and civil rights activist later in the nineteenth century. The struggle for "national belonging" is a hallmark of his career that begins with his enslavement and intensifies with his escape.[42] But, such is also the case for Harper, as a fugitive by law subject to enslavement or exile.[43] Choosing the latter, Harper fled the U.S. South and faced similar struggles as Douglass, but hers from the position of a triple minority—being Black, female, and freeborn in antebellum America. So, Harper appears less visible to the public.[44]

Consider, for instance, how Frances Harper's photographic archive is not as extensive as Frederick Douglass's. The few known images of Harper place her at different stages of her career, as an abolitionist lecturer/poet and, later, as a post-Reconstruction-era novelist. However, the set of engravings and studio portraits—I count at least five distinct images—were so often reproduced that the timeline of original production is difficult to determine. The earliest image of Harper appears as an 1872 engraving featured in *The Underground Railroad: A Record of Facts, Authentic Narratives, Letters, &c., Narrating the Hardships, Hair-Breadth Escapes and Death Struggles of the Slaves in their Efforts for Freedom, as Related by Themselves and Others, or Witnessed by the Author, by William Still.*[45] (See Fig. 1.3.) Harper is posed in a slight profile looking outward with a furrowed brow; her wavy hair is parted down the middle and neatly tucked in a thick bun. She is a striking woman of might, with a strong cleft chin, high cheekbones, broad nose, and full lips. Her complexion is deep and shadowed. The fine details extend also to her clothing: a coat with a wide, decorative collar and crisp light blouse with a bowtie. The engraving seems likely to have been based on a lost photograph. Harper appears as a freedom fighter (much like Douglass's 1840–50s images) as suggested by its publication in Still's anthology of fugitive sketches years after the Civil War. Beneath the engraved image, her full name appears, "Mrs. Frances E. W. Harper," which indicates that the image was created by or after 1860 when she married Fenton Harper. Similar to the engraving, a portrait of a middle-aged Harper was included years later in Hallie Q. Brown's *Homespun Heroines and Other Women of Distinction* (1926). That photograph authenticates the engraving's details, with matching physical features and similar clothing (though Harper now wears a bonnet). The third image of Harper is a "three quarter-length portrait, [of her] standing, facing front."[46] This studio portrait appeared as the frontispiece in several editions of Harper's poetry collections and her novel, *Iola Leroy*, in the 1890s.[47] She is dressed in a dark suit, with a high collar, and is posed clutching a chair;

MRS. FRANCIS E. W. HARPER.

See p. 755.

Fig. 1.3. Harper from Still's *The Underground Railroad.*
Library of Congress Prints and Photographs Division, Washington, DC.

the backdrop is blank to frame Harper's direct gaze into the camera. Since
Harper left Maryland by 1850–51, after the passing of the Fugitive Slave Law,
it is not likely that any of these early images are of Harper prior to that time.[48]

Collectively, though, the images of Frances Harper as a freeborn, exiled
southerner present a counternarrative to the black bodies stamped in fugitive
notices, framed in Louis Agassiz's scientific daguerreotypes, staged for abolitionist propaganda *carte-de-visites,* posed rigidly as domestic servants in various white slaveholders' "family" portraits, or crowded as contraband in Union
camps' photographic archives.[49] Harper perhaps used photography as other
free Black Americans did by the 1850s to "convey self-worth, dignity, beauty,
intellectual achievement, and leadership."[50] Harper does not appear, though,
to have used photography for self-promotion as did Douglass and Sojourner
Truth. Their portraits became personal calling cards and circulated as popular
abolitionist souvenirs, often sold while on their lecture tours. Truth and Doug-

lass constructed self-images for profit and political power, which propelled their celebrity as formerly enslaved people.[51] Harper's image of refinement and respectability also illustrates a national belonging for Black citizens, though hers was not as transformational, from being chattel property to becoming human. Harper, in other words, did not promote sensational abolitionism with photographic images. And, for that, she does not often appear in a picture gallery of nineteenth-century African Americans envisioning freedom. Picturing Harper and Douglass does suggest how southern cultural identity was/ is manufactured and consumed by audiences respective to white-supremacist notions of belonging in/to a "place" of privilege.

Camera Obscura: "I Am As Much Like the Picture"

So, what do southerners look like when framed by the circumstances of slavery and freedom in the nineteenth century and even today? On opposite ends of the spectrum, Frederick Douglass's and Frances Harper's photographs are exceptional cases of individual subjectivity constructed as southern. Though created by different circumstances, being a fugitive was an experience Douglass and Harper had in common, and it is from this perspective we may best understand their regional displacement. Both try to resolve their conflicting relationship between the self and a "place" with fluid dimensions (then and now).[52] While mostly noted for their use of the pen and the podium as abolitionists, fugitive photography was also an equally effective weapon of self-representation for Douglass and Harper.

Both of them used this technology at a time when few other African Americans could afford to have their portraits taken, as a private keepsake, when, instead, Harper and Douglass used photography to construct images of themselves as public intellectuals.[53] Given the popularity of photography as it evolved in America by the mid-nineteenth century, it was the most effective medium to present a common humanity for eloquent orators mindful of a dissecting white gaze. They used the medium to dispel racial myths, affect policy, and advocate for social justice. These photographs also preserve a historical record of slavery and freedom that undermines discourses of race and region as we seek to understand the complexities of being "Black" and "southern."

The simplistic operations of a camera obscura illustrate the phenomenon of how such constructed realities appear as inversions. Light reflected through an aperture makes images appear opposite from their natural state. (The addition of a mirror to the device rotates the image 180 degrees, which made photography possible.) The camera obscura turns the natural world upside-down when viewed through the device; it thereby produces a copy of the original that can be further manipulated for aesthetics. Laws of slavery created binary oppositions of "whiteness" (freedom, privilege, power) and "blackness" (oppression, persecution, subjugation), which become foundational for a plantation society based on discriminatory ideals of belonging in/to the U.S. South. The Fugitive Slave Law illustrates this inverted principle when enslaved Black people were returned to their owners as property, but most African Americans could not claim equal rights as citizens, especially in the region. In writing and life, Douglass understood this inversion process well; he seized every opportunity to reverse the perceived natural order of a world built by enslaved African Americans and not as imagined by white slaveholders. Rhetorically, in his written narratives and oratorical performances, the chiasmus trope was his favorite to explain how "a man was made a slave" and "how a slave was made a man." A capitalistic system created a "slave," which Douglass understood as an abstraction of humanity: "Douglass's job, the political work of his rhetoric, is to strip away the veil behind which this universe of illusion operates, defining its functional processes and machinery and unveiling its systems, apparatuses, and the functional processes by means of which it operates, thereby subverting its claims to be natural and fixed."[54]

Douglass makes us *see* not with just our eyes how Blackness is constructed: rather, we come to understand how the illusions of difference perpetuate systemic racism. And, in the same way, we should understand the arbitrariness of being southern as an illusion created for the benefit of those with privilege and power to claim it as solely their own. (Freedom, as innate quality, however, was attained regardless of circumstances as Douglass and countless other fugitive slaves achieved it.) Claiming the South then also allowed Douglass to give it meaning for himself and for others to do the same by visualizing a southern self in response to cultural displacement created by the black/white binary.

We must consider how such identifying factors continue to influence our perceptions of the U.S. South, and the (in)ability to map the contours of its fluid boundaries and recognize its diverse populations. Today, the most difficult task, it seems, is that we must also deal with the legacies of slavery and emancipation that haunt our imaginations still. Natasha Trethewey's poetry invites us to do just that. She often incorporates photographic media in her lyrics for mediation between the past and the present. Considering image manipulations with new media in the twenty-first century, like the very popular "selfie" phenomenon, I find Trethewey using twentieth-century flash photography to undermine assumptions about race, region, and constructed identities. Look, for example, at how her poem "Pastoral" illustrates the formation of southern identities under the weight of history:

> Say *"race,"* the photographer croons. I'm in
> blackface again when the flash freezes us.
> *My father's white,* I tell them, *and rural.*
> *You don't hate the South?* they ask. *You don't hate it?*[55]

Trethewey deconstructs a modern U.S. South using a visual-textual narrative in her ekphrastic poem. The photographic process intensifies racial anxieties about being and belonging for the nonwhite southerner. The artificiality of the scene—"Behind us, the skyline of Atlanta / hidden by the photographer's backdrop—/ a lush pasture, green, full of soft-eyed cows / lowing,"—and of the interracial image produced ironically reveals the truth about how regional identity is constructed by privilege and power.[56] To illuminate the scene, "the flash freezes us," bringing in full contrast light and dark while the loss of shadows implicates the photographer's careful manipulation of identity. Also, with the staging of the photo—by Robert Penn Warren and the Fugitive Poets— white males figure as the architects of a regional identity that is exclusive. But, with the speaker's insistence on lineage and place, the poet reveals the desire to present an authentic self.

The photographic process of producing southernness in the nineteenth century required "giving it form, color, space, and all the attributes of distinct personality," as Douglass understood this medium in general. These factors are most evident in the archive of Douglass's fugitive iconography. The claim I make here may seem to counter those of Henry Louis Gates, Jr., about Douglass's use of photography to create multiple "selves": "'the Negro,' 'the slave,' was various as any human beings could be, not just in comparison to white people, but even more important among and *within* themselves. [. . .] Not only do all black people *not* look alike, Douglass repeatedly is attesting through [his] photographs, but even one black subject doesn't 'look alike' over time; even he varies from self to self, remaining never static, a self always unfolding: dynamic, growing, changing, evolving."[57] However, Douglass seemed to maintain a static self-perception despite presenting "a range of selves over time" in his photographs.[58] This is the case when we consider the face of the fugitive as I discuss earlier. Also, Douglass suggests that not even time affects his constructed identity in photographs as he asked once of a foreign friend to remember him: "'I am as much like the picture she took of me as the wear and tear of thirteen years will permit me to be.'"[59]

Both Frederick Douglass and Frances Harper were conscious of the rhetoric and imagery used to racialize Black bodies as subhuman and noncitizens, and they took control over their self-image in ways in which we are only beginning to understand that many other African Americans envisioned freedom. Photography gave prominent figures such as Douglass and Harper the opportunity to exude Black pride, intelligence, and autonomy; their images also inspired viewers to take action in promoting the abolitionist agenda of civic engagement to achieve racially equality. Seeing the U.S. South as a region transformed by the actions of enslaved and free Black people but also as a space that did not also recognize their humanity and contributions to its cultural development in the nineteenth century is reason enough to consider Frederick Douglass's use of photography as a revolutionary tool.

NOTES

Note to the first epigraph: Douglass delivered a series of lectures on photography during the Civil War era: "Pictures and Progress" (1864–65), "Age of Pictures" (1862), and "Lecture on Pictures" (1861). Such works have become foundational for the study of Douglass's photographic archive, which contains over 160 known images. The lectures and many of Douglass's pictures appear in *Picturing Frederick Douglass,* eds. John Stauffer, Zoe Trodd, and Celeste-Marie Bernier.

1. Though I will not explore fully the connections between Douglass's photography and the reification of blackness marking bodies as deviant, criminal, and nonhuman within various forms of new media (especially on social media platforms) in recent years, my analysis in this essay may suggest ways of understanding the trajectory from the nineteenth to the twenty-first century.

2. Blackwood, "Fugitive Obscura," 95. Among the works of many other historians and literary scholars, Sarah Blackwood's investigation has drawn considerable attention to the narratives of slave notices, especially as evidence of "pre-photographic visual technologies" and how African American writers of the antebellum era responded to the development of photography.

3. Douglass, "Pictures and Progress," 367.

4. Ibid. He has indeed become the focus of numerous studies on African American photography in recent years, including Maurice O. Wallace and Shawn Michelle Williams's *Pictures and Progress;* Deborah Wills and Barbara Krauthamer's *Envisioning Emancipation;* John Stauffer, Zoe Trodd, and Celeste-Marie Bernier's *Picturing Frederick Douglass.*

5. Cooper and Rhee, "Introduction: Hacking the Black/White Binary." In this issue, the authors use "hacking as an analytic and technological tool that can richly complicate a multi-dimensional analysis of U.S. racial politics."

6. Foster, *A Brighter Coming Day.* Frances Harper's regionalist identity takes shape in her private letters to her abolitionist friends, namely William Still, that often were published. The way she describes her encounters with northern whites during the early years of her travels stands in contrast to the life she had in Baltimore's free Black communities, and her encounters with white and Black southerners during Reconstruction reveal the incongruity of the white/black as well as the fugitive/free binaries of southernness; Jones, "Engendered in the South"; Ramsey, "Frederick Douglass, Southerner." Frederick Douglass consistently recalls elements of slave culture (in rural and urban life), and scholars examine the lasting impact it had on him as revealed in his autobiographies; Ward, "My True South." Most recently, Jesmyn Ward's ambivalence about her southern heritage brings to mind Harper's and Douglass's conflicting identifications as I examine them in this essay.

7. The gendered and racial constructs of stereotypical and romanticized black southern identity I list here appear often in southern literature and cultural studies. Two works that have been most influential for my analysis are that of Riché Richardson's *From Uncle Tom to Gansta* and that of Kimberly Wallace-Sanders's *Mammy.*

8. Stauffer et al., *Picturing Frederick Douglass,* 572, n.12. Louis Daguerre (1787–1851) is mostly credited with inventing photography, in 1839. His use of the "daguerreotype" became popular in America, though another process, the "calotype," was invented simultaneously by an Englishman, Henry Fox Talbot (1800–1877).

9. Ibid., xxiv–xxv.

10. Ibid., 3–6. On a visit to Syracuse, New York, Douglass posed for a daguerreotype between July 30 and August 1 of 1843. He appears in a fine suit with crisp white shirt and necktie, staring off-center in a dignified profile. An engraving by John Chester Buttre (1821–93) of this image was published later in *Autographs for Freedom,* ed. Julia Griffiths (1854). A copy of a lost 1847 daguerreotype (unknown photographer) features Douglass in a dark suit, vest, and necktie. He is staring directly into the camera, which becomes his signature pose.

11. Blackwood, "Fugitive Obscura," 99–103. She examines a rare editorial found in Douglass's *The North Star* where he makes a "textual-visual assault on the fugitive slave notice" (101).

12. Douglass, "To My Old Master," 413. The original editorial was published on September 8, 1848.

13. Blackwood, "Fugitive Obscura," 103.

14. Douglass, "To My Old Master," 416.

15. Blackwood, "Fugitive Obscura," 103–4. She cites the work of Marcus Wood, who traces the origins of the running figure to European print culture and as it later appeared

in antebellum America in *Blind Memory: Visual Representations of Slavery in England and America, 1780–1865.*

16. Blackwood, "Fugitive Obscura," 101.

17. Gonzales, "The Face and the Public," 185.

18. Ibid., 190, 192.

19. Douglass, "Lectures on Pictures," 127.

20. This pamphlet includes "Country, Conscience, and the Anti-Slavery Cause," the first major speech Douglass delivered in the US after his almost two-year European exile. Douglass fled abroad after the successful publication of his 1845 autobiography; he was afraid of being captured and returned to his master given the visibility of his stature as a fugitive slave author. On returning to the US, Douglass delivered the address on May 11, 1847, at the thirteenth anniversary meeting of the American Anti-Slavery Society in New York's Broadway Tabernacle.

21. Quoted in *Picturing Frederick Douglass,* 78. The editors of this collection do not distinguish "southerners" as referring to white people only, assuming instead that only white people would recognize Douglass as the caricature while Black people would see an authentic image of Douglass and of Blackness itself.

22. Stauffer et al., *Picturing Frederick Douglass,* xxiv.

23. Buolamwini, "How I'm Fighting Bias in Algorithms."

24. Ibid., 6:07.

25. Douglass, "Pictures and Progress," 350.

26. Stauffer et al., *Picturing Frederick Douglass,* x.

27. Douglass, "Pictures and Progress," 166.

28. Stauffer et al., *Picturing Frederick Douglass,* xii.

29. Gonzales, "The Face and the Public," 195.

30. Hansen, *Bodies in Code.*

31. Gonzales, "The Face and the Public," 187.

32. According to Gonzales, British artist Keith Piper created the offline videogame as part of his *Relocating the Remains* (1997) exhibit. Hansen's analysis of it appears to dismiss the historical origins of the "raced image" of a fugitive (in "as in the act of running") as Gonzales counters and as I trace to antebellum print culture.

33. Gonzales, "The Face and the Public," 189. In the game, as Gonzales explains, it is not possible to win by arriving at a utopian alternate space.

34. Douglass, "To My Old Master," 418. Another explanation of what may account for the ways Douglass performs as southern in this public letter is to consider the theatrics of his abolitionist orations. Douglass would often use comic relief to explain the hypocrisy of slaveholders in which he played the exaggerated role of the white master or overseer.

35. Ibid., 419–20.

36. Ibid., 420.

37. Ibid., 418.

38. Frances Smith Foster reminds us, in "Afterwords," of the processes of constructing and reconstructing "the South" and cautions us to be more inclusive of all type of "southerners." She asks us to consider radical changes caused by the Haitian Revolution and the

1803 Louisiana Purchase, the War of 1812, and the Trail of Tears among other cultural trans-formations to the expansion of a southern region of the United States. The "new citizens" of New Orleans and other port cities along the Gulf South and southeastern border, for example, were often multilingual and created a multicultural society.

39. A few field-shifting studies that illustrate the altered/-ing perceptions of the litera-ture and culture of the nineteenth-century US South includes Coleman Hutchison's *Apples and Ashes* and Gina Caison's *Red States*.

40. Some pre–Civil War presses have described Harper as a "red mulatto," as "painted," or even as a "Cuban belle," which has caused much speculation about her ethnicity. My use of "native" in the lowercase here indicates both the possibility of her Native American ancestry and her birth origins in Baltimore, Maryland.

41. Johnson, "'In the Sunny South.'"

42. Sinha, "Frederick Douglass and Fugitivity."

43. With the passing of the 1850 Fugitive Slave Act, many free Black people fled the South fearing capture and sale into servitude. The controversial law paid anyone (with deputized powers) who recovered chattel property to return to their owners, and slave catchers profited from kidnapping free Black people as well. See Yale Law School's Lillian Goldman Law Library.

44. Harper is perhaps the only major African American author and activist other than Douglass in the nineteenth century that draws scholarly attention. My intent is to show how less "visible" she appears in southern studies specifically. Historians such as Martha S. Jones have broadened the scope for understanding free Blacks, especially in the South, and their struggles for belonging and rights of US citizenship. Jones's recent work *Birthright Citizens* examines the free Black community in Baltimore. In *All Bound Up Together,* Jones uses Harper as a case study for national belonging as Black activist women fought alongside their male counterparts (especially Frederick Douglass) for abolition and gender equality.

45. In their essays on the recovery of Harper's *Forest Leaves*, Carla L. Peterson, Eric Gardner, and Manisha Sinha all use this engraving of Harper, courtesy of the American Antiquarian Society in Worcester, Massachusetts. The same image appears on the cover of *A Brighter Coming Day*, which is a collection of her writings; it is archived at the Moorland-Spingarn Research Center at Howard University.

46. Tagged label of the photographic copy archived in the Library of Congress: https://lccn.loc.gov/97513270 DOA: April 25, 2019.

47. Different sources identify the image as appearing in *Iola Leroy, or Shadows Uplifted, Poems* (1898), and *Sketches of a Southern Life* (1891). I have not located a copy of an earlier edition of *Sketches* that may have included this image.

48. Two more images, of an older Harper, feature her as a dignified "race woman," as they are featured in various collections around the turn of the twentieth century. See the Schomburg Center for Research in Black Culture, Jean Blackwell Hutson Research and Ref-erence Division, New York Public Library: "Mrs. Frances E. W. Harper" and "Mrs. F. E. W. Harper, Author and Lecturer, Philadelphia, Pa."

49. Harper's images are a glaring omission in recent collections of interdisciplinary scholarship and archival Black photographs that seek to make more inclusive a burgeoning

field of visual culture and southern historiography: Wallace and Smith (eds.), *Pictures and Progress;* Willis and Krauthamer, *Envisioning Emancipation;* Fox-Amato, *Exposing Slavery.*

50. Willis and Krauthamer, *Envisioning Emancipation,* 14.

51. Enslaved in upstate New York and freed by 1820 laws that abolished slavery in the state, Sojourner Truth presents an interesting take on identity politics, as I argue in this essay. Truth took control of her image as a free woman; she used photography as did Douglass to correct the public's perceptions of African Americans as a denigrated race. See Nell Irvin Painter, *Sojourner Truth: A Life, a Symbol.*

52. I see this conflict not only as a struggle for national belonging, but also as a personal struggle for two orphans who became crusaders of justice. Both Douglass and Harper were orphaned as young children, experiences that lack intimate details in their writing about growing up southern in Maryland among its enslaved and free Black populations. Douglass's autobiographies are more revealing about other slaves at times than about his own family relations. Likewise, Harper's early life remains a mystery with few biographical details about growing up in Baltimore until she reached the age of twenty-five. (Douglass was about twenty years old when he escaped in 1838.) Other than brief sketches by William Still and others, a full-length biography, Melba Joyce Boyd's *Discarded Legacy: Politics and Poetics in the Life of Frances E. W. Harper, 1825–1911,* is most often cited.

53. Willis and Krauthamer, *Envisioning Emancipation,* 2.

54. Gates, "Frederick Douglass's Camera Obscura," 201.

55. Trethewey, "Pastoral,"11.11–14. The speech here is inspired by William Faulkner's *Absalom, Absalom!* (1936), as spoken by Quentin Compson: "I don't hate it," he responds when asked by Shreve, his Canadian roommate at Harvard, "Why do you hate the South?"

56. Trethewey, "Pastoral,"11. 3–6.

57. Gates, "Frederick Douglass's Camera Obscura," 203, emphasis in the original.

58. Ibid., 203.

59. Quoted in Stauffer et al., *Picturing Frederick Douglass,* 254, n.3.

BIBLIOGRAPHY

Blackwood, Sarah. "Fugitive Obscura: Runaway Slave Portraiture and Early Photographic Technology," *American Literature* 81, no. 1 (March 2009): 93–125.

Boyd Melba Joyce. *Discarded Legacy: Politics and Poetics in the Life of Frances E. W. Harper, 1825–1911.* Detroit, MI: Wayne State University Press, 1994.

Buolamwini, Joy. "How I'm Fighting Bias in Algorithms." Filmed November 2016 at TEDxBeaconStreet, Brookline, MA.: Video, 8:37. https://www.ted.com/talks/joy_buolam wini_how_i_m_fighting_bias_in_algorithms.

Caison, Gina. *Red States: Indigeneity, Settler Colonialism, and Southern Studies.* Athens: University of Georgia Press, 2018.

Cooper, Brittany, and Margaret Rhee. "Introduction: Hacking the Black/White Binary," *Ada: A Journal of Gender, New Media, and Technology,* no. 6 (January 2015). http://dx.doi.org /10.7264/N38S4N6F.

Digital Public Library of America's collections: http://digitalcollections.nypl.org/items/510 d47de-1bfe-a3d9-e040-e00a18064a99; http://digitalcollections.nypl.org/items/510d47 da-7113-a3d9-e040-e00a18064a99.

Douglass, Frederick. "Lectures on Pictures" (1861). In *Picturing Frederick Douglass: An Illustrated Biography of the Nineteenth Century's Most Photographed American,* edited by John Stauffer, Zoe Trodd, and Celeste-Marie Bernier, 126–95. New York: Liveright Publishing Corporation, 2015.

———. "Pictures and Progress" (1864–1865). In *The Portable Frederick Douglass,* edited by John Stauffer and Henry Louis Gates, Jr., 345–63. New York: Penguin Books, 2016.

———. "To My Old Master." In *The Portable Frederick Douglass,* edited by John Stauffer and Henry Louis Gates, Jr., 413–20. New York: Penguin Books, 2016.

Faulkner, William. *Absalom, Absalom!: The Corrected Text.* Ed. Noel Polk. New York: Vintage, 1987.

Foster, Frances Smith. "Afterwords; Or, Whistling 'Dixie' on the Front Porch of My Southern Home." *Southern Quarterly* 45, no. 3 (Spring 2008): 177–84.

———, ed. *A Brighter Coming Day: A Frances Ellen Watkins Harper Reader.* New York: Feminist Press at City University of New York, 1990.

Fox-Amato, Matthew. *Exposing Slavery: Photography, Human Bondage, and the Birth of Modern Visual Politics in America.* Oxford: Oxford University Press, 2019.

Gardner, Eric. "Leaves, Trees, and Forests: Frances Ellen Watkins's *Forest Leaves* and Recovery." *Common-place.org.* 16, no. 2 (Winter 2016). http://common-place.org/book/leaves-trees-and-forests-frances-ellen-watkinss-forest-leaves-and-recovery/.

Gates, Henry Louis, Jr. "Frederick Douglass's Camera Obscura: Representing the Anti-Slave 'Clothed and in Their Own Form.'" In *Picturing Frederick Douglass: An Illustrated Biography of the Nineteenth Century's Most Photographed American,* edited by John Stauffer, Zoe Trodd, and Celeste-Marie Bernier, 197–216. New York: Liveright Publishing Corporation, 2015.

Gonzales, Jennifer. "The Face and the Public: Race, Secrecy and Digital Art Practice." In *The 'Do-It-Yourself' Artwork: Participation from Fluxus to New Media,* edited by Anna Dezeuze, 285–305. Manchester: Manchester University Press, 2012.

Hansen, Mark B. N. *Bodies in Code: Interfaces with Digital Media.* New York: Routledge, 2006.

Harper, Frances Ellen Watkins. *Iola Leroy, or Shadows Uplifted.* Boston: James H. Earle, 1892, and Philadelphia: Garrigues Brothers, 1892.

———. *Poems.* Philadelphia: George S. Ferguson Co., 1898.

———. *Sketches of a Southern Life.* Philadelphia: Ferguson Brothers & Co., 1891.

Hutchison, Coleman. *Apples and Ashes: Literature, Nationalism, and the Confederate States of America.* Athens: University of Georgia Press, 2012.

Johnson, Sherita L. "'In the Sunny South': Reconstructing Frances Harper as Southern." *Southern Quarterly* 45, no. 3 (Spring 2008): 70–87.

Jones, Anne Goodwyn. "Engendered in the South: Blood and Irony in Douglass and Jacobs." In *Haunted Bodies: Gender and Southern Texts,* 201–19. Charlottesville: University Press of Virginia, 1997.

Jones, Martha S. *All Bound Up Together: The Woman Question in Antebellum Public Culture, 1830–1900*. Chapel Hill: University of North Carolina Press, 2007.

———. *Birthright Citizens: A History of Race and Rights in Antebellum America*. Cambridge: Cambridge University Press, 2018.

Painter, Nell Irvin. *Sojourner Truth: A Life, a Symbol*. New York: W. W. Norton, 1997.

Peterson, Carla L. "Searching for Frances." *Common-place.org*. 16, no. 2 (Winter 2016). http://common-place.org/book/searching-for-frances/.

Ramsey, William M. "Frederick Douglass, Southerner." *Southern Literary Journal* 40, no. 1 (Fall 2007): 19–38.

Richardson, Riché. *From Uncle Tom to Gansta: Black Masculinity and the U.S. South*. Athens: University of Georgia Press, 2007.

Schomburg Center for Research in Black Culture, Jean Blackwell Hutson Research and Reference Division, New York Public Library. "Mrs. Frances E.W. Harper." New York Public Library Digital Collections. Accessed November 2, 2020. http://digitalcollections.nypl.org/items/510d47de-1bfe-a3d9-e040-e00a18064a99.

———. "Mrs. F. E. W. Harper, Author and Lecturer, Philadelphia, Pa." New York Public Library Digital Collections. Accessed November 2, 2020. http://digitalcollections.nypl.org/items/510d47da-7113-a3d9-e040-e00a18064a99.

Sinha, Manisha. "Frederick Douglass and Fugitivity." *Black Perspectives*. November 26, 2018. https://www.aaihs.org/frederick-douglass-and-fugitivity/.

Sinha, Manisha. "The Other Frances Ellen Watkins Harper." *Common-place.org*. 16, no. 2 (Winter 2016). http://common-place.org/book/the-other-frances-ellen-watkins-harper/.

Stauffer, John, Zoe Trodd, and Celeste-Marie Bernier, eds. *Picturing Frederick Douglass: An Illustrated Biography of the Nineteenth Century's Most Photographed American*. New York: Liveright Publishing Corporation, 2015.

Trethewey, Natasha. "Pastoral." In *Native Guard*, 35. New York: Houghton Mifflin Company, 2006.

Wallace, Maurice O., and Shawn Michelle Smith. *Pictures and Progress: Early Photography and the Making of African American Identity*. Durham, NC: Duke University Press, 2012.

Wallace-Sanders, Kimberly. *Mammy: A Century of Race, Gender, and Southern Memory*. Lansing: University of Michigan, 2009.

Ward, Jesmyn. "My True South: Why I Decided to Return Home," *Time* (July 26, 2018), 47–49.

Willis, Deborah, and Barbara Krauthamer. *Envisioning Emancipation: Black Americans and the End of Slavery*. Philadelphia: Temple University Press, 2013.

Wood, Marcus. *Blind Memory: Visual Representations of Slavery in England and America, 1780–1865*. Manchester: Manchester University Press, 2000.

Yale Law School. "The Avalon Law Project: Documents in Law, History, and Diplomacy." Lillian Goldman Law Library. https://avalon.law.yale.edu/19th_century/fugitive.asp.

SINCE TIME

S-Town and the Problem of Southern Temporality

DAVID A. DAVIS

I KNEW OF *S-Town* (2017) before I heard it. As soon as the podcast was released, people began asking me if I had listened to it, some of them caught up in the show's hype and many of them expecting me to opine about how the series depicted the U.S. South. I resisted the lure for a while but eventually succumbed. I was not alone, of course. More than ten million people downloaded the podcast in the first week of its release; more than forty million people downloaded it in the first month after its release; and, more than seventy-seven million downloaded it within a year of its release.[1] It won a Peabody Award for excellence in storytelling, and a major production company purchased the rights to make a film based on the story. *S-Town,* moreover, revolutionized the podcast genre into a bingeable format and established new conventions of storytelling, which has been dubbed "aural literature."[2] By releasing the entire series at once, rather than episodically like its predecessor, *Serial* (2014), producer Brian Reed was able to tell a story in a format more similar to a novel, developing characterization and narrative tension with plot twists and withheld information. While the format contributed to the podcast's success, most listeners were interested in the show's main character, John B. McLemore, an eccentric, colorfully cynical historic clock repairman from Woodstock, Alabama, a small town on Interstate 59 between Birmingham and Tuscaloosa, which figures in the podcast as the eponymous "Shittown." The podcast constitutes a new genre of southern literature based in an aural new media format that draws upon traditional conventions of othering the U.S. South as a perceptual region distinct from the United States, while using new forms of technology and storytelling to convey the narrative. When people asked me about the podcast, however, they rarely wanted to discuss its formal conventions or its record-setting popularity. Instead, they wanted to talk about its weirdness.

The defining characteristic of *S-Town*, even more than its narrative technique, is its preposterousness. The story opens with a seemingly irrelevant discourse about antique clocks and then veers into an unhinged and transparent conspiracy theory about a murder and an inept police cover-up. The supposed true crime theme harkens to *Serial*, the podcast produced by Sarah Koenig that spun off of the NPR storytelling series *This American Life* where Brian Reed is a senior producer. The first series of *Serial* investigated the murder of Hae Min Lee in Baltimore, and the show took an active role in investigating the murder and recording discoveries serially as they occurred, inserting the reporters into the investigation, rather than reporting on the case from the detached, past tense, cumulative perspective of traditional journalism. McLemore contacted *This American Life* to report a murder and cover-up in a small town in Alabama, which was sufficient to attract Reed's attention and lead him to investigate the tip. The first two episodes of *S-Town* focus on the murder, a plot that quickly dissipates as it becomes evident that the supposed crime is based on hearsay, exaggeration, and intoxication, but as Reed pursues the investigation, he focuses attention on McLemore, whose eccentric personality becomes the series' narrative center. The third episode of the series reveals that McLemore committed suicide by drinking cyanide and goes into lurid detail about the circumstances of his death. The remaining episodes explore facets of McLemore's life, including unfounded claims that he buried gold on his family's land, his work on antique clocks, his sexuality, his mental illness, his masochistic pain fixation, and his complicated relationship with Tyler Goodson. The series pries into the details of McLemore's life, allowing listeners to gawk at private aspects of his romantic relationships, his social milieu, and his southern hometown. The show's weirdness is crucial to its appeal because it allows listeners to eavesdrop on what appears to be a deviant subculture embedded in a regressive timescale.

One could argue, as I have, that the series should never have been made.[3] Since there is no crime to investigate, the series does not serve the public good, and many of the aspects of McLemore's life that the series explores were clearly personal and not intended to be revealed to the public. Some articles have rebuked Reed for making the podcast. Gay Alcorn calls it "morally indefensible" in the *Guardian*, and Jessica Goudeau questions if it should have been created in the *Atlantic*.[4] In an interview with *Time*, Eliana Dockterman asks Reed if he believes that he should have revealed details about McLemore's life, and he responds, "We weighed each one in terms of: what does this teach us about John? Is it important? How important is it? So there's a lot we left out. Honestly, it's a human judgment call. [. . .] But, I mean, the people who knew him best were very open and seemed to feel okay sharing a lot about his life. And we were judicious about what we included."[5] McLemore's family, meanwhile, has sued Reed and the podcast for exploiting details of his personal life to make money. The ethical issues regarding the podcast's depiction of McLemore are complicated and fraught. I contend, meanwhile, that the podcast also has serious problems regarding its depiction of the U.S. South.

The podcast allows listeners to eavesdrop on the sordid details of a person's life and to virtually participate in the projection of the U.S. South as a perceptual region, an area marked as distinctive based on historical, cultural, and, ultimately, imaginary characteristics. Unlike textual or visual media such as books or television, podcasts—which Dario Linares has labeled a "new aural culture"—depend solely upon listening to convey a story, appealing to the sonic imagination to develop an apparition of reality.[6] This represents a notable shift in media from visuality to aurality. In *Reason and Resonance* (2004), Veit Erlmann explains that modernity has privileged visual perceptions—from Descartes's emphasis on the notion that seeing is believing in his conception of rationality, up to developments of communication technologies that appeal to vision, such as film, television, and the internet. Erlmann asserts, however, that aurality involves both "the materiality of perception" and the "conditions that must be given for something to become recognized, labeled, and valorized as audible in the first place."[7] Auditory perception is heavily influenced by social context. Podcasts build upon a series of technologies, including phonographs, radio, and telephones, that use sound to communicate mediated experiences, so the new platform follows the contours of the media forms that preceded it. Ultimately, *S-Town* is a form of oral storytelling that combines the oldest form of human communication, which requires immediate intersubjective transmission, with a new form of media transmission that removes the requirement for immediacy.

In *The Audible Past* (2003), Jonathan Sterne states that historically, "new sound technologies had an impact on the nature of sound or hearing, but they were part of social and cultural currents that they did not create."[8] As a podcast, *S-Town* is a form of digital auditory media embedded in a specific social context, and its depiction of the U.S. South is predicated on stereotypes, biases, and assumptions that are deeply embedded in the American imagination. The program deliberately appeals to these ideas as it presents a distorted sonic

image of the region and its people, situating *S-Town* firmly within a long genealogy of southern storytelling. Each episode, for example, concludes with an
"eerie, melancholy" song titled "A Rose for Emily" by the English rock band
The Zombies.[9] First released in 1968, this song crafts a southern gothic soundscape befitting its literary inspiration—William Faulkner's 1930 short story
by the same title about a fallen, unwed, eventually decrepit southern belle
who turns to murder and necrophilia in her decline. McLemore intentionally
invites Reed to interpret Woodstock through the eyes of Faulkner's southern
gothic as he assigns "bedtime reading" on Reed's first night in Alabama, reading that includes "A Rose for Emily."[10] Podcasts may be a new means of deliver-
ing content, but *S-Town* ultimately engages in an old form of storytelling with
roots in southwestern humor and local color fiction. In this case, the story that
is being told depicts a long-enduring, exaggerated version of the U.S. South,
which makes the medium more relatable and potentially more bingeable because the message is familiar to the national imagination.

In addition to its exaggerated and gothic themes, *S-Town* also portrays
the U.S. South as temporally disconnected from the United States, suggesting
that it is an inherently deviant region situated in an imaginary historical space.
The podcast's emphasis on signifiers for time, such as clocks and sundials, reinforces this persistent narrative about temporality. Alexis McCrossen explains
in *Marking Modern Times* (2013) that, as the United States industrialized, mechanical linear time took precedence over organic cyclical time, and by the
early twentieth century clocks had become common symbols of modernity.
Time, however, is an arbitrary, socially constructed concept that is subject
to interpretation and differences in experience and perception. The podcast
contrasts the linear temporality associated with the contemporary experience
of modernity with an alternate version of temporality projected onto the U.S.
South. The podcast depicts McLemore's hometown and—by extension—the
entire U.S. South as a place stuck in the past and, thus, deviant. For example,
when he first visits McLemore's home, Reed asks McLemore's mother, whom
he describes as so old as to be virtually eternal, how long the family has lived
in this place, and she responds, "since time," implying that the family's inhabitation of rural Alabama extends outside the bounds of measurable time. Reed
verbally nods and winks at the statement, indicating his status as the arbiter
of "real time." He moves on, but this implication that the region exists in an
alternate temporal plane is a recurring trope throughout the podcast and a
persistent problem for discussions of the contemporary U.S. South. Under-

standing the narrative dynamics of the podcast reveals how new media reinforces old perceptions of the region.

Witness Marks: Signifiers of Temporality

During his initial visit to McLemore's home in Woodstock, Alabama, in October 2014, Reed describes himself driving into a remote location where he approaches "an old wooden house with three chimneys that looks like it hasn't changed since the Civil War."[11] The reference to the U.S. Civil War embeds the scene in the southern past, implying that the house—and the region—has not developed since the end of that war. He goes on to comment that "the whole place feels like it's of another time. And it is, literally. John doesn't follow daylight savings, so his property is on a time zone separate from the world around it."[12] Reed projects a palpable sense that McLemore's home exists in an alternate temporal frame where modern patterns of time and development have been suspended. The fact that McLemore evidently rejects normative time conventions reinforces the sense that the story takes place outside the present time. When Reed meets McLemore's mother, Mary Grace, she tells him, "where we live, it's real old."[13] The reference to the Civil War places the story in a past where, as the lyric from "Dixie" states, "old times are not forgotten," and the layered images of temporal discontinuity reinforce the sense that the U.S. South belongs more in the past than in the present. Later, Reed and a friend of McLemore's describe the sense of visiting the home as going "back in time."[14] The podcast's repeated references to time, timekeeping, and timepieces emphasize the sense of temporal discontinuity by bringing the listeners' attention to measurements and perceptions of time, and these repeated references function as a structural feature of the podcast, embedding temporality into the listeners' apprehension of the narrative.

Reed opens the podcast with a seemingly tangential discussion of clock repair. "When an antique clock breaks," he says, "a clock that's been telling time for 200 or 300 years, fixing it can be a real puzzle. An old clock like that was handmade by someone. It might tick away the time with a pendulum, with a spring, with a pulley system. It might have bells that are supposed to strike the hour, or a bird that's meant to pop out and cuckoo at you. There can be hundreds of tiny, individual pieces, each of which needs to interact with the others precisely."[15] From here, he describes the difficulty of repairing a clock that "doesn't come with a manual" and the importance of "witness marks": the "actual impressions, and outlines, and discolorations left inside the clock of pieces that might have once been there" that antique horologists use to guide their repairs.[16] The discussion of clock repair focuses the listeners' attention on the issue of temporality, particularly archaic devices for time measurement, and it also establishes a set of metaphors for the podcast's narrative exposition. The story, in effect, becomes an exercise in following witness marks. "I'm told fixing an old clock can be maddening," Reed says with a flat affect. "You're constantly wondering if you've just spent hours going down a path that will likely take you nowhere, and all you've got are these vague witness marks, which might not even mean what you think they mean. So at every moment along the way, you have to decide if you're wasting your time or not. Anyway, I only learned about all this because years ago an antique clock restorer contacted me, John B. McLemore, and asked me to help him solve a murder."[17] This introduction evokes the "once upon a time" trope that opens fairy tales, suggesting that the story takes place within an encapsulated temporal space while also implying that the story itself is a waste of time.

The repeated references to clock repair throughout the story, meanwhile, draw the listeners' attention to how we use and consume time. During the course of the podcast, Reed moves through the history of timepieces. "For thousands and thousands of years, we did not have clocks, or calendars, or any method for telling time in the way we think of telling time now," he explains. "And time was happening nonetheless. As humans, we must have sensed it. Maybe we heard it, the rhythm of it, as we sharpened a tool. It's amazing, if you think about it, the sheer variety of methods we've concocted over the centuries to keep track of time. We pour sand through a glass. We swing pendulums back and forth. We count the cycles of radiation coming off an atom. We count Mississippis."[18] This rumination about human fascination with time bookends the first episode, which began with the discussion of witness marks. It also entangles both the abstraction of time and its materiality in terms of objectivity ("sand through a glass," "pendulums") and geographic spatiality ("Mississippis"). His reference to "Mississippis" underscores a geotemporal construct of the U.S. South, as the State of Mississippi has been invoked as synecdoche for the region as a regressive space.[19]

Reed offers his thoughts about time measurement as McLemore shows him an astrolabe, which "looks kind of like a clock crossed with a compass. It's a flat dial with a map of the night sky laid over it, and a pointer, or I guess a sight, attached on top of that. You pick a star in the sky, and aim the sight at it, twist the sky map until it aligns with the sight in a certain way. And then the dial shows you your direction, as well as the month, day, and time."[20] Reed's description of the astrolabe collapses the abstraction of time measured by the "clock" and the geography invoked by a "compass," narrating how the tool renders for the user both their directional and temporal locations. He further explains that McLemore designed the astrolabe in his home himself, which indicates both his exceptional intellect and his enduring fascination with time. Later, Reed offers a similar discussion of sundials, another premechanical timepiece that McLemore designed. He says, "Before we had clocks, we had sundials, and I never thought about this until I started talking to John, but watching a sundial, which could be as simple as a stick in the ground, as the shadow crept along, you were actually witnessing the rotation of the Earth. It's so much less abstracted than a clock, a level closer to time itself."[21] Here, Reed temporarily abandons modern notions of time as a regimented, measured system and contemplates the idea of time being a natural process of orbital movement, which indicates the variability of temporal systems.

In addition to his interest in premodern time measurement, McLemore made his living as an antique horologist, a person who repairs old clocks, so the podcast delves into clocks and the community of people who collect clocks and people who repair them. Reed explains that "horology experienced a kind of heyday in the [19]90s, particularly as antique collectors took to eBay. But that boom has been over for a while, and especially with time so easily accessible now on our appliances and cell phones, it's definitely a dying trade."[22] McLemore gained a reputation as a capable clock restorer, partly because he was willing to use dangerous techniques to return pieces to their original condition, and he developed some close relationships with people based on their mutual interest in clocks. One of these people is a clock collector named Bill who explained the allure of clocks with a story about "a cheap kitchen clock in his grandparent's house."[23] Reed narrates that Bill watched his grandfather wind the clock every week, and "he was mesmerized by how this object suddenly became alive, ticking, hands turning. And he began crying as he told me. Is it that clock, I asked him, that was emotional for him? 'It's not any one personal clock,' he said. 'It was just the measure of time had something to do with me.' I didn't totally know what Bill meant by this—'the measure of time had something to do with me.' But I think he was saying that even as a kid the clock captured this feeling of time going by, going by, and never coming back."[24] Bill's emotional response to the clock indicates the complex relationships people have with clocks as fetishized objects and with time as a concept. As the podcast emphasizes, mutual fascination with the abstract concept of time and the materiality of its measurement created the community that largely comprised McLemore's social sphere during the heyday of his horology career. Where *S-Town* characterizes the concept and measurement of time as constituting McLemore's horology community, his physical community of Woodstock, Alabama, seems to be a place constituted *in* time, fixed in temporal alterity from the rest of the nation.

Time, indeed, lies at the core of most creation myths and, thus, religious systems, which locate the beginning of time as the origins of existence, and modern theories of physics still struggle to contemplate the moment when nothingness gave way to existence. Before the development of devices to measure time, people organized their lives according to the cyclical, diurnal patterns of seasons, days and nights, and births and deaths. The development of devices to measure time radically changed human relationships with temporality. Sundials, hourglasses, and water clocks used features of the natural world to mark the incremental passage of time, but these devices each had practical limitations. Mechanical clocks broke the perception of time free from the limitations of the natural world. As Barbara Adam explains in *Time* (2004), "as it is melded and worked into our social relations, decontextualized and disembodied, clock time facilitates an acute present orientation and sense of distance and disconnection from the physical world and external influences. When machine time, which has no consequences, no cause and effect, no accumulation, no irreversible change, no memory and no purpose, is employed as a synchronizing and organizational tool, an illusory set of temporal relations are set in motion that become real in their lived experiences."[25] Clocks fundamentally change our experience of time, and, as the community of clock collectors and horologists profiled in the podcast indicates, clocks have taken on value as fetish objects valued for their function, beauty, significance, and symbolism as well as for their ability to measure time. The podcast exposes its listeners to this subculture of time fetishists, which enhances the role of time as an element of the narrative, making the listener's binge, itself, a self-reflexive experience of temporality that consolidates Reed's months-long investigation, decades of McLemore's life, and generations of the McLemore family into 382 minutes or just over six hours. Whereas time historically has organized human labor, *S-Town's* complete release of episodic aural literature demonstrates how new forms of media have the capacity to invert that relationship. The binge format allows the listener to bend narrative time according to their prerogative.

This temporal flexibility raises another issue related to the representation of time in *S-Town*. The podcast draws attention to normative experiences of time and suggests the possibility that it can be experienced in other ways. In *Time Binds* (2010) Elizabeth Freeman describes the concept of chrononormativity, or "the use of time to organize individual human bodies toward maximum productivity."[26] She explains that the proliferation of temporal measurements and indicators, such as calendars, schedules, and clocks, inculcates a sense of regimented time that governs individual behavior. Monique Rooney builds on this idea, noting that the multiple forms of media represented in *S-Town* function as a form of intermedia, the depiction of numerous forms of media within a work demonstrating intricate networks of connectivity. She argues that the podcast's "intermediality" challenges the concept of chrononormativity and creates the possibility for alternative, or queer, experiences of temporality. She writes, "The significance of the podcast's intermedial structure for thinking about time, selfhood and the place of the South, focusing particularly on the temporally queer legacy of the Alabama clockmaker, on nonlinear aspects of the grammar organizing the spoken-drama and on temporally dissonant media incorporated within the podcast."[27] In her reading, McLemore "facilitates far-reaching concepts of time," but Michael Bibler disagrees with this position. He contends that *S-Town* limits the multiplicity of McLemore's temporality by "constraining it within the closed temporal field of the podcast's strictly sequential form."[28] This interpretation implies that the podcast itself also functions as a means of measuring time, along with calendars, clocks, and sundials. McLemore, therefore, exists enmeshed within a matrix of temporal technologies, which, considering his fascination with time, seems appropriate.

Fascination with time can also have a dark side. McLemore, who has clearly been interested in measuring and controlling time, manifests a paranoid fear that humans are inevitably facing an apocalyptic future, which may very well be true, but his obsession with these issues is clearly described by Reed as debilitating. As his mental illness progressed, he developed obsessive thoughts about climate change, socioeconomic instability, and impending cataclysm. When in a depressive state, he talks about "proleptic decay and decrepitude," suggesting an inevitable future decline.[29] Many people share this fear of impending apocalypse. In *Enduring Time* (2017), Lisa Baraitser suggests that, to some people, the idea of the future has been cancelled due to looming anxieties about inevitable crises, including violent conflict, growing inequalities, climate change, and the other apocalyptic qualities of the Anthropocene. These people feel that the future "has become emptied of its affective qualities such as hope, anticipation, longing, or the promise of satisfaction or betterment."[30] McLemore was unable to manage his obsession with time and his sense of a cancelled future. "His problem was a proleptic one," Reed attempts to explain. "He saw nothing but darkness in the future. Shittown, for John, was not believing that anything good would last. That we would inevitably mess it up. Relationships that are meaningful, the Earth as a place that can adequately support human life, even John's remarkable maze."[31] Reed uses McLemore's own eschatological visions to develop a theory that McLemore's use of vaporized mercury in antique clock repair damaged his brain, contributing to his depression and paranoia and, ultimately, leading to his suicide. Although credible, this theory could not be proved without physiological tests that would have to be conducted on living tissue, so we will never know for certain if McLemore's fascination with clocks led to his obsession with proleptic decay and decrepitude. Reed's elaboration of this theory in the podcast's final episode invites the audience to interpret McLemore through the mercury-poisoning theory, and this denouement suggests a kind of irony. According to Reed, McLemore's fascination with time led to a belief in its cancellation, and his individual disillusionment animates the podcast's broader temporal setting where Woodstock figures a geography where the future, modernity itself, never manifested.

To the average listener, that may not matter, as it did not seem to matter for the dozens of people who asked me about S-Town in 2017. The story's weirdness is more important than the proximal cause of McLemore's suicide, and the recurring motif of temporality reinforces a perception that Reed develops about the difference between himself and the place where McLemore lives. Reed uses allochronic discourse to describe McLemore's home in Alabama, the so-called Shittown. In Time and the Other (1983), Johannes Fabian argues that anthropologists often use allochronic discourse, or language that suggests that they, as observers, exist in a current temporal plane while their subjects exist in a detached, delayed temporal plane, to effectively deny coevalness to the subject.[32] The language of temporality in S-Town, including the repeated references to timepieces, horology, and conceptions of time, contributes to the sense that McLemore's community exists in a delayed temporal plane, trapped in an alternate past where "old times are not forgotten."³³ This sense that Reed and, by extension, the podcast listener voyeuristically observing McLemore's life through their headphones exist in the present—even as the podcast contains a digitally encapsulated segment of bingeable time—while Shittown exists in the past and feeds into persistent perceptions of the South as the United States' spatiotemporal other.

Shittown, Woodstock, and Uneven Development

Shittown, however, does not exist. McLemore uses the term to describe the place where he lives, and Reed borrows the term to title the podcast, thus situating the listener in a false reality—an imaginary, caricatured version of the U.S. South. In one particularly descriptive passage, McLemore uses the city's actual name, but he offers a vision of it that fits with his retrograde vision of the community:

> Yeah, Woodstock. This whole area needs to be defined. If you look at the demographics charts of the state of Alabama and go over the poorest counties, Bibb County is maybe the fifth worst county to live in. We are one of the child molester capitals of the States. We have just an incredible amount of police corruption. We have the poorest education. We've got 95 churches in this damn county. We only have two high schools and no secondary education. And we got Jebus, 'cause Jebus is coming and global warming is a hoax. You know, there's no such thing as climate change and all that. Yeah, I—I'm in an area that just hasn't advanced, for lack of a better word.³⁴

The podcast dwells on this notion that Woodstock "has not advanced" in wealth, public safety, education, or social engagement. Mocking Christianity, McLemore emphasizes the community's belief in spirituality and its denial of science-based evidence. While McLemore clearly works to "define" the community of Woodstock itself, Reed's position as a Jewish New Yorker narrating the weirdness of "Shittown, USA" creates an effect reminiscent of late-nineteenth century regional literature in which an educated outsider narrates and translates the region, here the South, to a fascinated "national" audience. In this way, the U.S. South is generalized as demonstrably not as developed as other parts of the nation.

Incorporating a genealogy of regionalism in its form of aural literature, *S-Town* invokes an imaginary southern soundscape. R. Murray Schafer uses the term "soundscape" to describe the auditory ecology of a place that brings together sounds of the natural world and sounds created by humans, which include both artificial sounds, such as horns and machines, and the sounds of human speech.[35] Soundscapes, thus, have a particular identity based on the accumulation of noises within an environment, so sound can be used to indicate a location. In "Listening to the Heard Worlds of Antebellum America," Mark Smith describes the phenomenon of auditory regionalism in which the North and South before the Civil War associated each other with specific sets of sounds. According to Smith, southerners associated the North with the cacophony of machines and cities, and northerners associated the South with the quiet of agriculture and the crack of the lash. "Where southerners found comfort in the sound of discipline on their plantations and reveled in the quiet industry of the Southern pastoral," he writes, "Northerners heard only the chilling silence and the deafening noise of immoral slavery, a politically tyrannous institution that retarded the industrial capitalist progress of the region."[36] These characteristics of auditory regionalism have endured for more than a century and a half, and *S-Town* trades on many of the same differences in soundscape. The soundscape in the podcast, however, is based mostly on the sounds of technology, such as the differences in recording equipment that Reed uses, some ambient noise, and human voices. In addition to The Zombies' Faulknerian tune mentioned earlier, the podcast's opening theme song, "Bibb County," composed by Daniel Hart, similarly adds to the southern soundscape with its folksy use of violin, cello, and percussion that one might mistake for sound of bare hands clapping to the rhythm. The tune might fit equally in a backwoods juke joint or around a campfire with moonshine. The most obvious marker of the southern soundscape, though, is the southern accent of interviewees, which Reed sometimes feels a need to translate for the listener, enhancing the sense of otherness between the listeners and the speakers.

Reed incorporates numerous signifiers for southern backwardness in the podcast. One of the obvious examples is the scene at Black Sheep Ink, a tattoo parlor in Bessemer, Alabama. On his second night in Alabama, Reed goes there to meet with Jake Goodson, the person who told McLemore about the alleged murder, and he finds a sketchy shop with a secret back room filled with "a collection of misfits, of self-proclaimed criminals and runaways and hillbillies."[37] Reed goes on at length describing the people there, including a shirtless fat guy with "feed me" tattooed on his belly, a man who has worn the same trucker hat for seven years, a man called Razor, and the obligatory tattoo artist named Bubba who uses racial slurs excessively and who displays "a rather fluent knowledge of the differences between various white supremacy groups."[38] This scene focuses on images of poverty and racism, illustrating a version of the U.S. South that impedes progress. The racist tattoo artist, in fact, articulates some troubling political opinions about social welfare that seem to align with reactionary white populism. Beyond this scene, the podcast features scenes of trailer parks, drug users, unwed mothers, holiness churches, the Ku Klux Klan, and numerous other images that are associated with backwardness and the region, reinforcing the persistent notion that the U.S. South "just hasn't advanced," to use McLemore's words.

Early in their relationship, Reed and McLemore have an exchange about McLemore's dissatisfaction with his hometown. McLemore laments being surrounded with "rednecks" who can't understand the consequences of climate change and are otherwise uninterested in intellectual pursuits, and Reed asks him if he can talk to anyone in the area for intellectual stimulation. McLemore launches into a typical rant, responding, "Ah, you're beginning to figure it out now, aren't you? So why don't I move?"[39] He veers into a long digression in which he compares himself to a person from Fallujah who feels a sense of obligation to family. The exchange recalls the scene in *Absalom, Absalom!* (1936) where Shreve asks Quentin, "Why do they live there? Why do they live at all?"[40] It indicates incredulity that people will live in the U.S. South of their own free will. Reed, for the record, does not express this attitude directly, but it is implied consistently throughout the podcast that McLemore's version of Shittown actually exists, even if it coexists with alternate versions of the same place. Another resident of Woodstock describes the community as a version of Mayberry, the idealized rural community in Andy Griffith's television show. For example, she idealizes the community's homecoming celebration, where everyone goes "to the turnip green supper, and there's a bonfire, and everybody you went to school with, and everybody brings a dish. I'm sure you know that Miss Laylor's made the turnip greens, and you know to, oh, try her coconut pie, Miss Daily's banana pudding, you know to get their Tupperware back to them."[41] In these contrasting versions of McLemore's hometown, we can see the usual poles of media representations of the U.S. South, which Lisa Hinrichsen, Gina Caison, and Stephanie Rountree describe as "a site of desire and fantasy, wonder and danger."[42] As a place both geographic and conceptual, Woodstock/Shittown appeals to the audience in its symbolic power to vacillate between contradictions without self-destruction.

None of these representations, however, reflect the actual town of Woodstock, Alabama. An exurban community on Interstate 59 between Birmingham and Tuscaloosa, Woodstock is located about five miles from Mercedes's largest North American automobile plant, and it is home to a large Thyssenkrupp materials manufacturing facility. The town was incorporated in 2000, and its population is 93 percent white and has a median family income of $48,750. While the median income is significantly lower than the national average of about $60,000, it is slightly higher than the Alabama average of $48,123.[43] The town is not old, and its economy is based more on contemporary global neoliberalism than on atavistic agricultural exploitation. While the town's racial imbalance suggests racial separatism and white flight, the community does not seem to reflect either the idealized agrarian community or the cesspool of white poverty that it appears to be in the podcast. As Bibler highlights, "the podcast deceptively portrays the area as *excessively* rural and remote. That deception not only gets this part of Alabama wrong, but also perpetuates a longstanding stereotype of the whole South as generally disconnected from the modern world, culturally and geographically."[44] The modern town of Woodstock, a white suburban bedroom community with a manufacturing-based economy, seems completely inconsistent with "Shittown," but they are the same town.

The representation of Woodstock as Shittown becomes even more confusing when we learn that McLemore was himself one of the city's founders. In 2000, the community of North Bibb, a crossroads near an interstate exit ramp, incorporated as the town of Woodstock. Cheryl Dodson, the original town clerk, tells Reed that McLemore had been an enthusiastic supporter of the town. He helped her with deeds and court records, stuffed envelopes, helped with the Christmas parade, and annexed his own property into the town. He, evidently, once believed in the value of Woodstock as a community, "but at some point," Reed says, "the town of Woodstock began to do what governments tend to do—disappoint him."[45] The town had some petty scandals, which soured his attitude, and he developed a strongly negative opinion about the town. In the podcast, Reed gives full voice to McLemore's perspective on the town and amplifies it with his own forays into caricature. This conversation with Cheryl Dodson about McLemore's involvement with the town's founding is the only opposing position that Reed offers in the podcast, and the primary purpose of the conversation is to chart the progress of McLemore's mental illness, not to give an alternative perspective on Woodstock. For the most part, Reed seems to be content to endorse McLemore's representation of his hometown, at least tacitly, which allows listeners to project their own images of the dirty South onto this so-called Shittown.

Reed's representation of Woodstock reinforces notions of uneven development that continue to define the South's relationship with the rest of the United States. As Neil Smith explains in *Uneven Development* (1984), capitalism fosters inequality across space, so the South's relative inequality is linked to the fact that its labor and resources have been consistently exploited to develop the nation's economy. Frequently, representations of the U.S. South in media use the region as a site for projections of deviance, distancing the nation from the region and suggesting that the South is at fault for its own delayed development. The podcast plays with these same projections, suggesting that Shittown (McLemore's imaginary version of his hometown) and Woodstock (the actual town in Alabama) are two different places that exist in two different temporal planes. Thus, the podcast obscures the modern exurban community to focus attention on bizarrely fantastic versions of the imaginary Old South.

The U.S. South and Temporal Fantasy

The notion of southern time as an alternate temporality has a long history and at least some basis in fact. Through the late nineteenth century, time was a localized construct, so different places were literally on different time scales. In many cases, local time was set on a public clock using an arbitrary designation of midday as noon, and local people would set their watches and clocks in reference to the public clock. The emergence of transcontinental railroads, however, created a need for standardized times and time zones to account for travel across long distances. On November 18, 1883, known as "the day of two noons," time was set according to a national standard.[46] This event illustrates that time as measured by machines is an arbitrary construct. Machine time is of varying utility depending upon local needs. In *Mastered by the Clock* (1997), Mark Smith explains that southern enslavers experimented with using clocks to regulate enslaved Black laborers, partly to emulate the time discipline of factory workers in urban northern factories, but the experiments were not

fully successful. Agricultural workers were less likely to use clock time to organize their work, and clocks were of limited use to southern sharecroppers well
into the twentieth century. Historically, the U.S. South depended less on clock
time than did some other parts of country, which establishes the legitimate
precedent for imagining the region as an alternate temporality.

In many representations of temporality, the U.S. South has been depicted
as slower, less progressive, and less modern than the rest of the United States.
The likely standard for national time is New York City, a place synonymous
with dynamism, cosmopolitanism, and industry, and the podcast frequently
contrasts New York as a signifier for the nation against Shittown as a signifier
for the South. Reed often reminds listeners that he is "a reporter from New
York," which means that he is a participant observer in the U.S. South representing the mainstream perspective among the weird southerners.[47] He tells
the listeners that his wife is a Black woman from the South, and he is Jewish
and a self-described "Yankee," points that he keeps to himself among the characters at Black Sheep Ink.[48] Meanwhile, the people he meets in Alabama frequently remind him that he *ain't from around here,* such as Kendall Burt, who
calls him "one of these left-wingers that we upset in the [2016] election."[49] In
an article in the *New Yorker,* Sarah Larson describes the obvious separation between Reed's listeners and his subject: "For a Northern, liberal NPR listener,
hearing such things levelled against mostly conservative Southern whites, in
a mellifluous spiel by a liberal Southern white man with a thick accent, is a
mind-bender in itself—you feel implicated somehow, and voyeuristic."[50] This
sense of voyeurism highlights the perceived difference between the mainstream North and the deviant South and the extent to which the U.S. South is
temporally and culturally othered in contemporary media.

S-Town contributes to a process of creating imaginary, othered souths that
is at least as old as the United States. In *Our South* (2010), Jennifer Rae Greeson theorizes that the U.S. South has functioned "as an internal other for the
nation, an intrinsic part of the national body that nonetheless is differentiated
and held apart from the whole."[51] This differentiation, which goes as far back
as the colonial period in works such as Thomas Jefferson's *Notes on the State
of Virginia* (1784) and Hector St. John de Crèvecœur's *Letters from an American
Farmer* (1782), allows the national narrative to depict the South as simultaneously a site of exploitation and one of differentiation. Leigh Anne Duck argues
in *The Nation's Region* (2009) that the U.S. South served a similar function in
the twentieth century. She claims that as the nation developed a narrative of

progress and modernization, writers imagined the U.S. South as the nation's dangerous, exotic, and backward other, the non-American part of America. In *The Real South* (2014), Scott Romine asserts that the narrative of the U.S. South as a place of otherness has effectively replaced the region as a reality. "The fake South," he argues, "has become the real South through the intervention of narrative. That the South is increasingly sustained as a virtual, commodified, built, themed, invented, or otherwise artificial territoriality—that is, as it becomes less imaginable as a 'natural' or 'organic' culture, if that antinomic construction ever existed—has hardly removed it from the domain of everyday use."[52] This paradigm of a constructed, fabricated, imaginary South as a site for projections of difference and deviance has consistently served the same purpose that it serves in *S-Town*, to be the nation's other. The South only exists in the national imagination to the extent that it deviates from the normative constructions of U.S. nationalism; otherwise, there would be no need to construct regional distinctions. Regions, in other words, are not spatial zones or geographic designations as much as they are "imagined communities," to use Benedict Anderson's phrase, that are imagined to be different from the nation. This differentiation extends back in time to America's earliest print culture, and, as we have seen in the adaptation of nineteenth-century techniques of literary regionalism to the southern soundscape of *S-Town*'s aural literature, it continues to persist as new forms of media technology develop. Throughout its genealogy, projections of difference onto the U.S. South reinforce the perception that it is out of synch with the nation. Indeed, such narrative imaginings of a temporally regressive region have historically assuaged national anxieties, conceptually quarantining violence and violation of civil liberties within the South, especially during times of national unrest.

At the time that *S-Town* came out, the nation had recently endured the divisive presidential campaign of 2016 and the resurgence of white populism. The usual constructions of conservative, rural regionalism have morphed into a political designation: red states. This term includes the South, as well as the Great Plains and parts of the Midwest, areas with lower population density but, by virtue of the Electoral College's nonproportional representation, sufficient political influence to determine the presidency. Trump's political emergence and the galvanization of his political base drove a wave of interest in rural poverty that made a semi-celebrity of J. D. Vance, whose book *Hillbilly Elegy* (2016) purported to explain the disintegration of the white working class in Appalachia. Residents of so-called blue states—populous states along the

Atlantic and Pacific coasts—were eager to understand the mindset of rural voters. This same wave of interest buoyed *S-Town*, which described the lives of marginalized poor white people and, as Maureen Callahan writes in the *New York Post*, "allows well-off liberals to congratulate themselves for listening while reinforcing their own sense of intellectual, financial and political superiority. For all the flaws of 'S-Town,' this is its greatest, most dangerous failure, one that can only widen the chasm between red- and blue-state America."[53] Setting aside the fact that the forty-fifth President was a New York businessman who transparently appealed to the values, grievances, and ingrained sense of marginalization among poor white people for his own political and commercial gain, the sense of marginalization that many people in supposedly deviant parts of the country feel is a result of the process of othering. John B. McLemore—who appears in the podcast as alternately queer, feminist, sexist, racist, progressive, cynical, intellectual, deranged, classist, poor white, rural, and otherwise deviant from every form of social normativity—acts as a microcosm of marginalization. The marginalization of subcultures, whether it is based on region, race, class, or any other criteria, necessarily fragments the social structure.

In form and content, the podcast *S-Town* temporally others the U.S. South, and it ultimately suggests that McLemore's fascination with time was responsible for his mental illness, leading to his suicide. In his horology business, McLemore used dangerous techniques to gild antique parts, some of them involving vaporized mercury, and he did not use proper safety precautions when handling mercury, which Reed documents when McLemore goldplates a dime. Inhaling vaporized mercury can lead to a host of neurological issues, including mental and emotional disorders such as depression. Reed hypothesizes that mercury poisoning caused McLemore's paranoia and was the underlying cause for his depression. The implication that McLemore's fascination with time led to his death is obvious. As Reed offers his nonexpert diagnosis, he describes one of John's tattoos, which seems prophetic, if not itself proleptic: "On the front of his body, one of John's tattoos is of a sundial, and John included a sundial motto there on his chest. The one he chose is *omnes vulnerant, ultima necat*—each wounds, the last kills. It refers to time, as in each minute wounds, the last minute kills. Time's a gift. It's also a punishment."[54] According to Reed, time is the root of McLemore's problem.

As a podcast, *S-Town* heightens the issues of temporality presented in the program. Because the podcast medium is based online and is available for download on demand, listeners control when they consume the show. In *Podcasting* (2019), Martin Spinelli and Lance Dann point out that "podcasts do not have the scheduling and timing constraints of broadcast media. They can be as long as they need to be and released whenever desired."[55] Podcasts do not follow the usual media parameters of production and serialization, and *S-Town* pushed the temporal boundaries even farther than its predecessor, *Serial*. Because Reed released the entire production at once, he allowed listeners to binge the program, collapsing their experience of the program's temporality. Simultaneously, because the program is available online, it can be consumed anytime, so listeners can have different listening experiences. Several million people listened to the entire show within days of its release, so they shared a cultural moment, which was intensified with numerous posts on social media and coverage in more traditional media, as well. These listeners had an amplified experience, but other listeners were able to consume the show at their own pace or at a later date, as I did, so our experience was somewhat different. Tim Barker describes this proliferation of multiple individual experiences of the new media environment of content on demand as "microtemporalities," which suggests that the development of new media has diminished the sense of collective experience that marked mass media, such as film, radio, and television.[56] Rather than discovering the program or participating in a communal experience, listeners encountered the program individually in their own timeframes, some after its initial release, some in the heat of media frenzy, and others with its reputation for genre-defining techniques and problematic storytelling already in place.

As I have argued here, time is a big part of the problem with Reed's storytelling about the U.S. South. By depicting the South as existing in an alternate plane of temporality, he others the region in a way that contributes to the perception of the South as deviant and backward. His storytelling separates Woodstock, which exists in the temporal present, from Shittown, which is a temporal fantasy of a southern landscape set in a backward, allochronic past. In truth, deviance and backwardness are not unique to the U.S. South. They are subjective perceptions based on asymmetrical power relations, and Reed uses his position as a reporter from New York to distinguish the South, in general, and John B. McLemore, in particular, as deviant. The podcast's recurring references to temporality, its juxtaposition between the imaginary Shittown and the actual Woodstock, and its engagement in temporal fantasy contribute to a media-based construction of the South as a problematic region. While the U.S. South certainly deserves this reputation for its history of slavery, racism, and labor exploitation, its reputation is, to some extent, a self-perpetuating culturally reproduced narrative that reinforces itself each time it is told. The pattern of projecting deviance and backwardness onto the South prevents the recognition that such problems have always manifested nationally, which impedes social progress. Whether Native dispossession and genocide, colonialism or plantation capitalism, slavery or segregation, public divestment from education or health infrastructure, every state in the Union bears the weight of these histories. Ultimately, the features that made *S-Town* fascinating to the millions of people who downloaded it also render it a troublesome depiction of the region. It represents the U.S. South as deviant and backward, caricaturing the region and the life of John B. McLemore. People listened to the show primarily because McLemore was strange and fascinating, but Brian Reed exploits a person living with mental illness to tell the story, and he fed into McLemore's delusions of the backward U.S. South. The reality, however, is much more complicated. Woodstock is just as much a part of modern America as New York City, and the United States is no more advanced than the South. Time, as any antiquarian horologist could attest, only moves in one direction.

NOTES

1. Moran, "New Podcast"; Quah, "*S-Town Has Exceeded 40M Downloads*"; Taylor, "'S-Town' Podcast Impact."
2. Waldman, "Gorgeous New Crime Drama."
3. Davis and Caison, "Gilded Souths and S-Towns."
4. Alcorn, "*S-Town* Never Justifies Its Voyeurism"; Goudeau, "Was the Art of *S-Town* Worth the Pain?"
5. Dockterman, "*S-Town* Host Brian Reed on True Crime Podcasts and That Major Twist."
6. Linares et al, "Podcasting and Podcasts," 6.
7. Erlmann, *Reason and Resonance*, 18.
8. Sterne, *The Audible Past*, 35.
9. Petridis, "The Story behind A Rose for Emily."
10. Reed, *S-Town*, chap. 1.
11. Ibid.
12. Ibid.
13. Ibid.
14. Reed, *S-Town*, chap. 4.
15. Reed, *S-Town*, chap. 1.

16. Ibid.

17. Ibid.

18. Ibid.

19. Malcolm X famously declared, "As far as I'm concerned, Mississippi is anywhere south of the Canadian border"; Haley, "Epilogue," 479.

20. Reed, *S-Town*, chap. 1.

21. Reed, *S-Town*, chap. 2.

22. Reed, *S-Town*, chap. 4.

23. Ibid.

24. Ibid.

25. Adam, *Time*, 115–16.

26. Freeman, *Time Binds*, 3.

27. Rooney, "Queer Objects," 158.

28. Bibler, "The Podcast and the Police."

29. Reed, *S-Town*, chap. 1.

30. Braitser, *Enduring Time*, 8.

31. Reed, *S-Town*, chap. 7.

32. Fabian, *Time and the Other*, 31.

33. Lyric from the song "Dixie," the widely popular, but unofficial, anthem of the Confederate States of America during the U.S. Civil War.

34. Reed, *S-Town*, chap. 1.

35. Schafer, *The Soundscape*.

36. Smith, "Listening to the Heard Worlds of Antebellum America," 152.

37. Reed, *S-Town*, chap. 2.

38. Ibid.

39. Reed, *S-Town*, chap. 1.

40. Faulkner, *Absalom, Absalom!* 142.

41. Reed, *S-Town*, chap. 7.

42. Hinrichsen, Caison, and Rountree, *Small-Screen Souths*, 2.

43. "2018: ACS 5-Year Estimates."

44. Bibler, "The Podcast and the Police."

45. Reed, *S-Town*, chap. 7.

46. McCrossen, *Marking Modern Times*, 113.

47. Reed, *S-Town*, chap. 1.

48. Reed, *S-Town*, chap. 2.

49. Reed, *S-Town*, chap. 7.

50. Larson, "*S-Town* Investigates the Human Mystery."

51. Greeson, *Our South*, 1.

52. Romine, *The Real South*, 9.

53. Callahan, "*S-Town* Is Just an Excuse for Urban Liberals to Rubberneck."

54. Reed, *S-Town*, chap. 7.

55. Spinelli and Dann, *Podcasting*, 8.

56. Barker, "Media in and out of Time."

BIBLIOGRAPHY

"2018: ACS 5-Year Estimates Data Profiles." *ACS Demographic and Housing Estimates, 2010*, prepared by the American Survey Program, United States Census Bureau, https://data .census.gov/cedsci/table?q=Woodstock,%20AL&tid=ACSDP5Y2018.DP05&hidePre view=false.

Adam, Barbara. *Time*. Cambridge: Polity, 2004.

Alcorn, Gay. "*S-Town* Never Justifies Its Voyeurism." *Guardian*. April 21, 2017. https://www. theguardian.com/commentisfree/2017/apr/22/s-town-never-justifies-its-voyeurism-and -that-makes-it-morally-indefensible.

Anderson, Benedict. *Imagined Communities: Reflections on the Origin and Spread of Nationalism*. Revised ed. New York: Verso, 2006.

Baraitser, Lisa. *Enduring Time*. New York: Bloomsbury, 2017.

Barker, Tim. "Media in and out of Time: Multi-Temporality and the Technical Conditions of Contemporaneity." *Le Sujet Digital*. 2014. http://sujetdigital.labex-arts-h2h.fr/fr/content/ media-and-out-time-multi-temporality-and-technical-conditions-contemporaneity.

Bibler, Michael. "The Podcast and the Police: *S-Town* and the Narrative Form of Southern Queerness." *Southern Spaces*. March 24, 2020. https://southernspaces.org/2020/ podcast-and-police-s-town-and-narrative-form-southern-queerness/.

Callahan, Maureen. "*S-Town* Is Just an Excuse for Urban Liberals to Rubberneck." *New York Post*. April 29, 2017. https://nypost.com/2017/04/29/s-town-is-just-an-excuse-for-urban -liberals-to-rubberneck/.

Davis, David A., and Gina Caison. "Gilded Souths and S-Towns." *About South*. July 21, 2017. https://soundcloud.com/about-south/s02-episode-3-gilded-souths-and-s-towns.

Dockterman, Elena. "*S-Town* Host Brian Reed on True Crime Podcasts and That Major Twist." *TIME*. April 3, 2017. http://time.com/4721146/.

Duck, Leigh Anne. *The Nation's Region: Southern Modernism, Segregation, and U.S. Nationalism*. Athens: University of Georgia Press, 2009.

Erlmann, Veit. *Reason and Resonance: A History of Modern Aurality*. Boston: Zone Books, 2014.

Fabian, Johannes. *Time and the Other: How Anthropology Makes Its Object*. 1983. New York: Columbia University Press, 2002.

Faulkner, William. *Absalom, Absalom!* 1936. New York: Vintage, 1986.

Freeman, Elizabeth. *Time Binds: Queer Temporalities, Queer Histories*. Durham, NC: Duke University Press, 2010.

Goudeau, Jessica. "Was the Art of *S-Town* Worth the Pain." *Atlantic*. April 9, 2017. https://www .theatlantic.com/entertainment/archive/2017/04/was-the-art-of-s-town-worth-the-pain /522366/.

Greeson, Jennifer Rae. *Our South: Geographic Fantasy and the Rise of National Literature*. Cambridge: Harvard University Press, 2010.

Haley, Alex. "Epilogue," In *The Autobiography of Malcolm X*, by Malcolm X, 441–523. New York: Ballantine Books, 1964.

Hinrichsen, Lisa, Gina Caison, and Stephanie Rountree. *Small-Screen Souths: Region, Identity, and the Cultural Politics of Television*. Baton Rouge: Louisiana State University Press, 2017.

Larson, Sarah. "*S-Town* Investigates the Human Mystery." *New Yorker.* March 31, 2017. https://www.newyorker.com/culture/sarah-larson/s-town-investigates-the-human-mystery.

Linares, Dario, Neil Fox, and Richard Berry. "Podcasting and Podcasts: Parameters of a New Aural Culture." In *Podcasting: New Aural Cultures and Digital Media,* edited by Dario Linares, Neil Fox, and Richard Berry, 1–13. London: Palgrave Macmillan, 2018.

McCrossen, Alexis. *Marking Modern Times: A History of Clocks, Watches, and Other Timekeepers in American Life.* University of Chicago Press, 2013.

Moran, Rob. "New Podcast from Serial Makers, S-Town, Breaks Download Records." *The Sydney Morning Herald,* last updated April 3, 2017, 10:57 A.M. https://www.smh.com.au/entertainment/tv-and-radio/new-podcast-from-serial-makers-stown-breaks-download-records-20170403-gvc4l2.html.

Petridis, Alexis. "The Story behind A Rose for Emily—And Why It's Perfect for S-Town." *Guardian,* April 17, 2017. https://www.theguardian.com/culture/shortcuts/2017/apr/17/rose-for-emily-s-town-zombies-podcast-john-b-mclemore.

Quah, Nicholas. "*S-Town* Has Exceeded 40M Downloads, Which Is Truly a Ton of Downloads." *Vulture,* May 4, 2017. https://www.vulture.com/2017/05/s-town-podcast-40-million-downloads.html.

Reed, Brian. *S-Town.* March 28, 2017. https://stownpodcast.org/.

Romine, Scott. *The Real South: Southern Narrative in the Age of Cultural Reproduction.* Baton Rouge: Louisiana State University Press, 2014.

Rooney, Monique. "Queer Objects and Intermedial Timepieces: Reading S-town." *Angelaki: Journal of the Theoretical Humanities* 23, no. 1 (2018): 156–73.

Schafer, R. Murray. *The Soundscape: Our Sonic Environment and the Tuning of the World.* New York: Knopf, 1994.

Smith, Mark. "Listening to the Heard Worlds of Antebellum America." In *The Auditory Culture Reader,* edited by Michael Bull and Les Black, 137–64. New York: Berg, 2003.

———. *Mastered by the Clock: Time, Slavery, and Freedom in the American South.* Chapel Hill: University of North Carolina Press, 1997.

Smith, Neil. *Uneven Development: Nature, Capital, and the Production of Space.* 1984. Athens: University of Georgia Press, 2008.

Spinelli, Martin, and Lance Dann. *Podcasting: The Audio Media Revolution.* Bloomsbury, 2019.

Sterne, Jonathan. *The Audible Past: Cultural Origins of Sound Production.* Durham, NC: Duke University Press, 2003.

Taylor, Drew. "'S-Town' Podcast Impact Still Felt in Woodstock, 1 Year Later." *Montgomery Advertiser,* last updated March 27, 2018, 11:46 A.M. https://www.montgomeryadvertiser.com/story/news/crime/2018/03/27/s-town-podcast-impact-still-felt-woodstock-1-year-later/462364002/.

Vance, J. D. *Hillbilly Elegy: A Memoir of a Family and Culture in Crisis.* New York: Harper, 2016.

Waldman, Katy. "The Gorgeous New True Crime Podcast *S-Town* Is Like *Serial* but Satisfying." *Slate.* March 30, 2017. https://slate.com/culture/2017/03/s-town-the-new-true-crime-podcast-by-the-makers-of-serial-reviewed.html.

NINETEENTH-CENTURY SACRED HARP SINGING AS NEW MEDIA PRACTICE

PAUL FESS

OVER THE COURSE OF its development shape-note singing has risen to the level of a metonymic figure for southern regional distinctiveness despite its origins in a New England buzzing with the religious energies of the Second Great Awakening. First appearing at the beginning of the nineteenth century, the shape-note method involved a seemingly minor shift in musical transcription practices wherein compilers of hymnbooks used notes with differently shaped heads as visual cues to help singers discern a given pitch, rendering a more accessible representation of music in print. Rather than its practitioners undergoing formal training or relying on the leadership of a musical precentor, singing from these tune books only required reading the shapes of the notes on the page. This method enabled a more congregation-centered singing experience and signaled a democratization of Protestant church music that took it out of the hands of specialists, leaders, and trained choirs and empowered churchgoers themselves to obey the biblical injunction to teach and admonish "one another in psalms and hymns and spiritual songs."[1]

By midcentury, however, church music moved away from shape-note and became increasingly aligned with a positivism celebrating the so-called scientific methods of the "better music" movement, which promoted trained choirs over congregational singing and rigid concepts about pitch and harmony over the homespun performances produced by shape-note singers. Now heard as old-fashioned by worshippers in northern cities, shape-note became associated with the backcountry. The practice, nevertheless, remained popular among people who moved south and west, and it merged with the Methodist and Baptist sects that proliferated throughout these regions as one element yoking together religious groups across the large frontier, gaining particular significance in the areas that would become Georgia and Alabama. Of the many shape-note tune books that appeared in the U.S. South at this time, the most enduring is Benjamin Franklin White and Elisha James King's *The Sacred*

Harp (1844). Unlike most of the other texts that used the shape-note method, *The Sacred Harp* became a basis for developing more elaborate traditions and practices around the egalitarian structure implied by shape-note singing pedagogy. As a result of this history, sacred harp singing has come to signify a quintessential element of a kind of communal southern folk culture even as it has gained an increasingly global network of enthusiasts.[2]

Others have treated the contours of this conventional—"North-South transit"—understanding of the history of shape-note and sacred harp singing extensively.[3] Here, I would like to focus on sacred harp singing as an instructive example of the tensions between new media practices and what scholars have described as the folkloric tendency in definitions of southern culture.[4] While not what we might conventionally think of as new media, shape-note did constitute a new way of mediating and disseminating music through print to audiences with little to no ability to read musical notation. Furthermore, the emphasis this practice placed on empowering singers also anticipated structural assumptions we hold about how users engage digital new media today, and sacred harp singers capitalized on this feature of the shape-note practice. If we take the radical recentering of user experiences as an important aspect of new media in our own moment, shape-note singing prefigures this structure by placing congregants themselves in positions to configure religious music-making events. Sacred harp singers expanded upon this attribute of shape-note by emphasizing this method's embodied, communal, and participatory qualities, seizing on the potential to facilitate the formation of nonhierarchical groups of singers, a tendency most obviously expressed through the figure of the "hollow square," the seating arrangement at sacred harp events. Within this milieu, King and White's *The Sacred Harp*, as well as the subsequent editions of this text, offered the potential to usher in new kinds of practitioners—such as the African American church groups that organized around the practice before and after the U.S. Civil War and the diverse sets of identity groups that participate in singing events today—modeling a more fluid religious social order and facilitating a sonic imagined community across the vast distances of nineteenth-century territorial expansion as well as what Kiri Miller has termed the sacred harp "diaspora" of today.[5] The history of sacred harp, thus, calls for a reconsideration of the old/new dichotomy that we commonly think of as underwriting the newness of new media.

Throughout this history, though, the potential for restructuring discourse implied by the sacred harp singing method has often been obscured by how it has been pressed into narrow definitions of southern identity. As the historical sketch above indicates, the moment shape-note singing fell out of fashion is also when it became "southern," a convergence that has rooted this practice from the very beginning in a kind of antimodern white southern folk culture. For sacred harpers, the U.S. South has signified homespun communal values, theoretically inclusive but underscored by a political quietism around controversial topics of the day.[6] To outsiders writing at the beginning of the twentieth century, on the contrary, sacred harp singing confirmed the U.S. South's persistent underdevelopment, its stubborn hold on rural ways.[7] Folklorists in the 1920s and 1930s answered this characterization by describing sacred harp songs along segregationist lines as examples of "white spirituals" in need of preservation against the "jigging, empty, banal" sounds of gospel, jazz, and other racially perceived musical threats to white southern folk life.[8] This estimation celebrated shape-note singing's place outside of the vanguard, dismissing nineteenth-century criticism that characterized it as unsophisticated, at a time when notions about southern whiteness became consolidated around fantasies of agrarian culture. More recently, sacred harp has been used to index an unspecified rural South vaguely connected to the years surrounding the Civil War, an association most clearly seen in its depiction in the 2003 film *Cold Mountain*. In light of this history, sacred harp presents an intriguing relationship between a media innovation that enabled more democratic modes of discourse and the longstanding forces of regional imaginary that have been subjected to a range of critiques by southern studies scholars. In this sense, sacred harp touches upon an age-old southern paradox: while gesturing toward the potential for social transformation, this practice has also been deployed for ideological purposes that reify ingrained notions about race, class, and the North/South binary. Thus, while *The Sacred Harp* and the social formations that have coalesced around it present a challenge to the modifier "new" in new media, this affiliation has also been overshadowed by the ways in which this singing practice signifies traditional, "old," and white notions about southern regional distinctiveness.

The Shape-Note Singing

Despite its associations with the U.S. South today, shape-note singing initially emerged in New England during the Second Great Awakening as a way to facilitate the shift from religious experiences rooted in Enlightenment rationalism to those structured by emotional excitement.[9] Among other things, this movement emphasized hymn singing as key to "mediat[ing] the new birth" of the evangelical Christian, and it used hymns as "primary vehicles of transcendence," as "the very wind of the Spirit itself."[10] Rather than simply listening to choirs or priests make music, however, members of the congregation needed to sing for themselves in order to foment their own individual salvation while, somewhat paradoxically, also aligning themselves with the scope of the doctrine of their broader Protestant community. As such, evangelicals during this period turned to hymns as important spiritual and pedagogical tools for proselytizing to the unconverted and educating children, placing more control in the hands of the congregation while maintaining church discipline by construing it as arising from within the motivations of each congregant. The spirit of this revivalism, then, involved a conception of music's relationship to power as Foucauldian: musical performance became a mechanism for implicating congregants within church discourse. This was a fundamental shift in the understanding of how religious music could serve as a basis for the formation of church communities; however, it raised questions about just how to involve churchgoers, many of whom had little or no musical training, in the production of hymns. Shape-note notation emerged as a method for mediating this dynamic in print, offering congregants a simplified way to collectively read and sing hymns without needing to know how to read music in the traditional sense. Shape-note singing thus aligned with the balance between disciplinary power and "democratic" religious experiences that emerged from the Second Great Awakening by conceiving of music making as a way for congregants to collectively produce hymns that was simultaneously circumscribed by religious doctrine.

There were other schemes designed to overcome the obstacles presented by musical illiteracy and allow the singer, reader, and user of hymnbooks to be more active within church services, but of these, shape-note and sacred harp singing resonate the most with our current expectations of new media as participatory practices. In addition to shape-note singing, for instance, another well-known methodology that gained popularity during this period was lining out, or "Dr. Watts singing" as it is sometimes called after the composer Isaac Watts. This practice confronted the problems of access presented by illiterate and poor worshippers by enlisting a precentor, who was often also the preacher, to choose a melody that fit a given hymn text and intone each line as the congregation repeated. Due to its structure, lining out dispensed with musical complexity, specifically the idea of harmony, focusing narrowly on instructing congregants in the texts and melodies of the hymns. In the United States today, lining out remains part of the services of Primitive Baptists and Old Regular Baptists. It is also recognized as an important aspect of African American culture as it emerged in the nineteenth century. Preachers from Richard Allen on deployed this technique to minister to people who, because of enslavement and other discriminatory policies, never had the opportunity to learn to read. In fact, scholars often link this method to the foundational African American sonic practices of call-and-response singing as well as improvisation.[11] Unlike shape-note singing, however, lining out implied a hierarchy wherein the precentor remained at the top of the microcosm of the social order represented by church services.

By contrast, shape-note enabled worshipers to learn the basics of reading musical notation quickly, which meant that they could enjoy a greater stake in the formation of church services. Of all the iterations of shape-note singing, sacred harp developed this egalitarianism to the greatest extent. To read music from a shape-note tune book, such as *The Sacred Harp,* one only needed to learn the correspondence between the shapes of the note heads and the solfege syllables, which in today's seven-note system begin with the familiar "do-re-mi." (Though, like the first shape-note tune books, *The Sacred Harp* only uses four syllables: "fa," "sol," "la," and "mi.") (See Fig. 3.1.) Unlike a traditional musical performance, the mechanics of this technique, as they are deployed in sacred harp singing, are more accurately understood as an ongoing, collective rehearsal that develops over the course of each song's performance, which in the parlance of sacred harp is also known as a "lesson." It has become customary for sacred harp events to begin with a pedagogical moment where singers join in a solmization of the solfege syllables of the song, singing them through without the song text once in order to grasp the melody, a practice that inspired the folklorist George Pullen Jackson, writing in the 1930s, to nominate sacred harp singers the "fa-sol-la folk."[12] Contrary to lining out, shape-note singing made it possible for "songs with harmony [to be] presented visually and systematically."[13] By learning to read the notes on the page, congregants could harmonize melodies and divide themselves into treble, alto, tenor, and bass parts, and to facilitate this advantage, editors and compilers wrote accessible arrangements. In *The Sacred Harp,* for example, White and King used simplistic intervals similar to the modal, chant-like singing one might hear in Renaissance polyphony.[14] (See Fig. 3.2.)

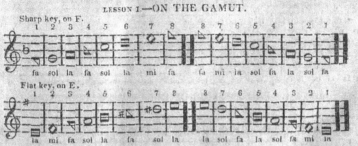

Fig. 3.1. Image of shape-note singing scale from David L. Clayton and James P. Carrell, *The Virginia harmony* (1831), Library of Congress Notated Music Division, Washington DC.

Fig. 3.2. Page from White et al., *The Sacred Harp*. Created by Sacred Harp Pub. Co. [1936]. Library of Congress Book/Printed Material Division, Washington, DC.

Shape-note implied a leveling of the kind of hierarchy that had traditionally existed in church services by demystifying the process of music making. This participatory quality is present in the first volume that featured shape-note, William Little and William Smith's *The Easy Instructor* (1802).[15] On the title page of this volume, for instance, the editors describe their project as imparting "the rudiments of music on an improved plan, wherein the naming and timing of the notes are familiarized to the weakest capacity," inviting the uninitiated—those who had the "weakest" understanding of music—to participate in the singing of songs contained in the book. They double down on this opening gambit by dedicating their collection to "those who have not had the advantage of an instructor."[16] The book itself made instruction "easy" by providing its users a path to quickly and painlessly internalize the process of reading musical notation so each member of a congregation could learn to read the melody and the rhythm, making this music accessible to a much wider array of singers.[17] Shape-note tune books thus mediated the distribution of musical knowledge throughout a given congregation by providing singers with the conceptual tools to create the service, and they broadened the base of music readers, both establishing important groundwork for church services and providing a communal basis upon which to construct religious events. Similar to how contemporary new media platforms place the consumer in control of the formation of content, shape-note offered congregants a cooperative way of mediating their experiences with church music through a new avenue for learning to read music and a new kind of engagement with print.

Shape-Note and Sacred Harp Singing as New Media

Shape-note singing might at first seem like an unremarkable development in music pedagogy; however, in the context of sacred harp, this method represents a proleptic staging of longstanding conversations about the relationships between consumers and technological and methodological media developments. The shape-note tune book, for example, anticipates Walter Benjamin's analysis of the changes wrought by the advent of mass media technology on visual artwork. Benjamin famously argued that developments in technological reproduction initiated a new kind of engagement with media wherein the work was divested of its "aura," or the sublime shock one might experience upon beholding the original, as technology made it more readily available through reproduction. Liberated from ritual, the artwork became a social experience available as a kind of language to be restructured and manipulated, which, for Benjamin, constituted a political struggle. Benjamin's analysis, here, straddles divergent understandings of the cultural significance of media innovation: one that views technological developments—such as the advent of print, photography, or sound recording—as determining the conditions of possibilities for cultural production and another that characterizes such innovation as arising from the needs, wants, and desires of communities of users. Similarly, sacred harp singing emerged at the convergence of the regional popularity of the shape-note method in the U.S. South—animated by the democratizing promise of this method—and the cultural forces that structured the nineteenth-century South. Like Benjamin's analysis of visual art, shape-note singing in general and sacred harp singing specifically can be seen as methods that dispense with the aura of musical performance in favor of allowing hymns to circulate more freely. In this vein, *The Sacred Harp* has been described as operating as "a teaching tool, propaganda vehicle, multivalent symbol, and transcendent canon all in one."[18]

The shape-note singer's orientation is analogous to Benjamin's analysis in that these tune books participated in the process of liberating hymns from conventional church ritual, atomizing their production across a given congregation and construing hymns as a kind of language. In the nineteenth century, the possession and use of hymnals became a way for expressing both the individual's social position and the theological commitments of the congregation. Like most hymnbooks during the period, in other words, shape-note tune books were objects around which congregations and church movements could organize, a feature that southern sacred harp singers emphasized in their practice. Hymnbooks were places where religious doctrine was continually renegotiated, and they came to be, as Christopher Phillips has argued, symbols for and influences on "who you were and who was with you; [they] could teach reading or preserve a self through various stages of its development; and [they] could open horizons in poetry as well as religion."[19] In the U.S. South, the market favored "entrepreneurial editors" who sought to guide churchgoers' belief systems through the hymnals they edited. The production and circulation of southern shape-note tune books indicate a robust competition for using hymns to set the terms under which churchgoers would engage religious worship. In fact, shape-note singing came to be one of the most heavily deployed methodologies for southern tune books.[20] David Warren Steel and Richard Hulan note that between 1801 and 1865 "at least 35 residents of the southern U.S. compiled and published sacred tunebooks in shaped notation."[21] The most popular of these during this period was William Walker's *The Southern Harmony and Musical Companion*, which is said to have sold 600,000 copies between its publication in 1835 and in 1866. Over the course of the second half of the nineteenth century White and King's *The Sacred Harp* overtook *The Southern Harmony* as the most popular shape-note tune book, as the former was continually edited, repackaged, and increasingly at the center of religious gatherings. This regional popularity inspired historians and folklorists to take up sacred harp singing as part of a revanchist, nostalgic remaking of social reality in the U.S. South during the late nineteenth and early twentieth centuries.

Only looking at this economy in terms of book sales or how the practice was repackaged by its first historians at the turn of the century, however, obscures the fact that in the sacred harp tradition the shape-note tune book circulated as more than simply an "agent of change" that determined a new frame for religious worship.[22] Sacred harp singers absorbed the methodology of shape-note within an already vibrant participatory religious milieu that, while somewhat inclusive, also formed alongside and in response to the transit networks and wealth created by the displacement of Native Americans and the subjugation of enslaved Africans. White and King structured their book around the idea of emphasizing entrenched communal practices concerning religious singing; however, true to well-established southern ironies, the sense of egalitarian co-creation that animated sacred harp singing traveled on a wave of exploitative economics. As Buell Cobb writes, the book "was conceived and nourished in a community situation."[23] White, in fact, organized singing events around his home in Harris County, Georgia, as he began publishing the first sacred harp hymn in his newspaper, *The Organ*, linking the production of the text to prevailing understandings of community organization. As this movement spread south and west throughout what would become the United States, this liberal understanding of religious community building, however, also supported colonial tasks associated with indoctrinating and managing Native Americans and enslaved Africans.[24] As David Warren Steel and Richard Hulan remind us, the economic prosperity that created the conditions of possibility for White and King to develop sacred harp singing in western Georgia was made possible by the expropriation of fertile lands from Native Americans and the strenuous labor performed by enslaved Africans. More to the point, both White and King lived on land formerly occupied by members of the Creek Confederacy following their forced removal as part of what is known as the Trail of Tears, and the families of future prominent sacred harp singers aided in this removal.[25] Additionally, this region hosted a robust circulation of music by enslaved Africans. The folklorists George Mitchell and Fred Fussell have noted the region's importance to the development of African American spirituals, fife-and-drum music, blues, and gospel, and Harris County is known as the birthplace of the famed enslaved piano prodigy Thomas "Blind Tom" Wiggins.[26] Sacred harp singers and hymn composers were in direct contact with these musicians, opening up questions about the origins and authenticity of sacred harp advanced by folklorists in the early twentieth century. This polyglot milieu, in fact, became the subject of segregationist disavowal in George Pullen Jackson's description of sacred harp tunes as examples of "white spirituals" in the 1930s.[27]

Sacred Harp Singing and the Camp Meeting Movement

Perhaps the most significant precursor to sacred harp singing that brought these threads of southern culture together was the nineteenth-century camp meeting movement. Beginning in Cane River, Kentucky, at the turn of the nineteenth century, around the same time that shape-note singing gained popularity in the North, camp meetings were important to the religious zeitgeist that fed shape-note's proliferation in the South. At these events, far-flung worshipers gathered and spent several days listening to sermons and singing hymns at makeshift campgrounds. These sites typically featured a central big tent, which hosted the main services, surrounded by smaller campsites housing attendees. Some of these smaller tents hosted secondary events for more marginalized segments of the population, such as poor white people and enslaved Africans brought as servants of wealthy white families.[28] This promiscuous arrangement caused these events to occupy a questionable place in nineteenth-century American religious culture. According to one historian, from the beginning the camp meeting's "value has been questioned [. . .] because of the noise and disorder prevalent at the services and the deliberate use of emotional excitement." As a result of this frenzied environment, "contemporaries introduced the legend that the woodland gathering was one long orgy of excitement," wherein religious zeal gave way to excessive, heretical displays.[29]

This movement was a crucible for southern American hymnody and religious practices. The singing styles that developed here would serve the basis for the participatory foundations of sacred harp, and the hymns that proliferated throughout camp meetings would provide much of the sacred harp repertoire, supplying much of the material for hymns that would be included in White and King's *The Sacred Harp*. As Buell Cobb writes, "By the time of the composition of the *Sacred Harp* in the 1840s, White and King could select from a field of songs generated by camp meetings throughout the span of the movement."[30] This influence can be heard, for example, in hymns such as "The Morning Trumpet" and "Turn, Sinner, Turn," both camp meeting songs that have remained part of the sacred harp repertoire since the book's original publication.[31] (See figs. 3.3 and 3.4.)

These two songs evoke the kind of community formation implied by the sacred harp tradition more generally. The conceit of "The Morning Trumpet" centers on the symbolic power of the trumpet blast that announces the second coming of Christ, a common theme for spirituals. In terms of its metaphorical and actual uses of sound, the song models the collective engagement and dispersal of power that came to structure sacred harp singing. Though sung by a full choir, the song imagines an individual contemplating his readiness to hear God's call figured in the repeated question when "shall [I] hear the trumpet sound in that morning?" The combination of the collective, amateur singing arrangement with this orientation toward religious power and salvation suggests the close proximity between the embodied communal practice of sacred harp, which aspired to sound single chords from many voices, and the individualistic, liberal undercurrents of southern evangelism, sonically elicited by the shared duties of four-part harmony paying homage to the singular sound of God's trumpet. "Turn, Sinner, Turn" conveys the same kind of worldview as the singers implore the sinner "today, if you will hear His voice, / Now is the time to make your choice; / Say will you to Mount Zion go? / Say will you have this Christ or no?"

"Morning Trumpet" and "Turn, Sinner, Turn" also index the unconstrained paths that songs emanating from camp meetings took. In addition to appearing in *The Sacred Harp*, "Turn, Sinner, Turn," for example, also finds its way into *Slave Songs of the United States* (1867), the first collection of African American sorrow songs, without any acknowledgment that it had also been part of the camp meeting movement or sacred harp. This association begs a comparison between *The Sacred Harp* and the *Slave Songs* projects: the latter was conceived as an effort to describe and preserve a dying culture, while the former sought to discipline and instruct the user within a cultural practice in formation. One might see these diverging impulses—occurring a mere twenty-two years

Fig. 3.3. "The Morning Trumpet," from *The Sacred Harp* by
Benjamin Franklin White and Elijah James King.

Fig. 3.4. "Turn, Sinner, Turn," from *The Sacred Harp* by
Benjamin Franklin White and Elijah James King.

apart—as symptomatic of racialized notions about how music could function;
one type of music was construed as only fit for preservation (*Slave Songs*), and
one type was the basis of a pedagogical system (*The Sacred Harp*). Interestingly, these terms get scrambled for sacred harp as this practice becomes the
subject of ethnographic recovery in the early twentieth century. George Pullen

Jackson took up this dichotomy in the 1930s to argue sacred harp occupied both positions, describing it as the authentic original of the sorrow songs and an important example of folksong circulation.

Sacred Harp Singing and Benjamin's Aura

Sacred harp singing originated at the convergence of the dissemination of shape-note tune books and the mores that structured southern society, where churchgoers, for example, expected a greater investment in an embodied, communal religious experience even as such encounters occurred upon an unequal landscape. Sacred harp, therefore, presents an example of how understandings of mediation and cultural history can combine in surprising and contradictory ways. Lisa Gitelman's definition of new media encapsulates this dynamic, by emphasizing that media innovation constitutes a relationship set in motion between technological and methodological advancements and the culture within which they take root. Gitelman asserts that new media developments are "less points of epistemic rupture" determined by the intervention of new technology than they are "socially embedded sites for the ongoing negotiation of meaning as such."[32] Her sense of the term "new media" emphasizes the dialectical interaction between media innovation and culture, the very relationship established between the shape-note tune book and sacred harp singing practice as they both channeled the religious energies on display at camp meetings and other events. Theorists W. J. T. Mitchell and Mark B. N. Hansen take this further in their definition of new media, locating its origins at a moment prior to any technological realization. They assert that "before it becomes available to designate any technically specific form of mediation, linked to a concrete medium, media names an ontological condition of humanization—the constitutive operation of exteriorization and invention."[33] While we might understand shape-note singing as purely a development in the mediation of music into print, sacred harp collapses any bright line distinction between this method and the culture it moved within as it traveled south, where one hears the sometimes conflicting pressures of an egalitarian methodology and a society structured by inequality.

Contrary to Gitelman's understanding, some scholars argue that new media developments tend toward the erosion of human agency and the erasure of cultural histories. In our own moment, for instance, computer and digital processing machines are increasingly created to talk to each other in coded language in order to exchange digitized textual, sonic, and visual information without ever needing to translate this material for human perception. One can now imagine, for example, the digital production of a hymn that originates in and travels between devices as code without ever being played for humans to experience. If this emphasis on automation has been the general thrust of media development across the twentieth and twenty-first centuries, then replacing both the work's uniqueness with a mass-produced copy (as Benjamin has described) and human agency with computer-driven data manipulation (the advent of digital new media)—so this technological determinist viewpoint goes—has taken the abstraction of the visual or aural object even further by reducing the work to code that technically need never be seen or heard.[34]

However, the figure of the hollow square in sacred harp singing practice offers a counterexample to this technological determinism because it illustrates sacred harp's investment in embodied experience as integral to the mediation of church music that structures this practice. As sacred harp developed in the nineteenth century, singers translated the organization of shape-note part singing at meetings, and it became common practice for them to sit in a square, "hollow" because of the space left open at its center for song leaders, with each side corresponding to a different singing part represented in the book (tenor, bass, alto, and soprano). Anyone could lead a song by moving to the middle of the square, and with a full day of singing, everyone who wanted to was granted a turn as leader.[35] Kiri Miller describes the hollow square as performing the dual work of "level[ing] the playing field" but also structuring relationships between singers, providing a framework for the event that exceeded the pages of the shape-note tune book on which it was based.[36] The hollow square is emblematic of the fact that sacred harp, as Buell Cobb has argued, is "not a bodiless, theoretical system of music," as shape-note itself might be construed.[37] Rather, like camp meetings, "it is a living thing, re-created anew by the singers who convene around the open square to tune their voices to its ancient chords."[38]

This configuration anticipates the more user-centered, culturally oriented thread that has emerged in definitions of new media that Gitelman and others have advanced. Hansen offers another compelling alternative to determinist understandings, arguing that one of new media's major contributions has been to allow consumers and users the ability to manipulate material by affording them idiosyncratic, individualized experiences, paradoxically also enabling a more embodied experience even as this material's circulation becomes more reliant on digitization. Hansen, therefore, concludes that new media holds the potential to revive a sense of the work's Benjaminian aura by engendering "a new, more or less ubiquitous form of aura: the aura that belongs indelibly to [a] singular actualization of data in [the] embodied experience."[39] The shape-note method foreshadowed Hansen's understanding of new media by giving congregants the tools to produce their own performances through sight-reading the music contained in tune books; however, through the hollow square sacred harp singers developed these ideas more fully by conceiving the reproduction of church songs as a collective, embodied, and democratic act, offering a renewed experience of the ritualistic aura—through the mass-produced shape-note tune book—that Benjamin would later claim was lost with the rise of mass media. Sacred harp singers conceived of music as a communal experience in which participants brought the song to life together through a social structure that pushed against hierarchical frameworks, even as it has continually been forced to contend with a social landscape structured by inequality. In a description that jibes with Hansen's understanding of new media, Kiri Miller writes that the hollow square "converts space into place and distraction or detachment into a body vibrating with voices coming from all sides," characterizing the sonic experience of sacred harp events as what Nina Sun Eidsheim might describe as an "unfolding phenomenon that arises through complex material interactions."[40] Against forces that might remove human agency, the hollow square "relies on inwardly focused voices, eyes and emotions to create an extroverted sense of place, a larger comment crossing temporal, geographic, and mortal boundaries."[41]

It is in the arrangement of the hollow square that we also see how sacred harp singing conceives of musical mediation as an activity, something one does, rather than as producing an artifact, such as a piece of sheet music. The hollow square, therefore, highlights sacred harp's attention to the act of music making, or what Christopher Small might call "musicking."[42] Small's work switches the focus of musical study from the notion of the supposedly stable, knowable text of a piece of music to the dynamic activity of music making, inviting us to pay attention to the relationships that coalesce in scenes of musical performance. At a time when music was becoming folded more and more into the commodification of print, the hollow square was geared to preserving the spectacle of the musical event. And, unlike other forms of religious music that featured choral, quartet, and solo performances, sacred harp encouraged attendees to participate, making the practice, as Sean Wilentz puts it, "firmly participatory rather than grandly performative," a feature that prompted George Pullen Jackson to describe sacred harp as music for singers, not listeners.[43]

Sacred Harp Singing and the South

These kinds of communal and participatory aspects of sacred harp singing were, in part, targets of proponents of the better music movement who began a campaign against shape-note singing in the 1820s and 1830s. The most ardent figure of this movement was Lowell Mason, a composer and music teacher, who rose to prominence in Boston, eventually serving as president of the Handel and Haydn Society and cofounding the Boston Academy of Music. Mason championed a Romantic, individualistic understanding of music education rooted in the work of Swiss pedagogical theorist Johann Pestalozzi. Mason was among the reformers who "turned to the rhetoric of progress, abandoning antiquarianism to adopt the cause of 'scientific' harmony," which, in turn, "provided an alliance with academic training and with the emerging unassailable truths of the natural world."[44] As shape-note singing fell into desuetude with the rise of the better music movement, its "historical continuity" was preserved in sacred harp singing in rural areas of the South that embraced it as homologous to traditions coming out of communal religious events like camp meetings.[45] As singers kept up the practice, they also kept White and King's book alive and current by continuing to edit and refine it into the twentieth century. In this process, shape-note singing became virtually synonymous with sacred harp singing, and both became quintessential aspects of southern regionalism.

As part of this process of regionalization, shape-note and sacred harp singing became swept up in the resurgent U.S. South. This association caused sacred harp to become part of the revanchism of the Democratic Party and champions of white southern folk culture in the 1920s and 1930s, most notably through the Southern Agrarians Donald Davidson and Andrew Nelson Lytle and folksong collectors like Cecil Sharpe and George Pullen Jackson. Lytle concisely sums up the prevailing characterization of sacred harp in his contribution to *I'll Take My Stand* (1930), where he asserts "these songs of the Sacred Harp are songs of an agrarian people, and they will bind the folk-ways which will everywhere else go down before canned music and canned pleasure."[46] Underlying this rhetoric about southern culture, however, abides an enduring claim that this singing style acts as a mediator, and in this case, it is being called upon to mediate the cohesion of a kind of rural, white nationalism. Seen as extending and supporting an antimodern agrarianism, sacred harp was characterized as a bulwark against industrialization and a unifying text that guarded against the alienation that followed. Davidson puts it in these terms when he claims "above all it represents a well-established habit of song and as such merits the serious attention of all who hope that an American music can be built upon native foundations," and of course, here, Davidson's phrase "native foundations" signifies a white, southern identity. Davidson, here, offers a definition of folk culture during a time when such definitions of folk, as Erich Nunn has argued, "worked to define racial whiteness and to insulate it from the cultural interracialism threatened by popular culture."[47] In a position that rhymed with the Southern Agrarians' viewpoint, George Pullen Jackson marshaled arguments to prove the white origins of sacred harp hymns, describing the practice in terms that both supported and were determined by a segregated society.

In a typical turn of events, this history conveys how sacred harp became tightly associated with whiteness, but in an equally expected part of the story, it also conceals African Americans' participation in the development of sacred harp. According to Jesse Karlsberg, the whitewashing of sacred harp stemmed from the twin pressures of George Pullen Jackson's "desire to identify a Scotch-Irish American folk music to form the basis of a new national folk-rooted culture" and interests within the African American community to forge a tradition distinct from white people, leading the musicologist and educator John Wesley Work III to turn away from black sacred harp singing.[48] Principally located in the Wiregrass Region, African American involvement in sacred harp first gained material form with Judge Jackson's self-published hymnbook *The Colored Sacred Harp* in 1934. Though it never received widespread recognition, even among African American singers, this text symbolized the efforts of these practitioners of the music to be accepted within the broader sacred harp community. Jerrilyn McGregory notes that the *Colored Sacred Harp* arose from Judge Jackson's own failed attempts to have one of his compositions included in revisions to the standard text. Additionally, as Joe Dan Boyd points out, the work undertaken by Judge Jackson and John Wesley Work indicates a robust tradition of African American sacred harp singing events in the years after the Civil War that are too often left out of accounts like George Pullen Jackson's *White Spirituals of the Southern Uplands*. Despite increasingly its being used to justify and expand the dominance of white culture, African Americans used the practice to aid educational projects and provide a medium around which to hold meetings and create community. McGregory takes this further to speculate that this practice provided a structure that left room for African musical techniques, such as call and response singing and polyrhythmic time signatures to endure.[49]

If the early twentieth-century history of sacred harp singing provides further evidence of typical understandings of the segregationist South, it also conveys how the methodology of shape-note helped new publics participate in the social institution of southern Protestantism. Understanding shape-note and sacred harp singing as a new media innovation requires holding these two thoughts at once. However, it also reveals more than the typical story of the disjointed relationship between progressivism and conservatism that is often said to structure U.S. southern society. Rather, by emphasizing that sacred harp arose from expectations about mediation we shift away from what Karl Hagstrom Miller has termed the "folkloric paradigm," which ultimately seeks to categorize music making into reified racial, class-based, and regional identities.[50] Instead, we begin to see the kind of work and surprising relationships sacred harp makes possible as a method of mediation. This perspective on the original *Sacred Harp* has been echoed by singers in the years since George Pullen Jackson wrote about sacred harp in the ways they have deployed various new media—cassette tapes, CDs, listservs, and digital recordings—to disseminate this singing style around the world, expanding its reach even further with the aid of good, old-fashioned digital new media.

NOTES

1. Eph. 5:19 (KJV).

2. Bealle, *Public Worship*, 44–45; George Pullen Jackson, *White Spirituals*, 16–23; Steel and Hulan, *The Makers of the Sacred Harp*, 4, 8–9.

3. See, for example, Bealle's *Public Worship*; Cobb's *Sacred Harp*; Eskew's "Shape-Note Hymnody in the Shenandoah Valley, 1816–1860"; Joe James Jackson's *A Brief History of the Sacred Harp and Its Author*; Kiri Miller's *Traveling Home*; Kay Norton, "Who Lost the South?"

4. Filene, *Romancing the Folk*; Erich Nunn, "Folk," 189.

5. Kiri Miller, *Traveling Home*, 28.

6. Ibid., 199.

7. Bealle, *Public Worship*, 90–93.

8. Davidson, "Sacred Harp in the Land of Eden."

9. Campbell, "'Old Can Be Used Instead of New,'" 171.

10. Marini, "Hymnody as History," 273.

11. Dargan, *Lining Out the Word*; Southern, *The Music of Black Americans*, 30–31.

12. Cobb, *Sacred Harp*, 9; George Pullen Jackson, *White Spirituals*, 3–11.

13. Cobb, *Sacred Harp*, 59.

14. Sean Wilentz, "1835," 229; Cobb, *Sacred Harp*, 32.

15. There are some competing claims to this milestone. See Cobb, *Sacred Harp*, 66; Bealle, *Public Worship*, 24–32.

16. Little and Smith, *The Easy Instructor*.

17. Cobb, *Sacred Harp*, 59.

18. Ibid., 96.

19. Phillips, *The Hymnal*, 24.

20. Eskew, "Sacred Harp," 128.

21. Steel and Hulan, *The Makers of the Sacred Harp*, 3.

22. Eisenstein, *The Printing Press as an Agent of Change*.

23. Cobb, *Sacred Harp*.

24. Ibid., 274.

25. Ibid., 16.

26. Ibid., 12–13.

27. George Pullen Jackson, *White Spirituals*.

28. Stauffer and Soskis, *The Battle Hymn of the Republic*, 19–20.

29. Cobb, *Sacred Harp*, 72; Steel and Hulan, *The Makers of the Sacred Harp*.

30. Cobb, *Sacred Harp*, 83.

31. Ibid., 72.

32. Gitelman, *Always, Already, New*.

33. Mitchell and Hansen, "Introduction," xiii.

34. This phenomenon is not unlike the future depicted in the videogame *Kentucky Route Zero* that Jae Sharpe examines in chap. 6 of this collection: "We Are Mere Gardeners in the Ruins."

35. Eskew, "Sacred Harp," 131–32.

36. Kiri Miller, *Traveling Home*, 74.

37. Cobb, *Sacred Harp*, 10.

38. Ibid., 40.

39. Hansen, *New Philosophy for New Media*, 3.

40. Kiri Miller, *Traveling Home*, 46; Eidsheim, *Sensing Sound*, 1–2.

41. Kiri Miller, *Traveling Home*, 75.

42. Small, *Musicking*.

43. Wilentz, "1835," 228; Jackson, *White Spirituals*, 122.

44. Bealle, *Public Worship*, 28–29, 44–45.

45. Kiri Miller, *Traveling Home*, 6.

46. Lytle, "The Hind Tit," 231–32.

47. Nunn, "Folk," 195.

48. Karlsberg, "Folklore's Filter," 1.

49. McGregory, 91–92; Boyd, 449–50.

50. Karl Hagstrom Miller, *Segregating Sound*, 9.

BIBLIOGRAPHY

Bealle, John. *Public Worship, Private Faith: Sacred Harp and American Folksong.* Athens: University of Georgia Press, 1997.

Boyd, Joe Dan. *Judge Jackson and the Colored Sacred Harp.* Tuscaloosa: University of Alabama Press, 2005.

Campbell, Gavin James. "'Old Can Be Used Instead of New': Shape-Note Singing and the Crisis of Modernity in the New South." *Journal of American Folklore* 110, no. 436 (Spring 1997): 169–88.

Clayton, David L. and James P. Carrell. *The Virginia harmony.* Samuel H. Davis, Winchester, monographic, 1831. Accessed March 9, 2021. https://lccn.loc.gov/2012562429.

Cobb, Buell. *The Sacred Harp: A Tradition and Its Music.* Athens: University of Georgia Press, 1989.

Dargan, William. *Lining Out the Word: Dr. Watts Hymn Singing in the Music of Black Americans.* Berkeley: University of California Press, 2006.

Davidson, Donald. "Sacred Harp in the Land of Eden." *Virginia Quarterly Review* 10, no. 2 (Spring 1934). https://www.vqronline.org/essay/sacred-harp-land-eden.

Eisenstein, Elizabeth. *The Printing Press as an Agent of Change: Communications and Cultural Transformation.* Cambridge: Cambridge University Press, 1980.

Eskew, Harry L. "Shape-Note Hymnody in the Shenandoah Valley, 1816–1860." Ph.D. Dissertation, Tulane University, 1966.

———. "Sacred Harp." *The New Encyclopedia of Southern Culture: Music,* edited by Bill C. Malone. 128–133. Chapel Hill: University of North Carolina Press, 2009.

Eidsheim, Nina Sun. *Sensing Sound: Listening as Vibrational Practice.* Durham, NC: Duke University Press, 2015.

Filene, Benjamin. *Romancing the Folk: Public Memory and American Roots Music.* Chapel Hill: University of North Carolina Press, 2000.

Gitelman, Lisa. *Always, Already, New: Media, History, and the Data of Culture.* Cambridge, MA: MIT Press, 2008.

Hansen, Mark B. N. *New Philosophy for New Media.* Cambridge, MA: MIT Press, 2006.

Jackson, George Pullen. *White Spirituals of the Southern Uplands: The Story of the Fasola Folk, Their Songs, Singers, and Buckwheat Notes.* Chapel Hill: University of North Carolina Press, 1933.

Jackson, Joe James. *A Brief History of the Sacred Harp and Its Author, B. F. White, Sr., and Contributors.* Privately printed, 1904.

Jackson, Judge. *The Colored Sacred Harp.* Ozark, AL: H. J. Jackson, 1992.

Karlsberg, Jesse P. "Folklore's Filter: Race, Place, and Sacred Harp Singing." Ph.D. diss., Emory University, 2015.

Little, William, and William Smith. *The Easy Instructor; or, a New Method of Teaching Sacred Harmony.* Albany, NY: Webster & Skinner and Daniel Steele, 1802.

Lytle, Andrew Nelson. "The Hind Tit." In *I'll Take My Stand,* edited by Susan V. Donaldson, 201–45. Baton Rouge: Louisiana State University Press, 2006.

Marini, Stephen. "Hymnody as History: Early Evangelical Hymns and the Recovery of American Popular Religion." *Church History* 71, no. 2 (June 2002): 273–306.

McGregory, Jerrilyn. *Wiregrass Country.* Jackson: University Press of Mississippi, 1997.

Miller, Kiri. *Traveling Home: Sacred Harp Singing and American Pluralism.* Urbana: University of Illinois Press, 2010.

Miller, Karl Hagstrom. *Segregating Sound: Inventing Folk and Pop Music in the Age of Jim Crow.* Durham, NC: Duke University Press, 2010.

Mitchell, W. J. T., and Mark B. N. Hansen. "Introduction." *Critical Terms for Media Studies,* edited by W. J. T. Mitchell and Mark B. N. Hansen. vii–xxii. Chicago: University of Chicago Press, 2010.

"The Morning Trumpet." In *Sacred Harp,* by Benjamin Franklin White, E. J. King, Thomas J. Denson, and Paine Denson. Sacred Harp Pub. Co., Haleyville, monographic, 1936. JPEG. Accessed September 17, 2020. https://sacredharpbremen.org/85-the-morning-trumpet.

Norton, Kay. "Who Lost the South?" *American Music* 21, no. 4 (Winter 2003): 391–411. https://www.jstor.org/stable/3250572.

Nunn, Erich. "Folk." In *Keywords for Southern Studies,* edited by Scott Romine and Jennifer Greeson, 189–99. Athens: University of Georgia Press, 2016.

Phillips, Christopher. *The Hymnal: A Reading History.* Baltimore: Johns Hopkins University Press, 2018.

Small, Christopher. *Musicking: The Meanings of Performing and Listening.* Middletown, CT: Wesleyan University Press, 2011.

Southern, Eileen. *The Music of Black Americans: A History.* Third Edition. New York: W. W. Norton, 1997.

Stauffer, John, and Benjamin Soskis. *The Battle Hymn of the Republic: A Biography of the Song That Marches On.* Oxford: Oxford University Press, 2013.

Steel, David Warren, and Richard H. Hulan. *The Makers of the Sacred Harp.* Urbana: University of Illinois Press, 2010.

"Turn, Sinner, Turn." In *Sacred Harp,* by Benjamin Franklin White, E. J. King, Thomas J. Denson, and Paine Denson. Sacred Harp Pub. Co., Haleyville, monographic, 1936. JPEG. Accessed September 17, 2020. https://sacredharpbremen.org/160b-turn-sinner-turn.

White, Benjamin Franklin, E. J. King, Thomas J. Denson, and Paine Denson. *Sacred Harp.* Sacred Harp Pub. Co., Haleyville, monographic, 1936. TIFF. https://www.loc.gov/item /68040523/.

Wilentz, Sean. "1835, *The Sacred Harp.*" In *A New Literary History of America,* edited by Greil Marcus and Werner Sollors, 225–30. Cambridge, MA: Harvard University Press, 2009.

II

FROM PLANTATION TO PLATFORM

Capitalism and the Extractive Economy
of Contemporary New Media

LISA HINRICHSEN

IN WRITING OF HOW U.S. slavery became "capitalized" in the nineteenth century, the historian Edward Baptist identifies how the plantation operates through technologies that interlock the local and the global, amplifying forms of inequity. "So push a button (with the index finger of your *right* hand) on the machine of the trading world, and things happen to benefit the man with sterling bills, a huge pile of cotton, a long roster of abundant credit that allows him to extend his reach across time and space," Baptist writes.[1] His words connect the colonizing "reach" of financialization to the ways in which between 1790 and 1860 human enslavement became subject to mechanization, standardization, and surveillance that ultimately resulted in an exponential increase in cotton production. Accelerated by the seemingly inexhaustible rotating saws of the cotton gin, the demand for enslaved labor swelled and took on newly brutal forms. Networked into global markets through the push of a button, the power of one (white) finger selling the labor extracted from hundreds, if not thousands, of enslaved hands found new ways to tilt fortune in its favor, securing economic and racial power by conceptually transforming subjects into objects of exploitation.

Just as historians have now begun to see the connections between enslavement, once thought to be premodern, and modern capitalism, we might think about the ways that the plantation anticipates the rigors of modern digital life, wherein humans are reduced to quantifiable bodies, and the affect and labor they produce, are increasingly available for exploitation, trafficking, surveillance, and data extraction. This section of *Remediating Region* seeks to trace connections between the present and the past, the postmodern and the modern, drawing connective lines between the workings of digital capitalism and earlier exploitative practices. In examining a range of digital platforms and their economic and social implications, we ask readers to think about the sometimes unpredictable effects of the push of a button: its power to command, erase, commodify, and objectify.

Against earlier predictions, like that of Peter Schwartz and Peter Leyden's "The Long Boom: A History of the Future, 1980–2020," which forecast that the rise of the digital would bring harmony and enlightenment, leading to a "great cross-fertilization of ideas, the ongoing, never-ending planetary conversation," the present-day state of the internet has tempered Western utopian visions of the future.[2] The logic of what Shoshana Zuboff terms "surveillance capitalism," or the trade in data as an exchange of influence and power, seems increasingly visible in everyday life. Noting the ever-increasing grab for "human experience as free raw material for translation into behavioral data," Zuboff emphasizes the proprietary claiming of the private through covert surveillance.[3] As she underscores, this operation is aimed less at controlling present realities and more at infiltrating and owning the future through the rise of what she terms "prediction products" that anticipate and direct future outcomes in ways that increasingly shape elections and human behavior, even feeling itself, stacking wealth and influence in the hands of those who already have it.[4]

Baptist points out that this drive toward accumulation was implicit in the plantation model, which used techniques of surveillance to ensure an asymmetry of knowledge as an asymmetry of power, striving for an ever-widening economy of scope. Amplified by computational power, algorithmic systems, and automated platforms, contemporary digital capitalism has seized ever more things that exist outside the market sphere, only to turn around to sell what was once "free" back to us as market commodities. Led by a drive for surplus and drawn to economies of scale, the digital increasingly intervenes in and modifies our understanding of the human, shaping it toward desired commercial outcomes and new forms of servitude, rather than forms of human reciprocity. Digital redlining, predatory ad-targeting, and other outcomes of digital tracking have inarguably contributed to the reification of racial and class stratification and, in many ways, the commodification of our own interior lives. In trading individual self-determination, autonomy, and freedom for convenience, personalization, and innovation, "connectivity" has offered not a utopian openness but instead increasingly segregated spaces of monopolistic power and serfdom, falling more in line with the vision of Lev Manovich than the "California ideology" he critiqued.[5] As Siva Vaidhyanathan argues, presenting a largely critical view of contemporary digital media, "social" media has, paradoxically, a largely *disconnective* and *anti*social character, which works in the service of leveling the information landscape, confusing conceptions of the "real" while also accentuating inequity and amplifying alienation.[6]

In reshaping the value and meaning of human labor and leisure, the extractive "efficiency" economy, itself drawn from forms of early twentieth-century Taylorism with roots in the plantation, seeks to control bodies and organize labor, while also obscuring profit- and decision-making processes behind opaque and impenetrable algorithms.[7] Made instrumental, binary, and spoken for, the individual is extracted into information that, as recent scholarship by Safiya Umoja Noble, Virginia Eubanks, and Lisa Nakamura argues, is indebted to the same source code of racial capitalism and settler colonialism that has long been the "southern" script.[8] Organized and governed by seemingly impersonal codes and abstractions, including highly digitized forms of financialization and computational capital, the immaterial power of algorithms translates back into material forms of dispossession and displacement. As Ruth Wilson Gilmore has claimed, underscoring the violence of abstraction into capital, racism itself "is a practice of abstraction, a death-dealing displacement of difference into hierarchies that organize relations within and between the planet's sovereign political territories."[9] Those practices of abstraction continue in digital realms, where they are amplified, drawing on power and wage differentials that have earlier origins. Commenting on this stratification, Jonathan Beller argues that "global communication and information processing utilizes planetary dispossession as its substrate," pointing to the role of the Global South in new media technologies.[10]

Through flattening out the lived and living environment into a computational field, digital policing and surveillance techniques underscore the violence of the commodity logic of abstraction and its link to white supremacy as a material system of relations. Such screen-mediated production of social difference can be seen, for example, in the operation of Nextdoor, an app launched in 2011 as "the first private social network for neighborhoods." The network was originally marketed as a virtual site designed to strengthen the bonds of offline geographical community, giving users a convenient space to sell used baby strollers, recommend an electrician, find lost pets, and review local businesses. Yet in making virtual a midcentury idea of community conversation, an ideal formed under Jim Crow segregation, the app amplifies forms of surveillance and exclusion, providing an outlet for racial profiling and for the harassment of the homeless through the ways it aggregates and imposes standards of normality and deviance that are linked to and reproductive of longer histories of racial and gendered violence. Between reports of lost dogs and advertisements of used treadmills for sale, users might come across posts warning of suspicious, and often racialized, outsiders. Rather than chart out new virtual modes of community engagement, Nextdoor's operations recall the broader history of midcentury housing, redlining discrimination, segregation, and homogenous perceptions of community and belonging. The site's geographic specificity and real-name policies make Nextdoor a powerful resource for law enforcement, something the platform has seized upon by partnering with "over 3,500 public agencies across the country—including police, fire, city, and emergency management departments," creating a direct line of communication between Nextdoor and government agencies.[11] While Nextdoor proclaims that "technology is a powerful tool for making neighborhoods stronger, safer places to call home," seeing the concept of "neighborhood watch" positively, many communities cannot forget the tragic consequences of race-based policing of residential spaces.[12] The death of Trayvon Martin, for example, illustrates the way that as Rahim Kurwa, in the journal *Surveillance & Society*, notes, neighborhood watch groups have been used as a tool to regulate race.[13]

In tracing the carryover of old systems of oppression into contemporary new media, this section reads against processes of datafication and digital control once envisioned, at least in the West, to liberate. James Bridle has aptly shown that the networks of the new, in the form of the "information superhighway," rest on old pathways: the networks of telegraph cables laid down to control old empires.[14] As old liberal economic ideas are unraveled in a contemporary new media economy, the once-secure logic of "possessive individualism,"[15] and now-naïve conceptions of the "free" market, have been replaced by the growth of what Stanley Aronowitz describes as forms of "wage slavery in which all the cards are held, mediated by technology, by the employer, whether it is the intermediary company or the customer."[16] Likewise, Jack Linchuan Qiu argues that we have "become deeply entangled in a planetary industrial system operating by and through digital media," one in which Western "productivity" is propped up by the exploitation of the Global South.[17] Beyond a mode of production capitalism is also, crucially, a mode of *social re-*

production. This means that to understand the future of neoliberal capitalism as it is mediated by platforms, we will also have to examine how these technologies reconfigure and reproduce the deeply gendered, classed, and racialized structures of law, knowledge, and life that combine to shape everyday U.S. life. Offline and on, these structures sustain labor, power, and capital accumulation, functioning as forms of capture.

Through pervading our everyday lives while reshaping relations and further blurring lines between the market, the state, and civil society, digital media platforms act as political, as well as economic, agents. In *Platform Capitalism* (2016), Nick Srnicek offers a sharp account of companies that mobilize platforms to create novel forms of value. As he and others argue, focusing on platform companies as primarily economic actors ends up obscuring the ways that these companies and the platforms they create, seek to act as new social institutions, transforming societies on a global scale.[18] The rise of extracting, processing, and analyzing data is not just an experiment with new forms of capitalist value-creation and extraction in the face of waning economic growth, but a wild-card experiment in human management that exceeds the traditional limits of behavioral economics. By monetizing human interiority, turning subject into object, monopolistic new media companies diffuse market logics and entrepreneurial rationalities into new, converged territories, altering working conditions and labor market norms in ways that ask for more and give less.

While critiques of what has been called "machinic enslavement" (Deleuze and Guattari), "digital slavery" (Fuchs), and "iSlavery" (Qiu) consistently make their arguments on a national and transnational scale, this section returns to region as a crucial lens through which to historicize and ground the digitization and commodification of the human experience.[19] As the introduction to this collection argues, the material impacts of digitization make places matter anew. Against the elusive flows of global digital interconnection and transnational capitalism, the region, as a unit of scale, makes visible vital historical, ecological, and interpersonal frames that can help us comprehend (and even rethink) global-scale forces and flows. By offering a human frame for the inhuman practices of contemporary capitalism, region decodes the dematerializing rhetoric of the global. In turn, new media theory prompts a rereading of the plantation as network, asking how its deadening paradigms of racial capitalism can be short-circuited. The following essays trace the representation of datafication, data tracking, and data-communications systems and focus on technology and media as they contain and constrain people in classification systems. Together, they dramatize how technology accelerates and automates the exploitation of human labor, extracting and circulating individuality, often without consent.

Margaret T. McGehee's "'It's a State of Mind': The Online Merch-ing of Whiteness" examines magazines and merchandise—such as a clothing store called Roots, complete with a cotton boll as its logo, and brands including Southern Marsh, Southern Tide, and Simply Southern—to trace the digital circulation of "southern" as signifier. McGehee uncovers the marketing of white power via what she terms "the virtual campfires of insularity, fueled by feedback loops."[20] Most of these companies, it turns out, are owned by white men from and in the U.S. South, and McGehee illuminates how in their ventures—and particularly in their online marketing and advertising campaigns—they "imitate and reproduce for the masses the perceived trappings of a southern white gentility, uniform and *uniformed* in its preppiness and elitism."[21] Yet these images also invoke how segregation, race and class relations in general have become "deracinated, uprooted, [and] detached from the larger history of the U.S. South."[22] Even when made "hip" by the *Bitter Southerner* or other alternative brands, online sales of "southern identity" ultimately bind the region to old myths, made newly monopolistic on the internet.

The online creation, reproduction, and mediation of racial difference is aided by the way digitalization dehistoricizes and dissolves distinctions. Addressing the relationship between the networked economy, the public sphere, and capitalist desire, Alexandra Chiasson's "#PlantationWedding: Fantasy and Forgetting on Instagram" focuses on how the plantation—a space now used by an industry that sells tradition, memory, and nostalgia—is now, more than ever, a place mediated by technology. In this essay, Chiasson argues that tagged wedding posts on Instagram provide testament to the marketability of this aesthetic. Marking a post with "#PlantationWedding" inserts an individual user's post into a larger public archive, creating app-based communities founded, in this case, on historical forgetting. Comparing marketing posts from wedding industry professionals and plantation estates' official accounts with that of personal accounts, Chiasson highlights how the platform encourages participation in the digital economy of the "simplantation," even when disavowing the notorious hashtag. Her exploration concludes by asserting that, if the field of southern studies collectively demonstrates how hyper-focus on regional subcultures creates a model for infinite other contexts, then new media studies, which grapples with this "infinite" directly as we consider the inestimable communities and their cultures spawning daily on the internet, can benefit from regional models of analysis similar to the #PlantationWedding case study provided in this essay.

While region can provide a comprehensible frame for analyzing the amnesia of late capitalism, the digital can provide its own forms of analysis. Jae Sharpe's "'We Are Mere Gardeners in the Ruins': *Kentucky Route Zero* and Modeling Collaborative Human Dignity in the Information Age" examines how, through fantastical and surreal gameplay environments, *Kentucky Route Zero* explores problems of alcoholism, poverty, the affective politics of urban desperation, and contemporary workers' rights in the Appalachian South, as the game's protagonists uncover a conspiracy engineered to protect corporate interests after a mining disaster. *Kentucky Route Zero* firmly establishes itself as the inheritor of twentieth-century American media traditions: in addition to its references to the work of Colombian novelist Gabriel García Márquez, one of the smaller, separate games that expands on the *Kentucky Route Zero* narrative, *The Entertainment,* pays homage to American literary icons such as David Foster Wallace in its examinations of addiction and contemporary visual media, while situating its examination of these problems in the specific social context of present-day Kentucky. The game thus focalizes an exploration of otherness and cultural identity through a speculative lens that places the U.S. media canon in dialogue with the influence of South American writers on the cultural identity of the U.S. South. The supplementary digital content (such as the narrative-related experimental television loop that plays on wevp.tv, the smaller point-and-click games released as downloadable content, and the publication of a printed script for *The Entertainment*) demands a high degree of interactive engagement for the player who wants to experience the full scope of the game's story. This need for sustained attention to fragmented and varied narrative forms makes the experience of playing *Kentucky Route Zero* one that privileges the deliberate curation of multiple styles of information and the intersection of old and new media.

Rounding out the consideration of platform capitalism, Jennie Lightweis-Goff, in "GIS South: Louisiana in the Lost and Found," interrogates how digital mapping technologies rely on static constructs of coastal cartographies frozen in time before the oil industry's extractive violence against the Louisiana landscape and the resulting land loss amid climate change. Emphasizing what she calls "intimate cartographies," Lightweis-Goff critiques corporate digital optimism for the way that it elides the lived realities of extractive capitalism in the Gulf South. She attends to place-based platforms that attempt to locate the user "in space," revealing that, rather than make concrete the challenges of New Orleans—and, indeed, the world—such platforms more often render them invisible in the service of selling a well-worn version of The City That Care Forgot.

These intersections between old and new, the embodied and the enminded, the human and the technical, are important to understand at this moment of late capitalism. In focusing on the ways that race, gender, and media co-constitute each other within the circuitries of capital, the essays in this section show that new media theory cannot responsibly operate without critical discussions of identity, politics, and history. The U.S. South, as the site of carceral slavery and human commodification, provides a scale from which to see the embodied, affective, political, and spatial histories and struggles that characterize capitalism from plantation to platform.

NOTES

1. Baptist, "Toward a Political Economy of Slave Labor," 40. Cotton production accelerated from 20 million pounds in 1805 to 2 billion pounds in 1860.

2. Schwartz and Leyden, "The Long Boom."

3. Zuboff, *The Age of Surveillance Capitalism,* 14.

4. Ibid., 10.

5. Manovich, *The Language of New Media.*

6. See Vaidhyanathan, *Antisocial Media.*

7. As Caitlin Rosenthal argues in *Accounting for Slavery,* Frederick Winslow Taylor's ideas in his 1911 magnum opus, *The Principles of Scientific Management,* and Henry Laurence Gantt's concept of the "task and bonus system" have a much longer history in methods of organizing labor under slavery. As she shows, planter-capitalists built sophisticated organizational structures for extracting human labor with brutal efficiency.

8. See Noble, *Algorithms of Oppression;* Eubanks, *Automating Inequality;* Nakamura, *Digitizing Race.*

9. Gilmore, "Fatal Couplings of Power and Difference."

10. Beller, *The Message Is Murder,* 19.

11. "How to Connect with Your Public Agencies," Nextdoor Blog.

12. "About," Nextdoor Blog.

13. See Kurwa, "Building the Digitally Gated Community." In 2015, Nextdoor was heavily criticized for the role it played in enabling racial profiling on the platform. The company responded by altering its algorithm, adding reminders to avoid racial stereotyping, and

requiring users to add other descriptors if they mention race. The company claims these reminders and alterations cut down on "problematic posts" by 75 percent. But, one can argue, these algorithmic tweaks did little to fundamentally alter the operational equation of race, class, and gender disparity in the United States and nothing to realize offline equality.

14. Bridle, *New Dark Age.*

15. Macpherson, *The Political Theory of Possessive Individualism.*

16. Cited in Natasha Singer, "In the Sharing Economy, Workers Find Both Freedom and Uncertainty." *New York Times,* August 16, 2014.

17. Qiu, *Goodbye iSlave,* 13.

18. Srnicek, *Platform Capitalism.*

19. Deleuze and Guattari, *A Thousand Plateaus,* 492; Fuchs, *Digital Labor and Karl Marx;* Qiu, *Goodbye iSlave.*

20. See McGehee, "It's a State of Mind."

21. Ibid.

22. Ibid.

BIBLIOGRAPHY

Baptist, Edward E. "Toward a Political Economy of Slave Labor: Hands, Whipping-Machines, and Modern Power." In *Slavery's Capitalism: A New History of American Economic Development,* edited by Sven Beckert and Seth Rockman. 31–61. Philadelphia: University of Pennsylvania Press, 2016.

Beller, Jonathan. *The Message Is Murder: Substrates of Computational Capital.* London: Pluto, 2018.

Bridle, James. *New Dark Age: Technology and the End of the Future.* London: Verso, 2018.

Deleuze, Gilles, and Felix Guattari. *A Thousand Plateaus: Capitalism and Schizophrenia.* Trans. Brian Massumi. Minneapolis: Minnesota University Press, 1987.

Eubanks, Virginia. *Automating Inequality: How High-Tech Tools Profile, Police, and Punish the Poor.* New York: St. Martin's, 2018.

Fuchs, Christian. *Digital Labor and Karl Marx.* New York: Routledge, 2014.

Gantt, Henry Laurence. "Task and Bonus in Management." In *Lecture Notes on Some of the Business Features of Engineering Practice* by Alex C. Humphreys. Rev. ed., 485–97. Hoboken, NJ: Stephens Institute of Technology, 1912.

Gilmore, Ruth Wilson. "Fatal Couplings of Power and Difference: Notes on Racism and Geography." *Professional Geographer* 54, no 1 (February 2002): 15–24.

Kurwa, Rahim. "Building the Digitally Gated Community: The Case of Nextdoor." *Surveillance & Society* 17, no. 1–2 (2019): 111–17.

Macpherson, C. B. *The Political Theory of Possessive Individualism.* Oxford: Oxford University Press, 1962.

Manovich, Lev. *The Language of New Media.* Cambridge, MA: MIT Press, 2002.

Nakamura, Lisa. *Digitizing Race: Visual Cultures of the Internet.* Minneapolis: University of Minnesota Press, 2007.

Nextdoor. "How to Connect with Your Public Agencies." Accessed March 20, 2020. https://help.nextdoor.com/s/article/How-to-connect-with-your-public-agencies?language=en_US.

Nextdoor Blog. "About." Accessed March 15, 2020. https://esblog.nextdoor.com/about/.

Noble, Safiya Umoja. *Algorithms of Oppression: How Search Engines Reinforce Racism*. New York: New York University Press, 2018.

Qiu, Jack Linchuan. *Goodbye iSlave: A Manifesto for Digital Abolition*. Chicago: University of Illinois Press, 2016.

Rosenthal, Caitlin. *Accounting for Slavery: Masters and Management*. Cambridge, MA: Harvard University Press, 2018.

Schwartz, Peter, and Peter Leyden. "The Long Boom: A History of the Future, 1980–2020." *Wired* (July 1, 1997). https://www.wired.com/1997/07/longboom/.

Singer, Natasha. "In the Sharing Economy, Workers Find Both Freedom and Uncertainty." *New York Times*, August 16, 2014.

Srnicek, Nick. *Platform Capitalism*. London: Polity, 2016.

Taylor, Frederick Winslow. *The Principles of Scientific Management*. 1911. Cosimo Classics, 2010.

Vaidhyanathan, Siva. *Antisocial Media: How Facebook Disconnects Us and Undermines Democracy*. New York: Oxford University Press, 2018.

Zuboff, Shoshana. *The Age of Surveillance Capitalism: The Fight for a Human Future at the New Frontier of Power*. New York: Public Affairs, 2019.

"IT'S A STATE OF MIND"

The Online Merch-ing of Whiteness

MARGARET T. McGEHEE

IN THE FLURRY OF social media posts that captured the Unite the Right Rally and the violence that ensued in Charlottesville in August 2017, journalists regularly commented on the "uniforms" of the white, predominantly male marchers: collared shirts, khaki pants, tiki torches. White robes and hoods had been replaced with Fred Perry polos. Or in the case of Peter Cvjetanovic, the twenty-year-old University of Nevada undergraduate whose image went viral on Twitter in the midst of the Charlottesville protest, the white cloak had been traded in for a seemingly generic white cotton polo monogrammed with the Identity Evropa's "Dragon's Eye" symbol.[1] On August 12, 2017, after posting images of multiple protesters in Charlottesville, asking readers to help identify them, and promising to "make them famous," @yesyoureracist shared images of Cvjetanovic, stating, "This angry young man is Peter Cvjetanovic, a student at @unevadareno."[2] These shirts and the white supremacists wearing them reflected age-old militaristic strategies of the erasure of the individual, reinforced marchers' white corporeal identity and white supremacist corporate ideology, and signaled their desperate desire for belonging and victory in the face of perceived loss and defeat, something that Twitter users foregrounded. Using the hashtag #PeterCvjetanovic, tweeters recirculated the now infamous image of Cvjetanovic mid-scream holding a tiki torch, an image taken by photojournalist Samuel Corum of the Anadolu Agency. One transformed it into a meme reading "We Are Taking Our Country Back!" while another juxtaposed it with an image of Adolf Hitler. Posting the image on August 13, 2017, Kurt Eichenwald of the *New York Times* tweeted: "Peter Cvjetanovic, a white nationalist, is upset that this photo of him has gone viral. So be nice: dont [*sic*] retweet this tweet 1000s of times."[3] Twitter users obviously did not heed his (sarcastic) plea.

Digital platforms and social media efficiently provide onlookers from across the nation and globe with a barrage of images and texts delivered in engaging, colorful, stimulating virtual environments. In some cases, a picture that goes viral via Twitter and that users transform into memes, such as the one of Cvjetanovic, overtly and directly points to white supremacy; a photo circulated a thousand times is indeed worth a thousand words. Certainly, Twitter's function in recirculating and critiquing white supremacy deserves close reading. However, it is also worth considering, as I do throughout this essay, the more subtle replications of elite white power that the digital world helps perpetuate and make accessible and purchasable through contemporary new media networks, whether online stores or digital zines. "Digital Southern" shirts, in particular, seem to be everywhere these days. The internet is host to many brands sporting "southern" in the title, including Southern Fried Cotton, Southern Shirt Company with its embroidered cotton boll logo, and Southern Point Company with its specialty line of "plantation flannel."[4] (See Fig. 4.1.) Most of these companies sell clothes—primarily shirts—that are a fitting marriage of preppy and outdoorsy. In examining issues of *Garden & Gun* and in perusing the merchandise of boutiques in places such as Covington, Georgia—including its clothing store Roots, complete with a cotton boll as its logo and merchandise supporting the Republican Party—one notes brands including Southern Marsh, Southern Tide, and Simply Southern, all founded in the twenty-first century. (See figs. 4.2a and 4.2b.)

Of course, these clothing companies are not the only ones selling southern-themed wear on the internet. The print publication *Garden & Gun* (*G&G*), also available in an online format, and the web-based zine the *Bitter Southerner*

Southern Point Co Sport Shirts are crafted for the superior gentleman seeking to exemplify the southern lifestyle. We have combined luxury and style in our shirts. Designed with the highest blend of Pima cotton, the Plantation Flannel Shirt sets itself apart from others.

custom designed pattern

100% flannel Pima Cotton

embroidered Greyton™ logo

laser engraved buttons

extra button closure to make sure shirt stays tucked in

imported

Fig. 4.1. "Plantation Flannel," by Southern Point Company. Screenshot by the author.

(*BS*) are home to online stores—the Fieldshop and the General Store, respectively. While the two publications differ in the wares they sell and in their missions and journalistic foci, they ultimately work together—alongside the shirt companies—to replicate white elite power via digital platforms and the material goods sold on such platforms. American in flavor, this politics is limited neither to the "southern" identities of their products' wearers nor really to "the South" at all. And while these publications and companies would no doubt contend that "the South" and "southern" are central to their causes and identities, there is no *there* there: consumers, whether readers or online shoppers, aren't purchasing commodities of southernness or southern identity. A

Fig. 4.2a. Southern Roots Outfitter (Covington, GA) logo with cotton boll. Cover photo, Facebook, January 23, 2020, 11:03 A.M.

Fig. 4.2b. Republican Party merchandise by Over Under Company, which advertises itself on its "About Us" page as selling clothing and accessories that are a "true staple for any Southern Gentleman." Screenshot by the author.

closer inspection of these brands' digital marketing campaigns reveals how their buyers are purchasing elite white identity made readily accessible via digital media. As Scott Romine argues in *The Real South*, "capitalism gives with the one hand what it takes away with the other: if it is, on some level, responsible for the broadly diffused experience of dislocation and disembedding, it also offers solutions in prepackaged and commodified forms of culture. This is why advertising comes so naturally to culture: both constitute attempts to replenish aura in an age of mechanical reproduction."[5] Online shirt companies and South-focused zines do just this, with a twist: they respond to a reader/viewer/consumer's "dislocation and disembedding" by offering dislocated bodies *virtual* spaces consisting of a shared vocabulary of images, tropes, and a seemingly infinite warehouse of commodities (articles, advertisements, material goods). These commodities reproduce—again, again, and again—the power structures underlying them, namely wealth, whiteness, patriarchy, heteronormativity, able-bodiedness, and more. Simply put, these sites are the virtual campfires of insularity, fueled by feedback loops. *Garden & Gun* and the *Bitter Southerner* drive this home fairly clearly through their donor programs that reinforce the notion of belonging as commodity. Membership in the exclusive Garden & Gun Society includes a "members-only event" at luxurious locations, such as Blackberry Farm in Tennessee, and *Bitter Southerner* offers readers the opportunity to "Join the Family."[6]

One might argue that the emergence of such companies reflects certain populations' anxiety about a disappearing "South" or southern identity, or an ongoing search for authenticity, for the "real" South, or a wishful longing to fulfill some lack. But the events of the second decade of the twenty-first century, including but not limited to the 2016 election, the backlash against Barack Obama's presidency, the alt-right's protest in Charlottesville, the numerous deaths of Black Americans caused by police violence, and the insurrection at the nation's Capitol in January 2021 might point us in other directions. What surfaces from the web pages of southern shirt companies or from the web pages of *G&G* is not anxiety. Rather, it's an unabashed, fearless loyalty to and pride in certain varieties and performances of elite whiteness that have been made possible by MAGA-hat-wearing inspired fantasies of regaining lost (white) power, especially for middle- and working-class Americans.[7] The *Bitter Southerner* may seem like an outlier in a larger project of white supremacy, especially given its staff members' and writers' progressive politics and the forward-looking, inclusive character of its articles and merchandise. Despite the editors' professed good intentions, *BS* nevertheless succeeds in reinforcing structures of white power in and beyond the U.S. South in that educated white folks, purporting to redefine "the South," ultimately reproduce hierarchies of power along racial and class lines. As accessible digital platforms, *BS, G&G,* and "southern" clothing companies online allow viewer-reader-shoppers to return repeatedly—free of charge and at any hour of the day—to such reproductions, a virtually (literally and figuratively) infinite journey on the web, and offer ways to purchase representations of the values they put forth. The ideas represented therein have the potential to—and do—travel beyond anything that scholars within southern studies have ever written. And they are traveling and selling, big time: in Covington, Georgia; in Nantucket, Massachusetts; in Westport, Connecticut; and beyond.

The photos and "About Us" statements on these "southern" companies' websites confirm the fashion options referenced above as the costumes for the performance of early twenty-first-century genteel whiteness by twenty-somethings. Take Southern Tide, for example, a company founded in 2006 by Allen Stephenson, a Greenville, South Carolina, resident who dropped out of the University of South Carolina during his junior year to start the company with help from his mother. "It was really quite simple," the Southern Tide website stated in early 2018:

> [Stephenson] wanted to take all the modern design elements of today's youthful trends and tie these in with his love for *old southern culture and lifestyle* to create a brand that stood for craftsmanship, clean lines, *classic* design and *rich heritage.* [. . .] From the unique sport shirts and casual pants, to the *classic* sweaters, swimwear and polos, the brand is the leader in youthful *Southern* style. No matter where one lives, anyone with an appreciation for *classic* design, good fit and craftsmanship, combined with *an affection for the coast and old-world heritage,* will quickly fall in love with the *charm* of the Southern Tide brand.[8]

Here, the use of "classic" three times, "heritage" twice, and phrases such as "old southern" and "old-world" works to link this company's products to ideals of an imagined genteel white past that continues virtually uninterrupted into the present. For those in and beyond the southern United States such terms function as shorthand for a particular kind of white planter class identity and perceived way of leisurely life that can be purchased and worn.

The company's CEO since 2014, Christopher Heyn, describes Southern Tide as "appeal[ing] to customers who incorporate Southern heritage and lifestyle into their wardrobe, even if they do not live in the South."[9] On its website today, Southern Tide states its ethos as follows:

> We're all about the CLASSIC AMERICAN LIFESTYLE: road trips across the country, quality time with our four-legged best friend, and low country boils on the coast. We have an affinity for all things BLUE, but we still live a COLORFUL life. From our wardrobe to our personality, we don't shy away from making a statement. Whether we're decked out for a special occasion or suited up for a dip in the ocean, WE'RE ALWAYS UP FOR A GOOD TIME. [. . .] To us, the South is more than a location, IT'S A STATE OF MIND.[10]

Again, the word "classic" surfaces, but it is followed by "American" rather than "southern," perhaps to appeal to a more geographically expansive consumer base. At the same time, regionally—and culturally—specific activities such as "low country boils" return "the South" to the products, and one could interpret the line "we don't shy away from making a statement" as speaking both to the often brightly colored wardrobes and the recalcitrant cultural history of elite white men in the South. Overall, though, the theme of leisure—"good times" historically made possible through whiteness and money—is what emerges most forcefully.

Store locations reinforce this theme as well. Southern Tide, according to *Shopping Centers Today*, "works with franchisers and seeks locations near resorts, country clubs, large college campuses," and it has stores not only in southern states but also in northern areas of extreme wealth such as Westport and Nantucket.[11] Such placement reinforces for whom these clothes are made: namely, white wealthy consumers who frequent (and are allowed into) resorts and private clubs and the young white people who may one day frequent such places. Southern Tide, in fact, has an "Ambassador" program for college students, all but one of whom appear to be white.[12]

However, it is the company's digital content—their website and accompanying promotional videos—that does the most work to signal for whom these clothes are intended. Southern Tide's clothing models are all young white men and women with the exception of one Black man, who also appears in the company's spring 2019 promotional video shot in the Bahamas. This video, set to Lady Bri's "Makin' a Move," features a white woman in various bikinis and outfits swimming in the ocean, a white man fishing, and a Black man who engages in leisure activities in some scenes (e.g., shooting pool, standing by a tree in the ocean, sitting in a beach chair) but who also appears as the white man's fishing guide. Outfitted in khaki guide wear and wearing a fanny pack, the Black model drives the boat and, in one scene, even poles the boat forward for his white passenger.[13] The white characters' visible enjoyment and happiness coming from their leisure-filled vacation largely depends on the labor of the Black guide, with Lady Bri, a Black woman singer, invisibly offering the rousing soundtrack to their exploits. In additional promotional videos, shot in Bermuda, the Bahamas, and Charleston, South Carolina, no people of color appear, though musicians of color, such as Chris Valentine, regularly provide the audio backdrop to the leisure depicted.[14] Collectively cloistered in their whiteness and wealth, the men and women roam comfortably and freely in the beautiful outdoor environments shown, unencumbered by the demands of daily life or the racial dynamics of the U.S. South or Caribbean islands.

Southern Tide is not the only shirt company in the business of selling a "state of mind" or to capitalize on commonly understood notions of "southern" as connected to a white leisure class.[15] Founded by two Louisiana State University students a year after Southern Tide and inspired in part by *Garden & Gun* magazine,[16] Southern Marsh describes its clothing line as follows:

> Known for its unique culture, beautiful people, and timeless dress—The South is an area of the country that still finds time to escape the hustle and bustle of big city life. Southern Marsh was inspired by that idea and influenced by those who understand the lifestyle as they take it with them everywhere they go. The friends getting up at 4 A.M. to make it to the blind before sunrise, the father cashing in vacation days to go fishing with his family, or the southern belle spending a timeless afternoon with great friends. The Southern culture is full of rich character that reminds us to give thanks for the little things that make life more enjoyable, everyday. At Southern Marsh, we do our best to make the highest quality products, out of the best materials and package up a piece of that charm to give you a snapshot into a life with a little *authentic southern class.*[17]

Sporting a duck logo on the front breast pocket, Southern Marsh shirts feature on the back a range of landscape scenes (e.g., mountains, marshes), images of animals and wildlife (e.g., hunting dog, duck, deer antlers), activities (e.g., chopping wood, fly fishing, deer hunting, canoeing), cocktails (e.g., the Mint Julep, the Hurricane), and floral or agricultural icons (e.g., peaches, magnolia blooms), along with the taglines "Classic Southern" and "Authentic Southern Class." (See Fig. 4.3.)

Like Southern Tide, Southern Marsh emphasizes stasis through its use of adjectives like "classic," "authentic," and "timeless" while also reifying notions of nature and country living more broadly as sources of positive values and "rich character," echoing Raymond Williams's analysis in *The Country and the City*. The company prides itself on its contributions to conservation efforts in the southeast, claiming that purchases have allowed them to place over eight thousand acres into conservation easements, a value of over $38 million, a gesture that could be read as positively contributing to environmental justice efforts.[18] However, in rhetorically presenting that conservation as a reclaiming

Fig. 4.3. "Cocktail Tee—Mint Julep—Long Sleeve," Southern Marsh Company. Screenshot by the author.

of "the [classic, authentic, timeless] country" they cast themselves as saviors of stasis in the process.

The cotton boll, fish, ducks, and other "southern" symbols referenced above may be to most consumers mere logos on the fabrics of their lives—deracinated, uprooted, detached from the larger history of the U.S. South and from a legacy of Black enslavement and exploitation. However, owned by white men in and of the U.S. South, these companies and their ventures, as represented in their online marketing and advertising campaigns, ultimately imitate and reproduce for the masses the perceived trappings of a southern white gentility, uniform and *uniformed* in its preppiness and elitism. With the exception of the one man of color on the Southern Tide site, the models are young white men and women; their wealth is implied by virtue of the fact that the clothes they sport range from $38 for a t-shirt to $95 for a polo shirt. What makes these shirts—and the publications discussed below—different than what has come before is their online presence, particularly how a dynamic and far-reaching digital platform allows for endless circulation of notions of uniformity and stasis. Viewers see the same people, the same shirts, the same symbols, over and over and over; companies such as Southern Tide repeatedly create an aura of stasis as they repeatedly remind consumers that the clothing styles they offer are "timeless" and "classic."

Magazines also participate in the digital reproduction and celebration of white elitism in southern clothing. Since its debut in the spring of 2007, the Charleston-based *Garden & Gun* has amassed "more than one million passionate and engaged readers," according to its website. The magazine's title, claims publisher Rebecca Wesson Darwin, is "a metaphor for the South—its land, the people, their lifestyle, and their heritage."[19] But whose metaphor is it? Which "people," "lifestyle," and "heritage" does it showcase, and whose notions—ideas *and* material goods—can be found within its matte-finished pages? Like the clothing companies discussed earlier, *G&G* plays a significant role in defining and commodifying the U.S. South and in producing and re-cycling a consumable popular imaginary for the region—one rooted in aristocratic activity and, at times, postbellum iconography. According to Ioanna Opidee and Stefanie Botelho in *Folio: The Magazine for Magazine Management*, "What both [*Garden & Gun* and *Cowboys and Indians*] have hit on is the wider appeal of their content, and the opportunity to export their sensibilities beyond the boundaries of a regional-focused magazine. Part of this is cultivating a sense of identity. [. . .] At *Garden & Gun*, the most resonant themes are a connection with the land and the sporting life."[20] But, as Opidee and Botelho go on to suggest, *G&G* also succeeds in ideologically linking populations who no longer reside in the U.S. South: "Both titles zero in on the large number of 'expats' who have moved from the region to other areas. Both magazines also aim at those who own vacation homes in the regions and strongly identify with their cultures."[21]

When *Garden & Gun* was first launched, the *New York Times* labeled its debut as "awkward," as it "arrived on newsstands just days before the shootings at Virginia Tech."[22] The title was clearly an issue for some, a title which in part refers to a popular bar-disco in Charleston in the late 1970s, the King Street Garden and Gun Club. In fact, it was "the first bar in the city," according to the Lee Brothers, "where people of all races and sexual orientations felt comfortable dancing together."[23] Though *G&G* suffered financially its first few years, it has been thriving in recent years. According to a 2012 article in the *Media Industry Newsletter* (*MIN*) entitled "'Garden & Gun' Is Having More Yankee Success than Robert E. Lee," *G&G* gained attention of "New York media circles," including *CBS This Morning* and *Morning Joe*. Their ad sales increased in 2012 "with a record 302 ad pages (+37% versus 2011's 221)" as did the newsstand sales and subscriptions (+28 percent and +25 percent, respectively). "Growing fastest," state the *MIN* editors, "is gardenandgun.com, where unique visitors are on a +330% clip this year."[24] A little over a year later, *MIN* reported both that *G&G*'s circulation rate had increased in 2012 by 11.5 percent to 305,280, with 41 percent of the non-South-based audience coming from California and New York, and that *G&G*'s first book publication, *The Southerner's Handbook*, was number 13 on the *New York Times* best-seller list in late 2013.[25] A 2016 *Wall Street Journal* article states that *G&G* "def[ied] the slump" experienced by print publications with its subscriptions slightly above 350,000 and its ad sales jumping 6 percent in 2015.[26] Reader demographics confirm the publication's wealthy, middle-aged, male base. The average household income for a *G&G* subscriber is $332,000. The majority of subscribers are male. The median age of *G&G* readers is fifty-four, though the initial goal was to target "readers in their 30s and 40s."[27] Statistics related to subscribers' race/ethnicity are not available, but it would come as no surprise if the majority identify as white. The U.S. South as a brand is a regional export thanks to older, wealthy, urban men.

But what about the audience for *G&G* online? At the very least, the digital platform has the *potential* to have a more diverse audience given its virtuality and the fact that a reader does not have to pay to access it. To what extent that potential shapes the content of *G&G* online is unclear. For example, up until the August 2015 issue, the print magazine's inclusion of people of color was pretty much limited to African American entertainers and servers/servants, with an occasional exception like Congressman John Lewis featured in the February/March 2015 issue.

G&G may have aspirations to represent "the amazing diversity" (*G&G*'s words) of a region and yet it is limited in its ability or willingness to do so.[28] It relies on a "lenticular logic," defined by Tara McPherson, in which texts present Black and white southerners (and really no one else) so "only one of the images can be seen at a time," in effect "repress[ing] connection."[29] There is little to no interrogation as to how lives and histories are intertwined, with one population's positionality secured by the other's; there is little consideration of history really at all. And so the white subject freely floats onward—in a $7,500 Visconti gown bejeweled with Swarovski crystal pearls, alone in a Mississippi cotton field, as pictured in the April/May 2015 issue of *Garden & Gun*—"each boll," to quote poet Natasha Trethewey, "holding the ghosts of generations" of Black southerners whose labor supported white planter-class extravagance.[30] (See Fig. 4.4.)

That said, shortly after the massacre at Mother Emanuel AME Church, located three-tenths of a mile from *Garden & Gun*'s headquarters, the magazine's editors published a letter on their website in which they showed their support for the removal of the Confederate flag and in which they reflected on their role as re-presenters of "the South": "we've been thinking a lot about what we do now. How we can do better, both individually and in our pages."[31] Neither that letter nor any other article about how Charlestonians came together after the massacre ever appeared in the "pages" of a print issue. That absence begs the question as to whether the editors were nervous to put it in print given their potentially unreceptive subscriber base, yet simultaneously emboldened to place it online given a potentially receptive virtual audience. Since that time, fuller articles about African American artists and families have appeared both in print and online. However, the efforts seem more like the "'additive' strategy" described by McPherson, in which "images of race [. . .] get tacked onto an initial image or narrative, but without a framework that allows us to understand the images or narratives in relation."[32]

Furthermore, *G&G*'s online store, the "Fieldshop," clearly targets a wealthy male (presumably white) readership as it offers such products as Sid Mash-

Fig. 4.4. High-end fashion in cotton field.
Garden & Gun, April/May 2015, 124–25.

burn ties featuring pheasants and gundogs at $125 each; a $175 quail money clip and $250 fly cuff links by Grainger McKoy; a $550 etched glass decanter by J. Hill's Standard; a $495 shotgun bag by Wren & Ivy; and, on the less expensive end, $40 magnolia trees.[33] (See Fig. 4.5.)

The magazine and its online wares clearly speak to and cultivate a communal ethos centered around a commodifiable, purchasable, and performative white elite masculinity and, to a lesser extent, femininity—aspects of which appear in the regular spread entitled "Good Hunting" that features the "finest southern commodities" and in the 450 pages of advertisements printed the magazine each year. (See Fig. 4.6.)

Fig. 4.5. "FieldShop by Garden & Gun" store merchandise for men, including a $175 quail money clip. *Garden & Gun* online. Screenshot by author.

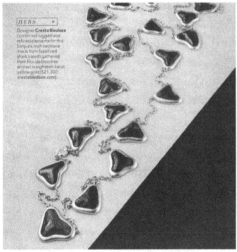

Fig. 4.6. "Good Hunting" merchandise for sale, including a $21,300 necklace made of fossilized shark teeth gathered from Florida beaches. *Garden and Gun*, February/March 2016, 50.

As *G&G* has flourished in the last decade, the *Bitter Southerner*—a progressively minded online zine out of Atlanta, Georgia, described in the *New York Times* as "a kind of kitchen-sink *New Yorker* for the region"—has also done well in terms of expanding its readership.[34] According to an article in *Forbes* in 2014, *BS* had "an average of 50,000 unique visitors" each week, twelve thousand subscribers to its newsletter, thirty thousand likes on Facebook, and eight thousand followers on Twitter.[35] In September 2017, the *New York Times* cited "100,000 visitors per month."[36] As of August 2019, *BS* had over 147,000 likes on Facebook and over 35,000 followers on Twitter.

BS claims that it is not "for" the conservative southern reader mired in Old South ideologies. The editorial team states:

> If you are a person who buys the states' rights argument [. . .] or you fly the rebel flag in your front yard [. . .] or you still think women look really nice in hoop skirts, we politely suggest you find other amusements on the web. The Bitter Southerner is not for you. The Bitter Southerner is for the rest of us. It is about the South that the rest of us know: the one we live in today and the one we hope to create in the future.[37]

This proclamation makes clear that those with Confederate, antebellum, and/ or racist leanings need not partake of the online zine. However, it's unclear to whom the "rest of us" or the "we" refers (both used twice). Progressive-minded readers? Liberals? Former editor Chuck Reese and his predominantly white staff? Reminiscent of Southern Marsh's claim that their shirts were influenced by "those who understand the lifestyle," the *BS* team is equally vague about what "the South" is: "the one" (singular) that "the rest of us know." However well-meaning in their mission, the editors' language here assumes and works to reinforce an insular superiority that continues to be rooted in the power to define who is in and who is out.

To some extent, the merchandise sold online in the *BS* "General Store" reflects their progressive values and goals of inclusion: t-shirts read "Abide No Hatred" and "Anti-Racist," "South" and "All Y'all" in rainbow colors, and imperatives such as "Love Everybody" and "Hug More Necks." These designs reflect their pro–gay rights and antiracist stance. Their "Power to the Women. No Delay." shirts reflect feminist sensibilities. Other t-shirts recapture in sans serif font clichéd southern expressions, including "Bless Your Heart" and "Have Mercy." Additional shirts refer to famed culinary pairings of the South, such as "Collards & Cornbread." And then there are the shirts that include phrases such as "Drink More Whiskey." At one point, the site included t-shirts that read "SOUTHERN AF" and "Hillbilly" as well as shirts that celebrated famed literary locations such as Flannery O'Connor's Milledgeville, Georgia, home Andalusia and Faulkner's imagined Mississippi county of Yoknapatawpha. The store also used to sell a "South without Borders" shirt featuring a map of southeastern states from Virginia to Florida and west to Texas, with the description reading: "The whole South, with no boundaries inside it. We like that idea. One big region that soaks up the power of every one of the hundreds of cultures inside it. We figured y'all could wear this one proudly." [38]

The *Bitter Southerner* undoubtedly desires to be inclusive and forward-looking. Perhaps the changes to the merchandise offered suggest that the BS editors have begun to realize in what ways its previous wares reinforced definitions they purported to critique. Perhaps they realized that in privileging Andalusia and Yoknapatawpha, they had forgotten Eatonton and Eatonville. Perhaps they realized that someone looking at the "South without Borders" shirt, whose map clearly depicts a bordered and bounded region, would not be able to see the hundreds of cultures within the region or Oklahoma, where the United States forcibly removed the majority of the region's Indigenous people in the nineteenth century. The shirt that read "Zora & Harper & Eudora & Flannery," referring to African American southern writer Zora Neale Hurston and three white southern writers—Harper Lee, Eudora Welty, and Flannery O'Connor—is no longer available. But one may purchase a shirt that reads "Zora & Alice & Maya & Jesmyn," referring to four African American southern writers—Hurston, Alice Walker, Maya Angelou, and Jesmyn Ward. One may now purchase a shirt that proclaims "Good Trouble Better South," a reference to the late John Lewis. However, their approach, like that of *G&G*, is at times additive and even moving the online zine in the direction of white virtue signaling.

Simply put, the items sold by the *Bitter Southerner*—as inclusive, progressive, or challenging to the definitions of "southern" as the editors mean for them to be—still ultimately project a singular and exceptional U.S. South. This time around, their "South" may represent a constellation of individuals united by their proclaimed progressive values and their shared emotional conflict over the region they call home. Readers are presumed to be "bitter southerners," too, and the hipster-cool t-shirts are no doubt cut from a different cloth. (In fact, it is a polyester, cotton, rayon blend.) But the items for sale don't do much to topple the monolith, to "dynamite the rails" (to borrow Patricia Yaeger's phrase), or to "shoot the jukebox" (to borrow Jon Smith's).[39] Rather, these items remain rooted in the categories that Yaeger, Smith, and many others within southern studies have tried to complicate over the last twenty years. As Yaeger writes,

The iron path, the official narrative along which the Dixie Limited has been bound, suggests that southern literature is about community (and not contestation), about place and the past (and not about the burden of underpaid domestic and agricultural labor, or the Great Migration, or the effects of the New Negro Renaissance on southern writing), about the preoccupations of an established white patriarchy (and not the weird conversations that take place among Black and white women writers), about the epic of race (and not about the recognition of patrilineal mystifications of miscegenation, or of "the" southern family, or of "the" spirit of the land, or of a peculiarly southern sense of place) [. . .] these traditional categories represent mystifications designed to overlook the complexities of southern fiction—its exploration of throwaway bodies, of a culture of white neglect, of the ways gender and racial politics work in the everyday, the commonplace.[40]

Extending the term "fiction" to include commodities sold on the internet, the goods may reflect a sincere attempt by the *BS* staff to redefine such notions in forward-looking ways, but they nevertheless fall short as the sellers continue to rely on a shared, merch-able idea of "the South"—and even more so, commodified names and phrases of southern Black people—that one may purchase *virtually* anywhere—whether in Georgia, New York, or Nevada.

Regardless of political outlook or agenda, these companies, their products, and their online platforms collectively monetize a dominant and limited definition of "southern identity" that scholars have worked for decades to complicate and resist. Even if the *Bitter Southerner* seeks to reframe the U.S. South in positive and more expansive ways, its wares—and those of *Garden & Gun* and southern-named shirt companies—ultimately reduce the diverse and troubled region to a number of stock images and phrases, thereby reinforcing the region's insularity and boundedness that equates southern-ness with whiteness and wealth, which affords not only the purchase of such shirts but the *leisure* in which one engages while wearing them. The internet additionally contributes to such reifications by allowing for the efficient, far-reaching reproduction of such ideas and for the facile consumption of their material manifestations. Add to that targeted marketing that links consumer sites to social media—that is, one visits the Southern Tide website and then ads for Southern Tide begin to appear in their Facebook and Instagram threads—and one comes to understand the illusion of agency in media consumption.

The use of online platforming makes it possible for a "state of mind"—or elite whiteness, to be more precise—to be visualized and subsequently purchased by anyone with internet access and a credit card. In turn, such definitions or conceptions travel further, presumably to more reader-viewer-consumers than the "old media" of journal articles, books, and conference papers within the field of southern studies. What southern shirts and their digital platforms signal then is the disconnect between what scholars write about in tomes, talk about in academic venues, post about in private groups on social media platforms, or even in online, open access academic publications (e.g., *Southern Spaces*), and what actually gets reproduced and consumed. We scholars seem to know what we are about, but who else "out there" *really* does? Our work typically lives behind paywalls or on university library shelves; most of us have little internet presence or engagement with online media in public ways. We may give an occasional lecture to a local club in our community, but most of us don't fully participate in forms of public scholarship, in part because that work is not what our institutions value. We tend to remain uninvolved in politics even as our work is deeply political. As Jon Smith reminded us in 2015, "it is also important to remember that there is a world of real bodies out there, and that getting full civil rights for all, and preventing massive environmental catastrophe for most, involves getting firmly in the way of those who are working very hard to preserve the status quo, those who are even working to increase disparities that are already at their highest levels since the Gilded Age."[41] He further called for a "post-postpolitical southern studies" which "could talk about—and help *do* something about—national phenomena such as Fox News and the Tea Parties."[42] In a digital world in which merch-able ideas of "the South" and "southernness" sell well, we have largely remained analog.

So how do we "go electric"? As much as this piece has pointed to contemporary new media as aiding in perpetuating a never-but-forever "South" recognizable to the masses, digital media also offers great potential for helping scholars to "*do* something" and to work collectively to take apart—in public and significant ways—the monumental narratives and symbols that refuse to die, not to mention the power structures that continue to feed them. *Southern Spaces* was an important start to such efforts, and some of us are lucky to be at institutions that encourage and promote digital scholarship. But most scholars don't have the resources, institutional support, or training to allow them to launch and successfully run a high-tech online publication. On the individual level, however, we do have the ability to "go digital" right at our fingertips at a relatively low cost, and many scholars have already taken the initiative. New media forms offer the means by which scholars might go viral, thereby reaching a broader audience, including the podcast (e.g., *About South, The Sound and the Furious, Southern Futures*), the TED talk (e.g., Riché Richardson's "The Hidden Life of Rosa Parks"), the online course (e.g., William Ferris's "The American South: Its Stores, Music, and Art" on *Coursera*), and the web series, to name a few. Such media may also offer a way for scholars to engage directly with those deeply invested in the online merch-ing of "the South," talking *with* rather than *at* them.

NOTES

1. Beery, "How Fred Perry Polos Came to Symbolize Hate"; Pearce, "A Guide to Some of the Far-Right Symbols Seen in Charlottesville."

2. Yes, You're Racist (@YesYoureRacist), "If you recognize," Twitter; Yes, You're Racist (@YesYoureRacist), "This angry young man," Twitter.

3. Eichenwald, "Peter Cvjetanovic, a white nationalist," Twitter.

4. "Plantation Flannel," *Southern Point Company.*

5. Romine, *The Real South*, 11–12.

6. "The Society," *Garden & Gun* online; "Membership," *Bitter Southerner.* One must call or email *G&G* to express interest in joining The Society; membership in the *BS* "family" is a one-time online payment of $25.

7. Nick Robins-Early, "How Far-Right Extremists Abroad Have Adopted Trump's Symbols as Their Own"; J. M. Berger, *The Alt-Right Twitter Census.* Numerous journalists have made the case that the Make America Great Again (MAGA) hats function as symbols of white supremacy. For example, journalist Nick Robins-Early points out that prior to killing six Muslim men at a mosque in Quebec City in 2017, Alexandre Bissonette had posted to social media a picture of himself in a MAGA hat. J. M. Berger's 2018 study of the alt-right's online presence points to "four overlapping themes" in that network, including "support for U.S. President Donald Trump, support for white nationalism, opposition to immigration (often framed in anti-Muslim terms), and accounts primarily devoted to transgressive trolling and harassment" (6).

8. "About Us," *Southern Tide.* Emphasis added; capitalization appears in the original.

9. Boswell, "Southern Tide Growing Store Network," 64.

10. "About Us," *Southern Tide.* Capitalization appears in the original. The website no longer mentions Stephenson by name, perhaps for two reasons: the company was purchased by Brazos Private Equity Partners LLC in 2013 and then sold for $85 million to Oxford Industries (owner of Tommy Bahama and Lily Pulitzer) in 2016, and also in 2016, Stephenson shot an intruder on his property in Greenville. In the *Greenville News* article about this incident, a link to the Southern Tide website conveniently appears alongside the story of Stephenson's acquittal when the judge deemed his actions a "justifiable homicide." As of 2019, the site reads: "Southern Tide was founded in 2006, by a then college student

who was inspired to create a premium lifestyle brand combining modern design elements with preppy, southern style." Daniel, "Brazos sells Southern Tide apparel brand to Oxford Industries"; Dixson, "Solicitor: Allen Stephenson Immune from Prosecution"; "About Us," *Southern Tide*.

11. Boswell, "Southern Tide Growing Store Network," 64.

12. "Ambassador Program," *Southern Tide*. See also "Southern Tide College Ambassador," *YouTube*.

13. "Southern Tide Spring 2019," *YouTube*. Southern Tide, according to *Shopping Centers Today*, has expanded its store presence in recent years. As of May 2018, they had fourteen stores and were planning to open four more by July of that year, setting their sites in some southern locations as well as in four towns in Massachusetts (Chatham, Lynnfield, Mashpee, and Nantucket). The article also states that Southern Tide distributes to "750 specialty stores across 45 states" and "over the past three years [. . .] has increased its department store presence from 15 stores to 95." Boswell, "Southern Tide Growing Store Network," 64.

14. For example, see the Southern Tide promotional videos for spring 2017, fall 2017, and fall 2018.

15. "About Us," *Southern Tide*.

16. Business Report Staff, "Stephen Smith and Matthew Valiollahi."

17. "About Us," *Southern Marsh* (emphasis in the original).

18. "Conservation," *Southern Marsh*.

19. "About Us," *Garden & Gun* online.

20. Opidee and Botelho, "Exporting a Local Sensibility to a National Market," 22.

21. Ibid.

22. Miller, "*Garden & Gun* Has an Awkward Debut."

23. Lee Brothers, "The Surprising Charleston Origins of the *Garden & Gun* Name."

24. Cohn, Manafy, and Smith, "*Garden & Gun* is Having More 'Yankee' Success than Robert E. Lee."

25. "'Garden & Gun' Has a Longer 'Growing Season' than Dixie," 10.

26. Trachtenberg, "How *Garden & Gun Magazine* Defies Industry Slump."

27. Saba, "New Publication: It's Laurel, Guns—and Money?"

28. *Garden & Gun* Editors, "Moving Forward."

29. McPherson, *Reconstructing Dixie*, 7.

30. Trethewey, "South," in *Native Guard*, 45.

31. *Garden & Gun* Editors, "Moving Forward."

32. McPherson, *Reconstructing Dixie*, 26–27.

33. "Fieldshop by Garden & Gun."

34. Fausset, "In Southern Magazines, Easy Pleasures and Hard Questions."

35. Robins, "'The Bitter Southerner' May be the 'Vice' of the South."

36. Fausset, "In Southern Magazines."

37. "Why We Created the *Bitter Southerner* in the First Place." The editorial team, as pictured on the website, appears to consist of four white men, one white woman, and one man of color. Cofounder Chuck Reece left *BS* in fall 2020.

38. "Southern AF t-shirt," *Bitter Southerner General Store*. This product is no longer

available on the website. *BS* cofounder Chuck Reece's wife, Stacy, screen prints the shirts and additional items such as tea towels available in the online General Store; Stacy Reece has her own online store called Down South House & Home, https://downsouth.house/; Joyner, "Why You Need to Know This Bitter Southerner: Heartlands' Interview with Chuck Reece, Part 3."

39. Smith, *Finding Purple America*, 48–49.

40. Yaeger, *Dirt and Desire*, 34.

41. Smith, "On the Limits of the 'Creating and Consuming' Paradigm," 89.

42. Ibid.

BIBLIOGRAPHY

"About Us." *Garden & Gun* online, accessed July 26, 2019. https://gardenandgun.com/about-us/.

"About Us." Over Under Clothing Company, accessed November 7, 2020. https://www.over-underclothing.com/pages/about-us.

"About Us." *Southern Marsh,* accessed June 2, 2019. https://www.southernmarsh.com/pages/about-us.

"About Us." *Southern Tide,* accessed June 1, 2019. https://www.southerntide.com/pages/about-us.

"Ambassador Program." *Southern Tide,* accessed August 3, 2019. https://southerntide.com/pages/st-ambassadors.

Beery, Zoë. "How Fred Perry Polos Came to Symbolize Hate." *The Outline,* June 20, 2017. https://theoutline.com/post/1760/fred-perry-polo-skinheads?zd=1&zi=ai2pdn2p.

Berger, J. M. *The Alt-Right Twitter Census.* VOX-Pol Network of Excellence, 2018. https://www.voxpol.eu/download/vox-pol_publication/AltRightTwitterCensus.pdf.

Boswell, Brannon. "Southern Tide Growing Store Network." *Shopping Centers Today* (May 2018): 64.

Business Report Staff. "Stephen Smith and Matthew Valiollahi." *Greater Baton Rouge Business Report,* April 30, 2013. https://www.businessreport.com/article/stephen-smith-and-matthew-valiollahi.

"Cocktail Tee—Mint Julep—Long Sleeve." Southern Marsh Company, accessed November 8, 2020. https://www.southernmarsh.com/products/cocktail-tee-mint-julep-long-sleeve?_pos=2&_sid=7c498fcae&_ss=r&variant=4053211585.

Cohn, Steven, Michelle Manafy, and Steve Smith. "'Garden & Gun' Is Having More 'Yankee' Success than Robert E. Lee." *Media Industry Newsletter* 65, no. 46 (2012): 20.

"Conservation." *Southern Marsh,* accessed June 25, 2019. https://www.southernmarsh.com/pages/conservation.

Daniel, Robert. "Brazos sells Southern Tide apparel brand to Oxford Industries." The *PE Hub Network,* April 20, 2016. https://www.pehub.com/2016/04/brazos-sells-southern-tide-apparel-brand-to-oxford-industries/.

Dixson, Romando. "Solicitor: Allen Stephenson Immune from Prosecution." *Greenville News,* last modified April 21, 2016. https://www.greenvilleonline.com/story/news/2016/04/19/greenville-castle-shooting-allen-stephenson/83228906/.

Eichenwald, Kurt (@kurteichenwald). "Peter Cvjetanovic, a white nationalist, is upset that this photo of him has gone viral. So be nice: dont retweet this tweet 1000s of times." Twitter, August 13, 2017, 12:21 P.M., https://twitter.com/kurteichenwald/status/896813863093587968.

Fausset, Richard. "In Southern Magazines, Easy Pleasures and Hard Questions." *New York Times*, September 5, 2017. https://www.nytimes.com/2017/09/05/us/south-magazines-bitter-southerner-charlottesvile-garden-and-gun.html.

"Fieldshop by Garden & Gun." *Garden & Gun* online, accessed July 22, 2019. https://www.ggfieldshop.com/.

Garden & Gun Editors. "Moving Forward." *Garden & Gun* online, July 6, 2017. https://gardenandgun.com/articles/moving-forward/.

"'Garden & Gun' Has a Longer 'Growing Season' than Dixie." *Media Industry Newsletter* 67, no. 5 (February 3, 2014): 10.

"Good Hunting." *Garden & Gun*. February/March 2016, 50.

Joyner, Alex. "Why You Need to Know This Bitter Southerner: Heartlands Interview with Chuck Reece, Part 3 of 3." *Heartlands*, September 21, 2018. https://alexjoyner.com/2018/09/21/why-you-need-to-know-this-bitter-southerner-heartlands-interviews-chuck-reece-part-3-of-3/.

Kappa Alpha Order–Delta Beta Chapter. "Southern Tide founder (and KA Brother), Allen Stephenson" explains how Kappa Alpha has helped him toward success." Facebook, May 20, 2012. https://www.facebook.com/199360540078976/posts/southern-tide-founder-and-ka-brother-allen-stephenson-explains-how-kappa-alpha-h/1382465096328294/.

Lee Brothers. "The Surprising Charleston Origins of the Garden & Gun Name." The *Lee Bros*, January 23, 2012. https://mattleeandtedlee.com/2012/01/23/the-surprising-charleston-origins-of-the-garden-gun-name/.

McPherson, Tara. *Reconstructing Dixie: Race, Gender, and Nostalgia in the Imagined South*. Durham, NC: Duke University Press, 2003.

"Membership." *Bitter Southerner*, accessed August 3, 2019. https://bsgeneralstore.com/pages/membership.

Miller, Lia. "Garden & Gun Has an Awkward Debut." *New York Times*, April 30, 2007. https://www.nytimes.com/2007/04/30/business/media/30garden.html.

Opidee, Ioanna, and Stefanie Botelho. "Exporting a Local Sensibility to a National Market." *Folio: The Magazine for Magazine Management*, 41, no. 2 (2012): 22.

Pearce, Matt. "A Guide to Some of the Far-Right Symbols Seen in Charlottesville." *Los Angeles Times*, August 14, 2017. http://www.latimes.com/nation/la-na-far-right-symbols-20170814-story.html.

"Plantation Flannel." *Southern Point Company*, accessed July 26, 2019. https://www.southernpointco.com/collections/plantation-flannel.

Robins-Early, Nick. "How Far-Right Extremists Abroad Have Adopted Trump's Symbols as Their Own." *Huffington Post*, April 6, 2019. https://www.huffpost.com/entry/trump-extremism-maga-hat_n_5ca5075be4b082d775dfca37.

Robins, J. Max. "'The Bitter Southerner' May be the 'Vice' of the South." *Forbes,* September 15, 2014. https://www.forbes.com/sites/maxrobins/2014/09/15/the-bitter-southerner -might-be-the-vice-of-the-south/#1dcde4b97062.

Romine, Scott. *The Real South: Southern Narrative in the Age of Cultural Reproduction.* Baton Rouge: Louisiana State University Press, 2008.

Saba, Jennifer. "New publication: It's Laurel, Guns—and Money?" *Editor & Publisher* 140, no. 3 (March 2017): 10. https://www.editorandpublisher.com/columns/new-publication -it-s-laurel-guns-and-money/.

Smith, Jon. *Finding Purple America: The South and the Future of American Cultural Studies.* Athens: University of Georgia Press, 2013.

———. "On the Limits of the 'Creating and Consuming' Paradigm." In *Creating and Consuming the American South,* edited by Martyn Bone, Brian Ward, and William A. Link, 72–94. Gainesville: University Press of Florida, 2015.

"The Society." *Garden & Gun* online, accessed August 3, 2019. https://gardenandgun.com/gg society/.

"Southern AF t-shirt." *Bitter Southerner General Store,* accessed February 1, 2018. https://bs generalstore.com/products/southern-a-f.

Southern Roots Outfitter Covington. Cover photo. Facebook, January 23, 2020, 11:03 A.M. https://www.facebook.com/188425511560210/photos/.

Southern Tide. "Southern Tide College Ambassador." YouTube, April 23, 2018. https://www .youtube.com/watch?v=W-EGPF9dpKQ.

———. "Southern Tide Fall 2017." YouTube, September 5, 2017. https://www.youtube.com /watch?v=fGGantIm5fM.

———. "Southern Tide Fall 2018." YouTube, January 25, 2018. https://www.youtube.com /watch?v=UAkg0nFIr5A.

———. "Southern Tide Spring 2017." YouTube. January 29, 2017. https://www.youtube.com /watch?v=gGPi5atIYqM.

———. "Southern Tide Spring 2019." YouTube, January 23, 2019. https://www.youtube.com /watch?v=7RUrNoep5Gw.

Trachtenberg, Jeffrey A. "How *Garden & Gun Magazine* Defies Industry Slump." *Wall Street Journal,* February 1, 2016. https://www.wsj.com/articles/how-garden-gun-keeps-growing -1454322601.

Trethewey, Natasha. "South." In *Native Guard,* 45. New York: Houghton Mifflin, 2007.

"Why We Created the Bitter Southerner in the First Place." *Bitter Southerner,* August 16, 2013, https://bittersoutherner.com/we-are-bitter.

Yaeger, Patricia. *Dirt and Desire: Reconstructing Southern Women's Writing, 1930–1990.* Chicago: University of Chicago Press, 2000.

Yes, You're Racist (@YesYoureRacist). "If you recognize any of the Nazis marching in #Charlottesville, send me their names/profiles and I'll make them famous #GoodNightAlt Right." Twitter, August 12, 2017, 12:43 P.M., https://twitter.com/YesYoureRacist/status /896502810971426818.

———. "This angry young man is Peter Cvjetanovic, a student at @unevadareno." Twitter, August 12, 2017, 6:45 P.M., https://twitter.com/YesYoureRacist/status/89650281097142 6818?s=20.

#PLANTATIONWEDDING

Fantasy and Forgetting on Instagram

ALEXANDRA CHIASSON

A PARTICULAR POST FROM the Instagram account @alowcountrywed captures the trajectory of plantation imagery and commentary as it has circulated on digital platforms in the twenty-first century.[1] Beneath a photo of a white antebellum house is a caption reading "Y'all, these Lowcountry plantations get us every time, and we love when couples select them as the backdrop for their big day. Tell us, what's your favorite plantation?"[2] (See Fig. 5.1.) Within this attempt at audience engagement, the question "what's your favorite plantation?" is particularly troubling: it suggests that "plantations"—not "antebellum" or "historical" homes or even "event venues," but "plantations" most specifically—are desirable, rankable, and free from complicated, often horrific histories of enslavement and economic exploitation. Given the history of violence and oppression that has stemmed from slavery, weddings held at a plantation should be considered wrong in practice. Yet perhaps the more troubling issue, and a problem central to this essay, is that content posted by Instagram users is currently contributing to a cultural memory-making phenomenon that normalizes replacing undesirable histories with fantastical notions of wealth and whiteness. Such historical revisionism is aided by Instagram's platform-specific functions and algorithmic rewards, which encourage individual users and small businesses to disseminate whitewashed photographs of chattel slavery sites refashioned as marketing strategy: #PlantationWedding.

This essay argues that scholars in southern studies have provided the tools needed to interrogate powerful symbols such as the plantation, and that such an interrogation can reveal how contemporary new media technologies actively rely on and sustain white supremacy as an economic principle. My specific concern is the unique way Instagram—a digital advertising platform that monetizes user-produced content—not only *reflects* the fantasy of wealth, whiteness, and power sustained by cultural amnesia that has allowed for the transposing of a violent plantation history with a pleasurable present, but also

Fig. 5.1. Image of Grove Plantation on Edisto Island, South Carolina, posted on @alowcountrywed Instagram account. Screenshot by author.

encourages and rewards forgetting more generally.[3] I tie the intuitive, collective decision to create and use a hashtag such as #PlantationWedding to the new media concept of the "like economy," the driving motivation for positive reinforcement of a post through the "like" and the cultural currency to which a "like" translates. In this sense, the like economy is a framework to understand why the Instagram user experience looks and feels the way it does, and why old location-based symbols of whiteness and wealth such as the plantation proliferate in a digital era. Operating within this framework, this essay relies on close examination of the content production phenomena of influencer culture and "Instagram tourism," photo trends and editing practices on the app, the "vision board effect" of a search, and the mindlessness of the infinite scroll to begin to illuminate the new media narrative of the plantation on Instagram.

As the sixth largest social media platform in the world—currently at over 1 billion active users and still rapidly growing—it is difficult to estimate the

extent to which Instagram has shaped and will continue to shape innumerable visual cultures in the coming years.[4] My choice to focus on region and
the plantation is inspired in part by Katherine Henninger's writing on photography and southern women writers. In *Ordering the Facade: Photography
and Contemporary Southern Women's Writing* (2007), Henninger shows how the
cultural idea of "the South" emerged alongside photography, and that the early
days of the visual medium "help constitute the visual legacy of the gendered,
raced, and classed hierarchies that characterized southern identity."[5] Henninger turns to the "words surrounding the pictures" to show how southern
literature, sans photographic object, can instruct a reader to look for the "cultural dynamics of vision and visual representation"—providing a "model" for
further analysis of visuality in other subcultural contexts.[6] Relatedly, this essay
pinpoints a seemingly small piece of Instagram's vast visual archive as an analytical strategy that can evolve to address many other interlocking contexts.

Analyzing the surface visuality of social media artifacts for deeper meaning in a new media context can benefit from the same narrowing of scope
and interpretive strategy Henninger proposes. As Henninger writes, "If a few
photographs can supplant thousands of words, it is only because thousands
of words have trained us to 'read' photographs."[7] What, then, can an Instagram post do, and where can we find the necessary training to "read" them for
cultural context? When one searches for images of contemporary plantation
spaces, particularly through tag searches for #PlantationWedding, the "words
surrounding the pictures" are more often than not some superficial variation
of "Tell us, what's your favorite plantation?" I argue that "reading" posts on
Instagram requires not just a consciousness of political negotiation of material
space and layered histories of photographed subjects, but also an understanding of platform-specific cultures and visual trends stemming from application
software design. The practice of capturing and distributing images of white supremacist fantasies is not new in practice, particularly in terms of photographs
of symbolic spaces such as the plantation house. Instead, users seeking to
maintain a deliberately ahistorical white supremacist narrative of heritage, tradition, and southernness are currently offered ample opportunity to do so at a
newly massive scale. This practice is aided and abetted by an Instagram user experience that rewards aesthetics stemming from fantasy with likes and speeds
the dissemination process with the enticement of quick, thoughtless scrolling.

In terms of mapping platform trends and cultural phenomena, marketing
content tagged "#PlantationWedding" reveals how the aesthetic of white fan-

Fig. 5.2. Image posted on @southernoaksweddings featuring the labor of Black men shaping the plantation's promise of "magic." Screenshot by author.

tasy functions as an implicit content organizing principle on the application. For example, in February of 2019, a popular New Orleans event venue called Southern Oaks Plantation posted a photograph on their Instagram business account of two Black men posing with an ornate, horse-drawn carriage (See Fig. 5.2).[8] The caption reads, "We are traditionally known for our grand columns and enchanting oaks. . [sic] but once you step inside the plantation—the magic continues!"[9] The limited textual component of the post focuses on the venue's "columns" and "enchanting oaks," alluding to the material "backdrop" for wedding and event photographs Southern Oaks advertises on its website.[10] How, then, do we interpret the accompanying image featuring the Black men and carriage except as a visual rendering of what Southern Oaks intangibly calls "magic"?

The post optically positions the photo's subjects as servants orchestrating a ceremony and is clearly functioning in service of a persistent fantasy of

Black labor in the plantation context. This Southern Oaks post exemplifies the "lenticular logic" Tara McPherson theorizes, capturing a nostalgic attachment to Blackness characterized by servitude that is tied implicitly to a plantation aesthetic yet abstracted in its omission of context and political commentary.[11] Without historical context and functioning as an advertisement in the Instagram economy, it is clear the marketing post is meant to appeal to a viewer's fantasy for their wedding day. In their introduction to the "Plantation Modernity" special issue of *The Global South* (2016), Amy Clukey and Jeremy Wells ask a vital question: "How did [the plantation] become in mass culture a sign of prestige and object of desire: a place one should long to obtain, to visit, or, Scarlett O'Hara-like, to go back to? Or to combine all these questions into a single one: what makes a garden like an outpost of empire like a forced labor camp like a garden again?"[12] Plantation studies now comprise many (often interconnected) answers to this question, but in this essay, I focus on the technological mediation of plantation imagery on Instagram—perhaps the most recent mass-media rendering of the plantation space as "garden," a place in which to celebrate and fantasize. For example, "Instagrammability" likely weighs heavily in the venue selection for many millennial couples, who often look for venues that reflect the couple's personality or "story."[13] As a result, effective Instagram marketing content construes the plantation as a perfectly packaged (and rentable) symbol of whiteness and wealth that can serve as a backdrop for other Instagram posts.

Owned by Facebook, Instagram is an advertising platform, which extracts user information, analyzes it, and uses the findings to sell advertising space to third parties.[14] This process of data extraction and analysis and the resulting ad sales comprise Facebook's primary source of revenue.[15] Thus, activity and user production on Instagram is monitored and analyzed by programs created by data scientists with the explicit purpose of boosting advertising on the platform. This underlying corporate motivation explains the design of the application, which creates a "user experience," or the creators' design for how a user will engage with the platform, meant to keep users scrolling and liking as much and as quickly as possible. The like economy and resulting platform cultures are consequential to this intentional "user experience" design.

Influencer and tourism cultures stem from Instagram's like economy and can help to explain the intensified importance placed on wedding venue choices—a connection that helps to illuminate how Instagram application functions encourage plantation weddings and shape how they are chronicled on the platform.[16] Likes correspond more or less to audience engagement levels, and there is a firm threshold for "like"-ability for personal private account users on Instagram when they do not tag their posts, allowing strangers to interact with them. This is the like economy: the cultural capital obtained and exchanged from such proof of audience engagement, no matter how fleeting. The like economy can explain the growing number of personal accounts using #PlantationWedding, a transparent act of self-branding and "aspirational" content production. To that end, two important pieces of Instagram culture are, on one hand, the related, platform-specific particularities of sponsored marketing and otherwise aspirational content posted by "influencers" and, on the other hand, the recent rise of "Instagram tourism," a trend toward documenting visits to "Instagrammable" geographic spaces.

The platform encourages the average user to participate in the marketing of themselves and their activities, essential to the economy of #PlantationWedding. Numerous hashtags posted in the caption or the comments by the poster allow these posts to appear in search results for specific tags. (See Fig. 5.3.) Such users are deliberate in their marketing to a greater audience and have developed strategies to reach audiences by employing platform-based strategies such as hashtagging. The purpose of such posts is to advertise a service, targeting Instagram users who are likely to search for a hashtag such as #PlantationWedding and other wedding-related tags. A hashtag such as #PlantationWedding or a general location-based tag inserts the user's post into a broader category, and the purpose of tagging is to earn likes and to be seen by strangers and corporations seeking brand ambassadors.

As new media scholar Diana Zulli puts it, "being looked at on Instagram is not only expected but also welcomed; users hope that their images will garner attention and that viewers will be interested in the content presented."[17] Furthermore, the tagging of posts creates app-based communities wherein the previously mentioned wedding industry businesses can target users with their advertising. As a result, many users are mimicking the style and presentation—even the strategy—of an Instagram advertisement, even when they technically have no service to advertise. The site is at once a digital archive of personal memories and a data mine of consumer habits driven by user-produced marketing content, fueled by the "like" as currency. Thus, as a memory tool, Instagram is not as useful as Facebook.[18] Rather, accounts for individuals on Instagram often reflect this desire to "be looked at," signaling participation in the like economy, where accounts with enough likes and fol-

Fig. 5.3. A white, newly married couple kissing in front of Nottoway Plantation in White Castle, Louisiana, and an example of hashtags that help plantation wedding fantasies circulate. Image posted on @ainsleyevents. Screenshot by author.

lowers earn company sponsorships for product placement and the fantasy of "influencer" status.

According to a recent survey of influencers worldwide, Instagram is the clear leader as the primary social media platform used for promotional content.[19] In her 2015 essay on influencer culture called "Instafame: Luxury Selfies in the Attention Economy," Alice E. Marwick describes Instagram as "a convergence of cultural forces: a mania for digital documentation, the proliferation of celebrity and microcelebrity culture, and conspicuous consumption."[20] Marwick argues that images representing the aspirational perform remarkably well on Instagram: influencers and microcelebrities—people whose fame exists due to their account activity and curated personal brands—are successful users who earn likes and followers because they showcase appearances, possessions, lifestyles, and social networks (especially proximity to more famous celebrities) that others want but typically cannot have. Most importantly, "these individuals have succeeded in gaining immense audiences on Instagram, a free, easy-to-use technology available to virtually everyone with a smartphone and a data plan. Thus, their fame seems attainable to the average onlooker."[21] It could be said that in the context of influencer culture, the number of likes a post receives is a measure of this desirability. The marketing term Marwick borrows to explain how influencers gain prominence is "aspirational" content: users feel compelled to like posts that capture an unfulfilled fantasy.[22]

Thus, Instagram posts that signal possessing wealth (and whiteness, in the #PlantationWedding context) can be called aspirational content, spawning fantasies for those who cannot afford or cannot have access to desirable material objects and geographic spaces. In plantation wedding culture, the historic house—the venue—is the backdrop for an Instagram post that signals wealth to followers. Consequently, posts tagged #PlantationWedding earning the most likes typically feature photographs centering the house as dominant motif, often with a white woman in the foreground.[23] Indeed, the overarching aesthetic of whiteness in such posts cannot be overstated: there is an abundance of white houses with white columns, white dresses, and white people.

The rising popularity of Instagram tourism can also help to explain trends in representations of the plantation wedding on Instagram. One #Plantation-Wedding-tagged post, for example, is captioned "You don't have to travel far to find a wedding venue that gives you that intangible feeling of being surrounded by natural beauty and centuries of history."[24] (See Fig. 5.4.) Ironically, what makes this "feeling" so "intangible" is in fact the omission of the "centuries of history," which are absent in any photographic rendering of the plantation as wedding venue. In this context, the house—like beautiful scenery in a foreign location inaccessible to those without the means to travel—becomes a different kind of destination, one where a venue rental for a photo backdrop becomes a demonstration of power. Reading the plantation wedding venue as a kind of geographically—and historically—based fantasy of access and ownership, no matter how temporary, sets the foundation for reading such posts as participation in the Instagram like economy and as a clear demonstration of wealth and whiteness.

Fig. 5.4. Instagram image posted on Rose Hill (@rose.hillevents) of white plantation home with a fountain in the foreground. The caption gestures to "centuries of history," but evades mention of slavery. Screenshot by author.

The plantation wedding is, in many ways, a destination wedding—the "destination" being the aspirational, immersive experience the plantation venue claims to offer. This destination is firmly rooted in the visual: many of the posts tagged #PlantationWedding contain the plantation house as the dominant motif. If a wedding at a "castle" (another popular destination venue for the wealthy) connotes "fairy tale" and "princess," the plantation sets the scene for the fantasy of the mythic southern belle.[25] For example, one #Plantation-Wedding-tagged post includes the caption "Imagine driving up the long gravel driveway to see this estate waiting for you."[26] The word "imagine" here markets the plantation venue as a space where fantasies become real: if a couple holds their wedding at this location, they can pretend they own this house for a day. Instagram is not just the virtual venue to market this destination: content on the platform suggests that the app experience encourages the production of these visual fantasies.

The enduring desirability of the antebellum house in American society—symbolizing the fantasy of wealth and status—and its functionality as a space for events denotes a dangerous brand of white supremacy characterized by deliberate forgetting and disavowal of history. As Matthew Pratt Guterl writes in his "Plantation" chapter for *Keywords for Southern Studies* (2016),

> Given [the plantation's] gruesome history, one would imagine that the material remains of the plantation complex would be a source of shame, with commemorations that match—in emotional tone—the deeply contemplative, melancholic ruins of the concentration camps of Europe. One would think that the hoopskirts and big white houses and accented mannerisms of the planter class would be subject to ridicule and consigned to the dustbin of history. Perversely, though, the plantation has endured instead as a symbol of an Old South deemed worthy of restoration and visitation, a likely site for family reunions, weddings, and getaway weekends.[27]

As evidenced by internet outcry in the wake of celebrity weddings like that between Ryan Reynolds and Blake Lively in 2012, the contemporary plantation wedding is a performance of whiteness that should not be tolerated.[28] Still, the plantation wedding maintains widespread cultural acceptability, implying that the social capital rendered by such a wedding—often expensive, as plantation venues generally charge thousands of dollars per hour of rental—retains its value.

Crucial to sustaining the fantasy of wealth, southernness, and white supremacy that the plantation wedding enables is a deliberate, systematic forgetting. As detailed above, for many users potential Instagrammability motivates and shapes any number of purchases, vacations, and life events—all working toward the photo opportunity that will earn likes, build social capital, and shape a personal brand. As I have argued, this desire to be seen can explain the abundance of plantation weddings chronicled on Instagram, including the proliferation of hashtags such as #PlantationWedding, as well as the focalization of the plantation as a venue in both marketing content by small businesses and individual posts. Moving beyond the app-based cultures and user-created content that reflect the longstanding legacy of the plantation as a symbol of wealth and white supremacy, I address two particular functions of Instagram: the infinite scroll and the search. Each of these are designed to boost user activity on the app and consequently create a user experience that contributes to mindless engagement and consumption.

The results for an Instagram search are almost purely visual: unless one clicks on a photograph and starts scrolling, the rest of the post—captions and other hashtags—are not immediately visible. Thus, searching for a hashtag assembles what amounts to a vision board: an archive of "Top Posts" appears immediately, without text or a caption. A vision board, also known as a "dream board" or "mood board," is a collage of images meant to inspire or motivate. It is also a popular wedding planning tool in deciding the aesthetic a wedding participant, typically a bride, wishes their wedding to embody. The Instagram search replicates this effect by compiling the top or most recent posts containing a searched tag. With a tag like #PlantationWedding dominated by marketing content, the assembled images are highly complementary and come together to provide a visual representation of class privilege and whiteness. Perhaps unsurprising, the dominant motifs of posts showing up in a #PlantationWedding search are white women and white houses. The lack of text in the listed search results—in other words a complete absence of contextualization—contributes to what Zulli has called "the glance as an economic enterprise."[29]

In other words, Instagram encourages surface-level engagement with user-produced content: the less time users spend looking at individual posts, the more posts users can view, and hopefully, like. The value of attention, as Zulli argues, is high, and marketing content and individual users imitating advertisements want to put their best foot forward, posting only the best photos that will stand out in a search and compel liking. Instagram users respond strategically to Instagram design, implying recognition of this typical, fleeting engagement with posts on the app. Zulli's concept of "transactional glancing" helps us to observe not only the existing cultural amnesia regarding plantation history but also the ways Instagram culture and platform design is likely facilitating an even more insidious kind of forgetting.

In his analysis of early nineteenth-century plantation paintings, John Michael Vlatch writes: "When planters commissioned paintings, not too surprisingly, they opted for pictures that confirmed their own centrality and their slaves' marginality, works of art that by and large managed to conceal the presence of black majority."[30] Centuries later, Instagram enables user participation in a similar project of erasure, but with much wider and far-reaching implications. A painting on the wall of a home or hung in a museum may be exposed

Fig. 5.5. The results of a search on the Instagram smartphone application for #PlantationWedding. The aspirational content centers on images of whiteness, including white people, white dresses, white plantation houses, and white tablecloths. Screenshot by author.

to a handful of viewers; a post on Instagram has the potential to reach one out of every seven people on the planet.[31] In the results for a searched tag, posts that fit certain visual parameters are more likely to earn more likes, thus fulfilling the transactional aspirations detailed earlier. These aesthetic parameters become the norm for certain categories of Instagram content and posted photos begin to look the same. For example, a quick scroll through results for a search of #PlantationWedding yields a lot of the literal whiteness mentioned earlier: zoomed-in shots of white neoclassical antebellum homes, close-ups of white women in white wedding dresses, and white tablecloths. (See Fig. 5.5.) This sameness, combined with the ability to scroll through posts indefinitely, contributes to the elimination of political context. In the new digital context of Instagram and the like economy, the deliberate aesthetic of whiteness and wealth in the geographic space of the plantation reveals systematic forgetting that traces back to visual tactics employed by nineteenth-century enslaver-planters.

A plantation wedding in 2020 provides evidence of this geographically focused fantasy of power and whiteness as an aesthetic that the plantation continues to represent. The plantation is, expectedly, strongly associated with a self-conscious identification with southernness: in one *New York Times* article on in-demand wedding venues, the writer describes how "couples are being drawn to the Southern charm of the plantations in and around Charleston, S.C."[32] That many restored antebellum mansions in the U.S. South are now used and marketed as event venues rather than converted into memorials honoring the enslaved people who built them testifies to how these venue operators have "obscur[ed] violence and conflat[ed] it with pleasure," as Lisa Hinrichsen describes.[33] The plantation as an enduring symbol of power sustained by a collective fantasy of white supremacy in visual culture is now further indebted to its representations on social media, perhaps especially on Instagram.

Instagram, by design, contributes to the production of contemporary plantation wedding culture—a narrative of plantation history guided by "lenticular logic."[34] Furthermore, it is now a crucial platform for sharing the "evolving set of images" that make up the U.S. South.[35] For example, a search for #SouthernWedding or #SouthernWeddings, like #PlantationWedding, yields thousands of results with posts featuring venue shots fitting predominantly into three aesthetic categories: plantation home and grounds, church, and barn. Orchestrating the fantasy of the plantation wedding requires a considerable amount of money, which can explain the wider desirability of such weddings. On Instagram, the spectacle of wealth- and status-signaling—contributing to the aspirational content that performs so well on the platform—uplifts a version of white supremacy and heterosexual privilege glamorized as mere class privilege and the desirable lifestyle that goes with it.

As one tech journalist noted in 2019, "Instagram is no longer just an app, but a visual lens through which we navigate physical spaces."[36] With Instagram now being used not just as a digital memory archive and space for social media community but also as a marketing tool, these iconographic images of southern geographic spaces help to shape a fantastical visual representation of a South that can be employed as a backdrop to (predominately heteronormative) wedding performance. This outlook is particularly insightful in light

of developments in the wedding industry, namely a series of 2019 announce-
ments that the wedding-planning community site The Knot Worldwide and
the social networking site Pinterest would no longer promote plantation wedding content.[37] Coverage of these new policies from two big industry players
resulted in numerous articles in which white couples share their regret at
hosting their weddings on plantation grounds. One woman in an interview
with *Buzzfeed* refers to the role Instagram played her venue selection: "Lauren,
who is white, said she first stumbled upon Boone Hall on Instagram, when she
was researching wedding venues and saw photos of a wedding at the Cotton
Dock. While touring wedding venues in South Carolina with her fiancé in
2017, she 'immediately just fell in love' with Boone Hall. She said she'd always
loved the sight of oak trees with Spanish moss, and 'that's exactly what Boone
Hall gave us.'"[38] It is crucial to note that this idea of "stumbling" upon photographs of plantations on Instagram and "falling in love," is a narrative that is
likely common based on current platform-based marketing practices. Instagram is designed to provide patterns of content, and the example of plantation
weddings can function as an effective and illuminating case study of the interplay between online visual culture, platform design, and historical amnesia.

Perhaps the plantation has always provided a photo (and, according to
Vlatch, a painting) opportunity in the United States, which seems intent on
forgetting its bloody past of slavery and its present of persistent oppression.[39]
Still, with the growth of destination wedding culture and the development of
an industry more combined with the chronicling and marketing of these experiences on a platform such as Instagram, the plantation becomes, in essence,
a photo booth. Thus, the new media narrative of the plantation mapped out
in this essay is perhaps not so new: it is one of white supremacist fantasy and
historical erasure tracing back to at least the nineteenth century. However, the
technological mediation of forgetting described here is something we must
continue to study and resist. Implicating Instagram in this specific type of cultural amnesia opens up opportunities for further analysis of the platform's role
in perpetuating and creating many other social problems. If the field of southern studies collectively demonstrates how hyperfocus on regional subcultures
creates a model for infinite other contexts, then new media studies—which
grapple with this "infinite" directly as we consider the inestimable communities and their cultures spawning daily on the internet—can benefit from
models of analysis similar to the one provided in this essay.

NOTES

1. Before focusing on objects of white supremacy and symbols of oppression, I first wish to acknowledge two organizations that actively resist the historical revisionism of the plantation space through work on Instagram and beyond. Organizers with Color of Change (@colorofchange) successfully led a recent movement to end the promotion of plantation "venues" on prominent wedding planning websites, as I discuss later. The curators and administrators at Whitney Plantation (@whitneyplantation), a Louisiana-based museum, work to reorient historical understandings of the plantation by centering the lives of enslaved people. As explicitly stated on their website, "Given the sensitive nature of the museum's focus, Whitney Plantation does not allow weddings or other private events" ("FAQ").

2. A Lowcountry Wedding Magazine (@alowcountrywed), "Y'all, these Lowcountry plantations get us every time," Instagram, May 22, 2018.

3. Pinterest, much like Instagram, allows users to post and share photos and web content—often themed through the creation of "Boards," which may be public or private. It is important to note that the "vision board effect" resulting from a search for the tag "#PlantationWedding" I describe in this essay is similarly produced with a Pinterest search for "plantation wedding"—perhaps with even more results. I choose to focus on Instagram in my analysis for several reasons. For one, Instagram has a far larger user base, and marketing content on the platform is exposed to a much greater audience. Furthermore, Pinterest, due to its functional design as an archive, works quite differently as both a personal and a collective memory tool. Many accounts for personal use are employed to collect and organize information deliberately (e.g., a board devoted to wedding planning ideas as opposed to an album of photos from the actual event). Most importantly, in late 2019 Pinterest adopted a policy that it will no longer promote plantation "venues" on the site. I discuss this later in the essay.

4. Constine, "Instagram Hits 1 Billion Monthly Users," *TechCrunch,* June 20, 2018.

5. Henninger, *Ordering the Facade,* 10.

6. Ibid., 9, 11.

7. Ibid., 1.

8. In 2020, presumably in response to recent movements to end weddings held at plantations, Southern Oaks Plantation rebranded their marketing materials and social accounts and is now known as "Southern Oaks Weddings" using the Instagram handle "@southernoaksweddings." It is also interesting and important to note that the house Southern Oaks uses for events was built in the mid-twentieth century. Thus, Southern Oaks successfully employs the plantation aesthetic I discuss in this essay to attract clients seeking a "backdrop" to signal wealth and whiteness.

9. Southern Oaks Plantation (@southernoaksplantation), "We are traditionally known," Instagram, February 7, 2019.

10. Southern Oaks (website), "The Essence of Southern Oaks."

11. McPherson, *Reconstructing Dixie.*

12. Clukey and Wells, "Plantation Modernity," 3.

13. Myung and Smith, "Understanding Wedding Preferences," 695.

14. Srnicek, *Platform Capitalism*, 49. Facebook bought Instagram in 2012.

15. Ibid., 53. In the first quarter of 2016, ad sales comprised 89 percent of Facebook's revenue.

16. "Influencer" is a general term for social media personalities, bloggers, and You-Tubers who are paid by companies to promote products on their accounts. "Instagram tourism" is used to refer to tourism driven by Instagram user activity and influencer travel habits. Many use "Instagram tourism" tongue-in-cheek, implying that a user goes on vacations primarily for the photo opportunity.

17. Zulli, "Capitalizing on the Look," 147.

18. For example, Facebook allows for photos to be uploaded and shared with friends as albums; has multiple "Memories" and "On This Day" notifications and features that encourage users to look back at previously posted content; and is searchable by date, relationship with friends (e.g., "See Friendship"), and events attended in the past.

19. Chadha, "For Influencers, Instagram is the Clear-Cut Favorite," *eMarketer*, January 30, 2018.

20. Marwick, "Instafame," 139.

21. Ibid., 147.

22. Ibid., 141.

23. The most-liked #PlantationWedding-tagged posts often have over a thousand likes.

24. Rose Hill (@rose.hillevents), "You don't have to travel far," Instagram, June 12, 2019.

25. Myung and Smith, "Understanding Wedding Preferences," 699.

26. Shining Light Photography (@ashleym_brown), "Imagine driving up the long gravel driveway," Instagram, January 31, 2019.

27. Guterl, "Plantation," 28.

28. Nerada, "Blake Lively and Ryan Reynolds Are under Fire," *Marie Claire*, February 20, 2018.

29. Zulli, "Capitalizing on the Look," 138.

30. Vlatch, *The Planter's Prospect*, 180.

31. This estimation is drawn from Constine, "Instagram Hits 1 Billion Monthly Users."

32. Logan, "Some Wedding Sites Also Play Hard to Get," *New York Times*, March 13, 2015.

33. Hinrichsen, *Possessing the Past*, 6.

34. McPherson, *Reconstructing Dixie*.

35. Stanonis, *Dixie Emporium*, 5.

36. Kwun, "Inside the most Instagrammable place on Earth," *Fast Company*, January 2, 2019.

37. Zola, another wedding planning platform, followed suit not long after Pinterest and The Knot.

38. Lim, "Brides and Grooms Who Got Married at A Former Slave Plantation Are Speaking out about Criticism of the Venues," *Buzzfeed News*, December 13, 2019.

39. Kimberly Juanita Brown, in an essay entitled "At the Center of the Periphery: Gender, Landscape, and Architecture in *12 Years a Slave*" (2017), describes the "memorial refraction" of plantation imagery in visual cultures, which "fram[es] the event of slavery as a

series of visual images held in place over time" (121). I highly recommend this article for those interested in contemporary depictions of plantations.

BIBLIOGRAPHY

Ainsley Events (@ainsleyevents). "This sweet couple said 'I do' under the oaks at the classically beautiful Nottoway Plantation." Instagram, May 22, 2018. https://www.instagram.com/ainsleyevents/

A Lowcountry Wedding Magazine (@alowcountrywed). "Y'all, these Lowcountry plantations get us every time, and we love when couples select them as the backdrop for their big day. Tell us, what's your favorite plantation?" Instagram, May 22, 2018. https://www.instagram.com/p/BjGsSOcjoHB/.

Brown, Kimberly Juanita. "At the Center of the Periphery: Gender, Landscape, and Architecture in 12 Years a Slave." *The Global South* 11, no. 1 (2017): 121–35.

Chadha, Rahul. "For Influencers, Instagram is the Clear-Cut Favorite." *eMarketer*, January 30, 2018. https://www.emarketer.com/content/for-influencers-instagram-is-close-to-the-only-platform-that-matters.

Clukey, Amy, and Jeremy Wells. "Introduction: Plantation Modernity." *The Global South* 10, no. 2 (Fall 2016): 1–10.

Constine, Josh. "Instagram Hits 1 Billion Monthly Users, up from 800M in September." *TechCrunch*, June 20, 2018. https://techcrunch.com/2018/06/20/instagram-1-billion-users/.

"Frequently Asked Questions," Whitney Plantation (website), accessed September 30, 2020, https://www.whitneyplantation.org/faqs/.

Guterl, Matthew Pratt. "Plantation." In *Keywords for Southern Studies*, edited by Scott Romine and Jennifer Rae Greeson, 22–29. Athens: University of Georgia Press, 2016.

Henninger, Katherine. *Ordering the Facade: Photography and Contemporary Southern Women's Writing*. Chapel Hill: University of North Carolina Press, 2007.

Hinrichsen, Lisa. *Possessing the Past: Trauma, Imagination, and Memory in Post-Plantation Southern Literature*. Baton Rouge: Louisiana State University Press, 2015.

Kwun, Aileen. "Inside the most Instagrammable place on Earth." *Fast Company*, January 2, 2019. https://www.fastcompany.com/90281989/inside-the-most-instagrammable-place-on-earth.

Lim, Clarissa-Jan. "Brides and Grooms Who Got Married at A Former Slave Plantation Are Speaking out about Criticism of the Venues." *Buzzfeed News*, December 13, 2019. https://www.buzzfeednews.com/article/clarissajanlim/bride-groom-plantation-wedding-slaves-criticism.

Logan, Liz. "Some Wedding Sites Also Play Hard to Get." *New York Times*, March 13, 2015. https://www.nytimes.com/2015/03/15/fashion/weddings/some-wedding-sites-also-play-hard-to-get.html.

Marwick, Alice E. "Instafame: Luxury Selfies in the Attention Economy." *Public Culture* 27, no. 1 (January 2015): 137–60.

McPherson, Tara. *Reconstructing Dixie: Race, Gender, and Nostalgia in the Imagined South.* Durham, NC: Duke University Press, 2003.

Myung, Eunha, and Katie Smith. "Understanding Wedding Preferences of the Millennial Generation." *Event Management* 22, no. 5 (October 2018): 693–702.

Nerada, Pippa. "Blake Lively and Ryan Reynolds Are under Fire for Their 2012 Wedding," *Marie Claire*, February 20, 2018. https://www.marieclaire.com.au/blake-lively-ryan-rey nolds-wedding-plantation-slavery.

"#PlantationWedding" (search). Instagram (in application), screenshot by author, accessed on September 30, 2020.

Rose Hill (@rose.hillevents). "You don't have to travel far to find a wedding venue that gives you that intangible feeling of being surrounded by natural beauty and centuries of history." Instagram, June 12, 2019, https://www.instagram.com/p/BynYd_EnSGy/.

Srnicek, Nick. *Platform Capitalism.* Cambridge: Polity, 2016.

Shining Light Photography (@ashleym_brown), "Imagine driving up the long gravel driveway to see this estate waiting for you! 😍 📷 The @countryplantationhouse was an absolutely breathtaking venue! • The wide porch is perfect for a small family style wedding or the brick paver [sic] patio out back is a cozy spot for an open-air dinner reception! 🌿♡," Instagram, January 31, 2019, https://www.instagram.com/p/BtTqTCGBrJ-/.

Southern Oaks Plantation (@southernoaksplantation). "We are traditionally known for our grand columns and enchanting oaks . . . [sic] but once you step inside the plantation—the magic continues! Read our latest blog post to discover 'The Essence of Southern Oaks!' Photo @studiotranphotography." Instagram, February 7, 2019. https://www.insta gram.com/p/BtmXM4GA5j7/.

Stanonis, Anthony Joseph. *Dixie Emporium: Tourism, Foodways, and Consumer Culture in the American South.* Athens: University of Georgia Press, 2008.

"The Essence of Southern Oaks," Southern Oaks Plantation (website), accessed May 13, 2019, https://southernoaksplantation.com/essence-southern-oaks-plantation/.

Vlatch, John Michael. *The Planter's Prospect: Privilege and Slavery in Plantation Paintings.* Chapel Hill: University of North Carolina Press, 2002.

Zulli, Diana. "Capitalizing on the Look: Insights into the Glance, Attention Economy, and Instagram." *Critical Studies in Media Communication* 35, no. 2 (June 2018): 137–50.

"WE ARE MERE GARDENERS IN THE RUINS"

Kentucky Route Zero and Modeling Collaborative
Human Dignity in the Information Age

JAE SHARPE

IN ACT I OF *Kentucky Route Zero* (2013–20), a delivery driver-protagonist named Conway helps a woman named Weaver fix the image on her old television set, failing to realize as he does so that she is a ghost.[1] As the flickering of the television resolves into a picture of a nearby barn, the diegetic layers of the game's reality themselves change, with the walls of the interposed buildings breaking off to reveal one entrance to the game's enigmatic highway, the Zero, running through a cavern. The fluidity of the real here signals to the player that electronic devices are inextricable from the physical topologies in which they are produced and used, and these devices act as a means by which the game can consider how channels, both digital and geographic, function as connective tissue, hyperlink-like, among local communities even as they generate waste in their wake. One of *Kentucky Route Zero*'s primary concerns is that of e-waste: images of burning or destroyed electronics are a primary feature of the game's aesthetic. What, the story asks, comes after the sandbox of hypertexts, poststructuralism, and metafiction, reliant as the digital manifestations of these movements are on the production of consumer gadgets?

Critics such as Jussi Parikka have called attention to the impossibility of divorcing media technologies from the material dimensions through which they arise, and *Kentucky Route Zero* prompts us to consider what happens when these virtual forms, never as disembodied as one might assume, find themselves susceptible to corruption, poverty, or rot.[2] Among the game's most striking qualities is its marriage of the electronic with decay and death: Shannon Marquez, one of the game's playable characters, receives messages from Weaver (her dead cousin) through broken televisions, and electronics throughout the game become not only gateways for the dead but also, through their status as physically damaged artifacts, stand-ins for the problems of structural decay in Appalachian communities—such as physical health and the deterioration of physical local infrastructure—that have been obscured by a focus on abstract, digital modalities of communal life in the Internet Age.[3] *Kentucky Route Zero* examines stereotypes about Appalachian life—those concerning poverty, industrial labor, substance abuse, and racial and national identity, among others—with a critical eye, considering the historical precedents that have led to the creation and circulation of such stereotypes. Stereotypes arise and circulate in part through their divorce from historical context and nuance. Part of the game's project is building into the gameplay experience the narrative space necessary for the player's exploration of such nuance. As a text-heavy game, one that involves more reading than traditional video games and thus makes gameplay a necessarily slower, more contemplative experience, *Kentucky Route Zero* centers the importance of Appalachian histories in understanding (and determining) the actions of the game's characters.

Kentucky Route Zero is an independent multiplatform game produced by the studio Cardboard Computer, which released its first act in 2013. The game's point-and-click mechanics are complemented by a hypertextual narrative and low-poly graphics that incorporate a wealth of experimental features, both formal and referential, bracketing the primary story that it tells about the U.S. South.[4] *Kentucky Route Zero* uses the form of the video game to bring different issues rooted in Appalachian histories into correspondence with one another and with their modern consequents. The visual aspects of game design allow the writers of Cardboard Computer to situate narratives of Appalachian politics physically alongside magical and technological elements on the player's screen. The story is structured as five acts, with its fifth and final act released in January 2020, and it features a wealth of intertextual references that provide evidence of the game's relevance not only to the canons of American film and literature, but also to poststructuralism as a movement with international forms and a relationship to the digital humanities.

Despite its status as a game from a small, independent studio, *Kentucky Route Zero* has received critical attention from such venues as IGN and Polygon, which has amplified its popularity.[5] The computer game format of *Kentucky Route Zero* introduces players to the U.S. South and many of its attendant social and political phenomena in a way that is interactive, immersive, and, most crucially, more accessible than much of the extant literature dealing with the U.S. South's complex history of labor and class throughout the twentieth century. In making use of a popular, easily accessible medium like a computer game, *Kentucky Route Zero* draws on the historical relationship of the U.S.

labor movement to easily shareable forms of popular media such as political cartoons and protest music.

The game is set in an imagined area of Kentucky around the region of Mammoth Cave National Park and the Green River and follows the efforts of Conway, an aging truck driver, to deliver the last package from a failing antiques business to an address that seems not to exist: 5 Dogwood Drive. Later flashbacks in the game reveal that Conway is struggling to come to terms with his own aging and that he has relied heavily on the business for not only his livelihood, but also for his sense of self, given his history of low-wage work and the alcoholism that has prevented him from keeping other jobs. In the course of Conway's attempts to locate Dogwood Drive, he is directed onto the Zero, a mysterious highway that exists in a state adjacent to reality, and in which the game's surreal elements become explicit. Driving with Shannon, Conway observes that they continually pass the same location, and a character later makes reference to trying "to unwind that damned tangled highway," a suggestion that the Zero's seemingly straightforward circular shape may be as illusory as its apparent function. The player shares in this confusion, becoming responsible for guiding the characters along the Zero: while the early parts of Act I involve driving on realistically structured Kentucky roadways. Given an aerial view, we see that the Zero—true to its name—is designed as a ring and is navigated not like the branching highways of the surface, but by the user going clockwise or counterclockwise until they hit one of the Zero's topographical markers and then reversing direction.

Although the gameplay involves directing the playable characters by using a point-and-click mechanism, *Kentucky Route Zero* functions primarily as a hypertext. The game's story is driven through a series of dialogue options that appear on the screen, through which the player can determine how the characters behave. While the characters' identities are largely fixed, the player can access different details about their backstories based on the dialogue choices made. The hypertext, a literary form that is predominantly digital, offers different narrative choices based on reader input, which often take the form of clickable hyperlinks. Michael Joyce's *afternoon: a story* (1990) is one of the genre's earliest texts, and similarly structured hypertexts have evolved into gamified forms, with one notable example being the widespread hypertextual platform Twine, which allows users to create text-based narrative games that incorporate internal hyperlinks.[6]

The hyperlink in *Kentucky Route Zero* represents a communal form—a structural logic that involves communal interaction by means of incidental discovery. The hyperlink, like the highway, relies on impulse and chance encounters, becoming a logic of the accidental that encourages local encounters. New media theorists such as Lev Manovich and Alexander Galloway have considered how the "logic of selection" becomes aestheticized in digital forms, and the logic of the accidental encounter, in this game, privileges human dignity, not only encouraging the player to meet and learn the histories of other characters, but also revealing overarching connective power structures, in the form of Consolidated Electric, that have given rise to the area's social difficulties.[7] The name of the corporation itself is not an accident: experiences of the local and incidental that comprise the majority of gameplay stand in direct contrast to the Consolidated's interest in efficiency, organization, and a hegemonic programmatical life.

Manovich has suggested a definition of new media that expands it beyond the boundaries of its associations with computers, emphasizing how new media is indebted to the technical innovations of cinema, and especially to avant-garde understandings of space and the formal manipulation of objects; and Kentucky Route Zero foregrounds these influences by making use of visual techniques that recall the work of the video artists of the 1960s and 1970s.[8] The WEVP-TV website, which publishes teasers for the game in the form of broadcasts from a fictionalized local television station, cites the work of Jon Cates and Phil Morton, linking to a digital reproduction of Morton's seminal COPY-IT-RIGHT manifesto.[9] Morton founded the Video Department at Chicago, which would later become a nexus for the Video Art movement and be used by the married couple Steina and Woody Vasulka, among other pioneers of the form. Morton assisted in the creation of the Sandin Image Processor and penned "NOTES ON THE AESTHETIC OF 'copying-an-Image Processor'" (1973), a manifesto guiding derivative use of his processor work.[10] COPY-IT-RIGHT represented an important step toward the open-source, technologically collaborative communities that are structured as horizontal and rhizomatic, rather than as hierarchical.[11] These new forms of artistic sharing function as an ethical model for the same interest in collaboration that guides the exploratory structure of the game—the stories that players choose to listen to from the characters they encounter fleshing out Kentucky Route Zero's narrative world.

Game artist Tamas Kemenczy's interest in experimental film also elucidates the game's plethora of weird visual effects: walls and ceilings fragment and fall away during important character interactions, foregrounds and backgrounds become visually confused (and, at times, interchangeable), and while in the Bureau of Reclaimed Spaces, the characters broach the question as to whether they are currently inside or outside. The epistemological uncertainty here—and the game's broader unwillingness to clarify the veracity of its surreal incidents—reflects the game's larger interest in positioning the player as partially responsible for the construction of meaning that emerges. The game's visuals are heavily stylized, with trees having diamonds as leaves, and its environments offer more of a low-poly impression of the organic than any attempt at realistic rendering. In this way, the game emphasizes its own fictionality and its understanding of itself as a digital artifact akin to those that appear to the characters within the diegesis.

Though these formal features are a striking part of the gameplay experience, Alexander Galloway has called attention to the political dimensions of new media and to the failure of theoretical premises that emphasize its "poetics and pure formalism." Galloway deviates from critics like Manovich, who, like "Kittler or Marshall McLuhan, [. . .] may discuss the embeddedness of media systems within social or historical processes, [but] ultimately put a premium on media as pure formal devices."[12] *Kentucky Route Zero* foregrounds the relationship between the electronic and the embodied lives of those who use it, considering how those users exist in a sociopolitical context that directly influences their relationships to technology. The game reveals that digital play has never been disembodied, as evidenced by the necessary audience interaction and experimental forms of the hypertextual. In this respect, the game engages with a body of contemporary critical theory in the digital humanities that attempts to emphasize the centrality of the embodied subject to digital evolution. In *How We Became Posthuman: Virtual Bodies in Cybernetics, Literature, and Informatics* (1999), N. Katherine Hayles builds on this work when she observes that "embodiment has been systematically downplayed or erased in the cybernetic construction of the posthuman" in a way that fundamentally misrepresents the centrality of the human body to epistemological perspectives, and that the tendency of the posthuman might be replaced by "a version of the posthuman that embraces the possibilities of information technologies without being seduced by fantasies of unlimited power and disembodied immortality, that recognizes and celebrates finitude as a condition of human being.[13] I argue that *Kentucky Route Zero* embarks on the same theoretical endeavor, albeit by utilizing its unique genre features as a computer game to demand the active participation of the game's player in this project.

Complementing its visual strangeness, *Kentucky Route Zero* incorporates numerous unconventional features of gameplay. Although players begin the game with Conway, their control expands as others join the troupe, introducing a fluidity of character perspectives that pushes back against a narrative rooted in singular subjective experience. Hayles considers how "the presumption that there is an agency, desire, or will belonging to the self and clearly distinguished from the 'wills of others' is undercut in the posthuman, for the posthuman's collective heterogenous quality implies a distributed cognition located in disparate parts that may be in only tenuous communication with one another," a phenomenon that the game's many characters and locations reinforce.[14] The linear progression of the game's narrative is interrupted not only by flashbacks detailing Conway's past, but by scenes narrated from the perspectives of nonplayable characters at undefined times in the future. Much of *Kentucky Route Zero* involves learning the stories of characters one encounters only in passing—hearing how each has a tangled and complex family history that is bound to the physical geography of Kentucky that the player is currently exploring. The game is also heavily indebted to magical realism as a genre. In the process of getting on the Zero, Conway encounters various strange figures, among them a trio of ghosts, the long-dead Weaver, a pair of cybernetic musicians, the operators of an underground lake's ferry, and a boy whose brother is a giant eagle. The game also includes a number of surreal locales that mirror the story's interest in the decline of social infrastructure in poor areas of America.[15] The uncanny spaces that the characters traverse function as channels through which *Kentucky Route Zero* broaches questions about the reuse, dilapidation, and decay of urban facilities in low-income areas, along with the displacement, lack of government funding, and loss of jobs to which such decay leads.

While accessing the Zero, Conway and his group enter a series of caves and encounter a party of academics led by a man named Donald in a sequence entitled "The Hall of the Mountain King." Accessed through another decaying structure—a bridge that has partially rotted away—this sequence brings to a head the game's interest in what comes after poststructural play in a digital era, its consequences and the further literary techniques that it might inspire. The caves are littered with technological debris, as "broken computers are placed precariously among the rocks" and "a pile of discarded electronics burns steadily in the center of the chamber," with this fire being the most visually pronounced element of the scene. In order to talk to the other characters in the sequence, Conway must move in a circle around this central fire, monument as it is to the broken machinery that becomes central to the scene in the form of the XANADU program that lies at the center of the academics' work.

The entire game, like the work of the academics, explores the question of "human-computer interaction" through the lens of the literary surreal, and the prominence of self-referential and metafictional themes in this sequence underlines that interest. XANADU, the broken computer, is named after Samuel Taylor Coleridge's "Kubla Khan," and Donald, when approached, is humming a country tune that makes use of the words of the poem: "where the old green river runs, through hills and caves not known to us, down to that sunless sea." This passage, more than any other, stresses the game's investment in human-computer exchanges and how electronics can function as totems of human meaning.[16] However, as the academic group was creating the simulation—a hypertextual story that the XANADU computer functions as hardware for— Amy notes that her libidinal project had unintended results when translated into the game-within-a-game's hypertextual form. "We don't even have to add any new functionality," she admits; "the bugs just grow on their own."

The computer system, plagued by the mold that grows inside the cave, has overstretched the control of its creators. Unlike a conventional dystopian parable, the computer system of *Kentucky Route Zero* becomes more, not less, natural as it evolves beyond the scope of human manipulation. Donald notes that "it looks like a harmless old computer, doesn't it? Like some beat-up mainframe exhumed from a university basement and left in this cave to rot [. . .] or to flower! No, it's no ordinary computer. I've modified it extensively, and in some pretty *experimental* ways, believe you me!" After asking Shannon if she knows anything about "the effects of mold growth on diffused-based transistor circuitry," Donald explains that not all mold will destroy a computer completely, as

some moldy filaments are more or less conductive than others, and it grows in non-linear, chaotic patterns. We can guide it a bit, through a simple application of classical horticulture, but we can't produce specific results, only *tendencies*. Thwarted and feeble, we hammer on this derelict keyboard: 'MY NAME IS REASON, KING OF KINGS!' But we are mere gardeners in the ruins. Our keystrokes echo off into the tunnels [. . .] boundless and bare, the caves stretch far away.

The logic of mapping, conceptual and geographical, expressed here is again that of accidents: the strange, organic (and notably rhizomatic) encounters become an alternative to the efficient, profit-maximized grids of Consolidated Electric.[17] The "Ozymandias" variations of this sequence figure contemporary post-Enlightenment reason itself as the monument that will be undone as digital systems grow and subsequently change our relationship to the natural world. In this regard, *Kentucky Route Zero* offers a compelling inversion of commonsense wisdom that aligns the digital with reason and rationality. Its references to Romantic poets in this scene instead gesture to the possibility that the electronic will become more natural, where "natural" becomes shorthand for an uncontrollable sublime that evades the human determination that originally produced it. This sequence is also one of the game's most playful and self-referential. In describing XANADU, Donald tells Conway and the others that he published an academic article about the program's data structures entitled "Literary Multitudes: Hypertextual Narrative as Poststructural Witness." While this title is arguably a joke that the game directs at its own formal self-awareness and at the hypertext-game-within-a-hypertext-game that the player is about to experience, XANADU also gives the player a clue to the game's understanding of anxieties surrounding rampant deterioration and structural decay. Donald tells Shannon: "I'm afraid you are too late, fellow hypertext enthusiast. As the mold accumulated on the circuitry, XANADU blossomed for a moment into something holy and enchanted [. . .] then all the charm was broken. Do you have any idea what it's like to spend your life building something, and then to sit powerlessly as your work declines into ruin?" The player is provided with three separate responses to this, one for each of the other characters in the group (Conway, Shannon, and Ezra), all of whom have lives characterized by a significant loss or sense of deterioration. The game suggests, moreover, that this deterioration is the natural end result of the characters' various struggles with poverty, addiction, and lack of access to medical help and treatment, a prediction that will be fully realized when the player discovers that the mold destroying the XANADU computers has grown because it feeds on the ethanol fumes produced by the nearby Hard Times Distillery.

It is an attempt to repair the XANADU computer that leads Conway's party to the distillery. After the workers have offered advice and the group has returned to the caves, they activate XANADU, which proves to be a narrative-based hypertextual game that the characters themselves can play about the origins of the academic project and their first encounter with the "others":

the skeletal distillery men. Donald recalls, "There was so much more to it: ornate labyrinths of memory, exhaustively-simulated parallel cave ecosystems. Real artificial intelligence built on sophisticated neural network algorithms! [. . .] And then it began to crumble, when the strangers came." The strangers, the game reveals, are associated with the Consolidated Electric Company. As the story unfolds, Consolidated is revealed to be responsible for the decay of most of the social resources of the fictionalized Kentucky. Critics, including Stephen Fisher and Barbara Smith, have noted how Appalachian settings are consistently othered within American political discourse because of their associations with "poverty, joblessness, low wages, and other economic woes," which bear witness to the often-obscured consequences of "modernizing" projects that are driven by corporatized global capital on locales outside of the urban sphere.[18] Others, such as Dwight Billings and Ann E. Kingsolver, have identified the multiplicity of identities and political subjects that constitute Appalachian experience, pushing back on the idea of a single, easily definable Appalachia.[19] In addition to the work of Anne Shelby on Appalachian stereotypes, John Gaventa has observed how such "stereotypes—laziness, apathy, ignorance—could all serve, if internalized, as forms of powerlessness" that "protect the legitimacy of the status quo."[20] As a means of interrogating the economic histories of place that serve as the source of these stereotypes, *Kentucky Route Zero* devotes itself to finding power in the sharing of stories among characters from different parts of Appalachia.

The threat of structural decay looms large over the game's story: Conway meets Shannon at the entrance to an abandoned mine system called the Elkhorn, where Shannon is reading a plaque memorializing coal miners whose lives were lost in a structural accident. Shannon explains that her parents were former miners, and she recounts details about their low-wage work to Conway. "You know," she tells him as the two explore the mine together, "the miners used to have to pay just to run the fans and the lights? Yeah, they got paid in these shitty plastic tokens—coal scrip, you know? And if you want to run the fans for a bit to clear the air up, well, you have to put a token in." As they attempt to operate the PA system, Shannon further remarks that they will need to free up some of the power being used elsewhere, because "everything is rationed" in the mine.

The game's interest in Appalachian histories of coal mining activism responds to a broader focus on workers' rights that has been described by Fisher as characterizing media set in the area, a phenomenon also observed by Bennett Judkins in his work on the Black Lung Association and Richard Cuoto's writing on the coal strikes of the 1980s.[21] Taking up the question of the health and physical impact of working (and living) conditions in Kentucky, the game emphasizes the personalized nature of such experiences by forcing the player to inhabit different characters, implicating them in the characters' actions and forcing them to acknowledge the narrowing of self-determinative choices that have been caused by histories of trauma and harm. *Kentucky Route Zero* thus considers how people understand their own fraught relationship with place, particularly when they have emotional attachments to a location that functions at once as both home and threat due to the intersections of global capital and poverty.

While *Kentucky Route Zero*'s Consolidated Electric is fictional, its presence invokes the history of real American entities such as the Consolidation Coal Company, the Duke Power Company, and Duke's subsidiary the Eastover Coal Company. Duke Power has a particularly notorious labor history, being the subject of the *Griggs v. Duke Power Co.* case of 1971, in which the company was found to have used hiring practices (particularly employment tests) that unfairly discriminated against Black workers. Duke Power systematically excluded these workers from high-paying departments within the company in violation of the Civil Rights Act.[22] The company was also involved in the Brookside Mine Strike in Eastover, Kentucky, in 1973, which was featured in Barbara Kopple's documentary *Harlan County, USA* (1976). The documentary explicitly tackles the corporate practices that render the miners' bodies expendable, exploring black lung disease and its effects, the explosion of the Mannington Mine in West Virginia that trapped seventy-eight men underground, the violence directed toward the miners on the picket line by company-hired strike breakers carrying guns, and the poor housing conditions provided by the company for its employees, with the homes having no "water and no indoor plumbing."[23] Like its historical antecedents, Consolidated Electric appears to have a monopolistic control on the power operations of the region.

The logic of maximizing production efficiency that monetizes health itself and puts a premium on physical well-being and access to safe environments reveals spaces that have always been unsafe to those who live and work in them, even before their abandonment, with a rural world in a state of decay that is constant, albeit appearing in different forms at different times. The story of the miners foregrounds how health itself becomes commodified for those who inhabit expendable bodies—or rather, bodies that have been deemed expendable by the corporate structures that function as powers-that-be. Needing to pay an additional cost to access healthier air and offset the environmental toxicity that they are inevitably exposed to in the course of their work, the miners become representative of the human cost involved when resources inherent to health and safety are understood through the conceptual frameworks of capitalist economics. As Hayles points out, the erasures of the bodily and the material from much posthuman rhetoric are not coincidental, but rather arise as the result of particular market conditions. She notes that the liberal self to which the posthuman responds "is produced by market relations and does not in fact predate them."[24]

Later in the Elkhorn sequence, the game reveals that Shannon's parents were killed when the mine became flooded, with Shannon noting: "The water came in pretty fast, and a lot of folks got trapped in the tunnels. I only heard parts of how it went from there—sanitized for the bereaved [. . .] you know how these big companies are. But there was gossip too. The trapped miners couldn't get the pumps going because the power was rationed, so they shut all the lights off. But even then it wasn't enough." These deaths are a direct result of rationing practices that typify the conditions of manufactured scarcity in the service of corporate profit that the miners work under, and the sequence as a whole thus forecasts the game's later revelation that the electric company is complicit in perpetuating the region's widespread debt and alcoholism through its influence with the Hard Times Distillery.[25] Even as the Elkhorn Mine is a site of tremendous loss of life and historical injustice, it is also home to old electronics and curios left behind by the miners after their deaths. The game invests these items with importance as markers of humanity, even in a rotted or dilapidated state. The miners took the trinkets offered by the company that they worked for and nonetheless used them to make markers of meaning and humanity. While the game is clearly interested in the practical details of the precarious lives of its subjects, it uses its supernatural features to further dramatize experiences of poverty and class, most notably by elevating the problem of debt—a condition that seems unavoidable for most of the game's characters, given how the social structures in which they live perpetuate it—to the stakes of a Faustian bargain. "If you want to die with any dignity, you've got to settle up," says one character who has already become part of the distillery's skeletal machinery. Shannon raises the problem early in Act I of the game, as the first thing she recalls when she and Conway enter Weaver's old house is the fact that her parents "took out a bunch of loans [to have] the place built." After asking Conway whether he has any debts, Shannon confides in him that her own parents attempted to avoid debt "until the company store found a way to get to them. For my dad it was tokens to run the fans and air purifiers, and for my mom it was canaries. Two solutions to the same problem," notably mechanical and organic solutions that serve a similar function. "Weaver had debt, too—a lot of it. All tuition." If Conway responds by asking how Weaver paid off her student loans, Shannon will tell him that "she didn't. She had no income, none of them did."

Kentucky Route Zero shows, rather than tells, the player how the problem of living under debt is perpetuated by a network of social problems—dangerous infrastructure and working conditions, a lack of health insurance, low wages, addiction as a makeshift coping mechanism—that create a cycle in which escaping precarity becomes nearly impossible. When all of these problems are interconnected, as the game shows them to be, they create a fatal system that the game mirrors in its central narrative and geography. The mold that is destroying the XANADU computer feeds on the ethanol fumes of a whiskey that is produced by the skeletons who work in the underground distillery. These skeletons are people who, in their lives, went into debt, and the skeleton Doolittle ties the exploitative work programs of the distillery to the electric company when he hints at the need for having a "Consolidated Plan" in order for a worker to pay off the debt that he has accrued. This phrasing suggests a conspiracy-like relationship between the distillery, whose working conditions seem purposefully to mirror those of the dead miners from decades prior, and the Consolidated Power Company.

The first hint to the distillery as a threatening technological presence in the game comes in an early sequence when Conway and Shannon meet Johnny and Junebug, cyborg musicians who have literally created themselves after having been produced as blank canvases to work as mechanical miners by Consolidated. Donna Haraway has, like Hayles, foregrounded the role of the body, and its various transformations, in an age of new technological sovereignty, observing that "by the late twentieth century, [. . .] we are all chimeras, theorized and fabricated hybrids of machine and organism; in short, we are cyborgs."[26] Although the cyborg is a psychological and existential state in addition to being a bodily one, much of Haraway's theorizing about it is predicated on the new fluidity of physical reality and her project aligns with that of

Hayles insofar as both are invested in the question of how technological use is rooted in the specificity of diverse bodily experiences.

Conway ends up working for the distillery because of his own alcoholism.[27] After injuring his leg in an accident with Shannon, they visit the mysterious Dr. Truman, who gives Conway the experimental drug *Neurypnol TM,* in a sequence that invokes the early twenty-first century's opioid epidemic with its possible origins in the availability of pain medication.[28] Truman waits until Conway is drowsy from the drug to talk about billing him for the procedure: the dialogue box becomes blurry and difficult for the viewer to read, but it is legible enough to show Dr. Truman saying that "the pharmaceutical company [he is] contracted with was recently acquired by an energy company," Consolidated Electric. Later, Truman will inform Conway that all of his medical payments "run through [his] electricity bill now. You can pay it all back in full on your next billing cycle, or you can get on an energy credit payment plan. You'd have to call Consolidated for more detail about that. [. . .] Something about generating electricity to send back into the grid." The interrelated structures of poverty, health care, and physical local infrastructure form a system in which the individual is subordinated to the efficiency of profit-making. The image of the grid here gestures to the organizations of power that underlie the cyclical, self-perpetuating structures of precarity that have characterized the region's long history as internal "colony" available for corporate exploit.

The game is keenly aware of the enormous cost of being poor in America. The doctor and the distillery both underscore the way that payment plans often take advantage of the working poor, or those who need a short-term infusion of liquid capital, in order to then charge them premiums, with the long-term result of keeping them in a state of economic precarity. When Conway and Shannon discuss the procedure later, Shannon, who comes from a family of Colombian immigrants, notes:

> We almost never had a regular doctor, or health insurance, or anything like that. Our immigration stuff was a mess for most of my childhood, so we only qualified for state programs in small patches before something or other would get contested. [. . .] If a cut got infected or her migraines were too much to handle, mom would talk to so-and-so who knew so-and-so— usually another miner—and end up with some pills. And instead of medical advice, every pill came with gossipy anecdotal warnings and superstitions.

These anecdotes about the sharing of medication and medical help, and the risks involved, highlight those whose lives in America are marked by a reliance on stopgap measures for health and safety and a dependency on casual familial and communal exchanges as a proxy for legitimate medical care. Shannon's recounting of her adolescent experiences highlights how such measures themselves take on a quality of folklore, with medication being passed along with family stories.

Before their encounter with Dr. Truman, Conway and Shannon visit the chapel that was relocated to a storage facility in search of information and Conway meets a caretaker named Brandon. Upon seeing Conway's injury, Brandon says, "I bet everyone's telling you to go see a doctor. Hey, I get it: too expensive. My dad cut his arm pretty bad on a job, but he stitched himself back up because we didn't have health insurance. But then his hand didn't work very well, and he got pretty depressed, and eventually he just sort of . . ." What remains unsaid in Brandon's elliptical trailing off sums up the position in which many of the game's characters find themselves—the precarity of living in poverty and coping with the ripple effects of intergenerational trauma involved perpetuates itself in subtle yet incessant ways. Having partial or unreliable access to health care, as the game stresses, can become a contributing factor for substance abuse, mental illnesses that are exacerbated by financial and medical stress, the necessity of low-wage, physically or mentally demanding jobs like mining, and a lack of access to meaningful government aid. This complex of social problems, whose many interconnecting nodes the game examines, forms its own highway-like network of desperation that leads to living people going without. With their lives characterized by a restriction of choices for maintaining their own survival, the game's own hypertextual form mimics such confinement's strategic closing of certain narrative choices. Moreover, *Kentucky Route Zero* reveals itself to be deeply invested in how this restriction of access to basic human rights spurs the formation of local community networks, in which one must rely for help on other people in similar situations due to the lack of overarching structural options.

Neurypnol has a number of strange side effects, and when Conway wakes after a short flashback sequence, the player sees that his leg has become skeletal and has taken on a strange, yellow glow, but none of the game's other characters seem aware of this change. Additional context clues suggest that only the viewer and Conway are able to see the distillery workers of Act III as the skeletons that they are. Other characters refer to them as "the others" and as "creepy distillery guys," and during their attempt to repair the XANADU computer, Conway and Shannon find the Hard Times Whiskey Distillery underneath a decrepit church. Doolittle the skeleton explains as part of a tour of the facilities that the workers are there to pay off the debts they've accrued according to a formula designed by Weaver prior to her death. The skeleton offers Conway a job and then a drink to celebrate his hiring. Conway, who drinks the whiskey before he can refuse the job offer, puts himself in debt to the distillery workers such that he must take the job to pay them off.

Kentucky Route Zero's supernatural features thus allow the game to examine the self-alienation inherent in addiction and alcoholism, with Conway's slow transformation making him a stranger to himself.[29] The visual elements and magical plot represent the emotional sensations involved in the experience of dealing with addiction—the actual subjective experiences of being subject to its deferred but inescapable consequences—in a way that is largely unavailable to the traditional codex and allows the viewer to share in the emotional stakes of the sequence. One of the rare moments in the game when the player's choice is restricted in service to plot is when Doolittle offers Conway the whiskey. Conway has to take the drink; the player is given no other choice for the progression of the story and thus shares in the sense of inevitability and Conway's culpability when the stakes of the drink are revealed.

Work, for the characters of the game, becomes a site of deep ambivalence, simultaneously representative of the exploitative conditions that cause direct bodily harm to workers but also a means by which structure and a sense of self can be established. In using Conway's last delivery for the antiques business as a narrative framework, the game examines the loss of sense of self that accompanies the loss of a job, especially for workers growing older who struggle with addictions or are part of the working poor.

Kentucky Route Zero is thus a game deeply invested in the posttechnological. Countering beliefs in technology as redemptive and democratizing, it asks instead how problems of poverty and structural deterioration continue, albeit in new—and, at times, more insidious—forms, while not foreclosing the possibility that the digital, like the buildings that cycle through the Bureau of Reclaimed Spaces, might be redeemed through the uniquely human meaning with which its users can imbue it. In Act IV, Poppy, a switchboard operator at Echo River Central Exchange, tells Shannon: "The power company came along, buying up all the lines, and one day they took the exchange as a throw-in, like it was nothing. Nothing! And they started phasing us out.

[. . .] After a few months, it was just me. A new automation strategy was announced, and this place was re-christened, 'Consolidated Auxiliary Switch Number 30.'" Shannon can respond by asking what Poppy does, given the new automation system, and Poppy responds that

> it's not *fully* automated. There are still gaps in functionality that need a human touch. [. . .] And, you know, it really is all about *touch*, here. Sound is a vibration, a touch you feel in your ear, so my voice is my touch. When we're talking, we're touching, even on the phone—that's an electrical touch, an intimate little shock. [. . .] So, short of replacing the whole thing, not to mention all the wiring, they'd have to work out the exact timing of every little human gesture that goes into routing a phone call.

In underscoring the ability to respond to "human gesture[s]" as a uniquely human quality in itself, *Kentucky Route Zero* poses the question of what humanity consists of in an age of widespread digitization, suggesting the inability of automated systems to do away entirely with human components, regardless of how deeply these aspects might be hidden. When Poppy later entertains what she considers "a dark thought"—"What if there is no cheap machine that's going to replace me? What if it's cheaper just to keep me here, filling in for the rhythm of the operators. [. . .] What if *I'm* the cheap machine?"—she manages to reassure herself by thinking that she is "keeping some part of [the Central Exchange] human."

The fifth and final act of *Kentucky Route Zero* reveals that the unnamed, flooded town in which 5 Dogwood Drive is located was once a settlement for power plant employees that had been developed by "the power company," presumably Consolidated Electric. The game tells us that the houses the company built were "rotten" and are now uninhabitable. Similarly, it failed to build a promised drainage ditch, which has led to worse damage from the flooding and the death of two horses. "When the plant shut down," we learn, "the company abruptly pulled out of the area and took a large part of the town's population with it," leaving the area in the care of its remaining residents. Near the end of the game, a town resident offers one reason why the power plant may have failed: a solidarity of workers in response to mistreatment. The resident tells the travelers, "You and our other visitors might not know about the Out-of-Towner. He came here to work for the company, to dig a ditch. And the company worked him good and hard, and for less than he was worth, but it wasn't enough. They had to use him up completely. After that, we became ungovernable. First out of shame, then grief, then anger."

Populated now by both living characters and singing ghosts (who share their memories of the town's earlier years with the player), the town is being investigated by the Bureau of Reclaimed Spaces for possible repossession, a process that would presumably corporatize the space and evict its remaining inhabitants. The game also suggests that some of the ghosts are from a period that predates the company homes: the horses who live in the area are from "generations ago," and they "came with the people from Central America [who settled in the region]. You know, the utopians—the 'People of Nothing.'" Many of the playable characters from Acts II through IV decide to stay at Dogwood Drive and attempt to preserve the town, even as the place's other inhabitants prepare to leave.

The interactivity of *Kentucky Route Zero* as a game forces the player to take an active role in the narrative, emphasizing the need for individual responsibility and regrounding in an era of corporate personhood. *Kentucky Route Zero* exemplifies the uniqueness of video games as a genre for exploring social responsibility, and the obligations that we have toward our local communities. Though it draws on the stylistic features of novels and films, the game's ability to collate the aesthetic qualities of its formal precursors with the ability to experience direct responsibility for a controlled character by choosing their behavior foregrounds the player's role as active co-creator of the story and allows the players to experience themselves as members of the game's local relationships in Appalachia. While the Consolidated Electric Company is an intangible, shadowy organization, the game forces players as human beings to recognize the stakes of—and take responsibility for—the lives that they encounter, an experience that the game suggests is fundamental to any preservation of meaningful personhood in an era of widespread digitization.

NOTES

1. *Kentucky Route Zero*, v. 22 (Cardboard Computer, 2020).

2. Parikka, *A Geology of Media*.

3. Literary and cinematic references abound in *Kentucky Route Zero*: the Marquez family, living at 100 Macondo Lane, functions with its Aunt Remedios as an homage to Latin American writer Gabriel García Márquez, and cousins Shannon and Weaver recall the theorists central to the creation of the integrated circuit and to communication studies more

broadly. One company featured in the game is "Laszlo Electronics," recalling the Jamf of Thomas Pynchon's *Gravity's Rainbow*. One of Cardboard Computer's intermissions for the game, *The Entertainment,* is a mock play about alcohol addiction whose authorship is attributed to Lem Doolittle, a character who appears in later acts of *Kentucky Route Zero* as a skeletal distillery worker, which suggests the infamous paralyzing media central to the plot of David Foster Wallace's *Infinite Jest*. One of the workers at the underground telephone exchange is named Dashiell Morse, in a nod to Dashiell Hammett, who is the author of *The Maltese Falcon*. Another sequence, entitled "In Bedquilt," evokes Dorothy Canfield. Conversations between the two cyborg musicians, named Johnny and Junebug after the Cashes, feature lines lifted from the plays of Beckett and the lyrics of Christian hymns. The game's references thus form an amalgamation of American cultural references together with postmodern and avant-garde media: it is deeply interested not only in the experimental textual structures that have inspired hypertextual traditions, but also in those that inform American culture more broadly. Having characters mimic lines from American texts with a reputation for being canonical and foundational—one makes reference to Whitman's "very well then, I contradict myself"—legitimizes an area of economic and structural scarcity, often caricatured as cut off from forms of high art in spite of its well-established literary and cultural history.

4. The game's hypertextual nature makes exact citations difficult—while some sequences are tied to specific acts, others appear at differing periods based on the player's choices, such that they can avoid certain areas entirely.

5. Marks, "*Kentucky Route Zero* Review"; Plante, "Why *Kentucky Route Zero* Is the Most Important Game of the Decade."

6. Joyce, *afternoon, a story.*

7. Manovich, *The Language of New Media*, 35, 123; Galloway, *The Interface Effect*, 3.

8. Manovich, *The Language of New Media*, 19, 50; in an interview for the now-defunct *Venus Patrol* website, game artist Tamas Kemenczy offers a brief catalogue of films that inspired his techniques of visual experimentalism, among them the films of Andrei Tarkovsky, Alexander Sokurov's *Russian Ark,* and the film art of Steina and Woody Vasulka. He points specifically to the "Scan Processor Studies" videos created by Woody Vasulka and Brian O'Reilly, citing the ability of their "deflecting cathode rays to make strange landscapes. They share a family resemblance to the Zero, and they are partly responsible for the tone of it and other map modes in KRZ." Boyer, "*Venus Patrol* Presents: The Kentucky Route Zero Guide to Film."

9. "COPY < IT > RIGHT!"

10. Morton, "NOTES ON THE AESTHETIC OF 'copying-an-Image Processor.'"

11. Christine Tamblyn notes that "Sandin eschewed the hierarchical organizational mode favored by television engineers that places all components under the control of one centralized unit. The unlabeled modules that comprise Sandin's machine can be connected incrementally to attain unpredictable and unprecedented results. Thus it is possible for users to devise their own personalized approach to operating the Image Processor and to develop unique, readily identifiable styles." Tamblyn, "Image Processing in Chicago Video Art, 1970–1980," 304.

12. Galloway, *Interface Effect*, 5.

13. Hayles, *How We Became Posthuman*, 3–4.

14. Ibid.

15. The Bureau of Reclaimed Spaces is responsible for taking the property of former institutions and repurposing them for use in other industries, transforming a hospital into the site of an auto dealership and a distillery into a graveyard. One scene involves the troupe of playable characters visiting a Museum of Dwellings, which showcases a number of homes and living spaces, still inhabited, collected in one large warehouse. A climactic moment in the game takes place at an old telephone exchange underground, accessed through a series of caves that serve as a bat sanctuary, and another in a chapel that has been relocated—via the Bureau of Reclaimed Spaces—to an old storage facility, where it continues to hold services in the absence of a congregation.

16. One academic named Amy tells the group that before working with the academics, doing debugging for their computer system, she used to write romance novels. She tells them how "suddenly it was all computers everywhere you went. I thought I might be able to do something with that. Inject a little libido into those ugly beige boxes."

17. See also Burnett, "Mold on the Cornbread," 162–165.

18. Fisher and Smith, "Introduction: Placing Appalachia," 2.

19. Billings and Kingsolver, eds., *Appalachia in Regional Context*.

20. Shelby, "The 'R' Word,," 153–60; Gaventa, "The Power of Place and the Place of Power," 91–110.

21. Judkins, "The People's Respirator," 225; Cuoto, "The Memory of Miners and the Conscience of Capital," 165–94; Fisher, "The Grass Roots Speak Back," 203–14.

22. Smith, *Race, Labor, and Civil Rights*, 1–2.

23. Kopple, *Harlan County, USA*.

24. Hayles, *How We Became Posthuman*, 3.

25. During this scene, the player can choose to turn off the light on the mine cart that Conway and Shannon are riding and witness the ghosts of the dead miners walking through the cave. The cave's ghosts indicate that these problems—low-wage jobs, the absence of worker's rights and access to medical care, mental illness—have, much like the Zero itself, a cyclical and self-perpetuating structure: the hard times of the past do not stay dead, but necessarily reappear and re-assert themselves in the present.

26. Haraway, "A Cyborg Manifesto," 150.

27. The *Kentucky Route Zero* intermission *The Entertainment* is set in a bar in the same universe as the game and examines more thoroughly the vicious cycles involved in alcoholism: addiction is subject to the self-perpetuating logic described above, in which characters living in economic precarity cope through a reliance on substances for which they will go deeper in debt.

28. Moody, Satterwhite, and Bickel, "Substance Use in Rural Central Appalachia."

29. As the game continues, Conway becomes progressively more skeletal, with his right arm following his left leg in appearance, and then, during a sequence with Shannon at the Echo River telephone exchange, his entire body has become a skeleton and other distillery workers come by in a boat to take him underground.

BIBLIOGRAPHY

Billings, Dwight, and Ann Kingsolver, eds. *Appalachia in Regional Context: Place Matters.* Lexington: University Press of Kentucky, 2018.

Billings, Dwight, Gurney Norman, and Katherine Ledford, eds. *Back Talk from Appalachia: Confronting Stereotypes.* Lexington: University Press of Kentucky, 1999.

Boyer, Brendan. *"Venus Patrol* Presents: The Kentucky Route Zero Guide to Film." Accessed November 20, 2018. https://web.archive.org/web/20170206105947/http://venuspatrol .com/2014/05//venus-patrol-presents-kentucky-route-zero-guide-film.

Burnett, Katharine A. "Mold on the Cornbread: The Spore Paradigm of Southern Studies." *PMLA* 131, no. 1 (2016): 162–65.

Cardboard Computer. *Kentucky Route Zero.* V. 22. Cardboard Computer, 2020. PlayStation 4, Xbox One, Microsoft Windows, Linux, Macintosh.

Cuoto, Richard A. "The Memory of Miners and the Conscience of Capital: Coal Miners' Strikes as Free Spaces." In Fisher, *Fighting Back in Appalachia,* 165–94.

Fisher, Stephen. "The Grass Roots Speak Back." In Billings, Norman, and Ledford, *Back Talk from Appalachia,* 203–14.

Fisher, Stephen, ed. *Fighting Back in Appalachia: Traditions of Resistance and Change.* Philadelphia: Temple University Press, 1993.

Fisher, Stephen, and Barbara Smith. "Introduction: Placing Appalachia." In Fisher and Smith, *Transforming Places, 1-16.*

Fisher, Stephen, and Barbara Smith, eds. *Transforming Places: Lessons from Appalachia.* Urbana: University of Illinois Press, 2012.

Galloway, Alexander R. *The Interface Effect.* Malden, MA: Polity, 2012.

Gaventa, John. "The Power of Place and the Place of Power." In Billings and Kingsolver, *Appalachian Regional Context,* 91–110.

Haraway, Donna. "A Cyborg Manifesto: Science, Technology, and Socialist-Feminism in the Late Twentieth Century." In *Simians, Cyborgs, and Women: The Reinvention of Nature,* 149–81. New York: Routledge, 1991.

Hayles, N. Katherine. *How We Became Posthuman: Virtual Bodies in Cybernetics, Literature, and Informatics.* Chicago: University of Chicago Press, 1999. 3–4.

Joyce, Michael. *afternoon, a story.* Massachusetts: Eastgate Systems, 1987. Microsoft Windows, Macintosh.

Judkins, Bennett M. "The People's Respirator: Coalition Building and the Black Lung Association." In Fisher, *Fighting Back in Appalachia,* 225–43.

Kopple, Barbara. *Harlan County, USA.* New York: Cabin Creek Films, 1976. 16 mm, 103 min.

Manovich, Lev. *The Language of New Media.* Cambridge, MA: MIT Press, 2001.

Marks, Tom. *"Kentucky Route Zero* Review." *IGN,* January 27, 2020. Accessed September 15, 2020. https://www.ign.com/articles/kentucky-route-zero-review.

Moody, Lara, Emily Satterwhite, and Warren K. Bickel. "Substance Use in Rural Central Appalachia: Current Status and Treatment Considerations." *Journal of Rural Mental Health* 41, no. 2 (2017): 123–35.

Morton, Phil. "NOTES ON THE AESTHETIC OF 'copying-an-Image Processor.'" 1973. Accessed

November 20, 2018. http://www.vasulka.org/archive/Artists4/Morton,Phil/Distribu tionReligion.pdf.

Parikka, Jussi. *A Geology of Media*. Minneapolis: University of Minnesota Press, 2015.

The Phil Morton Memorial Research Archive. "COPY < IT > RIGHT!" Accessed November 20, 2018. www.copyitright.org.

Plante, Chris. "Why *Kentucky Route Zero* Is the Most Important Game of the Decade." *Polygon*, November 12, 2019. Accessed September 15, 2020. https://www.polygon.com/2019 /11/12/20960055/kentucky-route-zero-the-most-important-game-of-the-decade.

Schumann, William, and Rebecca Fletcher, eds. *Appalachia Revisited: New Perspectives on Place, Tradition, and Progress*. Lexington: University Press of Kentucky, 2016.

Shelby, Anne. "The 'R' Word: What's So Funny (and Not So Funny) About Redneck Jokes." In Billings, *Norman, and Ledford, Back Talk from Appalachia*, 153–60.

Smith, Robert Samuel. *Race, Labor, and Civil Rights: Griggs versus Duke Power and the Struggle for Equal Employment Opportunity*. Baton Rouge: Louisiana State University Press, 2008.

Tamblyn, Christine. "Image Processing in Chicago Video Art, 1970–1980." *Leonardo* 24, no. 3 (1991): 303–10.

GIS SOUTH

Louisiana in the Lost and Found

JENNIE LIGHTWEIS-GOFF

Maps are approximate [. . .]; symbols like the boot are even more so.
—BRETT ANDERSON, "Louisiana Loses Its Boot"

Between Culture and a Void

Home lies between "culture" and "avoid." Danny runs a gallery among "rich hippies." Sharon is searching for a house in the "East Fixies." Shane tarries at "the Gentrification Station." Mike and Carol grew up halfway between "the Sopranos" and "cheap cigarettes." Tom finds himself among "quiet gays," though they're often so quiet as to blur the border with nice Midwestern church ladies. Dana rides her bike from "humans piled in concrete siloes" to run the back of the house in a Minneapolis restaurant. Katie and Burke are too far north, even by Minnesota standards, for anyone to map them, though a colleague once said that hilly Duluth was "the San Francisco of the Midwest." When I teach at the top of Mississippi, I am crowded by white suburbanites who fled Memphis for Southaven in successive waves of white flight. When I am in Memphis itself I live with "unhip hipsters and artists," dovetailing neatly with my partner Chip's sense that, born in the 1970s, we were hipsters that peaked too soon. Sometimes, by way of explanation for that condition, I tell people I grew up halfway between Asheville and Athens. Then they know I'm a product of the southern bohemia, such as it is.[1]

All of the descriptions of place in the paragraph above come from collo-quial city maps—usually Judgmental Maps, the internet's repository of inti-mate cartography—and the informal geographies our new neighbors teach us when we begin to put down roots.[2] At home in New Orleans, a city with four centuries of settler colonialism and four distinct nationalisms shuffling its place names, I have heard dramatic shifts in less than a decade on a single block in the Sixth Ward. When I got to the block, white neighbors called it

Lafitte and Black neighbors said Back of Town. Treme grew and so did Bayou St. John, though mainly from real estate agents wielding slick cardboard signs. Mr. Freddie likes to say Mid-City—as aspirational as that is for developers, and as inaccurate to municipal mappers—because he has lived here all his life and, even when flush with cash, has never felt the need for a car. "It is in the middle of everything," he says. If the city ever tears down the crumbling overpass that bifurcates the neighborhood from the richer, whiter portion of the Treme, the blocks once known as the Lafitte may yet be annexed by the French Quarter or reintegrated with what preceded the I-10 Corridor. The reunion might simultaneously restore traditional names and feather the nests of already richly remunerated developers.[3]

All this to say, my city requires an intimate cartography: that is, a mapping practice that shows the spaces that were, the spaces that exist, and the spaces that will come to ruin when the waters rise again. While new media mappers from the smartphone navigator to the local cartographer tease with these possibilities, they ultimately fail to chart landscapes built for capital. New Orleans is "a palpably vulnerable city on a shifting terrain," in Barbara Eckstein's words, but maps of the city fix the present in place.[4] This condition is paradoxically *most* harmful and *least* visible in a place where the margin of the water persistently moves to swallow habitable land, and where that same land sinks and cracks to displace inhabitants. An honest update requires minute-to-minute attention on interfaces seemingly designed for present, rather than future, orientation. Shapes like the Crescent and the Boot remain on branded maps despite land loss and rising waters. Contemporary digital media's collaborations with and dependency on capital produce the illusion of static, mapped space, albeit overlaid with touristic and affective landmarks, that this essay critiques. To borrow a phrase from new media theorist Wendy Hui Kyong Chun, regarding the flooded and flooding oil-rich zones of the Gulf South, we "update to remain the same."[5]

This essay begins with the intimate cartography of Judgmental Maps because such proximity seems possible, if not wholly accomplished by the mapping technologies that users carry in their pockets. Tracking the names appended to and rescinded from space matters, perhaps especially in coastal southern cities in danger from rising waters, in interior cities (like Nashville and Atlanta) that are bywords for gentrification, and in every place vulnerable to climate change (which is to say, every place). Bereft of notions of regional, racial, and political innocence (however false) that follow urban transplants to

Portland and San Francisco, southern cityscapes are shaped by displacements and erasures that become visible: mappable, even. Projects like Paper Monuments work toward that aim with their poster installation counter-memorials that augment the white-washed history of New Orleans, but they are decidedly analog, deliberately local.[6] This essay measures the distance between the smartphone map and the vulnerable city, traveling from a "tweetstorm" by game designer James L. Sutter to the prestige project of Rebecca Solnit and Rebecca Snedeker's *Unfathomable City: A New Orleans Atlas* (2013), and, finally, to a remapping of Louisiana by journalist Brett Anderson. At each turn, I consider not only what the digital makes possible, but also what the user—that unmappable variable—resists.

Bright Lines

Space is rendered diffuse by a dishonest public sphere in which we "make space" for new ideas and build "safe spaces" for their expression. Humans navigate concrete space. Cartographic intimacies offer vernacular names and local navigations, orientations provided by neighbors and natives, rather than by guidebooks and Yelp reviews. They are a kind of colloquial response to spatial critical theory and cultural geography. If smartphone mapping offers the potential to make sense of intimate locality, the difference between ideal and actual use has blunted much of that potential. On a linguistic level, a scholar looking for resources on mapping will be diverted by how often "mapping" simply means "conceptualizing" in the humanities and social criticism, despite accessible digital technologies that make mapping both literal and possible. The mapping and navigational technology of the small screen produces distance from urban environments, exacerbating conditions that have turned cities into branded and owned spaces.[7] For digital humanists, "curation—as opposed to automation—is the dominant paradigm [. . .] for the creation of digital resources in general, and for cartographic or geographical resources in particular."[8] Branded, static maps of a sinking city are in need of constant revision, the condition ignored by Sutter and addressed by Anderson. Popular digital media cartographies curate with surprising consistency from already-existing maps; indeed, their persistent strategy seems to be neither curation nor automation, but overwriting.

City-sized cartography relies on reader knowledge of the good and bad mall, the new and decaying Krogers and Wal-Marts within particular communities, but the maps often use a distanced template, sourced from Google Maps. With the exception of a single, jokey faux-nineteenth-century map of San Francisco for Gold Rushers, Judgmental Maps is a repository of screenshots, overwritten with text from MSPaint.[9] Are these routes *into* our places—especially southern spaces, so often graphed for prisons, cheap labor, and oil extraction—or routes *away* from them? With mapping technology at our disposal, do we stay on decontextualized blocks to which we have been navigated? Do we zoom out, an epistemological practice that locates us in space? Do we pinch, to place our bodies on a local landscape with less context? Do we find "random" buttons, which have seemed scarcer over the lifetime of the internet? Digital optimism, such as that espoused by media corporations and educational institutions, imagines alternative-to-paper projects as producing a more democratic public sphere; it proves an unpalatable extension of the internet-fueled, deregulatory zeal of the late millennium, and of the "disruption" mania of the last two decades.

Despite the necessary skepticism of new media theorists such as Wendy Hui Kyong Chun, the realpolitik roars back with reminders that we are governed by digital optimism. In a single week in February 2020, the Iowa Democratic Party tried (and failed) to count votes by smartphone app, and, using artificial intelligence, Barnes & Noble curated a list of "Diverse Editions" for Black History Month without a single Black writer.[10] According to the bookstore, the artificial intelligence they used defined editions by white writers who offered no racial designation for characters as "diverse." Flush with tech cash, even (and perhaps especially) liberals imagine disruption as the solution to persistent social problems, as though tech is a carbon-neutral alternative to the petrochemical industries of which they offer legitimate criticism. To each of the questions above, I offer the less optimistic option: navigational technology is directional, not random; atomizing, not social; distancing, not intimate.

Innovation is nonetheless possible by interrupting habituation, not simply to technology but to the built environment. Digital theorists Christian Ulrik Andersen and Soren Bro Pold figure the city as another interface, mediating human access to both urban space and urban time.[11] In their consideration of "territorial interfaces," they describe how two smartphone applications resist the cognitive encryption of Google Maps. British artist Graham Harwood's *Perl Routes to Manipulate London* simultaneously reproduces the visual effects of William Blake's multidimensional London, with its "charter'd streets" and "blackning Church[es]," and quantifies the exploitation he found there.

Ringed by Blakean river maps and vistas of the Thames, its Perl program code calculates "the gross lung-capacity of the children screaming from 1792 to the present" and "the air displacement needed to represent the public scream."[12] Harwood's intervention refuses to erase the history of capital in order to enable seamless (and guiltless) navigation of space; his GPS does not elide the miseries of coal, oil, and imperialism. Another application, Serendiptor, interrupts Google Maps' step-by-step directions through city streets to insert a little serendipity: bum a smoke, touch a statue, shred a receipt, accompany the lonely. Like the unwanted and infelicitous landing prompted by dice on a game board—those little maps—Serendiptor can send the flaneur backward or forward on urban streets. Produced by artist and architect Mark Shepard, it "dissolve[s] the boundaries of urban zones, such as the boundaries between the public and private, or work and leisure, and make[s] the adjoining moments, the travel and transportation itself, pleasurable."[13] While this situationist, phenomenological relationship to the city is possible through the apparatus of digital media, it is filtered by the structural biases of the algorithm.[14] When I went off in search of Serendiptor, my search engine recommended that I download Uber instead.

After years of contraction of and eulogies for "the good internet"—the harvest of often feminist, progressive, anti-authoritarian writing on sites like Gawker, Deadspin, Feministing, and Jezebel, sites that have receded as monopolistic platforms like Twitter and Facebook have swollen—we ought to acknowledge that Google Maps chose the side of the Bad Internet in 2016, when it began branding users' flânerie with instructions to "turn right near McDonald's" or "pass Dollar General on the left."[15] We pinch. We dislocate. Without intention, we choose the familiar. Capitalism produces more options and fewer choices. Urban space erupts with distractions, stickiness, inertia, collisions, and delay, the pleasures and dangers of people fricating together. Smartphone navigation of that space, by contrast, offers what Bill Gates famously described as the key benefit of the internet in the Bill Clinton years: "friction-free capitalism."[16]

The touristic vision of New Orleans proffers "a city-sized act of civil disobedience" against the "techno-driven, profit-crazy, hyper-efficient self-image of the United States."[17] The extractive economies of oil and private prisons are erased, even excused, in that vision. Long imagined as an exception to both national and regional norms, New Orleans was transformed into a fantasy landscape in a recent moment of viral mapping. "If this came in from a freelancer," wrote game designer James Sutter of the image of the city provided by Google Maps, "there are half a dozen things that would raise my eyebrows."[18] Sutter's nine-post Twitter essay critiquing New Orleans's "totally unrealistic" landscape earned viral boosts from reliable content aggregators including Bored Panda and DeMilked. (See Fig. 7.1.) Curated content under clickbait headlines affirmed preconceptions of New Orleans as somehow unreal, a place one might observe on a fantasy map. It is a place that has "no right to exist" by the rules of capitalism, or by the related logic of the navigable small screen.[19] Between New Orleans's body and its map lie many distinctions without differences since it is so often mediated by the tourist's imaginary and a sentimental rhetoric around climate change that positions it—but never, say, warming Nashville—as a preeminent city without a future. This notion of New Orleans as nearly fictional, passing into the mists like Avalon or Brigadoon, is not undone by more rigorous accounts of it as unfathomable, accidental, improvised, inevitable, and impossible.[20]

Sutter leaves the political dimensions of landscape untouched in his reading of New Orleans as fictional setting. To many of Sutter's readers, the notion that landscape is contingent and constructed would likely startle. But little could be as unnatural as New Orleans's putatively natural features highlighted in these tweets. In August 2017, a handful of blocks in New Orleans (including my own) accrued, in the course of a single, ordinary, unnamed afternoon rainstorm, more water than they received during Hurricane Katrina, calling attention to what Elizabeth Kolbert describes as "a sort of Trojan Solution. Since marshy soils compact by de-watering, pumping water out of the ground exacerbates the very problem that needs to be solved. The more water that's pumped, the faster the city sinks. And, the more it sinks the more pumping is required."[21] An ordinary day's flooding produced by a seemingly minor rainstorm should raise alarms. Apocalyptic destruction will not arrive during hurricane season, with the irregularity of the hundred-year storm; apocalypses will arrive with the frequency of bank holidays. Considering expansive land loss, the September 2017 (and May 2019) floods from unnamed storms might also highlight the optimal purpose of a digital media map: to enable users to see how the land shifts and recedes, to show how terrain disappears in real time. Residents of vulnerable terrain do not benefit from a digital climate that overlays words onto branded, static, corporate maps. The navigational technology of Google Maps has become ordinary, but, "habit + crisis = update."[22] Our lives may depend on an update that is not yet here.

Fig. 7.1. Mapping Industrial Fantasy. Screenshot by author.
Tweet by James L. Sutter, "And then there's this thing,"
March 18, 2018, 10:05 P.M.

The land is not simply slow and low, swampy and decadent, fantastic and wild. It is synthetic and industrial. Next to screenshots of "artificial" shipping outlets to the Gulf of Mexico, Sutter asks, "What even is this? A canal? More like your eraser tool slipped, and you didn't notice until it was time to color things and you were too lazy to go back and fix it. Sloppy."[23]

This flippancy abuts even the most destructive features of Louisiana's industrial, petrochemical landscape: most famously, the Mississippi River Gulf Outlet, or Mr. Go. The seventy-six-mile channel provided a shortcut between the Port of New Orleans and the Gulf of Mexico. Built with public moneys from the Army Corps of Engineers for the private benefit of the shipping industry—thereby socializing the risk and privatizing the profits—the channel invited even larger ships into the Port and intensified flooding after Hurricane Katrina. It breached nearly two dozen levees touched by its waters. By rare bipartisan environmental action, Mr. Go closed for traffic before Christmas 2007. According to a 2005 article in the *Washington Post*, Mr. Go crafted "a hurricane highway, a storm-surge shotgun pointed at the city's gut."[24]

I find myself riveted by the *Post*'s image of a gut-shot Louisiana, and by

Solnit and Snedeker's later specification of New Orleans as a fragile, filtering liver.[25] Seldom the first choice for an assassin, a bullet in the gut chooses maximum pain and a slow bleeding rather than the immediate kill. Thanks to the stylized violence of the movies, I now imagine New Orleans as a wounded Mr. Orange [Tim Roth], gray-skinned and nearly bloodless from the bullet in his belly at the conclusion of *Reservoir Dogs*. This is perhaps an apt image for a city both drowning in and drained of oil: drowning as it is drained, dried as it drowns.[26] Though the infamous graffiti reading "Katrina, you bitch" got far more attention, on a ruined house in the Lower 9th Ward, a resident spray-painted "use this to fill MRGO!" over the names of the displaced.[27] For the predominantly Black residents of the Lower Nine and their white working-class neighbors in St. Bernard Parish, Mr. Go was a leviathan, a murderer, the world ending in neither fire nor ice, but water. Google is not Exxon, and Twitter is not British Petroleum, but the present forms of digital mapping and navigation inhibit the collective capacity to see the connections between the environmental violence of industrial capital and the social distance produced by extractive economies. Friction-free capitalism has never gone away: our networks promise liquidity and immediacy, but they offer, through branded maps and #FollowYourNola posts, fixed images of land that is literally disappearing.

Screenshot maps nonetheless fix and capture, erasing the ground's disappearing act. An "interesting-looking design," Sutter writes, ablating the guiding hand of capital on the map of New Orleans. Digital optimism would have us hope that a person who wonders "what even is this?" at the sight of Mr. Go would simply look it up with the instruments at their disposal, since it is the same instrument they use to tweet. An online culture that enables and encourages users of these technologies to read, revise, and even critique geospatial maps can enable a more equitable distribution of a needful knowledge: that is, it can teach its readers that just as Hurricane Katrina was a manmade failure of flood protection, the geographical boundaries of a place are as constructed as its political and digital borders. The network of canals, waterways, and bridges that strikes Sutter as fantastical is, in fact, a too-real construction of the same "fever dreams" that brought finance capitalism to the Deep South to build plantations.[28] The lakes that are not quite lakes—Borgne, Pontchartrain—have been dredged to make room for massive oil tankers. The landscape is fantasy: the fantasy of men with dollar signs in their eyes. Industry carves a violent, nonconsensual cartography into the flooded, oil-rich United States and global souths that has profited a few and flooded the rest.

But smartphone mapping, too, may be defined by its "leakiness." Because of its centrality to the neoliberal economy, it "erodes the distinction between the revolutionary and the conventional, public and private, work and leisure, fascinating and boring, hype and reality, amateur and professional, democracy and trolling."[29] It might also make visible the invisible flows of capital. A responsive digital map could offer a key fleshed out not simply by scale, but by time and artificiality, by points and shadings that demarcate features built for oil and gas. In New Orleans, Mr. Go; in New York, dredge marks that show the expansion of Manhattan's land and the ghosts of its freshwater ponds. Instead, Sutter's tweet-storm evades or even excuses the slow-motion hurricane of Louisiana's land loss by asserting the unreality of a persistently vulnerable place; New Orleans becomes a city without a history. This distortion lands like another shot to the gut, considering how often its history has been celebrated as consolation prize for the notion that it has no future.

Freelancers in the business of fantasy—role-playing games, speculative novels—draw by hand, emblazoning unreal cities with Germanic fonts and Gothic features. But like the local cartographers of Judgmental Maps, Sutter simply uses screenshots from Google Maps with his own textual additions. As a result, he proffers a branded map, where the red names Crowne Plaza French Quarter and Renaissance New Orleans Warehouse District Hotel take up more space than labels for waterways. Four years before Sutter's critique, restaurant critic and Katrina survivor Brett Anderson wrote a long-form essay on *Medium* to fleetingly record the changed shape of Louisiana. Though Louisianans and people farther afield are accustomed to hearing that the state loses "a football field every hour to coastal erosion," we are simultaneously visually assailed with the branded image of its boot shape.[30] If we take climate change seriously, we must acknowledge not only the way land loss chips away at the state's shape, but that the small screens of our smartphones provide distance from that flux.

Cutlass or Compass

Lush with images of gators and pelicans, with sousaphones morphing into cypress trees, Solnit and Snedeker's *Unfathomable City: A New Orleans Atlas* shares with Sutter an inclination toward the fantastic, even if its tone leans toward passionate attachment to (not skepticism of) the Crescent City. Describing New Orleans as at "the bottom" of the continent and its riverways, but also "at the center of the American unconscious," it offers "immortal well-springs" of popular culture and "hard ground of disputed memory."[31] That is to say that the politics of the city are its environment, and its environment political. Considering that aesthetic (and the book's lavish production), it is curious that the maps within it are so hyper-realist, wedded to the same immediately identifiable templates used by Sutter and the wags at Judgmental Maps. They offer maps with names like "Ebb and Flow," "Sites of Contemplation and Delight," and "Snakes and Ladders" (wherein ladders are acts of Katrina heroism, and snakes are acts of destruction, often at the hands of the police). But the waterline is exactly where you would expect to find it, were you to imagine New Orleans as fixed in place, rather than harried by the River, the Gulf, and Pontchartrain.[32] Only one of its twenty-two maps offers the representational surreal necessary to represent the "specifically cartographic problem [. . .] of stuff that is neither solid nor liquid": images in the chapter "Oil and Water: Extracting Petroleum, Exterminating Nature" show the city beset by seabirds, casting shadows over the city and the state.[33] But there, below their vulnerable, oil-slicked wingspan is the Boot, a familiar shape that appears on every Louisiana highway sign. If you have ever had the dubious pleasure of sitting in a Louisiana courtroom or visiting one of its infamous prisons, you may also notice that the Boot provides an insouciant belt buckle for swaggering prison wardens and guards.

The marketing of the Boot is relentless. But for fourteen years, the state of Louisiana has failed to produce an updated paper map of its own borders, so the shape is merely memory of what has been lost since the last survey. As Solnit and Snedeker argue, a paper map enables you to "take charge," while digital mapping requires you "take orders."[34] To this I would add and affirm the paradox that this essay struggles with: the most flexible technology is, in fact, as unlikely to get an update as its analog parent. In early 2014, Brett Anderson began his remapping of Louisiana by searching for a paper map, documents once produced by the United States Geological Survey and the Louisiana Department of Transportation and Development. The former no longer produces paper maps, allowing analog navigators to print from their website instead. The latter prints in response to demand; in 2014, the organization still possessed a stockpile from 2000, so no demand existed or seemed to. This condition leaves Louisiana in a permanent stasis, where the paper map retains authority, while the ubiquity of the digital map delays its revision and reproduction. Travelers and residents alike depend on Google Maps, a resource "programmed to spit out the granular information we need to get from point A to point B."[35] That information does not, incidentally, consider the environmental effects of the driving it encourages and enables; its tendency to route drivers onto secondary roads to avoid delays has proven that their "perfect selfishness" leads to "deterioration of driving conditions."[36] Friction-free capitalism: move fast and break things.

With mappers and fishers, Brett Anderson went in search of the state's shape, and found a body butchered and bleeding: "on our map, the real map, the boot appears as if it came out on the wrong side of a battle with a lawnmower's blades. It loses a painful chunk off its heel in Cameron and Vermilion parishes. A gash cutting off the bird's-foot delta [. . .] from the center of the state is reason to consider amputation."[37] What startles me in this image is not the desiccated bird's foot displacing the Boot, but the tenuousness of its attachment to the rest of the national body. Louisiana, an ambivalent and belated entry to the settler-colonializing United States, sits precariously at the edge of a nation that once annexed it and is now determined to quarantine its coming climate catastrophe. Ideologically diffuse and motile, Louisiana's body is its objective correlative. Neoliberalism contracts state power, forcing those of us who live in space—which is to say, all of us—into such derealization that we cannot visualize the ground on which we are standing, or locate it through official channels. We rely, instead, on digital resources on the privatized internet. In resistance, Brett Anderson has made his revision of the Boot available for distribution. (See Fig. 7.2.) Long ago, another environmentalist, the poet Gary Snyder, said that his work "may be reproduced free forever."[38] But how long will forever last?

Below New Orleans, the land evaporates even on the inaccurate, obsolete Google Maps iteration of the state. Press a wet sponge and let the water burst from the pores, or sew tissue together and watch the needle "shred [. . .] and rip with every stitch."[39] Manhattan is a fist, and San Francisco is a heart, but New Orleans, as Solnit and Snedeker argue, is the fragile liver that swallows the poison the rest of the nation consumes. These images—the sponge of the sea, the sponginess of the body—will give one a firmer visual sense of Louisiana than any obsolete map or fixed navigational instruction can. "All the texture you've got going on in here? It looks rad, I'll give you that," writes Sutter. "But killing yourself like this in a map turnover is pointless, because no cartographer is going to bother recreating every little puddle."[40] The language used by Solnit and Snedeker, Anderson, and Sutter four years apart, and in

Fig. 7.2. The Revised Boot. Image in Brett Anderson,
"Louisiana Loses Its Boot," September 8, 2014.

dramatically different idioms, has a curious symmetry. Louisiana bleeds out in a surgical bay, its liver dissolving in a doctor's hands. Louisiana runs over its foot with a lawnmower. Louisiana kills itself. In the face of its self-injury, entirely too few people in power will map what has been lost, plan for the losses to come, or put the blame where it is due when catastrophe arrives on routes accelerated by and for industry.

Down in Terrebonne Parish, Anderson and his traveling companions see a watercolor by Brooks Frederick called "No Means No"; in it, a male-bodied figure who looks as though he has been plucked from a Kara Walker silhouette fucks Lake Pontchartrain.[41] (See Fig. 7.3.)

Louisiana appears as a representatively vulnerable and feminized body ripe for exploitation. So much is excused in New Orleans with regard to its decadence, its decay, and its status as a company town for Marriott and British Petroleum. Its decadence lures people here; its wild hurricane parties don't even leave the storm off the guest list. Often framed as an antonym for progress, decadence is a word that dogs New Orleans, but the word "fits squarely within the all-too-visible operations of so-called progress in the modern world, with all its excesses of production and consumption, extraction and exploita-

Fig. 7.3. Drill me deep and never leave. "No Means No," watercolor, courtesy of Brooks Frederick. Image featured in Brett Anderson, "Louisiana Loses Its Boot," September 8, 2014.

tion, waste and inevitable fallout in the pursuit of profit."[42] Suffice to say, it is not sex and license that hasten decay; a cash and carry economy kills. Mediated affective attachments to New Orleans remove friction from the path of petrochemical capitalism.

The mayor's office and municipal buildings where I vote and pay taxes (though paying *attention* is the far more essential qualification for living in New Orleans) sit on Perdido Street. After Katrina, there was a period of political tension about the presence and permanence of Latinx recovery workers; it was not uncommon to hear New Orleanians complain about the sound of Spanish conversation, as though the city were not itself part of the Spanish Caribbean. The contemporary mayor's office and city hall were built on a street with a Spanish name; it is scarcely the only one, though its name bears more symbolic weight than Salcedo, Lopez, Galvez, and Miro. *Perdido*, after all, means *lost*. Long ago, when I spent too much time on bar stools, I heard a potentially apocryphal story. According to my interlocutor, it was once the case that every neighborhood in New Orleans had a street called *Perdido*. Surveyors noted that people called the lowest-lying street in the neighborhood by that Spanish name because they could watch as it got lost under water when rain came. But in a functioning, modern city, it wasn't possible to have seventeen streets called Perdido: one for every ward. And so they were lost to regularized maps that militated against repetition. Power preserved Perdido Street for itself and, with it, the capacity to conceal our shape, our loss, and the ground we have ceded to the design of destruction. To borrow Sutter's phrasing: such are the "rules of a real-world city."[43]

NOTES

Dedicated to Tom Nehrbass.

1. This essay was written with research support from the Department of English and the Sarah Isom Center for Women and Gender Studies at the University of Mississippi, as well as intellectual support from Robert Tally (scholar of space) and Michele White (scholar of new media), who augmented my limited, exploratory claims about the spaces in which I live. This essay is therefore a collaboration between the familiar space of my city and the unfamiliar disciplines with which it engages. For driving and navigating, I offer thanks to Chip and to Tom.

2. Though Judgmental Maps is searchable by city, local maps do not generate unique web addresses for reference. Interested parties can look for New Orleans, Big Sur, Brooklyn, Atlanta, New Jersey, Milwaukee, Minneapolis, Mississippi, and Memphis.

3. Van Huygen, "How Nine New Orleans Neighborhoods Got Their Names." Among the curious spectacles of post-Katrina life in New Orleans is the persistent advocacy from left and right alike for the preservation of "traditional" lifeways, as though the age of name or durability of a practice is an argument for its maintenance, and as though there is one authentic habitation for one's subject position. Shannon Powell, New Orleans drummer and neighborhood fixture, reminded *Mental Floss* in 2017 that "Treme" is a name that is at once historical and bracingly new, winking at long-dead planter Claude Treme (1759–1828), who gave his surname to the blocks around Place des Nègres, or Congo Square. Before gentrification of the neighborhood, that name was not widely used—or even offered in its French pronunciation—by its longtime residents.

4. Eckstein, *Sustaining New Orleans,* 9.

5. Chun, *Updating to Remain the Same.*

6. Lee and Brand, "Claiborne Avenue." Committed to "equity, integrity, and collaboration," Paper Monuments produces ephemeral paper installations for display in New Orleans public spaces, from street corners to the lobby of the Public Library. Past projects are viewable on their website; they continue to take proposals for new ones. In this endnote, I link to the Paper Monument for Claiborne Avenue, the thoroughfare for African American cultural production that was eroded but not destroyed by the construction of the I-10 Corridor through Treme in 1968.

7. Ulrik Andersen and Pold, *The Metainterface,* 98. Digital media theorists Christian Ulrik Andersen and Soren Bro Pold argue that the jargon around smartphones establishes

a tension between "personal" and "private," words that have long been treated as virtually synonymous. Hence, users treat their phones as extensions of their bodies, but handle them with every expectation of state surveillance.

8. Brown, Baldridge, Esteva, and Zu, "The Substantial Words Are in the Ground and Sea," 326.

9. Burrito Justice, "Judgmental Map of San Francisco in the 1860s."

10. For information on the Shadow App and the chaotic caucus, see Schneider, "What We Know about the App That Delayed Iowa's Caucus Results." For a critique of Barnes & Noble's "literary blackface," see De León, "Barnes & Noble, Criticized for Book Covers, Pulls Plug on Diverse Editions Project."

11. Andersen and Pold, *The Metainterface*, 81.

12. Ibid., 108–9.

13. Ibid., 105–7.

14. See Noble's *Algorithms of Oppression*.

15. For a brilliant eulogy on the "good internet," and consideration of its place in the canon of required reading for undergraduates, see Maciak, "The Good Internet Is History." Maciak borrows the term "the good internet"—a name for the years in which ambitious editors curated early work by writers from Jia Tolentino to Hanif Abdurraqib—from Gawker founder Nick Denton, whose website was maliciously targeted for closure by Paypal founder Peter Thiel. Despite Thiel's legitimate frustration with Gawker, which outed him as gay, his willingness to fund onerous lawsuits against the organization has measurably reduced outlets for investigative journalism on the internet.

16. Gates, *The Road Ahead*, 180.

17. Baum, *Nine Lives*, xiii.

18. Sutter, "Holy cow."

19. Baum, *Nine Lives*, x.

20. These adjectives reference scholarship and popular writing on New Orleans. The texts include Cowen and Seifter, *The Inevitable City*; Lewis, *New Orleans*; Powell, *The Accidental City*; and Solnit and Snedeker, *Unfathomable City*.

21. Kolbert, "Louisiana's Disappearing Coast."

22. Chun, *Updating to Remain the Same*, 63. I borrow this phrase, which Chun uses to describe the minimization and habituation of catastrophe on platforms like Twitter, to think about what might be gained by a more responsive, adaptable new media environment.

23. Sutter, "And then there's this thing."

24. Grunwald and Glasser, "The Slow Drowning of New Orleans."

25. Solnit and Snedeker, *Unfathomable City*, 2.

26. Tarantino, *Reservoir Dogs*.

27. Moore, "10 Years Post-Katrina."

28. Despite the long associations of southernness and premodernity, the slow states of the Deep South were the fast-moving capitals of capital in antebellum America. "Already vital to the American economy by the start of the 1830s," writes Joshua Rothman, "over the course of the decade cotton crops brought to market by southwestern growers swelled capital accumulation that accelerated national economic development, furthered the rising

position of the United States as a global power, and cemented cotton's place as the most significant commodity on earth." Rothman, *Flush Times and Fever Dreams*, 3.

29. Chun, *Updating to Remain the Same*, 12–13.

30. Baurick, "Is Louisiana Really Losing a Football Field of Land Per Hour?"

31. Solnit and Snedeker, *Unfathomable City*, frontispiece.

32. Ibid., 20, 38, 125.

33. Ibid., 3, 48–49.

34. Ibid., 4–5.

35. Anderson, "Louisiana Loses Its Boot."

36. Madrigal, "The Perfect Selfishness of Mapping Apps."

37. Anderson, "Louisiana Loses Its Boot."

38. Snyder, "Smokey the Bear Sutra."

39. Solnit and Snedeker, *Unfathomable City*, 2.

40. Sutter, "Okay, all the texture you've got going on in here?"

41. Anderson, "Louisiana Loses Its Boot."

42. Azzarello, *Three Hundred Years of Decadence*, 7.

43. Sutter, "Anyway."

BIBLIOGRAPHY

Andersen, Christian Ulrik, and Soren Bro Pold. *The Metainterface: The Art of Platforms, Cities, and Cloud*. Boston: MIT Press, 2018.

Anderson, Brett. "Louisiana Loses Its Boot." *Medium*, September 8, 2014. https://medium.com/matter/louisiana-loses-its-boot-b55b3bd52d1e.

Azzarello, Robert. *Three Hundred Years of Decadence: New Orleans Literature and the Transatlantic World*. Baton Rouge: Louisiana State University Press, 2019.

Baum, Dan. *Nine Lives: Death and Life in New Orleans*. New York: Spiegel & Grau, 2009.

Baurick, Tristan. "Is Louisiana Really Losing a Football Field of Land Per Hour?" *Times-Picayune*, May 12, 2017. https://www.nola.com/news/environment/article_3128024a-cc03-57a0-9b37-18f5eb519d4b.html.

Brown, Travis, Jason Baldridge, Maria Esteva, and Weija Zu. "The Substantial Words Are in the Ground and Sea: Computationally Linking Text and Geography." *Texas Studies in Literature and Language* 54, no. 3 (Fall 2012): 324–39.

Burrito Justice. "Judgmental Map of San Francisco in the 1860s." *Judgmental Maps: Your City, Judged*, May 22, 2014. https://judgmentalmaps.com/post/86519094280/sanfrancisco1860.

Chun, Wendy Hui Kyong. *Updating to Remain the Same: Habitual New Media*. Boston: MIT Press, 2016.

Cowen, Scott, and Betsy Seifter. *The Inevitable City: The Resurgence of New Orleans and the Future of Urban America*. New York: St. Martin's Press, 2014.

Eckstein, Barbara. *Sustaining New Orleans: Literature, Local Memory, and the Fate of a City*. New York: Routledge Books, 2005.

Gates, Bill. *The Road Ahead.* New York: Viking Press, 1995.

Grunwald, Michael, and Susan B. Glasser. "The Slow Drowning of New Orleans." *Washington Post,* October 9, 2005. https://www.washingtonpost.com/archive/politics/2005/10/09/the-slow-drowning-of-new-orleans/7519e88e-e67d-4a2d-91a4-0100f340de7c/.

Judgmental Maps. *Judgmental Maps: Your City, Judged.* Accessed March 1, 2020. https://judgmentalmaps.com.

Kolbert, Elizabeth. "Louisiana's Disappearing Coast," *New Yorker,* March, 25, 2019, https://www.newyorker.com/magazine/2019/04/01/louisianas-disappearing-coast.

Lee, Bryan C., and Anna Brand. "Claiborne Avenue." *Paper Monuments: Imagine New Monuments.* Accessed March 1, 2020. https://www.papermonuments.org/pmplc-024-claiborne-avenue.

De León, Concepción. "Barnes & Noble, Criticized for Book Covers, Pulls Plug on Diverse Editions Project." *New York Times,* February 6, 2020. https://www.nytimes.com/2020/02/05/books/barnes-and-noble-fifth-avenue.html.

Lewis, Peirce F. *New Orleans: The Making of an Urban Landscape.* Chicago: Center for American Places Book Series, 1976.

Maciak, Phillip. "The Good Internet Is History." *The Week,* November 6, 2019. https://theweek.com/articles/875251/good-internet-history.

Madrigal, Alexis C. "The Perfect Selfishness of Mapping Apps." *The Atlantic,* March 15, 2018. https://www.theatlantic.com/technology/archive/2018/03/mapping-apps-and-the-price-of-anarchy/555551/.

Moore, Amanda. "10 Years Post-Katrina—Where Have You Gone, Mr. Go?" *Restore the Mississippi River Delta: Delta Dispatches,* June 8, 2015. https://mississippiriverdelta.org/10-years-post-katrina-where-have-you-gone-mr-go/.

Noble, Safiya Umoja. *Algorithms of Oppression: How Search Engines Reinforce Racism.* New York: New York University Press, 2018.

Powell, Laurence N. *The Accidental City: Improvising New Orleans.* Cambridge, MA: Harvard University Press, 2013.

Rothman, Joshua. *Flush Times and Fever Dreams: A Story of Capitalism and Slavery in the Age of Jackson.* Athens: University of Georgia Press, 2014.

Schneider, Avie. "What We Know about the App That Delayed Iowa's Caucus Results." *National Public Radio,* February 4, 2020. https://www.npr.org/2020/02/04/802583844/.

Solnit, Rebecca, and Rebecca Snedeker. *Unfathomable City: A New Orleans Atlas.* Berkeley: University Press of California, 2013.

Snyder, Gary. "Smokey the Bear Sutra" (1969). *Sacred Texts.* Accessed March 1, 2020. https://www.sacred-texts.com/bud/bear.htm.

Sutter, James L. "And then there's this thing." Twitter, March 18, 2018, 10:05 P.M. https://twitter.com/jameslsutter/status/975553879520690176.

———. "Anyway, big props to the South for convincing me that New Orleans was a real place—you really had me going there for a while." Twitter, March 18, 2018, 10:26 P.M. https://twitter.com/jameslsutter/status/975559035255635968.

———. "Holy cow—if you like fantasy maps, spend some time looking at New Orleans." Twitter, March 8, 2018, 9:54 P.M. https://twitter.com/jameslsutter/status/975550946884268032.

———. "Okay, all the texture you've got going on in here?" Twitter, March 18, 2018, 10:21 P.M. https://twitter.com/jameslsutter/status/975557805607239680.

Tarantino, Quentin, dir. *Reservoir Dogs*. Performed by Tim Roth and Harvey Keitel. Film. Hollywood: Paramount Pictures, Miramax Films, 1992.

Van Huygen, Meg. "How Nine New Orleans Neighborhoods Got Their Names." *Mental Floss*, July 31, 2017. https://www.mentalfloss.com/article/502045/how-9-new-orleans-neighborhoods-got-their-names/.

III

IN FORMATION

Mediating Identity through Space and Place

STEPHANIE ROUNTREE

ON FEBRUARY 6, 2016, Beyoncé broke the internet.

Maybe that's hyperbole. But it is no exaggeration that in the wake of her "Formation" music video debut and next-day Super Bowl performance, Beyoncé's "Unapologetically Black" aesthetic dominated U.S. public media discourse.[1] Podcasters, Insta-influencers, Twitter trolls, news pundits, and even *Saturday Night Live* all had something to say about it.[2] Proclaiming Queen Bey's entrée into the #BlackLivesMatter iteration of centuries-old African American social justice discourse, the video's audiovisual iconography firmly asserted her community allegiance to a legacy of Black survival, resistance, and excellence.[3] Amid the media frenzy, much discussion revolved around precisely such images of celebratory Black life against systemic racism: Beyoncé splayed atop a white NOPD car sinking beneath the water on flooded streets (Hurricane Katrina); the artist adorned in black against a white-columned pre–Civil War plantation house with her middle fingers to the sky (enslavement); a young Black boy in a hoodie dancing before a line of white, heavily militarized police officers (Trayvon Martin and Michael Brown). While the lyrics and images celebrate Black life unmitigated by respectability imperatives, they simultaneously underscore systemic threat to those same lives under white supremacy. Among the responses to these themes, many championed her #BlackGirlMagic and advocacy for Black communities. Others, mostly white people, derided her video and Super Bowl performance as an "anti-police stunt" that "attack[ed] police officers."[4] Still others, especially New Orleanians and Katrina survivors, condemned her for appropriating and capitalizing their lived trauma.[5] The popular and scholarly debates around these and other points are robust, yet all arguments in this media storm seemed to be circling a point where three themes converged: Beyoncé's identity, her position within (or without) particular communities, and her power to wield her media empire to intervene in national identity discourse.[6]

As the sections "Nothing New Here" and "From Plantation to Platform" have already demonstrated, this third section confirms the impossibility of an utterly "new" media formation divorced from historical antecedents or capitalist environment. Building upon these realities, the following essays challenge us to consider not only how such histories and economies shape emergent media, but also how evolving technologies work to negotiate identity formations for the networks of users, creators, and communities that such media indeed *mediate*. In this light, Beyoncé's "Formation" video offers a useful object lesson. It demonstrates the mechanisms by which history and capitalist enterprise converge in a new media artifact to constitute place-based identity, doing so explicitly through an audio and aesthetic compilation of antecedent media.

The "Formation" video is both a singularly innovative artifact in Beyoncé's artistic archive and a multidimensional, multimedia pastiche. It opens with the image of a white computer monitor as filmed from a camera. The words "parental advisory explicit lyrics" type across the white background, and a moiré pattern—horizontal white lines produced by the misalignment of the monitor's light frequencies and the camera's lens—calls the viewer's attention to the fact that their relationship to the monitor is mediated by a camera. The scene cuts, and the voice of Messy Mya, a queer Black YouTube personality and rapper who was murdered in 2010, plays over the image of Beyoncé atop a flooded police car. His YouTube declaration is sampled as a question; "What happened at the New Wildins?"[7] Beyoncé sings about the "paparazzi," and a host of photographers armed with mid-twentieth-century flashbulb cameras crowd the frame. Scenes filmed in high definition contrast with those depicted in 1980s-era VHS aesthetic, complete with a "PLAY ▶" icon in the lower right corner and fuzzy horizontal lines indicating the deterioration of analog video-recorded tape. The coloration of the plantation house scenes frequently washes out to a bright red hue, evoking the retro look of film stock burning on a projector bulb. The voice of Big Freedia, New Orleans bounce music artist and reality television star, fills the musical interlude between verses: "I did not come to play with you hoes. Ha! I came to slay, bitch. I like cornbread and collard greens, bitch."[8] Black women in Victorian attire evoke Julie Dash's 1991 film *Daughters of the Dust* while seated in a parlor adorned in nineteenth-century photography. Beyoncé dances in a hall lined with old books and oil portraiture.[9] Church congregants sing and dance in worship.[10] A man brandishes a newspaper with Dr. Martin Luther King, Jr. on the front page. Even the closing frame of Beyoncé atop the NOPD car succumbing to the rising waters incorporates an audio clip from the 2008 Katrina documentary *Trouble the Water*. The disembodied voice of Kimberly Rivers Roberts exclaims—"Golly! Look at that water, boy. Whew, Lord!"—as the car slips beneath the surface. Neither the first nor the last words of this smash-hit video are Beyoncé's. At the end, Roberts's audio from her 2005 camcorder footage close out the video's sonic landscape, an aural account of her and her husband Scott's survival while they watched a shipping canal swallow their Ninth Ward home. Hardly subtle, these manifold antecedent media formations prompt conscious recognition of their presence and diversity. The video's form and content are self-aware, drawing the viewer's attention to the mediated nature of the message by rendering it visible through layers of antecedent media. We are through the "old/new" media looking glass.

In this convergence, the "Formation" video constructs a performance of Beyoncé's individual and communal identity.[11] The lyrics (penned by five contributing writers) assert the performer's heritage as a proud, Black "Texas Bama" who is descended from her "daddy Alabama" and "momma Louisiana."[12] The material and mediated histories that animate the video likewise animate Beyoncé's public identity while simultaneously articulating her identification with a community of Katrina survivors who suffered under the Bush administration's neglect.[13] Even as the hurricane and ensuing governmental negligence manifested a very real, material crisis locally for people in New Orleans and the Gulf Coast, the tremendous volume of poor, Black survivors evince the racist logic of broader national infrastructures. Kanye West most memorably encapsulated the national scope of Black grief in his famous declaration while co-hosting NBC's televised concert benefiting Katrina survivors: "George Bush doesn't care about black people."[14] While those who bore the material brunt of neoliberal neglect inhabited a discrete regional place, their suffering as proliferated spatially through mass media resonated in Black consciousness nationwide. As Regina N. Bradley puts it, "Katrina is not just a historical event. It is a springboard for re-rendering southern trauma and its association with blackness."[15] It makes sense, then, that Beyoncé and, perhaps more accurately, her creative team identified New Orleans as an ideal geocultural site for her artistic engagement with Black social justice discourse, especially given her personal history as the daughter of a Creole woman from Louisiana and as someone who grew up in Houston, Texas, the site of the largest population of the Katrina diaspora.[16] However, her use of the 2005 storm's imagery in 2016 to compose a profit-generating video is still a source of pain for many who suffered materially through the storm and its aftermath.[17] Does mere *identification with* the community authorize Beyoncé to perform cultural *belonging to* communities of Katrina survivors?

Alongside the video's manifestation of Beyoncé's individual identity, its national circulation across varying platforms facilitated viewers' social negotiations, as well. Take, for example, the cultural life of Beyoncé's lyric "I got hot sauce in my bag, swag." After "Formation" dropped, this line proliferated widely across popular media in memes, social media posts, and advertisements declaring one's beloved (and portable!) hot sauce brand. Emerging as it did in the beginning of the 2016 U.S. presidential election, the lyric presented an opportunity for then Democratic presidential candidate Hillary Clinton to claim "authenticity" while trying to appeal to Black voters. In an April 2016 interview with the New York City hip-hop radio show "The Breakfast Club," Clinton shared her penchant for carrying "hot sauce" with her at all times.[18] Nearly immediately, social media erupted in debate over whether Clinton's #HotSauceInMyBag #swag claim was genuine or pandering.[19] True, reports of Clinton stockpiling "100 hot sauces" during her time as First Lady in the White House confirmed that her love for the condiment began well before Queen Bey's hit single.[20] But, as *Atlantic* writer Vann R. Newkirk II explains, "Sometimes hot sauce isn't just hot sauce."[21] Clinton's choice to emphasize her hot sauce affinity was both true and simultaneously an attempt to position herself as an insider within a community of people who identified with Beyoncé's lyric. Given the "unapologetically Black" themes of "Formation," many Black Americans read Clinton's comment as pandering. In this light, we might consider challenges to Clinton's authenticity in conjunction with Beyoncé's use of Katrina imagery. To what extent does motivation for the media message (votes or profit) impact the authenticity of the claim? Motivations aside, are such mediated utterances enough to authorize *belonging* to particular communities?

The essays that follow do not answer such questions. Rather, they draw our attention to the inherent futility of inquiries into "authenticity" as a stable category and begin from a constructivist principle. As scholars across disciplinary boundaries have asserted—including Jean Baudrillard in media studies, Scott

Romine in southern studies, Michael Omi and Howard Winant in critical race studies, and Judith Butler in gender studies, among many others—the ontological construction of meaning, place, and identity is produced through dynamic social engagement and not in some imagined "original" or a priori moment before socialization.[22] The methodological approaches demonstrated by the following essays help reorient our critical inquiry into the "Formation" object lesson by shifting our focus toward three key characteristics of evolving forms of media engagement at the intersection of region and identity: the constructivist role of media in identity formation, the inherent materiality of mediation, and the production of region—and thus regional identity—through collective ways of feeling.

First, it bears repeating that the essays that follow recognize how mediated identity renders visible a "myth of authenticity," the mistaken belief that identity precedes social interaction. Instead, as scholars such as Lisa Nakamura assert, individual and community engagement with innovative forms of media have long constituted community and identity formations in a constructivist framework.[23] For example, in Austin Svedjan's essay, "Cultivating/Contesting Identities: The Intersection of New Media and Rural Southern Queerness," he demonstrates how LGBTQ+ people living in rural, southern localities come to self-actualize queer identity through engagement in online platforms against pervasive national systems of what he terms "antisouthern normativity"— the notion that to be queer, one must repudiate any identification with rural southern community. The case studies he cites reveal how participation in online media facilitate self-constitution for many southern queer individuals in ways that still enable identification with rural southernness. In light of Katie R. Horowitz's extension of Judith Butler's well-worn theory of performativity, such online engagement might be read as constitutive acts that manifest individual identity in dynamic overlapping social processes, rather than diminishing their significance as mere play-acting that masks one's "authentic" interiority.[24]

Second, the following essays emphasize the deeply material conditions of media as they both inform user access/experience and effect material outcomes of identity-based mediations. As Abigail De Kosnik and Keith P. Feldman articulate, "Online spaces cannot be regarded as separate or distinct from the spaces in which fleshly bodies meet and do harm to one another."[25] They emphasize media's inherent materiality in a moment when the rise of hate groups, wielding labels such as "alt-right," "neo-Confederate," "neo-Nazi," "neofascist," and "incel," engage online in ways that are informed by and productive of physical, identity-based violence—a truth that was made all too clear in the January 2021 insurrection against the U.S. Capitol, as white supremacist groups who organized online sought violently to undermine the results of a secure and democratic presidential election. Indeed, Svedjan's essay indicates how such dangerous material conditions often compel LGBTQ+ rural southerners to engage in queer community via "safer" spaces online. While the materiality of media clearly has the capacity to activate violence, Svedjan's work demonstrates how it can simultaneously function to assert survival and vitality against erasure.

Such material possibilities manifest even more clearly in Jean-Luc Pierite's essay "áriyasɛma of Bits and Atoms: A Tunica-Biloxi Revitalization Movement Powered by Digital Fabrication." Following a long history of "Injunuity" that, since time immemorial, has continually revitalized the traditional material culture of the Tunica-Biloxi Tribe of Louisiana by innovating emergent technologies, Pierite narrates a twenty-first-century initiative by áriyasɛma, those who serve as "keepers of the medicine and the ways" as they "traditionally incorporate technology/science and pharmacology with the spiritual just as the elder man and elder woman had done."[26] By establishing fabrication labs—technologically equipped sites of material production—members of the Tunica-Biloxi Tribe incorporate centuries-old manufacturing techniques with modern digital technology to preserve community and national sovereignty within and beyond their ancestral lands. Pierite's work highlights the material conditions that both proceed from and return to media engagement. While tradition and history deeply inform Tunica-Biloxi use of digital technologies, so too do those technologies contribute to revitalizing forms of nationhood at the intersection of "community, land, tradition, and Injunuity."[27] Pierite's work reminds us how engagement in ever-evolving forms of "new" media manifests very material outcomes for humans who engage (or are engaged by) such media.

Where both Pierite and Svedjan affirm deep personal and communal investment in southern geographies and cultures, both Leigh H. Edwards and Sam McCracken evince how region itself and, by extension, regional identity are constituted through engagement with "new" media. Their scholarship aligns with the research of scholars such as Nicholas Greenwood Onuf and Hsuan L. Hsu who view national and regional production as a complex, ongoing negotiation of discourses and narratives "in relation to larger-scale phenomena such as migrant flows, transportation networks, and international commerce."[28] The dynamism of region and regional identity production explored in Edwards's essay "Digital Souths in Interactive Music Videos: Dolly Parton, Johnny Cash, and Media Convergence" emerges through crowdsourced music videos, which create an opportunity for establishing community among participants. Participants' mediated, collaborative work implicates national and global spaces in southern sensibility, as international users co-construct Johnny Cash's "Ain't No Grave" (2010) online crowdsourced music video, and world travelers collaboratively create imagery for Dolly Parton's digital crowdsourced music video "The Summer Adventures of Travelin' Dolly" (2010) for the artist's song "Travelin' Thru" (2005). In both cases, shared affect for southern markers of place and identity circulates in nonsouthern, even non-U.S. spaces to reify stable categories of an imagined U.S. South.

More often than not, such mass-circulated ideals of imagined souths and southern identities undergird white nostalgia for a racially homogenous region that indeed never was. Svedjan, Pierite, and Edwards underscore this truth through the constructivist, material, and regional contours of technologically mediated forms of identity. In this same vein, Sam McCracken's essay explores how the contraction *y'all* signifies southernness on Twitter in ways that reveal very old histories of exploited Black labor, white appropriation, and the application of southern mythology as troublesome panacea. In "Y'all Use *Y'all* Unironically Now, 'but Y'all Aren't Ready to Have That Conversation': Race, Region, and Memetic Twang on Twitter" McCracken examines the "digital second life" of *y'all* in three meme genres: (1) *y'all consider this a date?*; (2) *y'all mind if I . . . ;* and (3) *. . . but y'all aren't ready to have that conversation.*[29] Tracing the appearance of all three of these memetic forms to their Black creators on Twitter and Vine, McCracken interprets digital use of *y'all* as Barthean inflection, arguing that it "naturalizes its own deployment in the moment it is deployed, simultaneously calling up its predigital associations and seemingly muting them."[30]

At stake in McCracken's intervention is nothing short of this collection's first and foremost premise: all media were once new media, and thus, claims to newness reveal as much about users' efforts to distinguish themselves ideologically from oldness as they do about teleological progression "past" established technologies. McCracken's essay reinforces this point as he demonstrates the way *y'all*'s deployment on Black Twitter conveys a Black user's Blackness. When predominantly white Twitter users redeploy these racially specific meme genres, they can function to maintain very old systems of racial appropriation and exploitation. McCracken asserts, "The memetic *y'all* brokers a kind of plausible deniability in this way: it registers as blaccent and the (white) southern accent at once, conferring upon those users who engage with it the means to distance themselves from any interpretation that might pose them as participating in digital blackface by another name."[31] This plausible deniability enables the formation of both/and identification for users outside of Black Twitter communities. Perhaps white users intend to singularly signify their southernness; such an intention *can* engage *y'all*'s racially diverse, predigital use. Nevertheless, a white user's intention and the "authenticity" of their southernness does not negate the fact that *this* memetic digital utterance signifies Blackness within a racially specific Twitter community. As such, intentionally or not, white users engage in a digital performance that falls within a centuries-old genealogy of blackface, one that indeed affects very old ideological systems: white pleasure, white privilege, white power. Whether the user is Black (or not) and southern (or not) simply cannot define the totality of this regional remediation. McCracken's essay asserts that we must attend to the processes and histories of such mediated communication if we are to account for the multiplicities of meaning that emerge and recur across the time and space of networked communities.

Hence, the essays of this final section of *Remediating Region* serve as a collective caution against the myth of authenticity as a measurement of ethical access to identification and belonging in mediated spaces—a reality that returns us, once again, to the "Formation" object lesson. Beyoncé's mother *is* from Louisiana. Clinton *does* enjoy hot sauce. Neither of these facts endows "authentic" belonging in and of itself. To assert as much fundamentally demeans the experiences, systemic injustices, and community formations that have defined life for Black Katrina survivors, as they are, undoubtedly, at the heart of the "Formation" discourse. Instead, this section engages its critical inquiries through constructivist, material, and regional identity formations of the media object, taking up the term *formation* through its dual denotation as both process and product of mediating technologies. In doing so, we affirm the agency of individuals and communities to self-determine against institutional violence, oppression, and erasure. These methods approach the complexities of identity remediation across deep histories and economies, accessing significations of those who have come before while anticipating future users not yet engaged. Above all, such an inquiry takes up the processes of mediating between, among, and beyond networks of creators and users as technologies of ceaselessly revolving, remediated structures of self, other, place, and community. In this way, the authors featured in this section and throughout *Remediating Region* compel us to think of how identity, region, and media are most productively understood *in formation*.

NOTES

1. Hobdy, "Stop Everything!"

2. "The Day Beyoncé Turned Black," *Saturday Night Live*; "BEYmergency: Formation," *The Read*.

3. See Aisha Durham's "Class Formation: Beyoncé in Music Video Production" (2017) for a nuanced analysis of the artist's career-long representational evolution as it "mirrors the development of hip-hop feminism" (197).

4. *TIME* Staff, "New York City Protest Planned."

5. See Lewis's "'Formation' Exploits New Orleans' Trauma."

6. See especially Aisha Durham, "Class Formation"; Kira Marie Pratt, "Why We Need to Get in 'Formation.'"

7. Messy Mya, "Booking the Hoes from New Wildin": In the original video, Messy Mya begins by declaring, "The subject I want to talk about today, hoes, is what happened at the New Wildins." The trimmed sound bite plays in the "Formation" video while Beyoncé crouches atop a sunken "New Orleans Police" car with a neighborhood of flooded homes—recalling the ubiquitous media images of the Ninth Ward after Hurricane Katrina. Played over this New Orleans imagery of post-Katrina devastation, the audio clip invites the audience to understand Messy Mya's original statement as a question: "What happened at the New Orleans?"

8. See Jennifer DeClue's "To Visualize the Queen Diva!" (2017) for an important critique of Beyoncé's choice to visually omit Big Freedia's gender-queer embodiment from the video.

9. See Jarvis C. McInnis's "Black Women's Geographies and the Afterlives of the Sugar Plantation" for a fuller analysis of how Beyoncé's video manifests a "politics of insurgency" in depicting "Black women [who] have reclaimed the plantation house for themselves" (762).

10. See Paul Fess's "Nineteenth-Century Sacred Harp Singing as New Media Practice" for a history of church singing as new media practice in the nineteenth century.

11. My use of "convergence" here evokes Henry Jenkins's definition in *Convergence Culture* (2006): "Convergence represents a shift in cultural logic, whereby consumers are encouraged to seek out new information and make connections between dispersed media content" (4).

12. While Beyoncé's parents are indeed from the states named, Beyoncé is only one of the five writers who crafted "Formation"—including Asheton Hogan, Aaquil Brown, Khalif Brown, and Michael L. Williams II. Also, see Mehera Bonner's "The Surprising Story be-

hind Beyoncé's 'Formation'" for more on coproducer Mike Will Made-It and rapper Swae Lee's collaboration on the song's hook, "ok ladies now let's get in formation."

13. See Giroux's *Stormy Weather* (2006).

14. Strachan, "The Definitive History of 'George Bush Doesn't Care about Black People.'"

15. Bradley, "Getting in Line."

16. Godoy, "Tracking the Katrina Diaspora."

17. Davis-McElligatt, "HANDS UP, DON'T SHOOT," 120.

18. Breakfast Club, "Hillary Clinton Interview."

19. Newkirk, "On Hillary Clinton's Pandering."

20. Associated Press, "Clinton Will Have the Salad."

21. Newkirk, "On Hillary Clinton's Pandering."

22. See Baudrillard, *Screened Out*; Romine, *The Real South*; Omi and Winant, *Racial Formation in the United States*; Butler, *Gender Trouble*.

23. See Nakamura, *Digitizing Race*.

24. See Horowitz, "The Trouble with 'Queerness.'"

25. De Kosnik and Feldman, "Introduction," 11.

26. See Pierite, "áriyasɛma of Bits and Atoms."

27. Ibid.

28. Hsu, "Literature and Regional Production," 37; See also Onuf, *Making Sense, Making Worlds*.

29. See McCracken, "Y'all Use *Y'all* Unironically Now, 'but Y'all Aren't Ready to Have That Conversation.'"

30. Ibid.

31. Ibid.

BIBLIOGRAPHY

Associated Press. "Clinton Will Have the Salad, Not the Fried Chicken, Thank You Very Much." *New York Post*, December 21, 2016, https://nypost.com/2015/12/21/clinton-will-have-the-salad-not-the-fried-chicken-thank-you-very-much/.

Baudrillard, Jean. *Screened Out*. Translated by Chris Turner. New York: Verso, 2002.

"BEYmergency: Formation," *The Read*, hosted by Kid Fury and Crissle, LoudSpeakers Network, February 9, 2016, *SoundCloud*, https://soundcloud.com/theread/beymergency-formation.

Beyoncé (@beyonce). 2016. "Download Formation on Tidal 🐝🐝🐝." Instagram photo, February 6, 2016. https://www.instagram.com/p/BBdXpbXvw57.

Beyoncé. "Formation." Written by Aaquil Brown, Asheton Hogan, Beyoncé, Khalif Brown, and Michael L. Williams II. Produced by Beyoncé and Mike Will Made-It. Debuted February 6, 2016. Posted December 9, 2016, YouTube video. https://www.youtube.com/watch?v=WDZJPJV__bQ.

Beyoncé. "Formation. (clean)." Posted as unlisted February 6, 2016, YouTube video. https://www.youtube.com/watch?v=7xwrbrgngUo.

Bonner, Mehera. "The Surprising Story behind Beyoncé's 'Formation.'" *Marie Claire,* July 6, 2016, https://www.marieclaire.com/celebrity/news/a21391/beyonce-formation-explained/.

Bradley, Regina N. "Getting in Line: Working through Beyonce's 'Formation.'" *Red Clay Scholar* (blog), *WordPress,* February 7, 2016. https://redclayscholarblog.wordpress.com/2016/02/07/getting-in-line-working-through-beyonces-formation/#more-5.

Breakfast Club Power 105.1 FM, "Hillary Clinton Interview at The Breakfast Club Power 105.1 (04/18/2016)." Aired April 18, 2016. Posted April 18, 2016, YouTube Video, https://www.youtube.com/watch?v=oRZd861Pogo.

Butler, Judith. *Gender Trouble: Feminism and the Subversion of Identity.* New York: Routledge, 1990.

Coscarelli, Joe. "Beyoncé Releases Surprise Single 'Formation' Ahead of Super Bowl Performance." *New York Times,* February 6, 2016. https://www.nytimes.com/2016/02/07/arts/music/beyonce-releases-surprise-single-formation-ahead-of-super-bowl-performance.html.

Davis-McElligatt, Joanna. "HANDS UP, DON'T SHOOT: Teaching Black Lives Matter in Louisiana." *south: a scholarly journal* 50, no. 2 (Spring 2018): 114–25. doi:10.2307/26610372.

"The Day Beyoncé Turned Black." Skit on *Saturday Night Live,* Season 41, episode 13. Aired February 13, 2016, on NBC. Posted February 14, 2016, YouTube video, 3:24. https://www.youtube.com/watch?v=ociMBfkDG1w.

DeClue, Jennifer. "To Visualize the Queen Diva! Toward Black Feminist Trans Inclusivity in Beyoncé's 'Formation.'" *TSQ: Transgender Studies Quarterly* 4, no. 2 (May 2017): 219-25.

De Kosnik, Andrea, and Keith P. Feldman. "Introduction: The Hashtags We've Been Forced to Remember." In *#identity: Hashtagging Race, Gender, Sexuality, and Nation,* 1–19. Ann Arbor: University of Michigan Press, 2019.

Durham, Aisha. "Class Formation: Beyoncé in Music Video Production." *Black Camera* 9, no. 1 (2017): 197–204.

Giroux, Henry A. *Stormy Weather: Katrina and the Politics of Disposability.* 2006. New York: Routledge, 2016.

Godoy, Maria. "Tracking the Katrina Diaspora: A Tricky Task." *NPR,* August 25, 2006, https://legacy.npr.org/news/specials/katrina/oneyearlater/diaspora/index.html.

Hobdy, Dominique. "Stop Everything! Beyonce Just Dropped the Most Unapologetically Black Video of the Year." *Essence,* February 6, 2016. https://www.essence.com/entertainment/stop-everything-beyonce-just-dropped-most-unapologetically-black-video-year/.

Horowitz, Katie R. "The Trouble with 'Queerness': Drag and the Making of Two Cultures." *Signs: Journal of Women in Culture and Society* 38, no. 2 (2013): 303–26.

Hsu, Hsuan L. "Literature and Regional Production." *American Literary History* 17, no. 1 (Spring 2005): 36–69.

Jenkins, Henry. *Convergence Culture: Where Old and New Media Collide.* New York: New York University Press, 2006.

Lewis, Shantrelle. "'Formation' Exploits New Orleans' Trauma." *Slate,* February 10, 2016. https://slate.com/human-interest/2016/02/beyonces-formation-exploits-new-orleans -trauma.html.

McInnis, Jarvis C. "Black Women's Geographies and the Afterlives of Slavery." *American Literary History* 31, no. 4 (Winter 2019): 741–74. https://muse.jhu.edu/article/745439.

Messy Mya, "Booking the Hoes from New Wildin." Posted August 20, 2010, YouTube video. https://www.youtube.com/watch?v=daKqgdcypTE.

Nakamura, Lisa. *Digitizing Race: Visual Cultures of the Internet.* Minneapolis: University of Minnesota Press, 2008.

Newkirk, Vann R., II. "On Hillary Clinton's Pandering." *Atlantic,* April 19, 2019. https://www .theatlantic.com/politics/archive/2016/04/hillary-clinton-pandering-radio/479004/.

Omi, Michael, and Howard Winant. *Racial Formation in the United States.* 3rd ed. New York: Routledge, 2014.

Onuf, Nicholas Greenwood. *Making Sense, Making Worlds: Constructivism in Social Theory and International Relations.* New International Relations. New York: Routledge, 2012.

Pratt, Kira Marie. "Why We Need to Get in 'Formation': The Rhetoric of Beyoncé." *Young Scholars in Writing: Undergraduate Research in Writing and Rhetoric* 14 (2017): 70–87. https://youngscholarsinwriting.org/index.php/ysiw/article/view/242.

Romine, Scott. *The Real South: Southern Narrative in the Age of Cultural Reproduction.* Baton Rouge: Louisiana State University Press, 2008.

Strachan, Maxwell. "The Definitive History of 'George Bush Doesn't Care about Black People.'" *HuffPost,* Posted August 28, 2015. Updated September 9, 2015. https://www.huff post.com/entry/kanye-west-george-bush-black-people_n_55d67c12e4b020c386de2f5e ?ncid=engmodushpmg00000006.

TIME Staff. "New York City Protest Planned against Beyoncé's Super Bowl Half Time Performance." *TIME,* February 6, 2016. https://time.com/4215030/.

DIGITAL SOUTHS IN
INTERACTIVE MUSIC VIDEOS

Dolly Parton, Johnny Cash, and Media Convergence

LEIGH H. EDWARDS

AS NEW MEDIA PRACTICES continue to alter the way audiences think of concepts like "region," the interactive digital music video form has particular potential to spark evolving fantasy projections of multiple "souths." The U.S. South is always already a fantasy projection, but as Scott Romine has argued, in a late capitalist context, narratives try to claim different versions of a so-called "authentic" South as a commodity; of course, no "real" singular South exists, only simulacra created through such narratives.[1] I have argued elsewhere that discourses about the U.S. South and authenticity take on particular force in some recent media genres that are articulating new versions of southern exceptionalism, such as on reality TV shows that focus on the South or on country music.[2] As part of a larger cultural trend, media in the digital era continually turn to concepts of what is real versus what is fake in order to try to use ideas of "authenticity" to anchor truth claims or to assuage fears about how any digital text can be faked.[3] In the context of these larger anxieties about the digital world, I argue that new media texts about the U.S. South can often be seen as taking part in a new iteration of southern exceptionalism, one in which the South becomes a shorthand for "authenticity" or truth in a way that is nostalgic not just for some fantasy projection of the South as somehow premodern and pastoral, but also for media that seems more trustworthy rather than faked.

In this essay, I contend that one relevant trend is interactive country music videos that can be seen as examples of southern "digital folk culture" defined as folk culture texts that are made via the interactions of a group, albeit collective work that is occurring online through the internet rather than in person.[4] Using textual analysis and media theory, I demonstrate this dynamic in two case study examples: the 2010 crowdsourced digital video for Dolly Parton's "Travelin' Thru" (2005) and the crowdsourced online music video for

Johnny Cash's "Ain't No Grave" (2010). This essay analyzes digital interactive music videos that demonstrate how some new media texts and practices are creating distinctive spaces for projecting versions of the U.S. South. These interactive videos are staged through fan-targeted websites that can function a bit like a smaller-scale version of an "imagined community," Benedict Anderson's term for how audiences use media to think of themselves as members of a larger group or entity.[5]

The digital interactive music video as a form involves networked cultural production that depends on media convergence, specifically combining old media and new media, since the old music video format is now staged on an interactive digital network that incorporates user-generated content. As such, these texts depend on what Pierre Lévy terms "collective intelligence," meaning pooled knowledge on digital networks.[6] They also depend on what Henry Jenkins celebrates as "participatory culture," meaning the active consumption of fans who will seek out media content across multiple platforms as they add value to a media text by sharing it on social networks or contributing content to it themselves.[7] I argue that fans who consume such new media can help shape online-imagined versions of a twenty-first-century U.S. South in important ways.

However, such online interactive videos raise complex ethical questions, since media companies are profiting from the free labor of fans who contribute content. In the case of these Dolly Parton and Johnny Cash videos, the user-generated content is integral to the finished product. Are such videos merely staging stereotypical versions of the South and exploiting consumers for marketing and profit, or do they offer meaningful intersubjective performative spaces for expressive fan culture? While critics like Jenkins have argued for potential co-creation models in networked cultural production in the context of media convergence, others have warned that the user-generated content trend exploits consumers and hijacks the internet's democratic promise of greater media access.[8]

In the case of these new media texts about the South, the videos' cultural politics depend on the sociohistorical contexts. While these videos do not constitute co-creation, they do have a substantial level of collaboration with users, thus they are examples of new media that can grant audiences greater access to media production and distribution. At the same time, that audience agency is limited because the media companies involved control the content, distribution, and profit, although the Cash video does include a provision that allows for some small degree of profit sharing. While limited, these particular videos are examples of those that can create a possible space for expressions of southern digital folk culture.

Through their engagement with ideas of the U.S. South in relation to the genre history of country music, both videos meditate on the imbrication of folk culture and mass media and speak to the ability of folk culture to adapt and survive in our digital era. In these texts, the South becomes, variously, a kitsch object, a historical archive, the staging ground for a participatory fan community, and a source for digital folk culture. In imagining new media Souths, these videos offer another take on the way U.S. popular culture reinforces rhetorics of southern exceptionalism, narratives that southern studies scholars continue to explicate and critique.[9]

To explain why I classify the Dolly Parton and Johnny Cash videos named here as "digital folk culture" and why it matters, let me provide a critical definition. "Digital folk culture" is a contested term, with scholars debating whether or not one could apply the concept of folk culture in a digital context, since some critics insist that the internet would not count as folk culture and would instead categorize it as mass culture defined in opposition to folk culture. Folk culture as a category was originally an industrial-era concept that was specifically posed in opposition to an emergent mass culture. However, the very definition of folk culture versus mass culture has long been called into question, with scholars pointing out that the folk culture versus mass culture distinction is an arbitrary one and that the two categories intersect with and inform each other. Folklorist Dan Ben-Amos provides a foundational early scholarly definition of folk culture that is frequently referenced. For him, folk culture means "artistic communication in small groups."[10] More recently, critics in folklore studies have sought to underscore the performative features of folk culture in the way that they define the concept. For example, scholar Kiri Miller dubs folk culture "a form of expressive culture transmitted through intersubjective performance."[11] In my own understanding of the category, I concur with scholars who aver that digital culture can be a carrier for folklore, meaning that the internet can be viewed as both a mass culture form and a storehouse for folk culture because what is happening on digital networks (ranging from YouTube videos fans share with each other to fan websites for musicians) does replicate the one-on-one personal interaction that characterizes folk culture, simply in a new, online environment.[12] In such a view, the concept of digital folk culture itself highlights the way folk culture and mass culture are intertwined as conceptual categories. Digital folk culture, in addition, further breaks down the very distinction between folk culture and mass media because it underscores how that distinction is based on subjective category differences in the first place.[13]

Dolly Parton, Digital Symbols, and the South as Kitsch

The Parton video "The Summer Adventures of Travelin' Dolly" (2010) is a crowdsourced web film that can be understood as a piece of digital folk culture, one that stages complex ideas of the South, country music, authenticity, and Dolly Parton's media image. The official Parton website at the time asked fans to print out a copy of a Parton cut-out image, an exaggerated drawing of her, from the website and take it with them to places that they traveled that summer and to document it by sending in video footage or photographs of this so-called "Travelin' Dolly" from around the world. Producers then collated that fan material into "The Summer Adventures" music video. This humorous gimmick, similar to the Travelocity garden gnome commercials or to a *Where's Waldo* conceit, had fans holding up a kitschy gingham-clad image of Parton, with her immediately recognizable stage persona, as they stand in front of backgrounds ranging from the Appalachian Trail to the Taj Mahal. Kitsch can be defined as excessively garish art that is knowingly tacky or in "bad taste" and can be consumed in an ironic way. Parton's image juxtaposed with these backgrounds symbolizes a kitschy version of the U.S. South that can circulate around the world and, at the same time, stage collective cultural histories of country music and Appalachian folk culture. Parton represents a symbol of the U.S. South because she is so strongly associated with the region through her well-known autobiographical tales of growing up in the Great Smoky Mountains and becoming an icon of country music, which is still symbolically associated with the U.S. South and southern rural folk cultures even though it has always circulated beyond that region.

To take a closer look at the music video itself, "The Summer Adventures" crowdsourced web film depended on networked cultural production and is part of Parton's extensive digital presence, which includes musical content, promotional material, tie-ins with her Dollywood theme park, and copious space for fan interaction online. The video is for her Oscar-nominated song "Travelin' Thru," which she wrote for the soundtrack to the film *Transamerica* (2005). The crowdsourced fan video was advertised and screened on what was her official website at that time.[14] While her country song plays, the images in the video are comprised of the fan submissions of the Travelin' Dolly from across the globe. The drawing itself is a caricature of her Daisy Mae country sexpot persona. In it, she is wearing a red gingham minidress that is low-cut and focuses on her cleavage, with a white fringe around the hem and sleeves. The very short dress, red high heels, long platinum blonde wig, and excessive makeup are all standard parts of her image. Seated with her legs crossed, she is pictured holding one of her signature retro microphones, but the caricature makes the microphone appear even more phallic.

One could classify the video as a crowdsourced web film or as a collective digital music video. The fan submissions include video images of Parton in front of different kinds of scenes, with symbolism that depends on her icon status, in settings related to her biography, to the pastoral, to kitsch, to Americana, and to humorous juxtapositions where her presence is incongruous. Again, because of her country star status and well-known biography, she functions as a symbol for country music and for the U.S. South, and as she pops up in different settings around the world, the video taken as a whole suggests that this symbolism is evident all over the globe. Some of the places she is pictured relate to her own autobiography, such as in front of the statue of her in her hometown of Sevierville, Tennessee. In that scene, the Travelin' Dolly cut-out is the kitschy, ironic companion to the more reverential statue of Parton meant to be a monument to her. Likewise, she is pictured in the Great Smoky Mountains National Park. Parton is an ambassador for that park, and she is often presented as a symbol of it. In the video, the Parton cut-out suddenly jumps out on the Appalachian Trail and the Blue Ridge Parkway, in keeping with that pastoral symbolism. Other pastoral footage pops up, with Parton pictured in front of mountains from around the world. Some images focus on a kitsch setting, such as the one of Parton posed in front of an oversized moonshine jug and sign, or where she appears in front of the Pez factory. Some other images of her emphasize a kitschy show-business context, as when a fan hoists the Travelin' Dolly cut-out up near the "Welcome to Fabulous Las Vegas" iconic sign, or when a fan waves the Parton cut-out image alongside Vegas showgirls in regalia. Other scenes include Americana references, as when she is put in front of the W. C. Handy "Father of the Blues" Museum, marked as a historic blues site in Florence, Alabama. Some scenes place her in settings where she incongruously jumps out, a joking juxtaposition, as when she appears in front of a NASA rocket, Weeki Watchee Springs in Florida, and her appearance with a Mooresville, North Carolina Little League team. Meanwhile, some pictures are from tourist locations in Australia, New Zealand, and England, which emphasize her global reach. The video ends with the graphic message "Thank you, Dollyites [. . .] for sharing a little piece of your world [. . .] with us!" The tag line is directed at her online fan-club members at that time, with a graphic quotation of lines from the song: "Oh sometimes the road is rugged, and it's hard to travel on / But holdin' on to each other, we don't have to walk alone," and it wishes them all good luck on their own travels.[15]

From these juxtaposed images, "The Summer Adventures" video thus takes the message of solidarity from the song, directed at transgender acceptance in the movie, and reframes it in terms of fan community in this context. The song's lyrics are about a weary traveler trying to find their way back home or to make their own way home. The fan video reframes that idea as one in which a fan community is united in their fandom, regardless of where they travel, just as their fan expression here indicates their degree of involvement in that community. In addition to this crowdsourced web film example, Parton's fan-hosted websites are also particularly numerous and extensive, evidencing a high degree of fan labor.

Country Music Contexts, Folk Culture, and Mass Culture

To contextualize the Parton image in the broader context of images of country music and images of the U.S. South, it is important to note the fact that it is a drawn caricature of her, because the picture is speaking to her iconic, almost mythical status, rather than presenting a realistic photographic image of her. As such, the cartoonish drawing is referencing her media image in a comedic way that focuses more on the exaggeration of Parton's media image and less on Parton the person; it also speaks to the connotations about southernness associated with that image. Both Parton and the U.S. South here are circulated as kitsch images removed from original contexts and reframed in new, sometimes incongruous contexts around the world. The humor of having Parton pop up in unexpected places depends on audiences visually recognizing that she is out of context: that is, while they would normally see her on a country stage or at Dollywood, they suddenly see her in front of the Eiffel Tower. When she circulates as a digital image, then, she brings her original context with her because fans would recognize her image from that original country music context. Her image references the U.S. South because country music is still symbolically associated with that region, even though its audiences have always been broader, and because Parton's costuming and star image also depend on southern references. Here, the Parton image becomes a shorthand for the U.S. South. When fans contribute their creative expression and content online, they are interacting with and sharing that imagery and generating digital folk culture around it.

My argument that this participatory fan culture could be seen as digital folk culture also must be contextualized in terms of country music's ongoing authenticity debates involving folk culture versus mass culture. The genre has long been fixated on what counts as purportedly true or genuine country music versus what is a "fake" or sell-out, manufactured version of country. As part of the stereotypical rhetoric of a genuine country music, the genre's origin stories keep insisting on a rural, folk culture basis for the music as opposed to a commercialized, fallen mass culture. As scholars have noted, one can find many examples of this tension between authentic and manufactured in rhetoric framing the genre.[16] That tension manifests itself, for example, in lyrics that express nostalgia for a supposedly "simpler time" and an earlier, rural, agricultural way of life. This supposedly genuine folk vision, again based on stereotypes, is set in opposition to a corrupting idea of mass culture and the conditions of modernity, meaning the conditions of social life after the rise of industrialization and capitalism. Ironically, country stars sing mass-produced songs that are mass commodities, yet the lyrics are often about the wistful nostalgia for some noncommercial, simpler life on the farm. That kind of contradictory dynamic, in which modern mass culture expresses nostalgia for previous folk culture that it has commodified or marginalized, is part of a larger trend evident in mass culture more generally.[17]

It is important to note, of course, that country music's authenticity versus the market binary is an inaccurate fantasy belied by historical facts because country music always had commercial elements, from the beginning of its mass distribution in the 1920s as well as in its precursors in folk and old-time music in earlier epochs.[18] Likewise, in terms of U.S. culture more generally, the notion of a stark line between mass market products versus folk culture is a falsehood; in folk music, the popular or commercial was always mixed with the folk, and other folk practices did not see a tension between authenticity and the market. That tension was imposed on folk music in the early twentieth century by academics and song collectors who began trying to catalogue folk music.[19] In terms of the folk culture imagery that country music is popularly associated with, country music has also been symbolically associated with a rural, white, southern, working-class culture, even though, again, the genre's origins and audiences have always been broader than that.[20] The country music authenticity rhetoric is also gendered, with supposedly authentic "hard country" framed as masculinized versus purportedly "sell-out" country-pop framed as feminized.[21] The problematic valence of these symbols of folk authenticity along the lines of race and gender becomes even more evident given the ongoing struggle for Black country artists, LGBTQ+ artists, and women artists to have access to country radio.[22]

In my book on Parton, *Dolly Parton, Gender, and Country Music* (2018), I make a longer argument about how Dolly Parton's oeuvre and media image intervene in country music's authenticity debates, suggesting that she makes a gender critique of country music's authenticity rhetoric and rewrites it using feminist and gay camp. Allow me briefly to summarize that argument here, so that I can build on it in my discussion of this different media trend of digital interactive country music videos. I argue that Parton claims both sides of that binary, both folk culture and mass culture, the vernacular roots of country music and the highly commercialized mass culture version of it; her work is both folk and mass, real and fake, and it questions the distinctions between those categories.[23] She incorporates features of old-time Appalachian ballads in her songwriting, and her work is often described as folk-inflected in what she dubs her "blue mountain" music (a term she uses to refer to her mixture of Appalachian folk and traditional music as well as bluegrass). At the same time, her pioneering, highly commercially successful work in country pop secured her wider fame in a crossover genre associated with mass culture.

My larger argument in the book about her entire oeuvre is that Parton's media image also combines the folk and the mass because she uses two specific gender tropes from country music history: the innocent mountain girl and the scandalous "backwoods Barbie" tramp. She incorporates her autobiography into her media image—her story of growing up in the Smoky Mountains in East Tennessee and then succeeding in a male-dominated country music industry—and she talks about mixing the "real" and the "fake," her true sincerity and her artificial, exaggerated media image. Parton mashes up the "pure" image and the "fallen" one. In one famous quotation, she jokingly describes her inspiration: "I kinda patterned my look after Cinderella and Mother Goose—and the local hooker."[24] She critiques gender stereotypes by merging her image of the "pure" mountain girl with what she calls her "poor white trash hillbilly hooker," showing them both to be limiting stereotypes, a version of the long-running virgin-whore dichotomy in Western culture. Her mountain girl image critiques how the Appalachian girl has been idealized and has created a limiting stereotype of the white working class in country music history. Likewise, her tramp image criticizes how the "hillbilly" has been framed as the "low Other" in country music history, another limiting, negative, working-class stereotype. Her exaggerated, campy parody of the tramp creates ironic distance from that stereotype; elsewhere, I detail how she makes use of camp as a style and performance mode of over-the-top theatrical artifice that grew out of twentieth-century gay subculture.[25]

Parton's gender image of the pure versus fallen woman ties into country music's authenticity rhetoric about pure versus fallen popular music because those genre tensions are also gendered. Again, country music authenticity narratives draw on harmful gender stereotypes because they define authentic "hard country" music as masculinized and linked to idealized folk culture roots, versus "soft" country-pop that is feminized and corrupted by mass culture.[26] That idea of mass culture as corrupting and feminizing is part of a more general negative stereotype evident in U.S. cultural history, one that frames mass culture as a feminizing, "fallen," corrupting, commercialized force in U.S. culture.[27]

For this case study here, those two Parton gender tropes are evident in "The Summer Adventures" video because the cut-out picture of her emphasizes her use of the "tramp" stereotype: the picture is highly sexualized and even more exaggerated than usual, with Parton holding the phallic microphone and wearing her standard "tramp" image, involving, again, a big blonde wig, elaborate makeup, five-inch heels, long fake nails, and a custom-made campy outfit. At the same time, the imagery also invokes her mountain girl trope, because she is dressed in the red gingham and her lyrics include references to her autobiography, with the music referencing her Appalachian childhood and the folk "blue mountain" roots of her music.

The song itself strongly critiques gender stereotypes and supports LGBTQ+ rights. In this pro-transgender song, Parton sings from the point of view of the film's transgender protagonist. In her songwriting here, Parton nods to her mountain girl authenticity trope because she references "I am a Pilgrim" and the folk ballad "The Wayfaring Stranger" in her lyrics. For instance, she deploys a folk ballad style for a stanza in which she sings the lines "Like the poor wayfaring stranger that they speak about in song / I'm just a weary pilgrim trying to find what feels like home." She emphasizes her music's links to a folk tradition. This line about trying to find "what feels like home" is in an earlier stanza, while a later stanza in the song revises the line to read trying to find "my own way home." The earlier line suggests a theme of making a new sense of home based on a feeling, perhaps not in the original home space, while the latter returns the speaker to an original imagined home, albeit by a different path. Since Parton is rewriting well-known folk ballads there, her lyrics suggest a metacommentary on reworking folk culture to fit new contexts, whether through emotional realism or metaphorically different paths to the same folk destination.

Another, regular music video for the song (as opposed to the crowd-sourced video with fan content) intercuts images of Parton singing in the studio with footage of the film's transgender character, merging her own authenticity narratives with advocacy for transgender rights as acceptance for people "as they are," in her rhetoric. In an IFC behind-the-scenes documentary about the making of that official music video, Parton describes writing the song after watching a rough cut of the film, and she emphasizes the emotional realism of the song and her empathy with the film's main character. In an interview, she says that she was drawn to do music for the film because she saw it as having a "very sensitive subject" and being a "wonderful idea for a movie," and that she thought anyone could relate to the emotions of the film's protagonist, who is "feeling trapped, wanting to be known for who you are."[28] Director Duncan Tucker talks about how it was important to him to have folk music on the soundtrack, and that he specifically wanted Parton because he views her as an "icon of family values and self invention, and a life force."[29] He asked her for a song about traveling and redemption that could be effective in different contexts, saying he wanted a song "that could be sung in dance halls and churches." Lead actor Felicity Huffman talked about how Parton's iconic status could help gain support for their film. Parton joked behind the scenes about more analogies with her own life, exclaiming: "I'm road weary, telling all my secrets."[30] She draws analogies between the film and her struggles for acceptance and other challenges audiences could face. Their rhetoric about the film and the context for it emphasizes how Parton functions as a symbol for sincerity and acceptance, and also how she navigates her own media image as a process of self-invention. These narratives also emphasize a connection between Parton and the southern folk culture roots of country music, and specifically for Parton as a symbol of that folk culture link to the U.S. South.

Taken together, the song and official music video, alongside the crowd-sourced fan music video, all speak to how the interactive digital video itself functions in the context of folk culture as well as mass culture. Since it incorporates fan contributions, the fan music video also exhibits digital folk culture. More specifically, it links to Parton's long-running iconography where she mixes her gender tropes of the "tramp" and the mountain girl. It connects with that Parton imagery while also turning her into a symbol of southern culture, specifically Appalachian culture. This version of the South—as a literal cut-out symbol that fans can tuck in their pocket and travel around the world with—is one of projected nostalgia as well as campy humor, the sincerity and imagined country music notions of "authenticity," as well the more complex reality of its mass culture production. The video's version of the South, like Parton's own image, is manufactured authenticity, mixing an imagined version of the folk with the mass.

Johnny Cash and Digital Fandoms

Because both the Parton and Cash fan videos are interactive and circulate globally, they let fans around the world feel a connection to a digital folk culture version of the South. The high level of fan response to the interactive Cash video illustrates that idea, with different fans talking about what it means to them to have been involved in that video. In a video that filmmaker Chris Milk did about the making of the Cash music video, he notes that over a quarter of a million fans from 172 countries participated within the first year of the website's launch (2010).[31] His "behind the scenes video" depicts fans discussing why they participated and what Cash meant to them, often talking about how his body of work affected them emotionally or even spiritually, and that they felt that a collective online fan art project was one meaningful way to connect with a larger community and to express their fandom.[32]

The fans' affective investment in Cash in the response video is evident, but it is an interactive digital, mediated version of Cash that they are responding to here: it is a digital crowdsourced Cash. The Cash web film is also a transmedia narrative because it takes imagery and narratives told on other media platforms and extends the storytelling into to an online interactive environment in a coordinated way. The Cash video website invites fans to draw on frames from documentaries and then director Chris Milk combines those frames into an animated video.[33] Some users create quite elaborate artwork. The video's content also depicts a musician and genre associated with southern folk culture in a digital context. In the historical footage, drawn from documentaries, Cash journeys home to his childhood Arkansas cotton farm, then to the Virginia grave of A. P. Carter, the uncle of his wife June Carter Cash and patriarch of the Carter Family, who helped usher in commercial folk or "hillbilly" music in the 1920s, based on recordings of earlier folk songs. As the Cash video uses an interactive digital format and fan participation to explore this historical journey, it meditates on the southern folk roots of country music as an art form that combines folk culture and mass culture. Here the video turns the folk culture roots of country music into a theme. The form of the video itself, much like the Parton one, as a crowdsourced interactive web film, means that the video takes on the resonance of folk culture because it is created through a collective interaction, even though that interaction happens online, as a piece of digital folk culture.

On the website itself, Milk frames the video as a "unique communal work" that serves as the official music video for Cash's cover of the song "Ain't No Grave." Milk writes there: "Through this interactive website, participants may draw their own portrait of Johnny Cash to be integrated into a collective whole. As people all over the world contribute, the project will continue to evolve and grow, one frame at a time."[34] He goes on to describe how each fan's interaction with the website will be included in different versions of the final product: "Submit your drawing to become a part of the new music video for the song 'Ain't No Grave.' Strung together and relayed in sequence your art, paired with Johnny's haunting song, will become a living, moving, and ever changing [sic] portrait of the legendary Man in Black."[35] I have argued elsewhere that Milk uses the language of community in a problematic way that, on some level, tries to hold up the South as an idealized commodity, a nostalgic version of "authenticity."[36] The video nevertheless does give users at least some limited agency because it lets them have access to copyrighted material and lets them retain the ability to sell and circulate their own frames to which they add their own artwork.

For the purposes of this case study of a trend in interactive digital country music videos, my key point is that the video allows fans to engage in collective online activity that involves creating and circulating versions of southern digital folk cultures. In critic Ioana Literat's formulation of different levels of interactivity in digital music videos, the Cash video would not constitute actual co-creation, but it would land somewhat high on her scale of interactivity because users are free to draw what they like, even though they do not control what the larger finished product is.[37] For the Parton video, the users might have a bit less interactivity and access. While they can decorate the Parton cut-out image, their creativity is in how they juxtapose that image in different locations, and they do not control how producers integrate their images or videos into the final product. Importantly, in the case of the Parton video, they are not given express permission to profit off of those images if they so desire.

Meanwhile, for the Cash video, not only can the fans profit from their artwork, but also the hundreds of different versions of the Cash video do showcase fan creativity. A famous image of Cash striding down the train tracks into the setting sun, his guitar slung over his back like some kind of outlaw superhero, originally comes from a Cash documentary about trains, *Ridin' the Rails*. In the fan video, it takes on many different connotations and levels, with many religious or familial messages. Some fans write "RIP Johnny," or "See you in heaven," while others include personal messages about family members who have passed away or who were Johnny Cash fans. One user drew an image of Jesus looking over Cash; another scribbled crosses. Meanwhile, for a later image in the video of Cash walking beside sheep, someone else wrote a personal message, "The Shepherd: God bless you for finding me this morning," and they wrote "Black sheep" next to one of the sheep, with Cash dressed in black and a halo drawn around his head. One fan drew an image of June Carter Cash in the sky, staring down at Johnny Cash as if from heaven. Other fans take their imagery in a more pop direction or add humor to it, with the barreling train becoming Darth Vader's mask from *Star Wars,* or a supine Johnny Cash with a cigarette is suddenly joined by a dinosaur. Some are poignant and add different layers of cultural references from other cultural traditions, as in one frame where his face becomes a Mexican Day of the Dead skull.

The context for the song itself mixes folk culture, mass culture, and a certain image of the South and country music. Released on the posthumous album *American VI: Ain't No Grave* (2010), the song was produced by Rick Rubin as part of the producer's reframing of Cash in an Americana roots music context beginning in the 1990s, which was necessarily a marketing of Cash as a symbol for an imagined version of southern folk culture in a mass culture context. The "Ain't No Grave" song itself was the last studio recording Cash made before his passing in 2003, and it is his cover of a song Pentecostal Holiness preacher Claude Ely wrote in 1934 about a Christian judgment day resurrection, where the speaker will "rise right out of the ground" when Gabriel blows his horn. The video shows documentary footage of Cash walking down train tracks near a herd of American bison or walking by the Sea of Galilee. It includes footage of him returning to see his abandoned childhood home in Dyess, Arkansas, what was a cotton farm on a Depression-era federal farm colony. It also pictures him going to visit the A. P. Carter grave in Hiltons, Virginia, and lying on it while smoking a cigarette and swigging alcohol from a bottle. The final images have him walking down the train tracks toward the horizon, as if on an endless spiritual quest. Milk pulled the images of Cash from archival footage as well as from the documentary Cash starred in about train history (*Ridin' the Rails: The Great American Train Story* [1974]), a religious film Cash scripted and appeared in about Jesus's life (*The Gospel Road* [1973]), and a documentary about his touring in the late 1960s and his trip to visit his childhood home (*Johnny Cash: The Man, His World, His Music* [1969]).

Cash routinely mixed both folk culture and mass culture in his work, in which he would imagine the folk culture roots of country music in A. P. Carter's song collecting or in Cash's search for old cowboy songs, even as he noted their mass culture afterlife in his recorded mass culture music or in Hollywood cowboy films.[38] For example, on his Western concept album, *Johnny Cash Sings the Ballads of the True West* (1965), Cash argues that modern audiences should listen to Old West ballads on their modern radios, and they will still hear the "true west" coming through that mass mediation. On "Reflections" on that album, a spoken word recording, Cash says: "We aren't sorry for the modern sounds and modern arrangements on classics like 'I Ride an Old Paint' or 'The Streets of Laredo'; after all, they were meant to be heard on twentieth-century record players and transistor radios! For today that same West wind is blowing, although buckboards and saddles are lying out there turning to dust or crumbling from dry rot." The image he paints is of country music as a genre that mixes both mass culture and folk culture, here in reference to fantasies of the Old West. In the case of the fan-crowdsourced Cash music video, and equally for country music more generally, the imagined landscape is also most centrally the South, of course. In this web film of Cash's, audiences can project their own imagined version of the South, or indeed, what they think Cash's version of it is, as somehow an "authentic" picture of it that they can consume and interact with via mass media and that they can circulate as a symbol for southern authenticity in a global context.

For this video, the historical footage of Cash combines with the fan expression literally drawn onto those frames, yielding a composite digital text, comprised of the historical artist and the layers of fan responses, turning Cash into a crowdsourced mythological figure. Here too, Cash as symbol of country music is turned into a larger symbol of the South that fans around the world can comment on and turn into their own imagined version. When the images are collated together by Milk, they become this composite, constantly changing group of symbols, as the video plays through different compilations of images each time, and fans can even vote for which specific fan artwork frames play at which times.

In Milk's behind-the-scenes video in which fans discuss their artwork, they describe their contributions to the music video in a way that illustrates how they relate to Johnny Cash and his music and experiences, and how they imagine their fandom as a global community. Many comment on how his experiences as a country music star from the U.S. South were different from theirs in other parts of the world, but they feel like they are a part of a fan community dedicated to him. The specific work the fans did to contribute to the video also makes them feel like an active part of this fandom community in a way reminiscent of a digital folk culture version of an imagined community. The talking head, behind-the-scenes video is comprised of video and audio footage that fans submitted discussing their experience of contributing to the music video. Each fan is identified by the frame number that they drew and by where they are from, not by their name. One fan from California describes how he watched many different iterations of the video and saw it as an "organic," living thing that kept changing as more people contributed to it. Many of the fans reference the fact that one can watch videos of the drawing session for other fan art (the audience can see the brushstrokes as they were drawn into the custom drawing tool that runs on Google Chrome here), and one woman says the drawing tools let the viewer "focus on what [they] wanted to say."

A number of comments focus on an emotional connection to the musician, as well as on a growing sense of emotional connection to a global fan community, as enacted by this website. One thoughtful man from Edinburgh explains his motivation for participating in the Cash project, and his comments capture his affective investment in Cash: "I felt really sad when he died, and I just thought it would be wonderful, it would be really nice to contribute something to his memory." Likewise, a woman from San Francisco explains, "It really allows this last recording of his to be a living, breathing memorial. I am honored to have inadvertently made a contribution to something so magical." A male punk rocker from California explains, "For all of the frames to be drawn by fans, each individual frame, it's got a very powerful feeling to it." A man from Tennessee, his hair styled in a rockabilly pompadour tribute look, details his sense of how fans are working together from all over the world: "It's just amazing to see so many Cash fans collaborate on some of his final work. The artists that contributed, I mean, I've seen everybody from Japan, to Venezuela, to the states, to Knoxville, Tennessee." Bridging this sense of the global and the local, a man from Croatia says: "As much as it's different from frame to frame, it really is personal." His remark speaks to the affective investment fans can have in their own user-generated content.

The fan comments here emphasize the emotional realism, not just of Cash but also of their fan expression. Scholar Annette Hill has argued that in reality television, fans look for moments of believable selfhood or genuine depictions of feelings to which they can relate, as something viewers can believe in, even when they know many of those images can be faked or loosely staged.[39] Viewers seek what Stuart Hall and Paddy Whannel call "emotional realism" in popular music, in which they argue that while popular music is a manufactured mass commodity, it nevertheless combines elements of so-called authentic cultural expression, particularly in these moments of emotional realism.[40] I argue that media about the South can often emphasize those moments of sincere emotional realism as a way to ground truth claims, with the South becoming a marker for sincerity.[41] That dynamic is evident here in the new media fan culture for that Cash video. Along those lines, in the behind-the-scenes video, a young woman from Glasgow observes: "I didn't know that I could connect to someone with such a different background as mine and for it to mean quite as much as it does." Describing his drawing as a process of discovery, an Edinburgh fan says: "Watching back the video as I drew, I can see me not understanding at the beginning of it, and I just worked and worked through problems, until my little wee battles that I was fighting within the picture all began to resolve themselves." He goes on to describe his own identification with Cash in the process: "You can actually see the point where I know what I'm doing, and a light and a dark comes into it, and in a weird way, that's what I actually like about Johnny Cash's music as well, that it's the sum total of his life, all the things that happened, you know the bad things, the good things, you're hearing a person's life." The fan enacts his emotional identification with Cash through the process of creating his own fan content for the website, through this process of generating collective digital folk culture. Likewise, a New York fan describes how his work on this video content and his relationship to Cash's work "has helped me in my own personal spiritual struggle and journey through life," referencing a larger spiritual framework for his fandom.

Both the Cash and the Parton videos demonstrate how new media can create space for the staging of multiple souths, made distinctive by a digital folk culture context, with a more interactive, mediated framework for thinking about the U.S. South as a region. This interactive video trend suggests that we will continue to see different digital folk culture iterations of multiple souths. Just as the convergence of old and new media has created these new trends in interactive digital folk culture, the convergence of different local, regional, and global versions of the U.S. South creates ever more complex ideas about that South in terms of the content of this folk culture. For any media that uses symbols of the U.S. South, those symbols can take on multiple possible different significations of multiple souths. In the case of the Parton fan video, the text stages a certain kind of Appalachian idealized version of the U.S. South, but because of Parton's complex identity formulation involving gender, it also layers on kitschy ironic images to that idealized South; thus, it circulates a version of southern exceptionalism but also offers critiques of it. For the Cash crowdsourced video, it stages the U.S. South as an imagined pastoral nostalgia, one that could easily be critiqued, and it depicts a constructed sense of authenticity as well as community. Here, both singers are symbols of a region in different ways, yet they also show how a version of digital folk culture about the U.S. South can easily circulate globally, creating new types of fan communities and new types of interactive imagined versions of the U.S. South, as part of networked cultural production in the context of media convergence.

NOTES

1. Romine, *The Real South,* 9.
2. Edwards, *Dolly Parton;* Edwards, *"Big Smo,"* 184–99.
3. Fetveit, "Reality TV"; Dovey, *Freakshow.*
4. Jenkins, *Convergence,* 136.
5. It is important to note that Anderson was using the term he coined to refer to citizens in the eighteenth century as they began to think of themselves as part of nation-states via reading newspapers and literature and projecting themselves as part of a larger entity. Of course, I am only loosely adapting his concept for digital fandoms; Anderson, *Imagined Communities.*
6. Jenkins, *Convergence,* 4.
7. Ibid.

8. McChesney, *Digital Disconnect*; Terranova, "Free Labor."

9. Greeson, *Our South*; Bone, *Postsouthern*; McPherson, *Reconstructing Dixie*; Smith, *Finding Purple America*; Romine, *Real South*.

10. Ben-Amos, "Toward a Definition," 13.

11. Miller, "Grove Street Grimm," 280.

12. Blank, ed., *Folk Culture in the Digital Age*, 4.

13. Blank, ed., *Folklore and the Internet*, 20.

14. "Travelin' Dolly."

15. Parton, "The Summer Adventures of Travelin' Dolly."

16. Ching, *Wrong's What I Do Best*; Peterson, *Creating Country Music*; Jensen, *The Nashville Sound*; Fox, *Real Country*; Pecknold, *The Selling Sound*; McCusker and Pecknold, eds., *A Boy Named Sue*.

17. Lipsitz, *Time Passages*, 3, 22.

18. Malone, *Singing Cowboys*.

19. Filene, *Romancing the Folk*.

20. Malone, *Singing Cowboys*; Jackson, ed., *The Honky Tonk on the Left*.

21. Peterson, *Creating Country Music*.

22. Hubbs, *Rednecks, Queers, and Country Music*; Hubbs and Royster, "Introduction: Uncharted Country." Cottom has argued that Parton's cultural framing and reception in terms of country music as a genre reflects structural racism. McMillan Cottom, "The Dolly Moment."

23. Edwards, *Dolly*, 7.

24. Bufwack and Oermann, *Finding Her Voice*, 363.

25. Edwards, *Dolly*, 31.

26. Peterson, *Creating Country Music*.

27. Huyssen, *After the Great Divide*.

28. Transamerica, "Travelin' Thru."

29. Transamerica.

30. Ibid.

31. Milk, "Johnny Cash."

32. Ibid.

33. Milk, *The Johnny Cash Project*.

34. Milk, "Johnny Cash."

35. Ibid.

36. Edwards, "Johnny Cash's 'Ain't No Grave.'"

37. Literat, "The Work of Art."

38. Edwards, *Johnny Cash and the Paradox of American Identity*.

39. Hill, *Reality TV*.

40. Hall and Whannel, *The Popular Arts*, 269–83.

41. Edwards, *Dolly*, and "Big Smo."

BIBLIOGRAPHY

Anderson, Benedict. *Imagined Communities: Reflections on the Origins and Spread of Nationalism.* 1983. London: Verso, 2006.

Ben-Amos, Dan. "Toward a Definition of Folklore in Context." In *Toward New Perspectives in Folklore,* edited by Américo Paredes and Richard Bauman, 3–15. Austin: University of Texas Press, 1972.

Blank, Trevor J., ed. *Folk Culture in the Digital Age: The Emergent Dynamics of Human Interaction.* Logan: Utah State University Press, 2012.

———, ed. *Folklore and the Internet: Vernacular Expressions in a Digital World.* Logan: Utah State University Press, 2009.

Bone, Martyn. *The Postsouthern Sense of Place in Contemporary Fiction.* Baton Rouge: Louisiana State University Press, 2005.

Bufwack, Mary A., and Robert K. Oermann. *Finding Her Voice: Women in Country Music, 1800–2000.* Nashville: Country Music Foundation/Vanderbilt University Press, 2003.

Ching, Barbara. *Wrong's What I Do Best: Hard Country Music and Contemporary Culture.* New York: Oxford University Press, 2001.

Dovey, Jon. *Freakshow: First Person Media and Factual Television.* London: Pluto, 2000.

Edwards, Leigh. "'Backwoods Barbie': Dolly Parton's Gender Performance." In *Country Boys and Redneck Women: New Essays in Gender and Country Music,* edited by Diane Pecknold and Kristine M. McCusker, 189–210. Jackson: University Press of Mississippi, 2016.

———. "*Big Smo:* Reality TV, Hick Hop, and Southern Stereotypes." In *Small-Screen Souths: Region, Identity, and the Cultural Politics of Television,* edited by Lisa Hinrichsen, Gina Caison, and Stephanie Rountree, 184–99. Baton Rouge: Louisiana State University Press, 2017.

———. *Dolly Parton, Gender, and Country Music.* Bloomington: Indiana University Press, 2018.

———. *Johnny Cash and the Paradox of American Identity.* Bloomington: Indiana University Press, 2009.

———. "Johnny Cash's 'Ain't No Grave' and Digital Folk Culture." *Journal of Popular Music Studies* 27, no. 4 (December 2015): 186–203.

———. "Transmedia Storytelling, Corporate Synergy, and Audience Expression." *Global Media Journal* 12, no. 20 (Spring 2012), https://www.globalmediajournal.com/open-access/transmedia-storytelling-corporate-synergy-and-audience-expression.pdf.

———. *The Triumph of Reality TV: The Revolution in American Television.* Santa Barbara, CA: Praeger, 2013; *Society* 21, no. 6 (November 1999): 787–804.

Filene, Benjamin. *Romancing the Folk: Public Memory & American Roots Music.* Chapel Hill: University of North Carolina Press, 2000.

Fox, Aaron. *Real Country: Music and Language in Working-Class Culture.* Durham, NC: Duke University Press, 2004.

Greeson, Jennifer. *Our South: Geographic Fantasy and the Rise of National Literature.* Cambridge, MA: Harvard University Press, 2010.

Hall, Stuart, and Paddy Whannel. *The Popular Arts*. London: Hutchinson, 1964.

Hill, Annette. *Reality TV: Factual Entertainment and Television Audiences*. London: Routledge, 2005.

Hubbs, Nadine. *Rednecks, Queers, and Country Music*. Berkeley: University of California Press, 2014.

Hubbs, Nadine, and Francesca T. Royster. "Introduction: Uncharted Country: New Voices and Perspectives in Country Music Studies." *Journal of Popular Music Studies* 32, no. 2 (2020): 1–10.

Huyssen, Andreas. *After the Great Divide: Modernism, Mass Culture, Postmodernism*. Bloomington: Indiana University Press, 1986.

Jackson, Mark Allan, ed. *The Honky Tonk on the Left: Progressive Thought in Country Music*. Amherst: University of Massachusetts Press, 2018.

Jenkins, Henry. *Convergence Culture: Where Old and New Media Collide*. New York University Press, 2006.

Jenkins, Henry, Sam Ford, and Joshua Green. *Spreadable Media: Creating Value and Meaning in a Networked Culture*. New York: New York University Press, 2013.

Jensen, Joli. *The Nashville Sound: Authenticity, Commercialization, and Country Music*. Nashville: Country Music Foundation/Vanderbilt University Press, 1998.

Lipsitz, George. *Time Passages: Collective Memory and American Popular Culture*. Minneapolis: University of Minnesota Press, 1990.

Literat, Ioana. "The Work of Art in the Age of Mediated Participation: Crowdsourced Art and Collective Creativity." *International Journal of Communication* 6 (2012): 2962–2984.

Malone, Bill C. *Singing Cowboys and Musical Mountaineers: Southern Culture and the Roots of Country Music*. 2nd ed. Athens: University of Georgia Press, 2003.

McChesney, Robert W. *Digital Disconnect: How Capitalism Is Turning the Internet Against Democracy*. New York: New Press, 2013.

McCusker, Kristine M., and Diane Pecknold, eds. *A Boy Named Sue: Gender and Country Music*. Jackson: University Press of Mississippi, 2004

McMillan Cottom, Tressie. "The Dolly Moment." *Essaying*, February 24, 2021.

McPherson, Tara. *Reconstructing Dixie: Race, Gender, and Nostalgia in the Imagined South*. Durham, NC: Duke University Press, 2003.

Milk, Chris. "Johnny Cash—Ain't No Grave [Official HD]." *The Johnny Cash Project*. 2010, https://youtu.be/WwNVlNt9iDk.

———. *The Johnny Cash Project*. 2010, http://www.thejohnnycashproject.com/.

Miller, Kiri. "Grove Street Grimm: Grand Theft Auto and Digital Folklore." *Journal of American Folklore* 121, no. 481 (2008): 255–85.

Parton, Dolly. "The Summer Adventures of Travelin' Dolly." YouTube, November 22, 2010, https://www.youtube.com/watch?v=bGq4zwNXK8U.

Pecknold, Diane. *The Selling Sound: The Rise of the Country Music Industry*. Durham, NC: Duke University Press, 2007.

Peterson, Richard. *Creating Country Music: Fabricating Authenticity*. Chicago: University of Chicago Press, 1997.

Romine, Scott. *The Real South: Southern Narrative in the Age of Cultural Reproduction.* Baton Rouge: Louisiana State University Press, 2008.

Smith, Jon. *Finding Purple America: The South and the Future of American Cultural Studies.* Athens: University of Georgia Press, 2013.

Terranova, T. "Free Labor: Producing for the Digital Economy." *Social Text* 18, no. 2 (2000): 33–58.

Transamerica "*Travelin' Thru*." IFC Films, 2012, https://vimeo.com/30147832.

"Travelin' Dolly." 2010, http://www.DollyPartonMusic.net.

CULTIVATING/CONTESTING IDENTITIES

The Intersection of New Media and
Rural Southern Queerness

AUSTIN SVEDJAN

IN HIS FOREWORD TO *Queer Online: Media Technology and Sexuality* (2007), Larry Gross asserts that the proliferation of new media "create[s] opportunities for the formation of new communities [. . .] permitting the coalescing of interest-based networks spanning vast distance[s]."[1] As part of the recent social media boom, contemporary online communities have largely departed the chatrooms of yesteryears in favor of new social media platforms. So, too, have queer communities migrated to these new modes of cyber-connectivity. Consequently, queer and media scholarship have had to reorient themselves within the context of these contemporary mediations. However, often exalted in the reoriented scholarship surrounding social mediation is the notion that these ever-expanding networks of accessibility have, almost hyperbolically, rendered a number of disguised queer subjects visible.[2] Similarly, scholars have argued that the rapid expansion of visibility has facilitated an *access* to queer identifications by subjects who may find themselves secluded from others "like them."[3] As the title of this essay urges, in such an era of visibility and access, how might we consider southern queer people, particularly queer-identifying subjects who live in, come from, or otherwise attach to rural spaces and communities in the southern United States, who are commonly perceived as occupying spaces hostile to their sexual or gender identities? Complicating things further, all three of the facets of investigation marked by these subjects—the regional, the queer, and the digitally mediated—actively resist essentialist delineation and constantly shift in their expanse. I wish to confront this question by reframing the manner in which scholarship, queer and digital alike, engages with rural southern queer subjects in their interactions with social media, particularly as a mode of various identifications: rural, southern, and queer.

Consider, for instance, the Instagram account @lgbt_history, which recently surpassed 650,000 followers, managed by New York couple Matthew

Riemer and Leighton Brown. While the username @lgbt_history presumes all of queer sexual and gender histories everywhere—a claim that Riemer and Brown further adorn by repeating the adage "We Are Everywhere"—the reality of the page's representational content, made up of snapshots of queer history, runs contrary to this ambitious aim.[4] Of the pair's most recent one hundred posts, forty of the photos are from historical moments in New York, with the majority of others being from the District of Columbia and California.[5] From that same pool, only eight are located in the U.S. South and zero are from rural spaces. This poor visibility of southern and/or rural queer people does not originate from an absence of queer existence in these areas, or from a lack of their documentation, but instead from the rendering of rural and/or southern queer subjectivity as less visible.[6] What @lgbt_history illustrates, and representationally reenacts, is the notion that it is irreconcilable to be queer in the U.S. South, something that has likewise become an axiom in popular queer discourse. American queer identifications have historically been constructed through a process of unfolding and revealing, a movement from *closeted* to *out*. Allan Bérubé's archetype asserts that queer subjects who are not out—that is, those who have defined and assumed an identity but have yet to explicitly disclose that identity—experience isolation as a result and consequently migrate to urban spaces in order to remedy their seclusion by living an out life among a concentrated collective of queer people.[7] In *Men Like That* (1999), John Howard echoes this claim, arguing that "the predominant theoretical model of American lesbian and gay historiography scripts gay identity and culture formation as linked to capitalist industrialization and urbanization."[8] What both Bérubé and Howard are observing in their evaluations of queer identity construction is the shared perception that the cultivation of such an identity necessitates the inhabitation of urban space. This presumption constructs what theorist Jack Halberstam terms "metronormativity," a concept Halberstam argues "reveals the conflation of 'urban' and 'visible' in many normalizing narratives of gay/lesbian subjectivities. Such narratives tell of closeted subjects who 'come out' into an urban setting, which in turn, supposedly allows for the full expression of the sexual [and, I would add, the queerly gendered] self in relation to a community of other gays/lesbian/queers."[9] While Halberstam's conceptualization of metronormativity does well to underscore the assumption of rural spatiality as antithetical to queer identity, it concurrently presupposes that any urban environment is perceptually identical to another in its capacity to enable queer identity cultivation. However, as Donna Jo Smith reminds us, when considering the "obvious bias towards East and West Coast urban centers," aspects of ostensible southernness, both rural *and* urban, are depicted as adverse to queer identity.[10]

In this context, I employ *antisouthern normativity* as a term adjacent to Halberstam's—a locus from which to resituate the queer subject into a regional context. Although this term seems to set up a reinvigorated binarism, my preference for the *anti* prefix denotes more than just "not southern." Fantasizing a queer community "out there," queer people leaving the U.S. South often seek out urban places that are more than merely removed from the region.[11] These *anti-Souths* are not a set of rigidly defined, stable locales of exodus per se but instead are nominally dependent on the motivations for their pursuit. And yet, it might be too limiting to conclude that antisouthern normativity solely stresses the favoring of sites of queer urbanism such as New York, Los Angeles, and San Francisco over their southern counterparts—New Orleans, Raleigh, Houston, Atlanta, Birmingham, etc.[12]

The impetus of antisouthern normativity as an analytic frame at once uncovers a line of thought analogous with "you can be gay, so long as you aren't southern" and also facilitates a broader acknowledgment of identity intersections. Rendering the boundaries between gendered, erotic, and regional subjectivities as less definitive, an acknowledgment of antisouthern normativity is to acknowledge the risk for a preemptive foreclosure of the identity potential of any composite identity in which the relinquishment of any one subjectivity would detract from the whole.[13] While the conglomeration of queer people, both geographically and in terms of an organizing identity, has served an obvious political purpose, these conglomerations have, in the same motion, eclipsed spatial identifications perceived as antithetical to identities these organizations have also cultivated.[14] Interpreting a social media archive like @lgbt_history through both metronormativity and antisouthern normativity can emphasize this eclipsing and bring into relief the subjectivities they obscure. It is this obscuring through the hegemonic construction of queerness that @lgbt_history proliferates and assumes as the entirety of queer history, offering little latitude for the inclusion of historically excluded subjectivities.

Could the emergence of social media in this way, which presents rural southern queer subjects with newfound access to larger queer communities without stipulating their physical migration from spaces of rurality and/or southernness, disrupt the more ontological functions of metronormativity and antisouthern normativity? In *Out in the Country* (2009), Mary L. Gray provides testimony from rural queer subjects (some of them southern) revealing the methods in which media has enabled their access to community and thereby facilitated their cultivations of queer identities. Amy, from Central Kentucky, tells Gray that

> I was over at my friend's house one night joking that I only watched "Bay-watch" (my favorite show at the time) for the girls. After I said this, I realized it was true. It wasn't until about a year later, when I got on the Internet and found other people like me that I actually said to myself that I was bisexual. I've always been attracted to both sexes, but I found my *true identity* on the Internet [emphasis added].[15]

What Amy's testimony affirms is that while rural southern subjects may be aware that they have a queered sexual desire/gender expression, the sense of a queer *identity* arises once there is access to a community-cultivated label encompassing enough of that previously vague expression of sexuality/gender. Likewise, Zarah C. Moeggenberg presents a similar testimony from Martha, a genderqueer lesbian from North Carolina: "Visibility is important. Particularly for individuals who are looking for answers or identities or like-minded politics (which is one of the things that I think Tumblr provides with relative safety). I wonder if Tumblr had existed when I was 16 what my identity would look like today—if it would be the same, or if I would have come to some answers *sooner* [emphasis added]."[16] Martha's testimony builds upon Amy's insofar as her account of coming out is temporal, a matter of *when* rather than *if*. According to Martha, however, the eventual realization constituting this "when" can be expedited through access to digital mediation; the "answers" (identities) she came to are the same, but she wonders if she would have come to them sooner if she had had access to social media earlier.

While both Amy and Martha access community-cultivated queer identities through media, in lieu of potentially migrating from their spaces of rurality and/or southernness, what both of their testimonies expose is the continuation of identities being perceived as deterministic, manifesting once queer subjects integrate with a larger community. Amy and Martha express that their current identities are something that digitally mediated communities have taken an active role in materializing, suggesting that our focus for locating migrations within the scope of online platforms should not be on physical movements from spaces of rurality/southernness to urbanity/antisouthernness, but rather affective movements from ostensible isolation to community integration.

Yet, space is far from a benign component in rural southern queer people's relation to media and consequent interactions with(in) communities online. Since the late 1990s, discerning sites of virtual mediation as spaces remains a particularly contested nexus of argument among media scholars. Moeggenberg postulates that queer subjects "migrate from space to space [online] due to safety."[17] Borrowing José Esteban Muñoz's concept of "disidentification"—wherein one adapts the codes and spaces of a dominant culture, leaving "a newly available site of identification"[18]—Moeggenberg argues that queer subjects are continuously enacting processes of disidentification online, "leav[ing] spaces and com[ing] back."[19] Conversely, Nancy K. Baym argues that the distinction between online and offline space is exponentially more vague than it appears: "How online spaces are constructed and the activities that people do online are intimately interwoven with the construction of the offline world and the activities and structures in which we participate, whether we are using the internet or not."[20] While the online can certainly be considered a site of mediation between a number of subjects who may otherwise not occupy the same space (the rural and the urban, the southern and the antisouthern, etc.), and while it might then be identified as its own distinctive space, Baym's call to recognize the online's interlacing with the offline is significant.

Supporting Baym's claim, Zachary Blair's surveys digitized bigotry in Chicago's LGBTQ neighborhood Boystown, arguing that online community pages "allowed residents to publicly produce and engage with bigoted attitudes, ideologies, and discourses through photographs, videos, and concurrent threaded comments. As a result, Boystown was transformed into an environment where the racist, classist, and transphobic subjectivities that proliferated online could be easily reproduced and publicly displayed."[21] What is striking about Blair's anthropological research is that it emphasizes not only how offline discourses impact online space, but also how the distinctly online proliferation of those discourses correspondingly influence offline life. Within Blair's acknowledgment of the reciprocal exchange between the online and offline lies the essence of Baym's argument. It is necessary to conceptualize the online "cyberspace" as a unique extension of offline space, wherein discursive affects and ideologies originating in the offline impact the online, and vice versa.

To further complicate matters, Moeggenberg's subjects introduce a pluralized view of online space. Jordan, a bisexual woman from the Pacific Northwest, "organiz[es] her performance in each space to reflect an aspect of who she is—the activist on Instagram, the bisexual queer on Tumblr, the straight friend or family member on Facebook, the literary scholar on Twitter. Jordan generates a constellation of points for identification across these various digital platforms, a kind of migratory nexus that makes her survival as a bi, queer Latina woman possible."[22] Jordan's testimony compels us to contemplate how, in the framework of queer identities, online spaces are actively intersecting, overlapping, and potentially impacting offline spaces of rurality and southernness.

As Jordan's narrative indicates, there are aspects of spatiality at work in the lives of queer people online. It is important, however, that these spaces not be considered independent of their offline counterparts. I wish to move forward with a perspective of online spaces which are distinct from the offline, removed from the material concepts typically associated with "space" but attached via a permeable barrier.[23] This concept of online space as permeable acts to emphasize the production of distinctive online spaces while concurrently acknowledging that it is ultimately assembled by and reliant upon artifacts of the offline. In this regard, the identities accessed in online communities are not unique to these sites of digital mediation but rather are extensions of identities produced offline and subsequently proliferated within communities online, retaining any associated perception of region.

So, let us return to the concept of digitally mediated space as experienced by the rural southern queer person, who, due to compounded senses of metronormativity and antisouthern normativity, is potentially vulnerable to perceiving themselves as contrary to the queer communities they interact with online. If one is, at the very least, to acknowledge online social media as a distinctive albeit permeable space, then one must consequently consider: if the migration to that space is rendered compulsory for rural southern queer people in the same manner that movements to urban sites have been previously, then is this merely the same emperor in new, virtual clothes?

For example, Darrin, a gay seventeen-year-old from rural Kentucky, "sees websites [. . .] as 'a place to feel at least somewhat at home [. . .] a place to go when I don't feel I can connect to others where I am.'"[24] At a glance, it would seem that some form of migratory movement is taking place, as Darrin's experience certainly aligns itself with Halberstam's metronormativity in that a "spatial narrative within which the subject moves to a place of tolerance after enduring life in a place of suspicion, persecution, and secrecy" has ostensibly occurred.[25] Although Darrin is not migrating physically, he is acknowledging that he must "figure out how to make that home here too."[26] And yet, in terms of Darrin's construction of identity, this compulsion to migrate physically is made negligible, as Darrin is still accessing a digitally mediated space which has imparted an identitarian discourse of what constitutes queerness. Likewise, Gray urges scholars not to analyze media as autonomously producing effects upon subjects, but rather to examine how subjects impact and shape the media with which they interact.[27] We might regard, then, these identities as domains of identification which predate the emergence of online media and are later applied to online communities not encompassed in their entirety in the "ether" of the online. In this sense, because rural queer southerners are continuing to seek outside communities in which to name and essentially construct their identities, there *is* a migration occurring.

These essentialized identities sought out by rural southern queer people through migration to cyberspace offer nominal flexibility, particularly for those whose multitude of individual identifications do not align with what Wayne Brekhus refers to as the "auxiliary characteristics," or the agreed-upon and highly uniform components vital to being "authentically gay."[28] As Jeffrey Weeks has argued, identity "is about belonging, about what you have in common with some people, and difference from others. At its most basic it gives you a sense of personal location, the stable core of your individuality."[29] In that regard, the identities that rural southerners are now actively accessing through digital mediation are cultivated by both endorsing and rejecting identificatory objects. Recalling @lgbt_history, to claim the entirety of queerness in all its (perhaps infinitely) various forms in a finite format will inevitably exclude some facets of queer experience. Identical to the overarching narratives of queerness that precede the advent of social media, @lgbt_history futilely attempts to somehow name all that cannot be named and locate all that cannot be located, crafting an ultimately essentialized image of queer identity. A particular problem arises, especially, when one considers @lgbt_history's Instagram verification, represented by a visible blue check mark at the top of the page. This verification distinguishes a social media account, whether of a corporation or celebrity, from potentially fraudulent accounts posing as that corporation or celebrity. In essence, while the symbol of verification may seem superficially trite in the larger survey of an account, it is in actuality a symbolic differentiator from the otherwise counterfeit, insofar as the authority of the social platform has visually signified the verified account as authentic. As such, @lgbt_history's inevitably nonce representation of queer identity, observed here as motivated by presumptions of metronormativity and antisouthern normativity, becomes conflated with a universal authenticity.[30]

For rural southern queer people, accessing this form of "verified" queer identity produces a perceived viability of queer subjectivity only as it relates to this hegemonic version of queer identity. As Gray notes, "the Internet are where most stories of queer desires transpire. These representations translate queer desires into LGBT-specific identities. [. . .] As such, media are the primary site of production for social knowledge of LGBT identities. It is where most people, including those who will come to identify as LGBT, first see or get to know LGBT people. In other words, media circulate the *social grammar, appearance*, and *sites* of LGBT-ness."[31] These specific performative artifacts of hegemonic queerness that Gray highlights communicate the criteria by which rural and southern subjects have largely been relegated to the margins of a universalized queer identity. As a result, rural southerners attempting to appraise and delineate their own internal dialogue with sexuality and gender within these online communities appear to consequently become what Brekhus terms identity "univores," which are able to "label the central attribute of his self," as opposed to "the identity omnivore [which] considers his self as defined by so many competing attributes that it is hard to choose the most important."[32] Similar to the multiple sites of identity prioritization displayed earlier by Moeggenberg's "constellation of points for identification," identity omnivorism facilitates the arranging of identities on various platforms.[33] However, rural southern subjects must perceptually forgo the performance of their rurality/southernness in order to adopt uniform queer identities—foundationally metronormative and antisouthern. This is, as I have argued, epitomized by accounts such as @lgbt_history, and here we see it in Jordan's prioritization of familial and amicable identities on Facebook.

Whereas Brekhus's identity univore "has a hierarchical identity structure where one attribute reigns and the other serve as auxiliary characteristics,"[34] what might typically be seen as supportive attributes are, for the rural southerner, perceptually antithetical to the reigning identity of queerness, leading to a form of compulsory, singular veneration of queer identity. For example, consider a monarch's ontological existence if ruling over a domain of antagonistic subjects: the monarch's reigning hierarchal attribute is called into question by a want of supplementary, though not undermining, subjects. In

222 • AUSTIN SVEDJAN

a similar process, one's multidimensional subjectivity is foreclosed when the reigning hierarchical identity (in this case, queerness) demands the omission of characteristics that are conceptually contradictory to its existence (in this case, southernness and rurality). In this sense, rural southerners adopting a hegemonic queer identity through digital mediation can be regarded neither as univores nor as omnivores, but rather as identity *solovores*, which signifies the distinction of those whose otherwise intersecting identities must be perceptually elided in order to "properly" and singularly exalt a community-cultivated queerness (i.e., being queer on the condition one is not southern and/or rural). Whereas omnivores acquiesce with all aspects of their identity simultaneously and univores hierarchize one reigning identity in the company of all auxiliary ones, solovores must obscure and exclude their "antithetical" auxiliary identities in order to render stable their dominant identity. In the context of a regional identification conflicting with queer identity, a queer subject might only be able to access a sense of stable queerness through identity solovorism. A person from Brooklyn might be queer first, then a New Yorker (univore), but a person from Thomasville, Georgia, is compelled to be only queer and nothing else (solovore). In such a formulation, rural southern queer people may gain identitarian subjectivity, visibility, and inclusion within the larger queer community in exchange for relinquishing of their "contrarian" southern and rural attachments, thus generating a uniform and seemingly stable identity wherein all of the characteristics that both compose and distinguish a "queer identity" are agreed upon and enforced by the collective.

Judith Butler warns against the installation of margins of visibility in identities that claim to define those margins: "There is no question that gays and lesbians are threatened by the violence of public erasure, but the decision to counter that violence must be careful not to reinstall another in its place. Which version of lesbian or gay ought to be rendered visible, and which internal exclusions will that rendering visible institute?"[35] Concepts of rurality and southernness have been historically treated as those "internal exclusions" and elided in order to facilitate the development of identity solovorism during the physical migration to the antisouthern metropolitan center as a facet of Bérubé's coming-out model. However, with the advent of new media's expansive accessibility, a shift is transpiring (potentially for the first time) for those who are remaining in rural and southern areas. Heightened by contemporary development in digital media, social platforms are producing what Rob Cover sees as identity being "always online."[36] Coupled with my earlier observation that the virtual space is permeable, Cover's sentiment stresses how indistinguishable our online identities are from our offline ones. This presents a particularly precarious mode of being for subjects whose online queer identities are compelled to exclude potential secondary southern and rural identities yet who are no longer obliged to physically leave the rural South that defines those identities. If one is adopting Butler's opinion of identities as seemingly misleadingly expressions of a "reality" of being,[37] might we speculate that queer people, who assume distinctly urban and antisouthern queer identities through social media online but who also continue to inhabit sites of rurality and southernness offline, could reinforce those identities masquerading as essential truths through means external to digital mediation: the superimposition of the urban and antisouthern onto the rural South?

Moreover, through digital actions of following, unfollowing, blocking, and muting, social media platforms present a heightened possibility for the community policing of online spaces.[38] Queer people who find themselves insufficiently defined by a uniform (uni- or solovore) identity, and who subsequently wish to argue against that artificially uniform identity, may be rendered invisible through these functions of platform personalization. Although this customization is an individualized act, there are several examples online of a unified consensus to block or unfollow en masse a specific individual, with users even posting screenshots of their individual blocking as a more performative call to action.[39] Although digital ecologies have traditionally been perceived as sites of contestation and discourse, the propagation of uniform identities online suggests that the online has lost some of that discursive sheen. It is possible that, if these platform personalizing actions were to be excised from social media practices, it would increase the amount of negotiation occurring in identity constitution across boundaries. Though it is equally as possible that this personalization lends itself to the formation of a protected community, what Reed sees as the "new spaces for discreet connection and community formation" safe from "the anonymity and disinhibition allowed by online discourse [unleashing] a great flood of rhetoric that is viciously homophobic."[40]

To view a potential synthesis of these possibilities in which a community has not foreclosed on the subjective negotiations of identity and has—at least outwardly—avoided mass homophobic violence, one may turn to the Instagram account @queerappalachia.[41] The social imprint of the Electric Dirt Collective, @queerappalachia boasts just under 200,000 followers while lacking the symbolic blue check-mark verification from the moderating platform.

224 · AUSTIN SVEDJAN

Whereas @lgbt_history, as the name would imply, posts almost exclusively historical events, @queerappalachia's content encapsulates a varied collection of identificatory vignettes, which range from art installations and local political protests to Corvettes on monster truck tires and biscuit tattoos. In the spirit of this nuance, the Electric Dirt Collective notes that "the concept of Identity throughout Appalachia and the South is complex and nuanced. [. . .] We are all in the process of defining, refining, and reclaiming our identities."[42]

In the context of @queerappalachia's situated regionalism, the Electric Dirt Collective allows for the community cultivation of identity within the locale of distinctly rural and/or southern spaces. This elective positioning lends itself to the material outreach the Electric Dirt Collective has facilitated through @queerappalachia. For instance, in November of 2018, @queerappalachia operated their first "Rural Queer Coat Drive," which received over three hundred requests from predominately Indigenous and queer people of color. A testimony from one coat-solicitor included in the post reads, "I desperately need any clothing help y'all can spare. All the community closets in my area only give out gender specific clothing. My license list[s] me as a wom[a]n, I'd rather freeze than wear a god damn pink parka. I've tried to explain the situation to the church volunteers that staff it."[43] Another reads, "I am in desperate need of a coat. I lost my job due to calling out my racist boss calling [me] tranny to the entire staff. My antidepressant medication I have been on this past year has helped stabilize my mental health, I have gained 40 pounds on it and nothing I own fits me. QTIPOC should come before me."[44] In these instances, @queerappalachia's online presence is actively queering an offline life tied intimately to a distinctive regional location, a process Gray considers as perhaps more common than popular media representations would have us believe:

> Should we presume rural queer and questioning youth treat new media technologies as the latest vehicles of escape? Is it possible that, for the rural youth who stay put [geographically], new media serve not primarily as "opportunities for the formation of new communities . . . spanning vast distances"[45] but as opportunities to create and consolidate networks much closer to home that are otherwise absent from mass-media representations?[46]

In this regard, @queerappalachia certainly appears to consolidate a particular network of rural and/or southern queers.

Perhaps more important, however, is that @queerappalachia not only amalgamates subjects in the rural U.S. South who already identify as LGBT but also forms a space for cultivation of new identities. Indeed, @queerappalachia does not present a unified sense of identity, thus contrasting the shared history @lgbt_history presumes. Instead, @queerappalachia cultivates various avenues of being through identity, echoed on the Electric Dirt Collective's website, which lists various potential self-identifications that configure race, class, nationality, region, gender, and sexuality in highly idiosyncratic ways.[47] Echoed in something even as subtle as a rhetorical shift from "lgbt" to "queer," @queerappalachia opens up a possibility of various identifications always to be developed at the whim of the singular self rather than discovered and adhered to en masse. One might do well to think of those interacting with @queerappalachia as dutiful readers of Eve Kosofsky Sedgwick, insofar as they seem to epitomize the "important senses in which 'queer' can signify only *when attached to the first person*."[48] On the contrary, @lgbt_history, in its perpetuation of metronormativity and antisouthern normativity, forecloses the possibility of ambiguous identifications that might otherwise blur the boundaries between what are presently considered separate spheres of an intersectional identity (e.g., race, class, region, sexuality, gender). However, @queerappalachia consciously values the continual unsettledness of identity, offering instead a location in which rural southern queer people may safely negotiate their own identificatory possibility. In a similar impetus, Patricia Hill Collins's formation of Black feminist thought argues that offering subordinate groups "new knowledge about our own experiences can be empowering. But activating epistemologies that criticize prevailing knowledge and that enable us to define our own realities *on our own terms* has far greater implications."[49] In this sense, @queerappalachia offers the resources by which identity may be cultivated *by* the subject as opposed to cultivated *for* the subject, to name oneself rather than be named.

Juxtaposed against the queer solovorism of @lgbt_history, @queerappalachia ostensibly presents a form of identity univorism, in which queerness is still the unifying identity—and thereby prioritized—but other identities are not compelled to be overlooked in order to facilitate that prioritization. However, even that prioritization is often troubled by the content @queerappalachia posts. In a recent post, the account solicits reading material for (primarily Indigenous) activists protesting the construction of the Mountain Valley Pipeline.[50] Can one assume that in this instance eroticism or gender is still the prioritized identity? If a particular subject's sexual/gendered queerness is intimately associated to their identity as Indigenous, as it is for Two-Spirit people, can a singular prioritized identification be specified? In the adoption of a broader appreciation of queerness as "a more thorough resistance to regimes of the normal,"[51] @queerappalachia constructs an avenue of omnivoric possibility, expanding the boundaries of *queer* to acquiesce with any number of unique subjectivities without sacrificing a collective sense of community.

In this contemporary moment of new media wherein social media is increasingly integrated into the way members of society participate with online communities, queer subjects who have typically been perceived as existing on the margins are often rendered more visible. As I have articulated in this essay, such visibility largely remains conditional on the adoption of uniform queer identities that predate the internet but are now perpetuated and proliferated in online communities. Region can function crucially within these queer identities, particularly in perceiving queer inhabitants occupying spaces of rurality and southernness—regardless of whether or not those inhabitants have formed an identity encompassing regionality. With the development and propagation of new media, rural queer southerners are at risk of being unable to adopt these identities, which offer "cognitive and emotional coherence to experience," without having to forfeit another identity or the ability to form identity based on region.[52] Queer people occupying spaces of rurality and southernness who have no desire to alter either of those qualities—motivated possibly by familial, sentimental, economic, and/or other considerations— may find some of their sense of self lost via myths of metronormativity and antisouthern normativity when they assimilate into larger queer collectives through digitally mediated platforms. Perpetuating and distributing uniform identities across a wide spatial expanse via social media in the name of visibility may very well appear to offer new, brighter, horizons for queer individuals. Yet, this pursuit of visibility through community building on social media has the capacity to install new or adjusted forms of hostility for those who remain in the margins of a uniform identity. Suzanna Danuta Walters warns, "I believe there are ways which this new visibility creates new forms of homophobia. [. . .] We may be *seen*, now, but I'm not sure we are *known*."[53]

However, media reflections of larger queer communities such as @queerappalachia offer an alternative to this exchange of inclusion and visibility for subjectivity. This alternative challenges the typical mode of identity cultivation, facilitating an epistemology of knowing oneself. But what margins might even this alternative instill? What progress might be made from questioning the conditions in which those too easily dismissed in queer communities— minorities of race, region, class, and other marginalized identity formations— are folded into the larger community, online or off, and rendered visible: being made *visible* but not being made *known?*

NOTES

1. Gross, Foreword, ix.

2. In that spirit, Rosser, Oakes, Bockting, and Miner insist that new media best serve "individuals who in the past may have experienced significant social isolation, marginalization from mainstream society, and internalized shame regarding their sexual interests or identity," offering them new opportunities to "tap into a ready source of peer support and common bond"; Rosser et al., "Capturing," 51.

3. One such example of this inclination is Matthew G. O'Neill's assertion that for trans- and genderqueer youth "YouTube offers a valuable performative and discursive space, allowing the individual to become aware of their chosen gender identity"; O'Neill, "Transgender Youth," 36.

4. This idiom was proliferated during the post-Stonewall liberation movement and is the title of Riemer and Brown's book *We Are Everywhere: Protest, Power, and Pride in the History of Queer Liberation;* Riemer and Brown (@lgbt_history), "Our book," Instagram, April 30, 2019.

5. As of May 13, 2019.

6. As readers of John Howard's *Men Like That* and James Sears's *Rebels, Rubyfruit, and Rhinestones* can attest.

7. Bérubé, "'Fitting In,'" unpublished speech taken from Smith's "Queering the South," 373.

8. Howard, *Men Like That,* 12.

9. Halberstam, *In a Queer Time and Place,* 36.

10. Smith, "Queering the South," 370.

11. This conceptualization of antisouthern normativity moves, at least in part, to build upon Scott Herring's call to "attend to the specificities of lesbian and gay ruralities as they align together and as they depart from one another"; Herring, *Another Country,* 27. We might also consider how Jennie Lightweis-Goff has investigated how metropolitan centers, resisting the belief "that which is not urban is southern; that which is southern can never be urban," can maintain a sense of perceptual southernness (Lightweis-Goff, "Solid Souths," 295). While these cities may, indeed, act as regional sites of migration for queer people while still being read as southern, they concurrently appear to lack a cachet enjoyed by New York and San Francisco in larger constructions of queer identity. It is with this motivation, then, that potential southern queer expatriates seek urban centers collectively believed to reject everything the U.S. South is perceived to encompass, while concurrently embodying everything the U.S. South is perceived to lack.

12. I do not present antisouthern normativity here as a contrarian method to disregard the viability of Halberstam's metronormativity, nor to disregard its plethora of implications. Instead, I wish to question how these terms might be compounded upon one another in the queer subject occupying spaces of both ruralism and southernness.

13. See my article in the *Southern Quarterly*, "The Queer Art of Leaving: (Anti)Southern Expatriatism and the Organizing of Spatial Identity in *Breakfast at Tiffany's*," for a more dedicated meditation on these "composite" identities.

14. This political purpose of queer conglomeration could be considered a form of what Gayatri Chakravorty Spivak has noted as a "*strategic* use of positivist essentialism [original emphasis]." Though Spivak additionally notes that while this strategic essentialism may serve a useful purpose in organizing subjects on the basis of singular identity, it can only be strategic in its temporary deployment (Spivak, *In Other Worlds*, 281). Similar to Spivak's acknowledgment of strategic essentialism's productivity being conditional in its provisional usage, Judith Butler notes that lesbian and gay identities may be considered excessively exclusionary in the future once that political usage has dulled—a time I believe one could argue we now find ourselves in: "Can the visibility of identity *suffice* as a political strategy, or can it only be the starting point for a strategic intervention which calls for the transformation of policy? [. . .] That any consolidation of identity requires some set of differentiations and exclusions seems clear. But which ones ought to be valorized? That the identity-sign I use now has its purposes seems right, but there is no way to predict or control the political uses to which that sign will be put in the future. [. . .] If the rendering visible of lesbian/gay identity now presupposes a set of exclusions, then perhaps part of what is necessarily excluded is *the future uses of the sign.* There is a political necessity to use some sign now, and we do, but how to use it in such a way that its futural significations are not *foreclosed*? How to use the sign and avow its temporal contingency at once? [original emphasis]" (Butler, "Imitation," 19).

15. Gray, *Out in the Country*, 121.

16. Moeggenberg, "Keeping Safe (and Queer)," 231.

17. Ibid., 229.

18. Muñoz, *Disidentifications*, 41.

19. Moeggenberg, "Keeping Safe (and Queer)," 230.

20. Baym, "Finding the Quality," 86.

21. Blair, "Boystown," 298.

22. Moeggenberg, "Keeping Safe (and Queer)," 233.

23. For further reading and what might prove to be a welcomed representation of what I deem a "permeable" barrier between the offline and online, see Rowan Wilken's "Twitter and Geographical Location." In the essay, Wilken observes how geotagging offline spaces within online tweets heightens Twitter as a "locative platform," which I believe encapsulates my perception of the online/offline spatial dilemma nicely.

24. Gray, *Out in the Country*, 127.

25. Halberstam, *In a Queer Time and Place*, 36–37.

26. Gray, *Out in the Country*, 127.

27. Ibid., 12.

28. Brekhus, *Peacocks*, 42.

29. Weeks, "The Value of Difference," 88.

30. Readers of Eve Kosofsky Sedgwick might notice that my use of "nonce" here gestures toward the "nonce-taxonomic work" Sedgwick attempts to amplify in the then burgeoning field of queer studies. While @lgbt_history is indeed producing nonce taxonomies, it should not be confused with the "work" Sedgwick touts. Rather, such nonce taxonomic representations are an inevitable corollary to the "self-evident fact" that "people are different from each other." The issue arises, however, when social media venues—of which @lgbt_history, while my primary object of critique here, is not the exception—represent those nonce taxonomies as a singular, universalizing representation of queerness; Sedgwick, *Epistemology*, 22–23.

31. Gray, *Out in the Country*, 12 (emphasis added).

32. Brekhus, *Peacocks*, 114.

33. For instance, Jordan prioritizes her various identities on different platforms (activist on Instagram, queer on Tumblr, literary scholar on Twitter); Moeggenberg, "Keeping Safe (and Queer)," 233.

34. Brekhus, *Peacocks*, 201.

35. Butler, "Imitation," 19.

36. Cover attributes the position of always being online as "always performing ourselves online because even when we are nowhere near a digital communication device (which is now extremely rare), we leave traces all over the Internet, social-networking pages, blog, Twitter, and other sites that are actively contributing to elements of our identity"; Cover, *Digital Identities*, x.

37. In Butler's exact phrasing, identities seemingly "[express] in some indirect or direct way a psychic reality that precedes it" (Butler, "Imitation," 24).

38. Introduced in 2014, Twitter's "muting" function allows users to negate another's visibility without blocking or unfollowing them. Paul Rosania notes on Twitter's official blog that "muting a user on Twitter means their Tweets and Retweets will no longer be visible in your home timeline, and you will no longer receive push or SMS notifications from that user. The muted user will still be able to favorite, reply to and retweet your Tweets; you just won't see any of that activity in your timeline. The muted user will not know that you've muted him/her, and of course you can unmute at any time" (Rosania, "Another way," Twitter Blog, May 12, 2014).

39. I do not wish to cite any tweets without the original poster's permission and will not directly quote a tweet anonymously, because—utilizing Twitter's search function—one would be able to easy dissolve that purposeful anonymity. If one desires to look for examples of unified community blocking, I would suggest using the search function for relevant terms.

40. Reed, *Digitized Lives*, 118.

41. Since the initial writing of this essay, @queerappalachia has changed ownership and has not posted since August 7, 2020. This change in ownership appears to have been in response to a *Washington Post* article detailing an alleged misuse of donated funds; Eisenberg, "The Tale."

42. "About," Queer Appalachia (website), The Electric Dirt Collective.

43. Queer Appalachia (@queerappalachia), "We have gotten over 300 request [sic] for winter coats," Instagram, November 1, 2018.

44. Ibid.

45. The nested quote from Gross appearing within Gray's assertion is the same used in the first paragraph of this essay. See endnote 1 for the citation.

46. Gray, *Out in the Country,* 12.

47. Some of these identities are: "Fag Hillbilly, Dirt Femme, Chocolate Spoonie, Latinx, Queer, Farm-Her, Two Spirit, Affrilachian, Swamp Diva, Muslim, Indigenous, Thaibilly, Faggot Farmer, Veteran, Black, Dirt Witch . . ."; "About," Queer Appalachia (website).

48. Sedgwick, *Tendencies,* 9 (emphasis in original).

49. Collins, *Black Feminist Thought,* 292.

50. Queer Appalachia (@queerappalachia). "For the past 260 days," Instagram, May 29, 2019.

51. Warner, "Introduction," xxvi.

52. Bauman, *Story,* 113.

53. Walters, *All the Rage,* 10 (emphasis in original).

BIBLIOGRAPHY

"About." Queer Appalachia (website), the Electric Dirt Collective. Accessed May 13, 2019. https://www.queerappalachia.com/who-why.

Bauman, Richard. *Story, Performance, and Event Contextual Studies of Oral Narrative.* Cambridge: Cambridge University Press, 1986.

Baym, Nancy K. "Finding the Quality in Qualitative Research." In *Critical Cyberculture Studies,* edited by David Silver and Adrienne Massanari, 79–87. New York: New York University Press, 2006.

Bérubé, Allan. "'Fitting In': Expanding Queer Studies beyond the 'Closet' and 'Coming Out.'" Unpublished speech presented at the Contest Zone Conference, Pitzer College, Claremont, CA, April 1990. Excerpt taken from Donna Jo Smith's "Queering the South: Constructions of Southern/Queer Identity," in *Carryin' On in the Lesbian and Gay South,* edited by John Howard, 373. New York: New York University Press, 1997.

Blair, Zachary. "Boystown: Gay Neighborhoods, Social Media, and the (Re)Production of Racism." In *No Tea, No Shade: New Writings in Black Queer Studies,* edited by E. Patrick Johnson, 287–303. Durham, NC: Duke University Press, 2016.

Brekhus, Wayne. *Peacocks, Chameleons, Centaurs: Gay Suburbia and the Grammar of Social Identity.* Chicago: University of Chicago Press, 2003.

Butler, Judith. "Imitation and Gender Insubordination." In *Inside/Out: Lesbian Theories, Gay Theories,* edited by Diana Fuss, 13–31. New York: Routledge, 1991.

Collins, Patricia Hill. *Black Feminist Thought: Knowledge, Consciousness, and the Politics of Empowerment.* 2nd ed. New York: Routledge, 2009.

Cover, Rob. *Digital Identities: Creating and Communicating the Online Self.* London: Academic Press, 2016.

Eisenberg, Emma Copley. "The Tale of Queer Appalachia." *Washington Post*, August 3, 2020. https://www.washingtonpost.com/magazine/2020/08/03/popular-instagram-account -raises-funds-lgbtq-people-appalachia-its-not-clear-where-those-donations-go/.

Gray, Mary L. *Out in the Country: Youth, Media, and Queer Visibility in Rural America*. New York: New York University Press, 2009.

Gross, Larry. Foreword to *Queer Online Media Technology & Sexuality*, edited by Kate O'Riordan and David J. Phillips, vii–x. New York: Peter Lang Publishing, 2007.

Halberstam, Jack. *In a Queer Time and Place: Transgender Bodies, Subcultural Lives*. New York: New York University Press, 2005.

Herring, Scott. *Another Country: Queer Anti-Urbanism*. New York: New York University Press, 2010.

Howard, John. *Men Like That*. Chicago: University of Chicago Press, 1999.

Lightweis-Goff, Jennie. "Solid Souths, Fluid Souths: *The Wire*, *Treme*, and David Simon's Urbanism." In *Small-Screen Souths: Region, Identity, and the Cultural Politics of Television*, edited by Lisa Hinrichsen, Gina Caison, and Stephanie Rountree, 294–311. Baton Rouge: Louisiana State University Press, 2017.

Moeggenberg, Zarah C. "Keeping Safe (and Queer)." In *The Routledge Handbook of Digital Writing and Rhetoric*, edited by Jonathan Alexander and Jacqueline Rhodes, 225–36. New York: Routledge, 2018.

Muñoz, José Esteban. *Disidentifications: Queers of Color and the Performance of Politics*. Minneapolis: University of Minnesota Press, 1999.

O'Neill, Matthew G. "Transgender Youth and YouTube Videos: Self-Representation and Five Identifiable Trans Youth Narratives." In *Queer Youth and Media Cultures*, edited by Christopher Pullen, 34–45. Houndmills, Basingstoke, Hampshire: Palgrave Macmillan, 2014.

Queer Appalachia (@queerappalachia). "We have gotten over 300 request [*sic*] for winter coats from last nights post alone!" Instagram, November 1, 2018. https://www.instagram.com/p/Bpp8c8qg7sP/.

———. "For the past 260 days about a dozen people have lived in the woods, some in tree's [*sic*] & others on the ground supporting them, literally standing in the path of the #mountainvalleypipeline." Instagram, May 29, 2019. https://www.instagram.com/p/ByByl_oFvXj/.

Reed, T. V. *Digitized Lives: Culture, Power and Social Change in the Internet Era*. New York: Routledge, 2014.

Riemer, Matthew, and Leighton Brown (@lgbt_history). "Our book, 'We Are Everywhere: Protest, Power, and Pride in the History of Queer Liberation,' comes out one week from today (May 7)." Instagram, April 30, 2019. https://www.instagram.com/p/Bw4snJapd5U/.

Riemer, Matthew, and Leighton Brown. *We Are Everywhere: Protest, Power, and Pride in the History of Queer Liberation*. Emeryville, CA: Ten Speed Press, 2019.

Rosania, Paul (@ptr). "Another way to edit your Twitter experience: with mute." Twitter Blog, May 12, 2014. https://blog.twitter.com/en_us/a/2014/another-way-to-edit-your-twitter-experience-with-mute.html.

Rosser, B. R. Simon, et al. "Capturing the Social Demographics of Hidden Sexual Minorities: An Internet Study of the Transgender Population in the United States." *Sexuality Research and Social Policy* 4, no. 2 (May 12, 2007): 50–64.

Sears, James T. *Rebels, Rubyfruit, and Rhinestones: Queering Space in the Stonewall South.* New Brunswick, NJ: Rutgers University Press, 2001.

Sedgwick, Eve Kosofsky. *Epistemology of the Closet.* Durham, NC: Duke University Press, 1990.

———. *Tendencies.* Durham, NC: Duke University Press, 1993.

Smith, Donna Jo. "Queering the South: Constructions of Southern/Queer Identity." In *Carryin' On in the Lesbian and Gay South,* edited by John Howard, 370–85. New York: New York University Press, 1997.

Spivak, Gayatri Chakravorty. *In Other Worlds: Essays in Cultural Politics.* New York: Routledge, 2006.

Svedjan, Austin. "The Queer Art of Leaving: (Anti)Southern Expatriatism and the Organizing of Spatial Identity in *Breakfast at Tiffany's.*" *Southern Quarterly* 57, no. 3 (2021): 69–82.

Walters, Suzanna Danuta. *All the Rage: The Story of Gay Visibility in America.* Chicago: University of Chicago Press, 2001.

Warner, Michael. "Introduction." In *Fear of a Queer Planet: Queer Politics and Social Theory,* edited by Michael Warner, vii–xxxi. Minneapolis: University of Minnesota Press, 1993.

Weeks, Jeffrey. "The Value of Difference." In *Identity: Community, Culture, Difference,* edited by Jonathan Rutherford, 88–100. London: Lawrence & Wishart, 1998.

Wilken, Rowan. "Twitter and Geographical Location." In *Twitter and Society,* edited by Katrin Weller, Axel Bruns, Jean Burgess, Merja Mahrt, and Cornelius Pusc, 155–67. New York: Peter Lang, 2014.

Y'ALL USE *Y'ALL* UNIRONICALLY NOW, "BUT Y'ALL AREN'T READY TO HAVE THAT CONVERSATION"

Race, Region, and Memetic Twang on Twitter

SAM McCRACKEN

> Culture has a habit of not being where and when we are presently.
> —SCOTT ROMINE, *The Real South*

MY MOTHER, ONE OF the most articulate, well-spoken people I know, is an ardent supporter of her smartphone's preinstalled speech-to-text software, but I regularly question if the feeling is all that mutual. For years she has sent me semi-unintelligible messages as a result of her phone's apparent inability to de-cipher the downhome Georgia accent that structures her parlance: over text, "Ford" might take the place of "forward," "aroma" might replace "are on my." And when on rare occasion context clues fail me—like when I struggled to see "talk to text so you'll get my chest" for what it ought to have been, "so you'll *get the gist*"—I turn to reading my mom's texts aloud with a heaping dash of twang to reverse-engineer what she originally intended to convey. Mileage varies.

This essay, in the spirit of the above, explores how the accent characteristic of the U.S. South is and has been (re)configured, appropriated, deployed, and elided in the context of contemporary digital communication. While the auditory-transcription systems in place on my mother's smartphone might be less conducive, if only anecdotally, to recording in written form her and still other varieties of everyday, accented speech, there stands no shortage of ways by which people like her—or anyone whose dialect falls outside of the largely prescriptivist purview of "Standard" American English (SAE)—may commu-nicate through internet-communication technologies and preserve choice el-ements of their typical spoken dialects on the screen. This essay enters into a discussion of the same, if somewhat conversely, cataloguing the digital second life of one southernism, *y'all*, on one Web 2.0 platform, Twitter, and unpacking the implications of its current use as well as the conditions of its rise to relative popularity.

The sweetheart of American English's second-person pronouns, *y'all* now routinely surfaces and spreads across the English-speaking corners of Twitter (2006–), the international microblogging platform possessing of some 330 million monthly users as of August 2019.[1] A fixture in certain viral tweets and memetic tweet formats, *y'all* has gone from a "shibboleth" of southern speech in as recently as the 1990s to a working, if reluctant, metonym for its U.S. region of origin in the span of just three decades.[2] *Y'all* acts as a powerful piece of rhetorical shorthand on Twitter, an expedient means of expressing the range of communicative functions—from the diminutive *bless your heart* to the evocative *come quick!*—with which it has been organically, diachronically loaded. This remains true even inasmuch as its present-day adopters may seek to distance themselves from the same homespun, backwoods, hyperbolic affect it carries as part and parcel of its digital prehistory in vernacular speech. Nevertheless, reading the contraction as exclusively southern would fail to exhaust the scope of connotations *y'all* offers up in typed form. To the extent that this argument might urge that we think of its peculiarly regionalized register, it problematizes the same, exposing how *y'all*'s perceived southernness conceivably operates as a kind of pretext for the invisible recentering of whiteness on a platform in many ways built on the affective labor of Black tweeters and the wider dialogue-shaping online community of people of color known as "Black Twitter."[3]

For the purposes of such a line of inquiry, this essay necessarily supposes that the southern accent on Twitter—or wherever else it might be transcribed in silent text—is as monolithic in shape as its presentation in the singular here and in popular discourse would suggest, notwithstanding the veritable gulf of mutually (un)intelligible dialects one comes upon between Shreveport and Winston-Salem. That is, for their generally shared vocabularies, the plurality of accents peppered across the U.S. South coheres in a curiously, paradoxically blank synecdoche for the region at large. While, for example, *kyarn* ("carrion") might find little purchase outside of greater Appalachia, words thought common throughout southern localities would seem to consolidate the differently accented souths into a more readily recognizable, reproducible amalgam. Barbara Johnstone's work on how nonsoutherners attempt to emulate so-considered southern speech demonstrates the primacy of certain words in its legible performance, even when her research subjects provide otherwise "not

[. . .] very accurate imitation[s]."[4] What maintains the coherence of her interlocutor's technically questionable impression of a southern accent, Johnstone
suggests, is his "inclusion of *y'all*" in this instance, although she also underscores that "southerners typically do not need to call prosodic attention to the
fact that they are using *y'all* the way [he] does."[5] All other factors being equal,
y'all indexes the performance's aspiration to relativized southernness because,
she finds, "as with *literary representations* of dialect, a carefully selected subset
of dialect features may be enough to suggest the dialect."[6]

The triangulation Johnstone maps between *y'all*, perceived southernness,
and the written reproduction of dialect does much to orient the present exploration of the contraction as it appears on Twitter, a primarily text-based but increasingly multimedia-friendly social network. Twitter stands relatively unique
among other platforms of the Web 2.0 internet for the strict character limit it
imposes on user publications, "tweets," which were restricted to just 140 total
characters between 2006 (the year of its public launch) and 2017, when the
platform doubled this original figure to the current maximum of 280. Lacking
in the majority of instances the aural data necessary for conventional phono-
logical analysis, tweets betray dialect on the level of orthography above all else,
effectively collapsing the audible differences that distinguish one English accent from another, southern and not, and blurring any remaining distinction
between the authentic and inauthentic performance of dialect. Accordingly,
at least insofar as the textscape of Twitter may be concerned, accent manifests
as a visual component of user-compositions, observable in the words, spellings, or syntactical arrangements a given user provides in their tweets.

Linguist Taylor Jones arrives at a similar conclusion in his 2015 study of
Black Twitter and regional dialect. Mining the platform for tweets containing a set of previously documented Black regionalisms, Jones compiles the
available geolocation data embedded in such tweets by people of color across
the United States to assert that "individual Twitter users, even without location services enabled, could hypothetically be assigned to their cities of origin
based on the informal spellings they choose."[7] Jones's analysis produces a functional cartography of linguistic variation among the users of his study's sample
population, leading him to determine that "tweets have an 'accent.'"[8] Nevertheless, Jones is right to qualify the claim, however persuasive or reproducible
as, with the scare-quotes he places around "accent," it may prove here, and not
only because the term typically describes deviations in spoken language from
an alleged standard form.

Rather, because the platform itself restricts so liberally the length of its constitutive tweets, Twitter complicates our ability to understand any seeming linguistic quirks as directly or indirectly reflective of a user's real-world lived experience or spoken accent, particularly in the absence of other identifying information. The formal constraint, like any other, sparks invention, compression, and play with language in its users and increases in the value of abbreviations, acronyms, and nonverbal signs. As some have remarked, moreover, *y'all*—in contrast to, say, "you guys"—is gender-neutral, accommodating both those of binary gender identifications and nonbinary folks alike.[9] *Y'all* achieves gender neutrality while also retaining its second-person orientation, unlike "people" and "everyone," which conjure up an abstract third-party bloc of individuals and fail to directly address a plural audience in the manner that *y'all* does naturally.[10] More to the point, *y'all's* inherently gender-indiscriminate, plural mode of second-person address corresponds well to Twitter's platform design, as the audience with which one communicates through tweets is, far more often than not, composed of multiple people of different genders.

If we cannot determine in any consistent or verifiable way the identities or objectives of Twitter users from their tweets alone, we are left to take them quite literally at their word(s): the locus of interpretation shifts to *what* they say, not *why* they might say it, the *how* of the matter supplying a kind of provisional, contextually derived logic through which we might account for some semblance of the latter to the former. The richness of *y'all* as a communicative sign opens the door to this sort of reconstruction, but for its seeming syntactical suitability to the platform—as, again, an abbreviated second-person plural pronoun—the contraction's appearance on Twitter risks being written off as the product of circumstance alone. But Occam's razor tends to leave ingrown hairs.

For the same reason that we might attribute *y'all's* on Twitter to the mere concision it offers or to the gender inclusivity it imparts, we may equally point to *y'all's* enunciation as always already supplemental in the context of tweeted communication. Put differently: if we assume the conditions of audience address that *y'all* conceivably fulfills on the platform as true of every tweet—or at least implied by Twitter's organizational structure—*y'all's* inclusion becomes redundant, its ostensible functions more superfluous than self-evident. After all, on a network that by design places the speaker before a multitude of individually discrete potential listeners, what purpose does *y'all* serve? And for that matter, what does *y'all* satisfy that could not be achieved by the second-person singular *you* or by the imperative verb tense, with its embedded second-person directionality?

Sociolinguistics teaches that "to the extent that speakers are agentive, we can indeed say that they are always performing language, they have an awareness of alternative choices and their social meanings."[11] And provided Twitter's restriction on publication character-counts, this premium upon *choice* arises in every utterance posted on the platform, implicitly or explicitly, as an integral part of composing a tweet within the parameters allotted. When not reflexively, unconsciously adopted by its tweeter, *y'all's* appeal proves one of tone: stripped of discernible informational value by nature of its redundancy, it adds—or aspires to convey—an element of affect, mood, personality, or voice.

The colloquialism therefore proves a sign of excess, one which differentially and subjectively evokes southernness, rurality, bucolic sensibility, and homespun authenticity over and beyond its syntactical function as a pronoun, if only on Twitter (though I suspect elsewhere, too). *Y'all*, for Americanist and southern studies scholar Sharon Holland, "indicate[s] belonging" and "endearment" across cartographies and peoples, with its "roots in the South" and "home on the tongues of African American communities," their analytical separation, here, gesturing to the pervasive myth of a white South inasmuch as it accentuates *y'all's* multivalent affective registers.[12] The order of cool, unaccented, self-effacing text into which *y'all* is entered on Twitter, in spite of (and in light of) its semiotic dynamism in spoken discourse, effectively renders it a unit of what Roland Barthes terms "mythical speech," which is to say neither "a lie" nor "a confession," but an "inflection" that confoundingly discloses and forecloses both interpretations in a single motion.[13] Barthes elaborates: "What causes mythical speech to be uttered is perfectly explicit, but it is immediately frozen into something natural; it is not read as a motive, but as a reason."[14] *Y'all*, in other words, naturalizes its own deployment in the moment it is deployed, simultaneously calling up its predigital associations and seemingly muting them. The contraction connotes southernness safely, from a distance, gesturing to the region in its digestible, family-friendly form with a wink, aware of its mythical fabrication; the southernness it hopes to evoke is one without a South, southern for the sake of being southern.

Following N. Katherine Hayles's call for "media-specific analysis," to understand how *y'all* operates mythically in tweeted form requires a closer examination of the platform in question.[15] Twitter's unique structural affordances make of it a medium on which authorial intention and audience interpretation indeterminately, differentially intersect and diverge. Stated otherwise, because Twitter users may speak to any number of real or imagined readers and likewise listen from a functionally unlimited range of subject positions, tweets necessarily disclose and delimit an equally boundless array of subjectively accessible meanings. The notion of "context collapse," coined by Alice Marwick and danah boyd, strives to reconcile the indeterminacy of address in the era of networked interaction. Surveying Twitter users of varying follower counts, the two write of a need for the platform's participants to "maintain equilibrium between a contextual social norm of personal authenticity" and a related desire "to keep information private, or at least concealed from certain audiences."[16] This split motivation results in "context collapse," which "creates an audience that is often imagined as its most sensitive members."[17] The concept explains user stance by way of two slippery least-common denominators, "authenticity" and "sensitiv[ity]," which would seem to configure the tweeter as an adherent to a strange species of moral philosophy: do not transgress the content expectations presumed to be held by the majority of one's followers, and obey this command while remaining "authentic"—whatever that might mean.

For all of its explanatory power, however, "context collapse" arrived in the critical lexicon with a seeming unawareness of Twitter's then-developing role in the greater economy of internet memes in the mid-2010s. Much of the existent critical literature on the matter poses the meme in visual terms.[18] We tend to conceptualize memes along the lines of "image macros," the widely recognizable Ur-memetic form in which a visually represented emotional archetype—often but not always imported from popular media—is made to voice irreverent commentary about a given topic, which is inscribed at the top and bottom of the image in question in white, capitalized Impact font. But the "meme," first imagined in biologist Richard Dawkins's 1976 *The Selfish Gene,* originally sought to identify a cultural equivalent of the gene. In practice, this initial definition captures how text-based memes travel on Twitter in the contemporary moment, flowing from user to user as do verbally transmitted jokes, taglines, corporate jingles, or urban legends via face-to-face interaction. The content made to fill a given "memetic form," by which I refer to its guiding organizational structure, adapts as a matter of its survival as users remix, repost, and remediate individual memes on other platforms—with or without attribution—before growing overly accustomed to or bored with the humor they convey or how they go about conveying it.

For one media scholar, reading the content with which memes are loaded requires "decod[ing] a multitude of hidden, Barthesian mythological meanings that contribute to stereotypization" because they both rely upon established cultural archetypes and continually reinvent them.[19] Memes tap into a reservoir of culturally specific myths relative to the context of their production and dissemination, and they endlessly juxtapose these myths, create space for internal commentary upon them, and are on an individual basis themselves converted into myths—meta-myths—as their circulation makes them more recognizable, more formally consistent. Ultimately, Ryan Milner's purposefully broad characterization of internet memes—as, generally speaking, "linguistic, image, audio, and video texts created, circulated, and transformed by countless cultural participants across networks and collectives"—affords them the sort of formal plasticity the present writing embraces, for Twitter's dedicated "retweet" function allows for the rapid diffusion of both visual memes as well as those of a decidedly *textual* nature.[20]

To speak of a cross-platform social economy in which memes participate perhaps runs the risk of overstating their value in contemporary (digital) culture. But consider, too, the dangers of understating their purchase. The advent of Web 2.0—the social, platform-rich internet, marked by the pervasive logic of "sharing"[21]—in the years surrounding 2007 has occasioned the rise of "influencers," microcelebrities whose sizable followings on Twitter, Instagram, and other social networks have presented them with branding deals, corporate sponsorships, and nontraditional avenues for earning a living from their social media activity alone.[22] The ready conversion of social and cultural capital online into real-world material capital per the "influencer" model is not restricted to those who share popular content oriented to particular markets— the beauty industry being among the most notable in this respect—as evidenced by the 2019 controversy surrounding the meme-aggregator collective Jerry Media, which has charged upward of U.S. $30,000 per promotional post on its fleet of well-followed Instagram accounts since 2016.[23] Mike Bloomberg, billionaire and former mayor of New York City, gestured to the political value of meme-centered influencers such as those under Jerry Media's management by recruiting them into his digital ad campaign during his short-lived 2020 presidential bid, paying them to post self-reflexive content that naturalized their own sponsorship.[24]

The social capital that memes may confer, as indexed by their ability to increase their posters' follower counts or quickly accrued "likes" online, does not always—and most often does *not*—neatly translate into a conduit for capital proper, and this is particularly true for Black and women creators.[25] Even so, the multiform delivery of memes as playful, nonsensical, cynical, or otherwise humorous, ideologically charged digital media objects bespeaks an underlying economy of references well suited for the logic of "sharing" upon which Web 2.0 was envisioned and under which it now operates, if in a somewhat accelerated fashion. Whether we understand them as exercises in free play on the contemporary internet or regard them more suspiciously as shareable commodities, memes refigure the audience-expectation metric Marwick and boyd propose in "context collapse." As contextually decipherable arrangements that spread across user bases before ultimately transforming, memes encourage a kind of viral-mindedness that supersedes and modifies traditional interpersonal norms. The type of mentality memes promote, differentially manifest in the posting habits given users, prioritizes an equilibrium somewhat distinct from that which the aforementioned critics identify, one in which meme posters would appear to strive for a balance between recognizability and novelty in their production of and engagement with memes and popular memetic forms.

To avoid overdetermining intentionality here, as Twitter users on the whole act out of any number of personal or socially cultivated motivations, one might ascribe this observable—but admittedly, necessarily general—tendency to the nature of memes as formally structured units of language. Limor Shifman's characterization of "meme genres," an analogue term for what this essay calls memetic forms, acknowledges the linguistic function of memes, describing them as "operative signs: textual categories that are designed as invitations for (creative) action."[26] Decisively, the invitation memes extend is of a twofold nature, both syntactic and semantic, for they at once provide *mutable* cultural scripts to their readers and elicit their creative reinterpretation. Framing memes as linguistic molds, structurally labile but semiotically intelligible, allows us to think beyond individual intention in their production (or consumption) and better understand their constitutive economy as something more organic than willed: memes hold space for speaking *differently* in the otherwise uninflected expanse of the digital, for telling the truth with Emily Dickinson's "slant."

As a repository of ready-made signs and stock characters, the U.S. South would seem on paper inclined to its discursive repackaging in internet memes. Predigital media have made no qualms about propping up so-identified "southern" imagery, parodic caricatures of southern people and folkways, or the southern accent itself toward any number of rhetorical or diegetic ends. The images that constitute the U.S. South in popular discourse flirt openly with contradiction, fabricating a region marked by geographical isolation and unruly violence (as in *Deliverance* [1972]), by a nostalgia for antebellum sophistication and pageantry (as in *Gone with the Wind* [1939]), and by ignorance, poverty, and crudeness (à la Georgia-born comedian Jeff Foxworthy), all of which are contingent upon—and uncritical of—an understanding of southern as categorically white and necessarily Other.[27] Although these familiar constructions of southernness certainly inform how the region takes shape on Twitter, the early-2000s cult of the "redneck [. . .] commodified and merchandised nationally as a source of humor and comedy" has largely lost the comic edge that lent it widespread currency in the popular imagination just a decade or two ago.[28] This is not to say that memes do not poke fun at southernness through the tropes common to earlier media, of course, for many do: *Know Your Meme*, the acclaimed archive of all things memetic, lists a variety of memes under tags such as "redneck," "hillbilly," "Dixie," "Alabama," and still other southern keywords. Rather, in the localized digital context of Twitter, it seems that humor at the *explicit* expense of southernness has come to occupy a relatively diminished position in the cultural dialogue of Web 2.0. The reason for such a general decline, while unclear, perhaps stems from the ever-globalizing reach of Web 2.0 technologies; although one would be hardpressed to contend that *no* Twitter users traffic in southern-directed humor, we might easily imagine that our collective frames of reference have become more national than regional.

Twitter's sheer breadth makes it difficult to characterize its goings-on with any great precision. In 2018, approximately 500 million tweets were published on the platform per day, amounting to a staggering near-5,800 posts every second.[29] The resulting deluge of tweeted commentary—of which around a third is written in English—defies straightforward discourse analysis, outpacing cultural criticism and requiring that one adopt focalizing parameters.[30] One way around the problem inherent to locating traces of southernness on a platform of such scale therefore lies in scanning for those discrete words which, following Johnstone, in other milieu conjure southernness in the public imaginary. And while her work suggests that *y'all* tends to ring southern, a search for the term alone reasonably returns millions of distinct entries.[31] Some appear to use *y'all* in a seemingly natural and syntactically productive way—as when one speaker replies to multiple others—and in other instances it seems altogether affective and supplementary. Distinguishing an "organic" *y'all* from a performative one ultimately requires context beyond what a single, isolated tweet can offer.

Still, as the preceding discussion tried to lay bare, the meme can be a helpful tool in this effort, as the intelligibility of a given meme rests upon the larger cultural imaginary out of which it arose and to which it speaks. For this reason, we may look to a key set of memetic phrases that prominently feature *y'all* as somewhat representative of the contraction's affective registers on Twitter, because their popularity and spread betray certain commonly held connotations as well as gesture to a shared vernacular origin on the platform. With attention to the remaining space allotted to the present argument, we will look at three memetic tweet formats of this type.

According to *Know Your Meme*'s entry, May 2017 witnessed the emergence of *y'all consider this a date?* on Twitter, attributed to a tweet by @TheVibeControl that poses the question in reference to an adjoining two-minute video in which two people of color create music together, smiling, dancing, and singing while an original beat plays in the background.[32] The question reads both playful and sincere, as the two appear openly enamored with one another even though the depicted events take place in what seems to be an apartment living room, a space we might not conventionally associate with a "date" in its most formal or traditional sense. *Y'all consider this a date?* in its earliest known iteration thus asks us to reconsider how we may conceive of romance, urging us through the rhetorical maneuver—dependent upon *y'all* insofar as it directs the question to the reader—to reflect upon the extent to which our ritualization and commodification of the "date" has precluded our ability to recognize care, affection, or desire in seemingly unconventional contexts.

This first tweet, for all of its outward sincerity, quickly sparked more discernibly playful variants. Within two weeks the form abounded: @Namastaywoke entered the fray by appending the question to a headline tweeted by Miami-based news station WSVN, "Venomous snake bites man, man bites wife in hopes they could die together." The user's clever, recycled quip amassed some one hundred thousand likes by the time of writing.[33] By the close of August of the same year, the meme had run its course, as evidenced by the joke's deployment as self-reflexive parody and a concomitant outpouring of tweets that take open issue with the form's apparent overabundance. The tweet @blackvial asks, "y'all consider this a date?" with an attached photo of a *literal* date, the fruit.[34] Another tweeter writes, "Ok enough with the 'y'all consider this a date?'

tweets. Yes. It is a date. Everything w bae is a date. Next."[35] Each of these ulti-
mate examples, which respectively have received 1,000 and 270 likes on the
platform, suggests that the form had fallen out of fashion and become hyper-
recognizable in just three months' time, achieving what I have elsewhere
called *critical mass*: the endpoint in a meme's initial lifecycle, the point at
which its mass popularization prompts it to enter dormancy.[36] Although *y'all
consider this a date* certainly retains some purchase in ongoing tweeted discourse, it now operates in a decidedly more lighthearted than truly curious
manner and appears with less frequency than during its original boom.

If the above *y'all*-structured tweet emerged from a place of relative sincerity before becoming something more thoroughly parodic through its memefication on Twitter, our next object of inquiry grew out of what would seem a
deliberately funny first application in audiovisual form. The memetic format
that begins with "y'all mind if I" and subsequently introduces a typically in-
nocuous action by most accounts owes its online revival to a July 2016 You-
Tube upload, "Drug Dealer dancing to New FLY YOUNG RED!!!! 'Throw It'"[37] In
the video, New Orleans–based rapper Fly Young Red plays a then-new single
of his, "Throw It," from his car stereo while driving by an unidentified Black
man. The musician asks the man if he has heard it yet; nodding his head to the
beat, the man responds that he has not, asking Fly Young Red, "y'all mind if I
wild out?" before breaking out into dance on the sidewalk.

The seeming incongruity of the moment depicted, incongruous insofar as
we might not imagine strangers on sidewalks dancing at first listen to the songs
we play, resembles the aforementioned *y'all consider this a date* at the level of
potential critique: *do* we mind if he "wild[s] out" in this way, even if it should
breach convention? The humor implicit to—and ostensibly intended by—
the juxtaposition of the question with what follows suggests that we should
indeed *mind*, at once undercutting the authenticity of the request and complicating the commentary it might conceivably seek to stage. Nevertheless, this
presumed source of the now-memetic *y'all*-anchored expression, while itself
fifty-eight seconds long, prompted an early outpouring of similarly oriented
content across the Twitter-owned Vine (2013–17), a highly popular social network distinctive for the six-second videos it allowed users to post during its
four years of operation.

Journalist and cultural critic Jeff Ihaza rightly understands Vine as a platform on which non-Black users regularly proved able to profit materially on
the fruits of Black creators' labor, appropriating and remixing the ephemeral

content posted by people of color without attribution. He observes that "the cultural capital exchanged on Vine—dances, memes and expressions like 'ayyy'—originate with the app's black users [. . .] shut out from the new celebrity status created on Vine."[38] Indeed, now-popular phrases such as "eyebrows on fleek," coined by Atlanta teenager Kayla Newman, materialized on the free-to-use Vine only to be subsequently incorporated into nationwide ad campaigns that offer no compensation to their readily identifiable Black creators.[39]

Although it has since 2016 undergone considerable memetic transformation, leaving intact only the syntactic frame of its first four words, *y'all mind if I*, follows in the tradition of cultural appropriation of Black content that writers such as Ihaza and Lauren Jackson find true of Vine, Twitter, and other social networks. The expression appeared on Black Twitter, indexed in vernacular, everyday descriptions by predominantly Black tweeters, well before its popularization in and after 2016. Sarah Florini characterizes "Black Twitter" not as any imagined, homogenous racial monolith, but rather as "Black users on Twitter networking, connecting, and engaging with others who have similar concerns, experiences, tastes, and cultural practices."[40] For Florini, as well as for scholars André Brock and Raven Maragh, Black Twitter is a body of users linked by shared discursive cultural practices such as "signifyin'," which is to say, "a genre of linguistic performance that allows for the communication of multiple levels of meaning simultaneously" that has its roots in predigital Black oral traditions, cultural forms, and ways of knowing.[41] On Twitter, culturally informed, Black linguistic practices like signifyin' serve to "enact certain complex articulations of blackness" and assert one's "racial authenticity" through text,[42] a strategy of digital self-presentation that both performs identity in a personally meaningful way and combats the presumption of whiteness and/or white masculinity often uncritically and inaccurately embedded in the nondescript terminology of "user."[43]

The circulation of textual arrangements like *y'all mind if I* among Black and non-Black tweeters calls into view the distinction between signifyin', which takes its cues from vernacular convention, and memetic play, which would seem to reduce all things to flattened mythical speech. Take, for instance, the ways in which the unaccented phrase surfaces throughout the Twitter feed of one @CaucasianJames, a white Wisconsinite man whose online self-fashioning as ostensibly self-effacing, (hetero)sexually frustrated, and—as his user name declares—white has allowed him to accrue some 1.1 million followers since 2011. Although he regularly deletes "low-engagement" tweets, @Caucasian-

James has used the *y'all mind if I* structure fifty-one recorded times in three years, merely repeating "y'all mind if i have a good week" in twenty-nine of them (as he has done on a semiregular basis since July of 2019).[44] That the user adopted the phrase after its wide popularization in the latter half of 2016 and subsequently began to treat it as a fixture of his developing online persona speaks to how he encountered it: as a meme, inherited from Vine, from YouTube, from Black people and Black users, stripped of its cultural specificity while curiously dependent upon it for the humor it seeks to generate. Put otherwise, because the joke implicit to his application of *y'all mind if I* rests upon his outward difference to the Blackness it registers, @CaucasianJames performs a kind of distanced—if perhaps unintentional—"blaccent" through his adoption of it. Two steps removed from its original circulation, *y'all mind if I*'s textual afterlife as a meme retains a link, if subtle, to its audiovisual forerunners, affecting blaccent in its purposeful delivery as humor, as hyperbole, as soundbite. Typed, *y'all mind if I* may not carry the palpable, racist verbal trappings or linguistic tics that often attend caricatures of Black speech in audiovisual or real-world performances of blaccent, but it nevertheless calls upon the cultural memory of its once-audible enunciation as part and parcel of its rearticulation as a joke.

The appeal of the phrase to @CaucasianJames, as well as to users like him, would not seem unfounded. In the thirty-two recorded times that he has tweeted "y'all mind if i have a good week," the user has yet to attract fewer than 21,000 likes on any one post (and once received as many as 75,000), speaking to the tastes of his follower-base as much as they may reflect his own.[45] Interestingly, too, when the user inexplicably released a line of branded merchandise, he included the phrase in his announcement: "y'all mind if i drop merch."[46] The following week, he repeated it in a sponsored post he tweeted at the behest of restaurant chain Dos Toros: "y'all mind if i get this money real quick?"[47] Incorporating the phrase in his earliest promotional tweets, the user betrays in his marketization of *y'all mind if I* his very distance from it. Treated as received knowledge, as a memetic a priori, its commercial deployment as an advertisement seeks to gain entry into a larger cultural dialogue and its constitutive consumer base. The user's articulation of *y'all* in the service of marketing thus signals a certain disinterest in sounding specifically southern, per se, or in suggesting any regional affiliation, for that matter. It rather indexes the expression's dilution and memefication to the point of its near-cultural non-specificity in spite of, and perhaps due to, its etiology in Black vernacular. As "postracial" as the performance might think itself to be, the phrase's seeming democratization in the memetic *y'all mind if I* follows in the extended legacy of Black cultural expropriation in the United States: the expression accrues perceived value for general audiences only after it has been coopted by non-Black mouthpieces.

Lauren Jackson's landmark 2017 *Teen Vogue* essay on "digital blackface" calls into question the widespread, largely unchecked overrepresentation of Black people (but primarily Black women) in reaction GIFs. Posing the phenomenon as a digital-age form of minstrelsy, Jackson underscores the audial perceptibility of verbal "blaccent" in the physical world as a point of distinction with digital blackface, which "uses the relative anonymity of online identity to embody blackness."[48] While the writer also notes a tendency for non-Black users to assume caricatured Black identities online, "operat[ing] under stolen profile pictures and butchered AAVE [African American Vernacular English]," Jackson's shrewd piece does not enter into any discussion of those who coopt Black vernacular as a means of producing humor through text, focusing instead on the way that those who perform digital blackface attempt to achieve the same through visual, image-based memes. But the all but invisible repurposing of decidedly Black enunciations of *y'all* in standardized memetic forms demonstrates cause to expand her critique's initial parameters. @CaucasianJames, along with countless others who follow in a similar pattern of tweet production or consumption, may not post GIFs, photos, or audiovisual material that call upon images of Black people with the explicit aim of "inhabiting a black persona" or expressing "hyperbolic emotions" through the visual shorthand of the GIF, but his recurrent appropriation of *y'all mind if I* for its perceived, tacit humor reads as a silent operation of blaccent enacted at the level of stylized text.[49]

If both *y'all mind if I* and *y'all consider this a date* developed organically in Black vernacular before diffusing memetically across Twitter and the broader Web 2.0 ecosystem, it should come as little surprise that our final example, *but y'all aren't ready to have that conversation,* shares the same relativized point of origin. Attached to the end of an expressed opinion, the phrase levels a critique at what its tweeter recognizes either as common misconception or underlying truth. Per the platform's advanced search function, *but y'all aren't ready* seems to have entered the discursive spotlight at the close of August 2018 with a tweet by @BrettMau5_, "Olive Garden is basically italian Applebee's but y'all aren't ready to have that conversation yet," which has been liked over forty thousand times.[50]

While adjusting the search's timeframe closer to the present reveals a wealth of playful iterations, scanning the network for prior examples returns only a handful, most of which are more serious in tone than the above and all of which are published by outwardly Black users. Its first recorded entry on Twitter, omitted here for the sake of privacy, casts light on the abusive nature of some approaches to parenting. Another lies nested in a series of tweets that probe the root causes of human conflict. But within a month of @Brett-Mau5_'s viral tweet, *but y'all aren't ready* devolved into a remark seemingly valued only insofar as it can reduce to hyperbole any ostensibly controversial perspective. As one user muses, "Spongebob is a wage slave brainwashed by Mr. Krabs' capitalist ways but y'all aren't ready to have that conversation."[51]

To say it unequivocally: the memetic *y'all* one tends to encounter on Twitter does not come from a place of southernness, performative or authentic, not in the conventional sense at least. It instead almost exclusively works in a tacit effort to mimic Black speech, retaining a veneer of neutrality to the extent that the term *also* evokes southernness in the American cultural imaginary. And this imagined southernness, lest it be forgotten, is of a lily-white variety, for as Tara McPherson observes—and importantly challenges—visions of the U.S. South often obey a certain "lenticular logic" under which the truly racially heterogeneous region is framed as either Black *or* white.[52] Coupled with the U.S. South's historical and contemporary imbrication within a regime of anti-Black racism, the representational logic obscures southern Blackness and the lived experiences of Black southerners, producing an image of the region that is, more often than not, lamentably white.

While it remains unclear to what degree this memetic *y'all* could account for the contraction's now-widespread uptake across Twitter, we might safely wager that only a comparably small number of the thousands of users who engage with those tweets constructed around *y'all consider this a date, y'all mind if I,* or *but y'all aren't ready* understand the contraction's inclusion with the level of personal intimacy or reflexivity we might find among Black and/or southern (and/or rural) users. Moreover, precisely because memes take part in a kind of economy of references in which the perceived value of the joke outweighs that of its source, and because they do so through the language of ostensibly depoliticized mythic speech and cultural archetypes, *y'all*'s center-stage position in a number of text-based Twitter memes lends it a curious currency in the contemporary moment, a cultural purchase that is pegged to its blaccented affect inasmuch as it may seek to blunt the same. The memetic *y'all* brokers a kind of plausible deniability in this way: it registers as blaccent and the (white) southern accent at once, conferring upon those users who engage with it the means to distance themselves from any interpretation that might pose them as participating in digital blackface by another name. And in effect, *y'all's* memefication on Twitter would seem to leave it neither accented nor unaccented but—in the Barthesian sense—still altogether *inflected*.

NOTES

1. Twitter, "Number of monthly active Twitter users worldwide from 1st quarter 2010 to 1st quarter 2019 (in millions)."

2. Montgomery, "A Note on Ya'll." 273.

3. Brock, "From the Blackhand Side," 530; André Brock describes Black Twitter as "Twitter's mediation of Black cultural discourse" and resulting "'social public'; a community constructed through their use of social media by outsiders and insiders alike."

4. Johnstone, "Southern Speech with a Northern Accent," 502.

5. Ibid., 503.

6. Ibid., 505; emphasis mine.

7. Jones, "Toward a Description of African American Vernacular," 428–29.

8. Ibid., 429.

9. Mitsch, "Let's talk about 'guys.'"

10. Carey, "How Gender Neutral is *Guys*, Really?"

11. Bell and Gibson, "Staging Language," 556.

12. Holland, "Editor's Note: Y'all," iii.

13. Barthes, *Mythologies*, 128.

14. Ibid.

15. Hayles, *Writing Machines*, 29.

16. Marwick and boyd, "I tweet honestly, I tweet passionately," 11.

17. Ibid., 13.

18. See, for example, Limor Shifman's *Memes and Digital Culture* (2014), Ryan Milner's *The World Made Meme* (2016), Linda Börzsei's "Makes a Meme Instead" (2013), and Marta Dynel's "'I Has Seen Image Macros!'" (2016).

19. Pavlović, "Internet Memes as a Field of Discursive Construction of Identity and Space of Resistance," 101.

20. Milner, *The World Made Meme*, 1.

21. John, "Sharing and Web 2.0," 167.

22. Hund and McGuian, "A Shoppable Life," 20.

23. Carman, "Comedians are coming."

24. Tiffany, "You Can't Buy Memes."

25. Jackson, "Memes and Misogynoir"; Ihaza, "The People's Platform."

26. Shifman, *Memes in Digital Culture*, 34.

27. See, for example, Riché Richardson's *Black Masculinity and the U.S. South* (2007), Tara McPherson's *Reconstructing Dixie* (2003), and Scott Romine's *The Real South* (2008) for more on the fictive whiteness that has come to define the South.

28. Jarosz and Lawson, "'Sophisticated People versus Rednecks,'" 12.

29. *Mention, 2018 Twitter Report.*

30. Richter, "Only 34% of All Tweets"; available data on Twitter's linguistic makeup are few and far between, but according to a 2013 report—the last year on record—English was the most-used language on the platform at just 34 percent of all surveyed tweets, followed by Japanese (16 percent), Spanish (12 percent), and Malay (8 percent).

31. See Johnstone's aforementioned "Southern Speech in a Northern Accent" as well as her co-authored article with Baumgart on early digital communication, in which the two refer to user commentary linking *y'all* specifically with the U.S. South.

32. *Know Your Meme*, s.v. "Y'all Consider This a Date?"

33. @Namastaywoke, "Y'all consider this a date?": retweeting WSVN 7 News (@wsvn), "Venomous snake bites man, man bites wife in hopes they could die together."

34. @blackvial, "y'all consider this a date?"

35. @bella_patella, "Ok enough with the 'y'all consider this a date?' tweets. Yes. It is a date. Everything w bae is a date. Next."

36. McCracken, "Critical Mass as Obsolescence."

37. Know Your Meme, s.v. "You Mind if I Wild Out?"

38. Ihaza, "The People's Platform."

39. Smith, "Vine was a place for black teenagers to seize mainstream culture. And now it's gone."

40. Florini, "Tweets, Tweeps, and Signifyin'," 225.

41. Ibid., 224.

42. Maragh, "Authenticity on 'Black Twitter,'" 601.

43. See, for example, Lisa Nakamura's research on race, racism, and the presumed whiteness of the internet in her *Cybertypes* (2002) and *Digitizing Race* (2008).

44. The user first tweeted the phrase on June 17, 2019, and has continued since that time to semiregularly repost it. In response to the COVID-19 crisis, on March 23, 2020, he began to add "indoors" to the end of "y'all mind if i have a good week" and has done the same as of April 17, 2020.

45. @CaucasianJames, "y'all mind if i have a good week," Twitter, June 17, 2019, 1:27 P.M.; @CaucasianJames, "y'all mind if i have a good week," Twitter, September 9, 2019, 11:11 A.M.

46. @CaucasianJames, "y'all mind if i drop merch."

47. @CaucasianJames, "y'all mind if i get this money real quick?"

48. Jackson, "We Need to Talk About Digital Blackface in Reaction GIFs."

49. Ibid.

50. @BrettMau5_, "Olive Garden is basically italian Applebee's but y'all aren't ready to have that conversation yet."

51. @BeefedUpBaddie, "Spongebob is a wage slave brainwashed by Mr. Krabs' capitalist ways but y'all aren't ready to have that conversation."

52. McPherson, *Reconstructing Dixie*, 26.

BIBLIOGRAPHY

"Y'all Consider This a Date?" *Know Your Meme*. Published June 13, 2017. Last modified March 27, 2017. https://knowyourmeme.com/memes/yall-consider-this-a-date.

"You Mind if I Wild Out?" *Know Your Meme*. Published September 15, 2016. Last modified March 31, 2020. https://knowyourmeme.com/memes/you-mind-if-i-wild-out.

@BeefedUpBaddie. "Spongebob is a wage slave brainwashed by Mr. Krabs' capitalist ways but y'all aren't ready to have that conversation." Twitter, October 1, 2018. https://twitter.com/BeefedUpBaddie/status/1046939797388849152?s=20.

@bella_patella. "Ok enough with the 'y'all consider this a date?' tweets. Yes. It is a date. Everything w bae is a date. Next." Twitter, August 30, 2017. https://twitter.com/bella_patella/status/903000784912220160.

@blackvial. "y'all consider this a date?" Twitter, August 30, 2017. https://twitter.com/blackvial/status/903050036371628032.

@BrettMau5_. "Olive Garden is basically italian Applebee's but y'all aren't ready to have that conversation yet." Twitter, August 31, 2018. https://twitter.com/BrettMau5_/status/1035642372183478272.

@CaucasianJames. "y'all mind if i drop merch." Twitter, September 19, 2019. https://twitter.com/CaucasianJames/status/1174836984700985346?s=20.

———. "y'all mind if i get this money real quick? thank u to the good people at @dostoros for partnering with me and officially making me an influencer baddie. bet she wishes she could have me now [. . .] #ad." Twitter, September 26, 2019. https://twitter.com/CaucasianJames/status/1177361838255857664?s=20.

———. "y'all mind if i have a good week." Twitter, June 17, 2019. https://twitter.com/CaucasianJames/status/1140672247914553345?s=20.

———. "y'all mind if i have a good week." Twitter, September 9, 2019. https://twitter.com/CaucasianJames/status/1171078667268775936?s=20.

@Namastaywoke. "Y'all consider this a date?" retweeting WSVN 7 News (@wsvn), "Venomous snake bites man, man bites wife in hopes they could die together." Twitter, June 14, 2017. https://twitter.com/Namastaywoke/status/875003176369434624.

Barthes, Roland. *Mythologies*. Translated by Annette Lavers. New York: Farrar, Straus & Giroux, 1972.

Bell, Allan, and Andy Gibson. "Staging Language: An Introduction to the Sociolinguistics of Performance." *Journal of Sociolinguistics* 15, no. 5 (2011): 555–72.

Börzsei, Linda K. "Makes a Meme Instead: A Concise History of Internet Memes." *New Media Studies Magazine* 7 (2013): 1–28.

Brock, André. "From the Blackhand Side: Twitter as a Cultural Conversation." *Journal of Broadcasting & Electronic Media* 54, no. 4 (2012): 529–49.

Carey, Stan. "How Gender Neutral Is *Guys*, Really?" *Slate*, February 10, 2016. https://slate.com/human-interest/2016/02/the-gender-neutral-use-of-guys-is-on-the-rise-but-it-s-a-slow-rise.html.

Carman, Ashley. "Comedians are coming for one of Instagram's biggest joke aggregators." *The Verge*, February 1, 2019, https://www.theverge.com/2019/2/1/18206914/.

Dawkins, Richard. *The Selfish Gene*. Oxford: Oxford University Press, 1976.

Dynel, Marta. "'I Has Seen Image Macros!' Advice Animal Memes as Visual-Verbal Jokes." *International Journal of Communication* 10 (2016): 660–88.

Florini, Sarah. "Tweets, Tweeps, and Signifyin': Communication and Cultural Performance on 'Black Twitter.'" *Television & New Media* 15, no. 3 (2014): 223–37.

Hayles, N. Katherine. *Writing Machines*. Cambridge, MA: MIT Press, 2002.

Holland, Sharon P. "Editor's Note: Y'all." *Southern Literary Journal* 47, no. 2 (2015): iii–iv.

Hund, Emily, and Lee McGuian. "A Shoppable Life: Performance, Selfhood, and Influence in the Social Media Storefront." *Communication, Culture and Critique* 12, no. 1 (2019): 18–35.

Ihaza, Jeff. "The People's Platform." *The Awl*, August 3, 2015, https://www.theawl.com/2015/08/the-peoples-platform/.

Jackson, Lauren M. "We Need to Talk about Digital Blackface in Reaction GIFs." *Teen Vogue*, August 2, 2017, https://www.teenvogue.com/story/digital-blackface-reaction-gifs.

———. "Memes and Misogynoir." *The Awl*, August 28, 2014. https://www.theawl.com/2014/08/memes-and-misogynoir/.

Jarosz, Lucy, and Victoria Lawson. "'Sophisticated People versus Rednecks': Economic Restructuring and Class Difference in America's West." *Antipode* 34 (2002): 8–27.

John, Nicholas A. "Sharing and Web 2.0: The Emergence of a Keyword." *New Media & Society* 15, no. 2 (2012): 167–82.

Johnstone, Barbara. "Southern Speech with a Northern Accent: Performance Norms in an Imitation." *American Speech* 93, no. 3–4 (2018): 497–512.

Johnstone, Barbara, and Dan Baumgardt. "'Pittsburghese' Online: Vernacular Norming in Conversation." *American Speech* 79, no. 2 (2004): 115–45.

Jones, Taylor. "Toward a Description of African American Vernacular English Dialect Regions Using 'Black Twitter.'" *American Speech* 90, no. 4 (2015): 403–40.

Maragh, Raven S. "Authenticity on 'Black Twitter': Reading Racial Performance and Social Networking." *Television & New Media* 19, no. 7 (2018): 591–609.

Marwick, Alice E., and danah boyd. "I tweet honestly, I tweet passionately: Twitter users, context collapse, and the imagined audience." *new media & society* 20, no. 10 (2010): 1–20.

McCracken, Sam. "Critical Mass as Obsolescence: Internet Memes and the Ephemerality of Digital Culture." Paper presented at the Politics of Aesthetics and Obsolescence Graduate Conference, University of Minnesota, Minneapolis, MN, October 2018.

McPherson, Tara. *Reconstructing Dixie: Race, Gender, and Nostalgia in the Imagined South*. Durham, NC: Duke University Press, 2003.

Mention. *2018 Twitter Report*. Mention Solutions, May 2018. https://info.mention.com/twitter-report.

Milner, Ryan M. *The World Made Meme: Public Conversations and Participatory Media.* Cambridge, MA: MIT Press, 2016.

Mitsch, Jessica. "Let's talk about 'guys.'" *CIO Blog,* November 18, 2016, https://www.cio.com /article/3142382/.

Montgomery, Michael B. "A Note on Ya'll." *American Speech* 64, no. 3 (1989): 273–75.

Nakamura, Lisa. *Cybertypes: Race, Ethnicity, and Identity on the Internet.* New York: Routledge, 2002.

———. *Digitizing Race: Visual Cultures of the Internet.* Minneapolis: University of Minnesota Press, 2008.

Pavlović, Lidija M. "Internet Memes as a Field of Discursive Construction of Identity and Space of Resistance." Translated by Ana Stevanović. *Art + Media: Journal of Art and Media Studies* 10 (2016): 97–106.

Richardson, Riché. *Black Masculinity and the U. S. South: From Uncle Tom to Gangsta.* Athens: University of Georgia Press, 2007.

Richter, Felix. "Only 34% of All Tweets Are in English." Statista. December 16, 2013. https:// www.statista.com/chart/1726/languages-used-on-twitter/.

Romine, Scott. *The Real South: Southern Narrative in the Age of Cultural Reproduction.* Baton Rouge: Louisiana State University Press, 2008.

Shifman, Limor. *Memes in Digital Culture.* Cambridge, MA: MIT Press, 2014.

Smith, Jack, IV. "Vine was a place for black teenagers to seize mainstream culture. And now it's gone." *Mic,* October 27, 2016, https://www.mic.com/articles/157879/vine-was-a -place-for-black-teenagers-to-seize-mainstream-culture-and-now-it-s-gone.

Tiffany, Kaitlyn. "You Can't Buy Memes." *Atlantic,* February 28, 2020, https://www.the atlantic.com/technology/archive/2020/02/bloomberg-memes-instagram-ads/607219/.

Twitter. "Number of monthly active Twitter users worldwide from 1st quarter 2010 to 1st quarter 2019 (in millions)." Statista. April 23, 2019. https://www.statista.com/statistics /282087/number-of-monthly-active-twitter-users/.

ÁRIYASƐMA OF BITS AND ATOMS

A Tunica-Biloxi Revitalization Movement
Powered by Digital Fabrication

JEAN-LUC PIERITE

AT THE BEGINNING OF all things, according to our tradition, is the Flood. The chief calls an elder man and an elder woman who present two different visions for the future of tayoroniku, meaning "the People." Facing rising waters and Earth changes, tayoroniku either dance in thanksgiving for an abundance of fish or rush to build a large boat. Following this story comes halnisapirati, meaning "the new completion of the Earth." The futures of tayoroniku are decided by our actions informed by the two visions. If we dance, we sink into the waters and become fish. Those who build a vessel continue as tayoroniku. Descendants of tayoroniku ultimately become part of tayoroniku-halayihku— the Tunica-Biloxi Nation—an amalgamation of Tunica, Ofo, Biloxi-Choctaw, and Avoyel. tayoroniku-halayihku continues because of community, land, tradition, and Injunuity. áriyasɛma, meaning "keepers of the medicine and the ways," traditionally incorporate technology/science and pharmacology with the spiritual just as the elder man and elder woman had done. Injunuity in tayoroniku-halayihku is characteristic of the work of áriyasɛma, though it is a quality found in all community members. The last traditional chief and áriya for tayoroniku-halayihku is Joseph Alcide Pierite, Sr., who walked on in 1976. As this essay discusses, tayoroniku-halayihku continue to preserve their ways with increasingly digital technologies.

An emergent phase of tayoroniku-halayihku cultural revitalization in-cludes the application of insights from artifact conservation and preservation, as well as language documentation and instruction. This coincides with a dig-ital revolution in fabrication, again uniting traditional practices with technol-ogy. This phase of the revitalization movement empowers individuals to find local solutions through current technologies. Digital fabrication tools and pro-cesses are integrated with Indigenous traditional tools and processes such as brain tanning, beadwork, and hand stitching. A global community of makers and innovation spaces, including a network of digital fabrication laboratories, or "fab labs," invite tayoroniku-halayihku and other Indigenous nations to join.

The idea of a fab lab is that a person can enter one, work on a project, then continue the work from any other node in the international network. That said, there are no cookie cutter installations. Walking into a fab lab means seeing students, architects, artisans, and engineers. Additionally, each fab lab is required to have a level of open access for community members. Each person is designing, making, and sharing projects locally and globally. There are mobile fab labs on trailers, trucks, and bicycles. There are super fab labs that host a variety of tools aside from the core set. Each lab has at least a laser cutter, a 3D printer, a vinyl cutter, a large CNC router, and a numerically controlled (NC) mini-mill. While fab labs are flexible to local realities, an intentional look at needs as defined by tayoroniku-halayihku requires further malleability to integrate into the local ecosystem and to be effective.

With the promise of new digital literacies and competencies, tayoroniku-halayihku face challenges rooted in Western social systems that struggle to stay in step with digital technologies.[1] In an open-source digital domain, intellectual property remains a concern for an Indigenous nation, such as tayoroniku-halayihku, who spent decades fighting for repatriation of sacred objects and human remains and nearly centuries for federal recognition of tribal sovereignty. Despite an "Internet of Things" with ubiquitous smart devices, Indigenous nations face digital divide and gaps in access for all members across age groups, whether within traditional Indigenous territory or in urban settings. In tayoroniku-halayihku revitalization movements, attitudes shift concerning questions of assimilation into outer communities, affirmation of self-determination, and Indigenization or Injunuity. Immediate concerns within our nation center educational outcomes, fostering citizen entrepreneurship, and integrating culture with government policy.

Digital fabrication technologies and education are currently integrated in Indigenous nations in North America. A network of tribal colleges and universities (TCUs) with essential advanced manufacturing facilities is established in a collaborative project between Sandia National Laboratories and the American Indian Higher Education Consortium (AIHEC). The first fab lab serving Alaska Native corporations in the United States continues operations at the Cook Inlet Tribal Council in Anchorage, Alaska. Onaki FabLab, located in Ottawa since 2018, is Canada's first Indigenous-centered fab lab educational space. A growing community of Indigenous voices shares knowledge with the broader international network of fab labs. In this proposal for applying digital fabrication technologies toward current cultural revitalization movements, tayoroniku-halayihku forges new alliances. Despite the challenges, the "Tunica Trail" extends from the province of Quiz Quiz to Marksville, Louisiana, on into the digital domain. It is also important to distinguish fab lab educational programming specifically through participation in an international network and a model of distributed education. This essay explores the generative capacity of new media and the promotion of digital fabrication literacy within Indigenous nations, such as tayoroniku-halayihku. The essay proposes applications of digital technologies toward a self-organized holistic cultural revitalization movement uniting cultural traditions and traditional technologies with Western technologies promoting cultural sustainability and sovereignty.

The challenge of implementing digital fabrication within the cultural revitalization movement of tayoroniku-halayihku is to overcome the perception that the particular set of tools and processes are foreign in nature to Indigenous peoples. Such a perception roots digital fabrication tools in technological fundamentalism or within the legacy of Western colonial structures. tayoroniku-halayihku is experienced in importing new tools and processes within the scope of cultural repatriation and language revitalization. In either capacity, tayoroniku-halayihku enhance and expand on the work of conservation and preservation of material culture informed by knowledge of ancestral technology embedded in heritage languages. Going beyond that, the needs of tayoroniku-halayihku to improve educational outcomes and foster citizen entrepreneurship require systemic change at the tribal government level. Centering our nation, the adoption of these digital technologies spirals out from classes to business proposals to acts of legislation. Whether tayoroniku-halayihku ultimately adopt digital fabrication toward the proposed application or not, the end result should always be to further self-determination as an Indigenous nation.

This essay is the result of four years of conversations, observations, and literature reviews concerning the international fab lab network. Most importantly, background information relies heavily on personal experiences of language documentation and revitalization projects done within my immediate family. As a tribal singer and legend keeper, my preference is to recognize the land and ecosystem and to center discussion on what best serves both. The fab lab network arose from educational outreach programming by MIT's Center for Bits and Atoms. With over 1,600 labs in over one hundred countries, the network members meet annually to discuss projects and initiatives locally, regionally, and globally. There is also work done toward the completion of Fab Academy, a distributed education program facilitated by the Fab Foundation. Students must document mastery of core competencies around fab lab activities and combine several into a final project. This essay would not be possible without the help of champions, gurus, colleagues, coworkers, and family. Among the honor roll are names including Walter Gonzales Arnao, John D. Barbry, Tomas Diez, Nettrice Gaskins, Neil Gershenfeld, Craig Hobern, Beno Juarez, Haakon Karlsen, Mel King, Pamela King, Sherry Lassiter, Judith Maxwell, Minh Man Nguyen, Wendy Neale, Donna M. Pierite, Michael R. Pierite, Elisabeth Pierite-Mora, and Victor Jose Santana.

Periods of Individual Stress and Cultural Distortion

Anthony F. C. Wallace's description of the generic structure of the revitalization process follows five stages: steady state, period of individual stress, period of cultural distortion, period of revitalization, and a new steady state.[2] For Wallace, "Stress on one level is stress on all levels."[3] The structure describes a population that at first navigates stress with culturally recognized techniques. Individual stress impacts the efficiency of established techniques. Cultural distortion arises from the failure of techniques and anxiety on changing behavior patterns. The revitalization process as described by Wallace centers the religious over the secular. The revitalization stage is initiated by a single leader or prophet.[4] The idea of a central charismatic leader is not limited to the revitalization process and is found in fab lab educational outreach. A "fab lab champion" is defined by the Fab Foundation as one who has a passion for community development through technological deployment.[5] Central to the ideas of this essay is a community consultation process which focuses less on individuals. Over the course of the essay, I use personal anecdotes to help illustrate experiences and challenges.

Jeffrey P. Brain asserts that tayoroniku-halayihku has survived from the late nineteenth century to the present day through the maintenance of tribal lands and culture. He credits a viable chieftancy, traditional ceremonies, sacred knowledge, and language.[6] The late nineteenth and early twentieth century is a steady state for tayoroniku-halayihku when observed through the structure of a revitalization movement. A period of individual stress happens earlier in the mid-nineteenth century. Brian Klopotek details the legal maneuvers of American colonists to steal land within tayoroniku-halayihku traditional Indigenous territory. This history climaxes in 1841 when Celestin Moreau, Jr., shot and killed Chief Melacon, known presently as Milikan Youchigant.[7] Chief Volsin Chiki, starting in the 1870s, initiated a stage of revitalization through the refurbishment of the cemeteries and the rejuvenation of *fête du blé,* the traditional green corn ceremony.[8]

Following the steady state of the late nineteenth and early twentieth centuries, tayoroniku-halayihku again take on a period of individual stress. Arsene Chiki, the mother of Chief Sesostrie Youchigant, dies on nearby railroad tracks after she is struck by a train in 1915. Four years prior to this, Arsene's brother Fulgence dies on the same tracks. The local court rules against Chief Youchigant when he brings suit against the railroad for wrongful death in his mother's case. Louisiana Supreme Court affirms the decision in 1920. Under the civil code of the State of Louisiana, Chief Youchigant's parents are not officially married—despite their marriage being officiated through our tradition.[9] The injustice renews federal recognition efforts with the United States which date back to the Louisiana Purchase. Chief Youchigant dies in 1940 as the last fluent speaker of luchi yoroni, meaning "Tunica language." The *fête du blé* also falls dormant at that time.[10]

Beginning in 1967 and culminating in 1985, the history of the "Tunica Treasure" furthers the period of individual stress for tayoroniku-halayihku. Without free informed and prior consent by tayoroniku-halayihku, Leonard Charrier excavates an ancestral village site at the Trudeau plantation near Angola, Louisiana. Charrier seeks the monetary value of what is the largest cache of the nation's sacred and funerary objects, and human remains. When Robert "Stu" Neitzel, a local archaeologist, is called to make an assessment, he alerts a colleague at the Peabody Museum at Harvard, which eventually leases the collection from Charrier. Litigation follows with claims of ownership from Charrier, the owners of the Trudeau plantation, and the State of Louisiana. Prior to federal recognition of the Tunica-Biloxi Tribe of Louisiana in 1981, the argument does not center on the lineal descendants with rights to the "Tunica Treasure."[11] Recounting the story of the Tunica Treasure, Klopotek argues for the importance of material goods in articulating identity in the context of a community's decline in distinctiveness.[12] Overlapping the previous and current revitalization movements is the arc of federal recognition by the United States. Previous to the Louisiana Purchase, the specific histories of tayoroniku and the politically allied Indigenous nations of the Biloxi-Choctaw, Ofo, and

Avoyel prominently feature the military and trade relations with European interests: France, Spain, and England. According to our tradition, current tribal lands outside of Marksville are remnants of a Spanish land grant to Bosra, halayihkuchÐha meaning "chief of the Biloxi." This grant should be upheld by Article VI of the Louisiana Purchase. President Thomas Jefferson's Indian agent, John Sibley, provides there a dismissal of the tayoroniku-halayihku and other Indigenous nations within the Louisiana territory. This initiates approximately 175 years of negligence by the United States towards their treaty obligations.

Prior to federal recognition, white supremacy and racial logic of federal policy influence tayoroniku-halayihku government decisions.[13] Intermarriage is a common practice among tayoroniku-halayihku. Tribal rolls are, however, closed to individuals of less than a quarter blood quantum or with African ancestry. At the same time, enrolled members with spouses of African ancestry are banished from the community outside Marksville. Families feel in the present day impacts from the disparities fostered by the above policies. In the process of writing this essay, the Tunica-Biloxi Tribe amended its enrollment code by referendum. This repealed a limitation on new enrollment applications to include any eligible person over the age of one year. Restrictions on intermarriage and discrimination based on mixed ethnic heritage are not part of the current tribal code.

Challenges Facing tayoroniku-halayihku Youth

Periods of individual stress concerning the demographic data of the present day shape social and economic development opportunities of tayoroniku-halayihku youth. Understanding this data means that community members can ask of their representative government to strategically set goals. Of immediate concern is improvement to educational outcomes. Broader impacts include economic development through the fostering of citizen entrepreneurship.

In exploring available data about tayoroniku-halayihku, there are several scopes to consider. In one set, there is data from the enrolled membership of the Tunica-Biloxi Tribe of Louisiana who reside in Central Louisiana. A second set considers all who have tayoroniku-halayihku heritage whether alone or in combination with another identity. The second set is qualified through the understanding that enrollment in the Tunica-Biloxi Tribe of Louisiana is independent of ethnic identity. Consistent with the idea that the Tunica-Biloxi

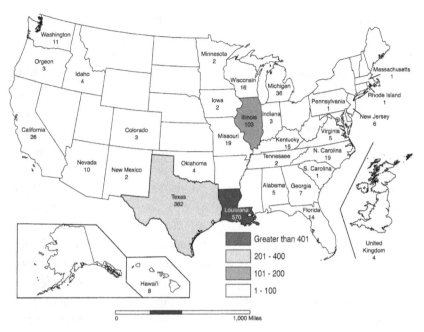

Map 11.1. Illustration of population density of Tunica-Biloxi Tribe of Louisiana enrolled membership by state and country. Courtesy Elisabeth Pierite-Mora.

Tribe of Louisiana determines its own membership, the blood quantum is currently lowered to 1/64 and African ancestry does not exclude members from enrollment. The tribal roll is, however, closed to all but children under the age of one year. There are adults who indeed have relevant heritage but do not qualify for enrollment by current tribal laws. A third set of data considers the national state of educational outcomes, economic development, and digital access for American Indians and Alaska Natives.

There are currently over 1,200 active tribal members who are enrolled in the Tunica-Biloxi Tribe of Louisiana (See map 11.1). Approximately 270 tribal members reside in Avoyelles Parish and are enrolled in school or eligible for primary or secondary school. In 2014, the dropout rate for tribal students is 40%, when compared to 32% for Avoyelles Parish, and 28% across the state of Louisiana. The Tunica-Biloxi Tribe of Louisiana further finds that for students with disabilities, 60% do not attain a high school diploma or GED. Factors contributing to tribal student dropout rates include: lack of transportation; disproportionate impact of mental health disorders and substance abuse; lack of awareness of social service resources; stigmatization based on seeking education assistance; and skepticism by tribal families toward assistance providers based on a perceived lack of confidentiality.[14]

The numbers cited by the U.S. Census Bureau are inconsistent with the population enrolled by the Tunica-Biloxi Tribe of Louisiana tribal membership. The selection of data from the American Community Survey American Indian and Alaska Native Tables includes Tunica-Biloxi Tribe of Louisiana alone or in any combination. While population estimates are lower than official registration, this difference in estimates does create an opportunity to involve a population in the broader tayoroniku-halayihku. The U.S. Census Bureau defines race as self-identification with one or more social groups.[15] Therefore, it is highly possible that these estimated members of tayoroniku-halayihku may or may not be enrolled through the government of the Tunica-Biloxi Tribe of Louisiana. This set of data specifically employs details outside of traditional Indigenous territory with the expectation of capturing facts on all who have tayoroniku-halayihku heritage. (See table 11.1.) Median family income increases by 166% between 2010 and 2015, from $45,491 to $67,571 respectively.[16] At the same time, the number of families with an income below the poverty level sees a decrease from 10% to 9%.[17] In regard to educational attainment for the population over twenty-five years old across tayoroniku-halayihku in 2015, male students do not complete secondary education at a rate of 12% while female students do not complete secondary education by 4%.[18] These rates are down respectively from 19% and 21% in 2010.[19] When considering this broader set of data, tribal enrollment status and geography are distinct factors. While some of tayoroniku-halayihku heritage may show higher wages and improved educational attainment, such progress may not reach tribal members in Avoyelles Parish. There is an opportunity for a distributed solution such as fab lab programming to support social and economic development.

As part of the National Assessment of Education Progress (NAEP), the National Indian Education Study (NIES) allows for more in-depth reporting on the achievement and experiences of American Indian/Alaska Native (AI/AN) students in fourth and eighth grade. This set of data reports for students in three mutually exclusive categories: students of Bureau of Indian Education (BIE) schools; students enrolled in public schools with AI/AN populations over 25%; and students enrolled in public schools with AI/AN populations under 25%. Distinct differences occur for the populations on the issues of eligi-

Table 11.1. Differences found to be statistically significant among populations of American Indian / Alaska Native (AI/AN) students

	FOURTH GRADERS (%)			EIGHTH GRADERS (%)		
	AI/AN students in BIE schools	AI/AN students in high-density schools	AI/AN students in low-density schools	AI/AN students in BIE schools	AI/AN students in high-density schools	AI/AN students in low-density schools
Eligible for National School Lunch Program	94	87	64	97	80	56
Attend rural schools	88	64	27	79	57	21
English language learners	49	12	6	39	9	3
Computer in home	56	63	74	55	68	82
More than 100 books in home	15	14	24	7	11	21
Parent(s) graduated from college	—	—	—	27	35	43

Source: "National Indian Education Study 2015: American Indian and Alaska Native Students at Grades 4 and 8," March 2017.

bility for the National School Lunch Program, attendance at rural schools, English language learners, computers in the home, number of books in the home, and whether parent(s) graduated from college.[20] For students in BIE schools, this data indicates that they are more likely low income, English learning, rural students with parents who do not have college degrees.

Finally, AI/AN youth face suicide rates at 2.5 times that of the national average. Suicide is the second leading cause of death for AI/AN youth between the ages of ten to twenty-four. It is further the third leading cause of death for AI/AN youth between the ages of five to fourteen.[21] AI/AN students face disparities in the disproportionate rate of disciplinary actions in school. Overall, AI/AN youth represent 2% of out-of-school suspensions and 3% of expulsions, despite representing less than 1% of the national student population.[22] In 2016, unemployment rates within the United States are at 4.9%. Disparities across race and ethnicity mean higher rates for AI/AN and African American populations with 8.9% and 8.4% respectively.[23] Tribal members, U.S. Census data, and NAEP data all confirm under supported/vulnerable communities that undermine education opportunities for tayoroniku-halayihku (and all AI/AN) students, and these income and educational conditions are further compounded by the mental and social health of AI/AN youth.

Contextualizing the local and national data across tayoroniku-halayihku, there are opportunities for further exploration of intersectionality. Because of our history of intermarriage, the personal experience of disparities may be complicated further by multiple identities, including African American and Latino. At the same time, some tribal students may benefit from white privilege. Local research does include data on impacts to students with disabilities. What the Tunica-Biloxi Tribe of Louisiana does not keep data on is its queer and two spirit population. Expectations reported are based on Louisiana census data of 3.2% of the adult population statewide.[24] Compared to the national data on English Language Learners in American Indian/Alaska Native student populations, most enrolled members of the Tunica-Biloxi Tribe of Louisiana speak English as a first language. luhchi yoroni is currently classified as "reawakening" by *Ethnologue*.[25]

How to Make (Almost) Any Fab Lab

To understand the possibilities of the local solutions provided by fab labs to communities such as tayoroniku-halayihku that are confronting issues of educational attainment and economic development, one must first explore the basic components: people, education, inventory, and an internet connection. The internet connection is a barrier to full participation. Fab labs in rural India, for example, may function without being regularly connected. Students, researchers, and instructors will travel with digital files to the next closest university to share their documentation and designs. These workarounds are important for Indigenous nations within the United States in whose communities there is a definite digital divide. While the digital divide is an issue, there is also opportunity for progress in social aspects. The flexibility of the fab lab physical specification allows for educational instruction in a variety of settings. The scale of "community based" fab labs is comparable to mainframes that once filled entire labs. The first research lab set up by MIT's Center for Bits and Atoms (CBA) is equipped with a $1 million inventory and is restricted in access to graduate students at the institution. The $100,000 iteration for communities contains approximately $50,000 of machines and $50,000 of materials. The inventories for these labs and the research lab are both curated by CBA. These costs present a question of priorities for Indigenous nations that must make budget decisions between infrastructure and social services.

Fab labs were created by CBA as part of the educational outreach effort associated with an original National Science Foundation project to study the scaling of information technology. The Fab Foundation is a nonprofit organization that emerged from CBA's educational programming in 2009. The mission of the Fab Foundation is to foster the growth of the international fab lab network. I joined the organization in 2014 when the network represented approximately 750 labs. The demand for labs since doubled year over year in quantity. I took over the procurement and logistics activities of the Fab Foundation while offering assistance with communications, particularly online and social media. Following the practice of centuries of tayoroniku-halayihku history, I chose to remain in the family business of trading and communicating with the world.

Despite the challenges presented to communities by internet access and inventory, people and education are less tied to finances. The inventories curated by CBA are centered on the curriculum for a Masters-level class at MIT called "How to Make (Almost) Anything." Each fall session, the class develops through "content deltas," and the inventory is responsive to the market.[26] New electronic components replace obsolete ones. Materials for molding and casting and compositing are vetted for best results and also for what is ecologically friendly. As the MIT class winds down each year, the distributed version of the class "Fab Academy" goes into preparations. Fab Academy takes the MIT course and distributes it across a "campus" of at least eighty different labs with hundreds of students. Each week, students participate in a three-hour lecture session in which they are introduced to a different competency. Homework happens in the lab with thirty-five hours of work on a specific project. This cycle continues through twenty-one weeks in which the students become familiar with the entire inventory. At that time, a final project presentation is made that combines as many different tasks as possible. Students will take on questions involving local problems and solve them through digital fabrication technology. All of this documentation is freely available online through an ecosystem of websites, repositories, and recorded video.

Fab Academy is one part of the distributed education model facilitated by the Fab Foundation and its global partners. Once a student learns how to make (almost) anything, they may then challenge themselves to build tools toward community-based DIY biology education in "How to Grow (Almost) Anything." While students learn to work with biological cultures and program DNA sequences, they also learn to think critically about the associated policy and ethics. There is the recent addition of Fabricademy, which is centered on work with textiles. A diploma thesis program recently branded as "Grow with Fab" challenges students to take their projects and prototypes and either conduct deeper research or introduce a product to the market. Each of these extensions demonstrates the flexibility of a community-based fab lab and challenges institution-based higher education. There is tuition associated with the administration of this programming. Through the online ecosystem, learning is not bound behind a paywall. As Neil Gershenfeld asserts, new sites join the fab lab movement to be a part of something bigger, a critical mass or network.[27] The fostering of relationships across borders and languages ensures that every class of students can dive deeper into the topic of how to make.

Learning to Make in Grandmother's Home

My lived experience as a language and culture activist with a focus on story and song tradition informs my personal expression of applications of fab lab programming in my community. This section focuses on the learning environment that fostered my personal maker education. The purpose is to illustrate how Indigenous learning is facilitated outside of the formal classroom. As the Center for Native American Youth (CNAY) at the Aspen Institute asserts:

> Across the country, CNAY hears from Native youth who are demanding an educational system that resides outside of the contemporary classroom setting. These youth are returning to more traditional forms of education, learning as their people have for generations in the hogan, longhouse, riverbed, and desert floor. It is within these settings that Native youth can engage in an education that reflects their needs, interests, and cultural moorings.[28]

My grandfather Joseph Pierite, Jr., was the first tribal chairman of the Tunica-Biloxi Tribe of Louisiana. He also gave me lessons in the ways in which our people make. His work centered on cypress and deer hide drums. Together, we regularly visited traditional Indigenous territories and sacred sites across Louisiana and Mississippi. On each of these trips or with every lesson, I received parts of our oral tradition. It was during one trip in my grandfather's truck that he turned down the radio and gave me this story: "There is a certain man. He has one arm, one leg, half a face, all covered with hair, and lives up in the trees. If you have a young boy in your house, you will get a knock on the door." tanap is a medicine keeper for the tayoroniku-halayihku people. He teaches young boys how to wrestle and challenges them to a match. If the boy can throw tanap on the ground, tanap will teach the boy how to be the best doctor in the world. The reason my grandfather knew this story to be true is because his father (and some other of our people) were áriyasema. I am personally affected by a mild case of cerebral palsy. This story in particular was gifted to me at a time when I experienced bullying for the way that I walk, how I write, and being set apart with in-school physical therapy. I learned about my role within tayoroniku-halayihku from this story.

These moments of storytelling from my paternal grandfather and maternal great-grandmother, Julia Descant Normand, form the basis of my immediate family's efforts to revitalize tayoroniku-halayihku heritage languages and culture. My mother, Donna Madere Pierite, documents each of these incidents of transmission of ancestral knowledge. Since 2007, these stories are retold each week in a regular cultural presentation. The presentations are part of a family tradition starting with my great-grandfather Joseph Alcide Pierite, Sr. Started in 2011, the Language and Culture Revitalization Project is a collaboration with Tulane University in New Orleans, Louisiana. Before these formalized programs and presentations, my parents set up a workshop at home for my mother's teaching materials. We designated an office room with a personal computer, scanner, and copy machine. With these tools, we designed and produced workbooks for luhchi yoroni language instruction. My mom taught French and Spanish in New Orleans Public Schools, until we lost our home in Hurricane Katrina. Although the technology was lost, we were able to retain the work. Copies were stored in plastic bins in the attic above the waters that devastated our neighborhood in New Orleans East.

Our work continued and our family was invited to University of Texas in Arlington (UTA) for the Institute for Collaborative Language Research (CoL-

ang) in 2014. I went to Arlington as a representative of my family. Coinciden-
tally, my work with the Fab Foundation started just prior to the trip. At the
same time as CoLang 2014, FAB10 in Barcelona was also underway. The FABx
series of events is an annual gathering of the international fab lab network. I
attended the institute at UTA for two weeks, regularly passing the university's
fab lab. I focused my training on language documentation tools and processes
through digital technologies. While the technology drove me to attend the
institute, the international network of academics and community language
activists helped to ground my own perspective.

CoLang motivated me to push for more deliberate and thoughtful fab lab
programming outreach in Indigenous nations. I dug into the repository of
Fab Academy to find examples of Indigenous students. At that point, I saw
a disparity of representation in the United States. Only the Cook Inlet Tribal
Council in Anchorage, which serves several Alaska Native corporations, had a
full fab lab within the international network. Further conversations made me
aware of the Advanced Manufacturing Initiative by the AIHEC. This initiative
is a collaboration between TCUs and the National Laboratories. Although the
technology is similar, the initiative was distinct through curriculum and geography. Tribal colleges and universities do not presently cross the east banks
of the Mississippi River.

My grandmother Fannie Lou Ben Pierite was from the Standing Pine community, Mississippi Band of Choctaw Indians. When I first learned how to
make, it was in her house sitting at a kitchen table stringing seed beads onto
single-strand necklaces of random colors. She was the first Choctaw woman to
graduate from a college in Mississippi. She was also the first Choctaw woman
to teach at a "white school." Both the distributed education model of making
in a fab lab and the traditional ways in which Indigenous elders teach their
students result in the promotion of collaboration to understand the world.

Growing up, I saw two pathways to self-determination. In central Louisiana, I saw Chairman Earl Barbry, Sr., and the tribal council take tayoroniku-
halayihku from reliance on federal assistance programs to investments in
tribal enterprises, to become the largest employer in Avoyelles Parish. In Mississippi, I saw the continuation of Chief Phillip Martin's leadership and the
vision of Choctaw self-determination. Chief Martin pushed for the Bureau
of Indian Affairs to advocate for the Mississippi Band of Choctaw Indians in
negotiations with General Motors. This push resulted in the establishment
of a wiring harness plant on Choctaw traditional Indigenous territory. This

business relationship supported by government and policy reform fostered economic development. Eventually, Choctaw tribal enterprises expanded to plastic manufacturing, electronics, forest products, retailing, and tourism. The ambition to develop Indigenous self-determination and self-rule through modern manufacturing technology was the result of contemporary Mississippi Band of Choctaw Indians identity.[29] It's important not to characterize enterprises that further self-determination as "modern." It perpetuates the false dichotomy of Indigenous epistemologies as "ancient." Ron Eglash argues in his approach to generative justice within digital fabrication that sources of unalienated value need not be "natural" or "pure." Instead, tayoroniku-halayihku are called to examine our relation to materials and the ecosystem.[30] More discussion on this point will come later in this essay.

Knowledge Creation as Ceremony

Centering the role of storytelling in the creation and transmission of knowledge, students are called to reflect on communication within their particular Indigenous nations. In order for this to be effective, the student must be paired with an elder or knowledge keeper to ensure the integrity of the values transmitted is maintained.[31] These concepts are again illustrated through storytelling tradition.

A day before the anniversary of the birth of René-Robert Cavelier, Sieur de La Salle, I traveled to the Conseil des Abénakis d'Odanak. As the board president of the North American Indian Center of Boston, I was accompanied by Gary McCann, policy advisor, Muhheconnew National Confederacy (MNC) Bureau of Political Affairs. The historical confederacy included nations such as Lenape, Pequot, Sokoki, Narragansett, Nipmuc, Wampanoag, Massachusett, Mohican (Mahican), and Abenaki. The confederacy was revived in 1991 on issues surrounding grave sites of Indigenous peoples interned on the Boston Harbor Islands during King Philip's War. While the purpose of my visit to Quebec was introductory, the letter that I delivered in English and French remarked on how intertwined tayoroniku and Abenaki histories were since King Philip's War and La Salle's claiming of "Louisiana."

While preparing to address Chief Richard O'Bomsawin and Chief Michel R. Bernard, I received an email from Sophie Tremblay at Onaki FabLab at Centre d'Innovation des Premiers Peuples in Canada's Capital Region. Earlier in June, the first Indigenous People's FabLab in Canada opened. Since that time, twelve

First Nations youth between the ages of seventeen and thirty years old completed 180 hours of digital fabrication and computer-aided design training, which was then followed by internships at the lab. Two of the students from the first cohort were then hired to assist the instructor, Phonesavanh Thongsouksanoumane, to teach a second cohort of students. One of the stated goals of Onaki FabLab is to "provide opportunities to modernize the art and Indigenous knowledge through the use of digital technologies. Valuing culture and Indigenous knowledge." Sophie Tremblay and her team at Onaki FabLab noted that the Honorable Julie Payette, at that time the governor general of Canada, had recently visited a fab lab. Sophie stated that the fab lab was cultivating a relationship with Governor Payette, who was a businesswoman, a member of the Canadian Astronaut Corps, and an engineer prior to assuming office.

The coincidence of timing of these events speaks to both the development of digital technologies and their adoption by Indigenous peoples. While the work is impacted and supports collaboration with outside communities, the knowledge is based on the formation of intertribal, international relations and confederacies, which hold histories since time immemorial. Before I, as a member of tayoroniku-halayihku, set foot in another's territory, I have to prepare. There are nonverbal modes of communication that I must follow. I need to have an offering of tobacco. If I carry a pipe, I need to consider the formalities of the calumet. Once the nonverbal mode of communication is met, we greet each other in a common language. In the southeast United States, we have the universal Mobilian Trade Jargon. Mobilian is a heavily Muskogean language which provides a means to communicate. As a luhchi yoroni speaker, those conversations are left to the intratribal and family level of communication. I chose to deliver letters to the Gran Conseil in English and French to be considerate to both francophones and anglophones on the matter of accessibility. The French letters also reflect a shared history between our peoples through the La Salle expedition. In this way, my position is established as a guest in Abenaki territory. I further inform them of a good intent and build rapport on extended kinship.

The effectiveness and efficiency of how one might navigate those Indigenous systems of communications are obviously enhanced by digital technologies. A keyword search in an online engine can provide access to libraries of historical records. However, this is no substitute for interpersonal communications. Storytelling and oral histories shared within and between Indigenous communities don't need the decoding and error correction of reports based on perspective through a Western lens. Thankfully, my company included Gary McCann, who previously worked closely with John "Sam" Sapiel (Penobscot), acting director of MNC Bureau of Political Affairs. It was after we crossed the border from Vermont into Quebec that we stopped at a Tim Horton's for coffee and sandwiches. There was a slight pause while Gary looked at me from the other side of the table. "So, should I tell you how your people connect to King Philip's War?" Despite Gary's identity as a non-Indigenous person, the pattern of communication matched what I knew from my grandparents, elders, and ancestors. The knowledge seeker is given a task or a journey. When the task is completed or the journey passes a point of no return, a story is imparted. While the story is being told, there's no room for interruptions or questions.

Fab labs embody the constructionist philosophy of Seymour Papert. Papert suggests that learning is most effective when the activity involves the making of a meaningful and shareable artifact.[32] The purpose of integration of language revitalization and conservation capacity of tayoroniku-halayihku is to enhance the constructionist model with culture-based education and language-centered learning. Depree Shadowwalker argues that Lev Vygotsky's theories of cognitive development parallel teachings that are experienced, witnessed, and researched in Indigenous nations. As opposed to Western pedagogies which center linear hierarchy, Indigenous systems spiral allowing for continual development through revisiting domains of knowledge.[33]

Applying this Indigenous flow of communication to the process of digital fabrication in a cultural revitalization movement for tayoroniku-halayihku, the discussion centers the space of a fab lab as part of the local ecosystem. A fab lab has specific machines. What distinguishes making in a fab lab as "digital fabrication" is the communication and control from pahitaniyu, meaning "computers." This connection results in the construction of devices that can control and communicate with each other. The process of causing a stepper motor to turn involves the making of a controller circuit board that can be locally fabricated. The circuit board is milled out on a numerically controlled (NC) mini-mill that receives instructions from pahitaniyu. People control and communicate with pahitaniyu. Building on the story tradition, people are an intermediary within a fab lab. This is analogous to how tanap is an intermediary between áriyasema and the local ecosystem. Each participant holds information that is circulated in a process that results in some work happening. So, there is collaboration: between motors and circuits, between machines and devices, between machines and pahitaniyu, between pahitaniyu and people. The collaboration spirals and extends out to the local ecosystem.

Choctaw Snake Dance and Peruvian Human Loom

"My grandmother is ninety-four years old as of this week. She was my first maker instructor. For her, I will share the Choctaw Snake Dance Song." As I said this, I stood before a morning session of FAB13 in Santiago de Chile. Representatives from seventy-five countries were in the audience of the morning session. It's through these annual gatherings that I connect with the broader Indigenous peoples' movement with fab labs. These multicultural demonstrations reflect collaborations and friendships fostered through the work of the international fab lab network. Starting at FAB12 in Shenzen, I collaborated with Walter Héctor Gonzales Arnao, professor at Peru's National University of Engineering (UNI) in the Department of Architecture, Urban Planning and Arts (FAUA). Walter is a Peruvian architect and industrial designer. While Walter holds many patents, his signature project is known as Fab Loom. The large-scale version is a traditional Andean loom constructed from parts machined out on a large CNC router. For workshops, Walter uses parts laser-cut from acrylic sheets. The workshops facilitated by Walter at FABx gatherings reproduce courses at UNI. His efforts to integrate digital technologies as a means of transmission of ancestral knowledge push Western norms to "Peruvianize" traditional handicrafts. Walter recounts in *El Impacto Technologico en La Artesania Peruana* an incident in which a male student was teased by his father for working on a backstrap loom. The Western norm associates weaving as a more feminine way of making. Work with textiles such as sewing and embroidery, even when controlled by digital means, is associated with women in the context of the international fab lab network. Despite these attitudes, Walter points to Taquile, or the Peruvian rainforest, for cultures where men take up work with looms.[34] I appreciate the spiritual side to collaborating with Walter as a member of an Indigenous nation within North America. Members of the Latin American regional network FabLat refer to Walter and myself as the Condor and Eagle.

A fabercise is a musical interlude scheduled to break FABx morning sessions with movement. Part cultural exchange, a fabercise reflects the social nature of the international network. Production of our fabercise collaborations involves waking up before sunrise and venturing outdoors to take photos with a stuffed toy llama. Regardless of the absurdity of poses, each of us represents our peoples through regalia and a shared reverence for the rising sun. These early morning expeditions are prayerful. Photos and video are edited to provide a backdrop to a five-minute sequence in which we share songs and invite the gathering to dance and collaborate with us. The audience becomes a human loom in these presentations as bolts of fabric or yarn are tossed around. For five minutes, the people assembled become the largest machine in the network. The users are Indigenous people. The end product is a spider's web of a rainbow of textiles, laughter, and love.

The last three sections have explored integration of the ceremony and oral tradition within fab lab educational programming. Andrew Jolivétte describes a model for Collective Ceremonial Research Responsiveness through three fundamental aspects: a shared collective endeavor between academics and community researchers; engagement with and cultivation of traditional knowledge keepers; and centering the needs and goals as defined by the community. Central to this approach is "radical love." Jolivétte says that radical love is "the activation of a deeply embedded and reciprocal devotion to holistic and ethnic specific self and community care through a balance of human feelings, emotions, and practices that reduce egocentrism while centering a symbiotic relationship between the physical and spiritual as co-constitutive factors of health promotion among Indigenous peoples and communities of color."[35]

Conclusion

For tayoroniku-halayihku, we are called to be áriyasɛma—keepers of traditional ecological and ancestral knowledge—of bits and atoms. Our nation continues because of community, land, tradition, and Injunuity. The way we interact with digital technologies of communication, computation, and fabrication is informed by our connection to the elders and ancestors through our material culture and heritage languages. There is no right or wrong way to apply fab lab educational programming, with the caveat that consultation and research directed by elders and knowledge keepers is a prerequisite. Beyond that, the step-by-step guide is written through the personal expression of youth and students. While improving educational outcomes is an immediate concern, the work spirals out to fostering citizen entrepreneurship and informing policy at the tribal government level. The international fab lab network is provocative in the promotion of finding solutions to local problems through social aspects over technical ones. If this network united beyond borders and languages is sincere in its convictions, then support for the preservation of Indigenous epistemologies globally remains a priority.

NOTES

1. Gershenfeld et al., *Designing Reality.*

2. Wallace, "Revitalization Movements."

3. Ibid., 266.

4. Ibid., 270.

5. The Fab Foundation, "Fab Foundation—Setting up a Fab Lab."

6. Brain, *Tunica Archaeology.*

7. Klopotek, *Recognition Odysseys,* 43–44.

8. Brain, *Tunica Archaeology,* 310.

9. Klopotek, *Recognition Odysseys,* 45–46.

10. Brain, *Tunica Archaeology,* 310.

11. Klopotek, *Recognition Odysseys.*

12. Ibid., 95.

13. Ibid., 221.

14. Tunica-Biloxi Tribe of Louisiana, "Tunica-Biloxi Education Program to Prevent Drop-Outs."

15. U.S. Census Bureau, "About Race."

16. U.S. Census Bureau, "Tunica Biloxi Indian Tribe of Louisiana Alone or in Any Combination"; U.S. Census Bureau, 2011–2015. American Community Survey American Indian and Alaska Native Tables, B19013.

17. U.S. Census Bureau, 2006–2010. American Community Survey American Indian and Alaska Native Tables, B17001; U.S. Census Bureau, 2011–2015. American Community Survey American Indian and Alaska Native Tables, B17001.

18. U.S. Census Bureau, 2011–2015. American Community Survey American Indian and Alaska Native Tables, B15002.

19. U.S. Census Bureau, 2006–2010. American Community Survey American Indian and Alaska Native Tables, B15002.

20. Ninneman, Deaton, and Francis-Begay, "National Indian Education Study 2015."

21. Center for Native American Youth, "Generation Indigenous," 13.

22. Ibid., 27.

23. Ibid., 36.

24. Tunica-Biloxi Tribe of Louisiana, "Tunica-Biloxi Education Program to Prevent Drop-Outs," 12.

25. SIL International, "Tunica."

26. "Content delta" in the context of Fab Academy means updates to the curriculum. The jargon is based upon how version control software such as Git stores and tracks changes to digital files in repositories.

27. Gershenfeld et al., *Designing Reality*, 23.
28. Center for Native American Youth, "Generation Indigenous," 33.
29. Jorgensen, *Rebuilding Native Nations*, 37–38.
30. Eglash, "Decolonizing Digital Fabrication," 44–59.
31. Lameman, Lewis, and Fragnito, "Skins 1.0," 107.
32. The Fab Foundation, "Scaling a Community of Practice," 7
33. Shadowwalker, "Vygotsky and Indigenous Cultures," 4.
34. Gonzales Arnao, *El Impacto Tecnológico En La Artesanía Peruana*, 76–77.
35. Jolivétte, *Research Justice.*

BIBLIOGRAPHY

Brain, Jeffrey P. *Tunica Archaeology.* Cambridge, MA: Peabody Museum of Archaeology and Ethnology, Harvard University, 1988.

Center for Native American Youth. "Generation Indigenous: The State of Native Youth 2018." State of Native Youth Report. Washington, DC: Center for Native American Youth at the Aspen Institute, November 2018.

Eglash, Ron. "Decolonizing Digital Fabrication." In *Fab City: The Mass Distribution of (Almost) Everything,* edited by Tomas Diez, 44–59. Barcelona: Institute for Advanced Architecture of Catalonia, 2018. https://issuu.com/iaac/docs/fabcitymassdistribution.

Fab Foundation, the. "Fab Foundation—Setting up a Fab Lab." Accessed March 15, 2019. https://www.fabfoundation.org/index.php/setting-up-a-fab-lab/index.html.

Fab Foundation, the. 2019. "Scaling a Community of Practice for Education in STEM through Digital Fabrication: Reflection and Playbook." https://www.scopesdf.org/wp-content/uploads/2019/02/SCOPES-DF-Playbook-1.pdf.

Gershenfeld, Neil A, Alan Gershenfeld, and Joel Cutcher-Gershenfeld. *Designing Reality: How to Survive and Thrive in the Third Digital Revolution.* New York: Basic Books, 2017.

Gonzales Arnao, Walter Héctor. *El Impacto Tecnológico En La Artesanía Peruana.* 2nd ed. Lima: Universidad Nacional de Ingeniería, 2018.

Jolivétte, Andrew. *Research Justice: Methodologies for Social Change.* Chicago: Policy Press, 2015.

Jorgensen, Miriam. *Rebuilding Native Nations: Strategies for Governance and Development.* Tucson: University of Arizona Press, 2007.

Klopotek, Brian. *Recognition Odysseys: Indigeneity, Race, and Federal Tribal Recognition Policy in Three Louisiana Indian Communities.* Durham, NC: Duke University Press, 2011.

Lameman, Beth Aileen, Jason E. Lewis, and Skawennati Fragnito. "Skins 1.0: A Curriculum for Designing Games with First Nations Youth." In *Proceedings of the International Academic Conference on the Future of Game Design and Technology- Futureplay '10,* 105. Vancouver: ACM Press, 2010.

Ninneman, A.M., J. Deaton, and K. Francis-Begay. *National Indian Education Study 2015: American Indian and Alaska Native Students at Grades 4 and 8.* Washington, DC: U.S. Institute of Education Sciences, Department of Education, 2017. https://files.eric.ed.gov/fulltext/ED572961.pdf.

SIL International. "Tunica." *Ethnologue.* Accessed March 15, 2019. https://www.ethnologue.com/language/tun.

Shadowwalker, Depree. "Vygotsky and Indigenous Cultures: Centuries of Language Centered Learning." Working paper, University of Arizona, Tucson, AZ, 2003. http://www.u.arizona.edu/~deprees/finalpaper.pdf.

Tunica-Biloxi Tribe of Louisiana. "Tunica-Biloxi Education Program to Prevent Drop-Outs." U.S. Department of Education, May 31, 2016. https://www2.ed.gov/programs/indiandemo/16awards/2016-299a-0104.pdf.

U.S. Census Bureau. "About Race." October 16, 2020. https://www.census.gov/topics/population/race/about.html.

U.S. Census Bureau. "Tunica Biloxi Indian Tribe of Louisiana Alone or in Any Combination." 2006–2010. American Community Survey American Indian and Alaska Native Tables, n.d. Accessed March 11, 2019.

U.S. Census Bureau. "Tunica Biloxi Indian Tribe of Louisiana Alone or in Any Combination." 2011–2015. American Community Survey American Indian and Alaska Native Tables, n.d. Accessed March 11, 2019.

Wallace, Anthony F. C. "Revitalization Movements." *American Anthropologist* 58, no. 2 (April 1956): 264–81.

CONTRIBUTORS

GINA CAISON is associate professor of English at Georgia State University. She is author of *Red States: Indigeneity, Settler Colonialism, and Southern Studies;* creator, host, and producer of the *About South* podcast (2016–19); and co-editor with Lisa Hinrichsen and Stephanie Rountree of the edited collection *Small-Screen Souths: Region, Identity, and the Cultural Politics of Television.* She is president of the Society for the Study of Southern Literature, 2020–22.

ALEXANDRA CHIASSON is a doctoral candidate in the Department of English and the Department of Women's, Gender, and Sexuality Studies at Louisiana State University. Her research is on discourses of sexuality and platform economics.

DAVID A. DAVIS is associate professor of English at Mercer University, where he also serves as associate director of the Spencer B. King, Jr., Center for Southern Studies. He studies modern southern literature and culture. He is the author of *World War I and Southern Modernism.* He edited reprints of *Not Only War* by Victor Daly and *Hard Times on the Southern Chain Gang* by John L. Spivak, and he is currently writing a book about sharecropping and southern literature.

LEIGH H. EDWARDS is professor of English at Florida State University. Her book publications include *Dolly Parton, Gender, and Country Music; The Triumph of Reality TV: The Revolution in American Television;* and *Johnny Cash and the Paradox of American Identity.* She is on the advisory board of the Institute for Bob Dylan Studies.

PAUL FESS is assistant professor at LaGuardia Community College (City University of New York). He specializes in American literature, African American literature, and sound studies. He is currently working on a book project that examines how music structured the politics and literature of race, enslavement, and citizenship from the U.S. abolitionist movement of the 1840s and 1850s to the end of the Civil War.

LISA HINRICHSEN is associate professor of English at the University of Arkansas. She is the author of *Possessing the Past: Trauma, Imagination, and Memory in Post-Plantation Southern Literature* and coeditor, along with Gina Caison and Stephanie Rountree, of *Small-Screen Souths: Region, Identity, and the Cultural Politics of Television*. She was president of the Society for the Study of Southern Literature from 2018 to 2020.

SHERITA L. JOHNSON is associate professor in the Department of English at the University of Southern Mississippi, where she specializes in nineteenth-century African American literature, Black women writers, Jim Crow literature and cultural studies. The author of *Black Women in New South Literature and Culture*, Johnson has served as guest editor of *The Southern Quarterly* for two themed-issues: "'My Southern Home': The Lives and Literature of 19th-Century Southern Black Writers" (Spring 2008) and "Freedom Summer 50th Anniversary" (Fall 2014). Since 2011, she has served as the director of the Center for Black Studies at the University of Southern Mississippi.

JENNIE LIGHTWEIS-GOFF is instructor of English at the University of Mississippi, where she teaches American literature with particular interests in critical regionalisms and feminist theory. She earned a PhD in English, as well as Graduate Certificates in Gender and Africana Studies, from the University of Rochester. The monograph based on her dissertation research, *Blood at the Root: Lynching as American Cultural Nucleus*, won the Susan B. Anthony Dissertation Award and the SUNY Press Dissertation/First Book Prize in African-American Studies. Her essays on urban studies have appeared in *south*, *American Literature*, *Signs*, and the *Southern Quarterly*.

SAM McCRACKEN is a doctoral student in the Department of Comparative Literature at the University of Michigan. He holds a BA in English and Spanish from Georgia State University and an MA in Comparative Literature and Intercultural Studies from the University of Georgia. His research centers on contemporary digital cultures and the ephemeral narratives shared on social media platforms.

MARGARET T. ("MOLLY") McGEHEE is associate professor of English and American Studies and associate dean for faculty development at Oxford College of Emory University. Her current book project, *Atlanta Fictions,* focuses on the Atlanta imaginary in the fiction and nonfiction of post–World War II women writers. She has published in the *Southern Quarterly, Southern Spaces, Cinema Journal, North Carolina Literary Review, Studies in American Culture,* and other journals.

JEAN-LUC PIERITE is president of the board of directors for the North American Indian Center of Boston. He was elected to the Community Linguist seat of the Advisory Circle for CoLang for the period 2016–20. Currently, Pierite volunteers with his tribe's Language and Culture Revitalization Program, which is a collaboration with Tulane University in New Orleans, and he is the International Procurement and Logistics Manager for the Fab Foundation.

STEPHANIE ROUNTREE is assistant professor of English at the University of North Georgia, where she specializes in U.S. literature and media, gender studies, and southern studies. She is coeditor, along with Lisa Hinrichsen and Gina Caison, of *Small-Screen Souths: Region, Identity, and the Cultural Politics of Television.* Her current monograph project, *American Anteliberalism: Literatures of Enslavement and Public Health,* explores legacies of enslavement in the evolution of US public health discourse as evidenced in post-Emancipation literature.

JAE SHARPE is a doctoral candidate at the University of British Columbia specializing in American postmodernism and the development of communication technologies in the postwar era. Her work examines the relationship between digital media platforms and national rhetoric as represented in fiction.

AUSTIN SVEDJAN is a doctoral student in the Department of English at Louisiana State University, where he studies American modernism, queer theory, and sexuality studies. His work has appeared in the *Southern Quarterly* as well as in the edited collection *Through Mama's Eyes: Unique Perspectives of Southern Matriarchy.* He is currently at work on a project concerning sexual fantasy, voyeurism, and antisociality.

INDEX

Page numbers in *italics* denote illustrations

Jackson, George Pullen, 74, 79, 81–82, 85, 86, 87; *White Spirituals of the Southern Uplands*, 86–87

Jackson, Judge, *The Colored Sacred Harp*, 86

Jackson, Lauren, 244, 246

Jacobs, Harriet, 28

Jefferson, Thomas, 258; *Notes on the State of Virginia*, 62

Jenkins, Henry, *Convergence Culture*, 189n11, 194

Jerry Media, 239

Jezebel, 166

Johnson, Sherita L., 8, 11, 21–22, 25–46

Johnstone, Barbara, 234–35, 241, 249n31

Jolivétte, Andrew, 271

Jones, Martha S.: *All Bound Up Together*, 43n44; *Birthright Citizens*, 43n44

Jones, Taylor, 235

Joyce, Michael, *afternoon: a story*, 143

Juarez, Beno, 256

Judgmental Maps, 162, 163–64, 165, 170, 171, 175n

Judkins, Bennett, 149–50

Karlsberg, Jesse, 86

Karlsen, Haakon, 256

Kemenczy, Tamas, 144–45, 158n8

Kentucky Route Zero (video game): overview, 12, 97; accessibility of, 142–43; and the accidental, logic of, 144, 147–48; addiction and alcoholism and, 151, 153, 155, 159n27, 159n29; and asymmetries of power, 144; and automation, 155–56; and commodification of health, 150–51, 152–54; and communal interaction, 143–44; and corporate labor practices, 150–57, 159n25; critical reception of, 142; and cyborgs, 152–53; decay and death as theme in, 141–42, 146–47, 148–49; development of, 142; and the embodied subject, 145; *The Entertainment* script, 97, 157–58n3, 159n27; epistemological uncertainty and, 145; and e-waste, 141; fictionality self-referenced in, 145; fluidity of character perspectives in, 146, 157; and human-computer interaction, 145, 147–49, 159n16; as hypertext, 142, 143–44, 145,

147, 154, 157–58nn3–4; and interactivity of the players, 97, 142, 145, 157; intertexual references in, 142; job loss and loss of sense of self in, 155; and labor activism, 142–43, 149–51, 156–57; literary and cinematic references in, 97, 144–45, 148, 157, 157–58nn3,8,11; magical realism and, 146; and the material dimensions of media technologies, 141–42; and poststructuralism, 142, 146; and poverty, 151–52, 153–54, 159n27; and the self vs. the posthuman collective, 146; setting of, 143; and social responsibility, exploration of, 157; South American writers and the cultural identity of the U.S. South, 97; and stereotypes, 142, 149; supplementary digital content and, 97; uncanny spaces in, 145, 146, 155, 159n15

King, Elisha James. *See* White, Benjamin Franklin and Elisha James King

King, Martin Luther, Jr., 183

King, Mel, 256

King, Pamela, 256

King Philip's War, 267, 269

Kingsolver, Ann E., 149

kitsch version of the U.S. South, 196, 197, 198–99, 209

Kittler, Friedrich, 145

Klopotek, Brian, 256–57

Knot Worldwide, The, 136, 138n37

Know Your Meme (archive), 241, 242

Koenig, Sarah, 48

Kolbert, Elizabeth, 167

Kopple, Barbara, *Harlan County, USA*, 150

Kurwa, Rahim, 94

labor activism, 142–43, 149–51, 156–57

Language and Culture Revitalization Project, 265

Larson, Sarah, 62

La Salle, Sieur de, René-Robert Cavelier, 267, 268

Lassiter, Sherry, 256

Latino identity, among Tunica-Biloxi Tribe, 262

law enforcement, Nextdoor app and race-based policing, 94

time fetishists and, 54–55; time pieces and clock repair in, 51–54, 56, 64; true crime theme of, 48, 52; Woodstock (Alabama) as setting of, 47, 54, 57, 59–61, 65–66

subjects transformed into objects of exploitation: plantation capitalism and, 91; platform capitalism and, 95–96

surveillance: critiques of the California ideology and, 13n1; Nextdoor app and, 93–94, 98–99n13; plantation-based systems as organizing society, 4; plantation capitalism and, 91, 92; smartphones and tensions between the personal/private and, 175–76n7; surveillance capitalism, 92. *See also* racial profiling

Sutter, James L., 164, 167–68, *168*, 169–70, 171, 172–73, 175

Svedjan, Austin, 12–13, 185, 186, 187, 214–32

systemic racism: Beyoncé's images of celebratory Black life against, 181, 182–84, 189nn7,9; country music and, 200, 210n22; illusions of difference as perpetuating, 38; new media technologies used to challenge, 8; slave notices as pre-photographic textual-visual culture promoting, 26, 28–30, 36, 40n2

Tamblyn, Christine, 158n11

Tarkovsky, Andrei, 158n8

Taylor, Frederick Winslow, *The Principles of Scientific Management*, 98n7

Taylorism, 93, 98n7

tayoroniku-halayihku. *See* Tunica-Biloxi Nation

technology/technologies: material, 9, 14n6; of power, 14n6

Teen Vogue, 246

temporality: disconnection/deviance of the U.S. South in *S-Town*, 50–51, 56–57, 61–62, 64, 65–66; microtemporalities, 65; podcasts and collapse of, 64–65

Tharps, Lori L., "The Case for Black with a Capital B," ix

Thiel, Peter, 176n15

This American Life (NPR), 48

Thongsouksanoumane, Phonesavanh, 268

time: machine time, 54, 61–62; national standardization of, 61, 62

Trail of Tears, 42–43n38, 79

transgender people: and accessibility of queer identifications, 227n3; Dolly Parton's song "Travelin' Thru" and acceptance of, 198, 201, 202; and "Rural Queer Coat Drive," 224

Tremblay, Sophie, 267, 268

Treme, Claude, 175n3

Trethewey, Natasha, 38–39, 111; "Pastoral" from *Native Guard*, 25, 39, 44n55

Tribe, Mark, 13n1

Trudeau plantation (aka Trudeau Landing), 257

Trump, Donald, 63–64, 118n7

Truth, Sojourner, 36–37, 44n51

Tucker, Duncan, 202

Tulane University (New Orleans), 265

Tunica-Biloxi Nation (tayoroniku-halayihku): African American ancestry and, 258, 259, 262; áriyasĐma (keepers of the medicine and the ways), 186, 253, 265, 271; as amalgamation of Tunica, Ofo, Biloxi-Choctaw, and Ayoyel, 253, 257–58; and assimilation, 254; citizen entrepreneurship, 258; and collaboration, 266; and community, 253–55, 256, 258, 271; and disabilities, people with, 259, 262; educational outcomes, 258, 259–62, *261*; and Injunuity, 13, 186, 253, 254, 271; intermarriage and, 258, 262; and intertribal Indigenous systems of communications, 268–69; and land, 253, 255, 256–58, 271; Latino identity and, 262; Marksville (LA) tribal lands, 258; median family income, 260; military and trade relations with European interests, 257–58; multiple ethnic identities and, 258, 259, 262; origin story of, 253; population of, 259; queer and two-spirit population, 262; suicide rates, 261; tribal enrollment code, 258–59; "Tunica Trail," 255; unemployment rates, 262; white supremacy and racial logic of federal policy and, 258; and youth, challenges facing, 258–62, 264

Tunica-Biloxi Nation revitalization movement: overview, 13, 186; artifact conser-

246–47; origins and functions of memes, 238–40; social- and capital economies of memes, 239–40, 243–44, 249n39; and southernness, generally, 240–41, 247; and Web 2.0 logic of "sharing," 239, 240; and *y'all* as linked to the U.S. South, 241–42, 249n31; *y'all consider this a date* memetic format, 242–43, 247; *y'all mind if I* memetic format, 243–46, 247, 249n44

United States as nation: New York City as signifier for, 62; projection of deviance and backwardness onto the South as denial of national histories, 61, 63, 65–66; time standardization, 61, 62
Unite the Right rally (Charlottesville, VA), 7, 12, 101, 104
University of Texas, Arlington (UTA), 265–66
U.S. Capitol violent insurrection, 7, 104, 185–86
U.S. Census Bureau, 260
users: as in control of content, shape-note singing and, 71, 76, 83–85; fictive whiteness of, 244; and narrative engagement with teleological dichotomies of old/new, 6; as never historically neutral subjects, 6–7. *See also* participation
U.S. Geological Survey, map production, 171
U.S. South: as the empire's regressive regional foil, 3; interactive country music and projection of multiple versions of; kitsch version of, 196, 197, 198–99, 209; Mississippi as synecdoche for the region as regressive space, 52, 67n19; as not exceptional in its deployment of media, 9; projections of deviance onto, as distancing the nation from the region, 61, 63, 65–66; as recent invention, 19; as region, vs. American South, ix; resilience of region in spite of evolving media forms, 3; temporal discontinuity/deviance of (*S-Town*), 50–51, 56–57, 61–62, 64, 65–66; *y'all* as metonym for, 234. *See also* fictive whiteness; othering of the U.S. South; southern accent; southernness; U.S. South, "new"

U.S. South, "new": and fantasies of connectivity, 2; and mythologies of "discovery," 17–19, *18*; rhetorics of, 5–6; uncanny likeness of "new" media to, 19

Vaidhyanathan, Siva, 93
Valentine, Chris, 107
Vance, J. D., *Hillbilly Elegy*, 63–64
Vasulka, Steina and Woody, 144, 158n8
Video Art movement, 144
video games: as genre for exploring social responsibility, 157; and racial erasure, 33, 42nn32–33. *See also* Kentucky Route Zero
Vine, 187, 243–44, 249n39
Vlatch, John Michael, 133, 136
Voyages, 14n22
Vygotsky, Lev, 269

wage slavery, 94
Walker, Alice, 115
Walker, William, *The Southern Harmony and Musical Companion*, 78
Wallace, Anthony F. C., 256
Wallace, David Foster, 97; *Infinite Jest*, 157–58n3
Walters, Suzanna Danuta, 226
Ward, Brian, *Radio and the Struggle for Civil Rights in the South*, 8
Ward, Jesmyn, 41n6, 115
War of 1812, 42–43n38
Warren, Robert Penn, 39
Washington Post, 168–69, 229n41
Watts, Isaac, 73
wealth: plantation weddings and fantasy/signaling of, 123–24, 125–27, 130–33, 135–36; as theme in online merchandising of whiteness, 107, 109, 110, 111–12, 116
Web 2.0: definition of, 239; ever-globalizing reach of, 241; logic of "sharing" and, 239, 240. *See also* internet; social media
weddings, #SouthernWeddings, 135. *See also* plantation weddings
Weeks, Jeffrey, 220
Wells, Jeremy, *The Global South*, 127
Welty, Eudora, 115
West, Kanye, 183

Whannel, Paddy, 208
white appropriation of Black creators' labor,
  the use of *y'all* on Twitter as, 187–88, 234,
  243–44, 245–46, 249n39
White, Benjamin Franklin and Elisha James
  King, *The Sacred Harp*, 70–71, 72, 74, 75, 77,
  78, 80–81, *81*, 85, 87
white/black binary: hacking of, 26–27, 41n5;
  laws of slavery as creating, 38; slave advertisements making visible, 28–30, 41–
  42nn11,15. *See also* race
white gaze, antebellum photography as challenge to, 37
white identity, uniforms of, 12, 101, 105–6,
  109, 118–19n10
White, John, *A Briefe and True Report of the
  New Found Land of Virginia*, 17–19, *18*
whiteness: plantation weddings and fantasy
  of wealth, power, and, 123–24, 125–27,
  130–33, 135–36. *See also* fictive whiteness;
  online merchandising of whiteness; white
  supremacy
white supremacist hate groups: the digital
  world as incubating real violence, 7–8,
  185–86; uniforms of, 12, 101
white supremacy: as economic principle,
  generally, 123; and federal policy affecting
  the Tunica-Biloxi Tribe, 258; inability to
  segregate radio airwaves, 8; MAGA hats as
  symbol of, 104, 118n7; shape-note/sacred
  harp singing and construction of white

"folk" culture, 22–23, 71–72, 85–87. *See
  also* online merchandising of whiteness;
  plantation weddings; racial profiling;
  racism
white virtue signaling, 115
Whitman, Walt, 157–58n3
Whitney Plantation, 137n1
Wiggins, Thomas "Blind Tom," 79
Wilken, Rowan, "Twitter and Geographical
  Location," 228n23
Willentz, Sean, 84–85
William, Raymond, *The Country and the City*,
  108
Williams, Michael L., II, 189–90n12
WiLL Made-It, Mike, 189–90n12
Wilson, Jim, 20
Winant, Howard, 184–85
Wired magazine, 13n1
Wood, Marcus, *Blind Memory*, 41–42n15
Work, John Wesley, III, 86

X, Malcolm, 67

Yaeger, Patricia, 115
y'all, use of. *See* Twitter, and the use of *y'all*
Youchigant, Seseostrie, Chief, 257
YouTube, 227n3

Zola (wedding planning platform), 138n37
Zuboff, Shoshana, 92
Zulli, Diana, 128, 133